MALCOLM BROWN

THE IMPERIAL WAR MUSEUM BOOK OF

1918

YEAR OF VICTORY

PAN GRAND STRATEGY SERIES

PAN BOOKS

in association with

The Imperial War Museum

First published 1998 by Sidgwick & Jackson

This edition published 1999 by Pan Books
an imprint of Pan Macmillan Ltd
Pan Macmillan, 20 New Wharf Road, London N1 9RR
Basingstoke and Oxford
Associated companies throughout the world
www.panmacmillan.com

ISBN 0 330 37672 1

A CIP catalogue record for this book is available from
the British Library.

Typeset by SetSystems Ltd, Saffron Walden, Essex
Printed and bound in Great Britain by
Mackays of Chatham plc, Chatham, Kent

THE IMPERIAL WAR MUSEUM BOOK OF

1918

YEAR OF VICTORY

We all certainly long for a really *peaceful* year, but I should never be happy in coming back a minute before my duty here was done. . . . No, if need be, dear ones, we *must* continue to suffer if needed for the permanent peace of the future – we should be cowards else.

Second Lieutenant Gordon Hassell, 8th Battalion, Tank Corps,
31 December 1917

Hurrah! Hurrah! Hurrah! At 11.00 this morning (or to be exact very shortly afterwards) I received a telegram ordering the 'Standfast' and the cessation of hostilities. The long looked for, worked for and prayed for victory has been achieved, and the downfall of wrong and the triumph of right are assured. Truly these are wondrous days. . . .

Acting Captain Gordon Hassell, 8th Battalion, Tank Corps,
11 November 1918

Surely this is the last war that will ever be between civilized nations.

Private Arthur Wrench, 1/4th Bn Seaforth Highlanders,
51st (Highland) Division, 11 November 1918

IN GRATITUDE TO ALL THOSE
WHOSE WORDS, WRITTEN OR SPOKEN,
I HAVE BEEN PRIVILEGED TO QUOTE
IN FOUR IMPERIAL WAR MUSEUM BOOKS
ABOUT THE GREAT WAR OF 1914–18

After Oxford and National Service in the Royal Navy, Malcolm Brown was for many years a BBC TV documentary producer, specializing in historical and military subjects. He became a full-time author in 1986 and has been a freelance historian at the Imperial War Museum since 1989. His other books include *Tommy Goes to War* (1978), *Christmas Truce* (1984), co-written with Shirley Seaton, *A Touch of Genius*, a biography of T. E. Lawrence co-authored by Julia Cave which was short-listed for the NCR Award for non-fiction (1989), *The Imperial War Museum Book of the First World War* (1991), *The Imperial War Museum Book of the Western Front* (1993), *The Imperial War Museum Book of the Somme* (1996) and *Verdun 1916* (1999).

CONTENTS

List of Illustrations

Section One

SECTION TWO

ACKNOWLEDGEMENTS

It is common practice for authors to give special thanks to their publishers, but in the present case my acknowledgements to William Armstrong of Sidgwick & Jackson go well beyond the conventional. I am most grateful to him for his support and encouragement, and for his belief in this book, from contract to publication. There could be no better gesture of confidence than that a publisher should take one's draft manuscript away to study over Christmas; there was satisfaction as well as relief when he subsequently disclosed that his festive season had been enriched rather than spoilt by the experience of reading it. His verdict on it suggested that it possessed the quality which I value above all in any book bearing my name: that it should be accessible, that it should invite anyone opening it to keep turning the pages. I see no reason why a work of history should not be as readable as a good novel, with the extra cachet of actually being true. Indeed, one might claim that the story of 1918, with its moments of high drama and amazing twists of fortune, is a thriller on the grand scale, which I hope will be found as interesting, exciting and moving to read as it was for me to write. Though even while making such a statement, I find it salutary to remind myself of the warning sounded by Revd 'Tubby' Clayton, the famous, kindly chaplain of Talbot House, Poperinghe, in a sermon preached at Oxford on Armistice Day 1928: 'I would not, if I could, turn the Great War into oratory. I can only try to tell you of my friends.'

To William Armstrong's name I should like to add the names of several others from the house of Macmillan (of which Sidgwick & Jackson is a constituent imprint) whose contributions have been of particular value: Peter Hull, who has now copy-edited three of my Imperial War Museum Books and done so with unfailing professionalism and good humour (though officially retired, he gladly returned from his Sussex sanctum to work on the book); Helen Surman, who has devised what I am not the only one to consider a most striking and effective dust-jacket; Wilf Dickie, who was the book's designer; and ML Design, who drew the maps.

Next I wish to express my great gratitude to the Imperial War Museum. The present book is the fourth that I have written about the First World War on its behalf and using its rich resources as basic seed-corn. This could not have been the case without continuing support from the Museum's leadership. I should therefore like to give special mention to the Director-General, Robert Crawford, with whom I can claim a friendly acquaintance going back twenty years, to the time when I worked on my first book in this area, Tommy Goes to War, and who is a stalwart believer in the concept of producing serious works of history under the Museum's name. I am also very grateful for the sustained support of Jane Carmichael, now Assistant Director, Collections, and of Dr Christopher Dowling, who has been in charge of the Museum's dealings with the publishers since the series was conceived back in the 1980s.

With regard to the central matter of research, I wish yet again to record my very warm thanks to Roderick Suddaby and the members of the Department of Documents of which he is the Keeper, among whom for the best part of a decade I have been allowed habitation: Nigel Steel, Simon Robbins, Stephen Walton, Penny Bonning (who has now left for family reasons), and Anthony Richards, not forgetting (how could one?) the cheerful support of Wendy Lutterloch and David Shaw. To these names I must add that of a previous member, Ann Commander (Mrs Ann Brooks). The riches of the collections held in this Department are such that working on any subject in which they are strong is a most rewarding exercise; and though much hard sifting is required to find the gold, gold there certainly is. If by nothing else a book of this nature is justified, I submit, by the sheer quality of the personal evidence given first publication in it.

Among other members of the Museum, very special thanks must go to Peter Simkins, its senior historian. His knowledge and understanding of 1918 are profound, and the book is undoubtedly the better for its having been subjected to his expert examination. As ever he offered me much wise advice, suggesting a number of additions and improvements as well as some most welcome corrections. Virtually all the text was also read by Roderick Suddaby; I am never happy at the thought of going to print before people of his and Peter Simkins' calibre have given it their magisterial overview. The blame and the responsibility are mine for any errors that might still remain.

My equally warm thanks go to those members of the Museum's Department of Printed Books who have been particularly supportive. Julie Robertshaw was the first person to read the whole book straight through from Foreword to Afterword, doing so at my request with a special eye for clarity, style and narrative flow; she not only reported positively but also contrived to come up with two significant early sightings of the key phrase 'the right stuff' (as discussed in the Foreword and Chapter 10). Sarah Paterson subjected the Bibliography to professional and, for me, valuable educative scrutiny; it is definitely the more scholarly for her intervention. I was also pleased to find in her a keen advocate of *The Distant Drum*, the outstanding, privately printed memoir of F.E. Noakes (who appears in these pages as Frederick or 'Fen' Noakes), a private soldier whose wartime letters are among the very best I have ever been privileged to read or to publish. He is the author of the remarkable testimonial to the historical value of the contemporary letter which is highlighted in the Foreword, and, additionally, has been given the accolade of being printed on the book's dust-jacket.

I am also grateful to the Department of Printed Books' former Keeper, Dr Gwyn Bayliss, for discovering and bringing to my notice the very moving 'influenza' letter – written on 5 November 1918 and sent to the Imperial War Museum at its then address in Great George Street, Westminster – which is reproduced in Chapter 9.

The Photograph Archive has as ever been most helpful in the provision of illustrations; here I am specially conscious of the friendly assistance of Bridget Kinally and the staff of the archive's reading-room, and of Ron Brooker and his colleagues of the All Saints' dark room. The Department of Art has also been generous with advice and help in the persons of Mike Moody and Pauline Allwright.

There are a number of people outside the Museum to whom I wish to register my very warm thanks. Patrick Quinn, an American scholar who is strictly a Professor of English Literature at a British university but is no slouch in the area of his own country's history, kindly read the principal chapter on the United States' contribution to the war; I am particularly grateful to him for introducing me to the wartime writings of Coningsby Dawson. Dr John Bourne of the University of Birmingham offered me valuable information on the subject of senior officer casualties. Gigi Horsfield, researcher for the Oxford English Dictionary, presented me with some useful findings in the matter of 'the right stuff' (as already mentioned). Jenny Suddaby and Neil Smith, companions with Roderick Suddaby and myself in a visit to the Chemin des Dames, were early and valued readers of Chapter 5 (and also of the Foreword); additionally Jenny Suddaby did noble work as expedition photographer during that fascinating and memorable journey. I am pleased to have been able to include one of her photographs among the book's illustrations.

Another long-suffering but still remarkably benevolent reader to whom I am more than grateful, and who has as ever retrieved my manuscript from numerous verbal pitfalls, is my wife Betty; yet again I apologize for the general state of disarray to which the domestic scene unfailingly deteriorates in the final stages of a book.

Two valuable contributions of a different provenance from that standard in the book came from letters received in the course of research and writing. I found Mr Alan Brodrick's letter on the impact of the war among the ex-soldiers he knew in his childhood, written after reading my *Imperial War Museum Book of the Somme*, so relevant and moving that I asked, and was graciously given, his permission to quote from it in the Afterword. I am also pleased to have been able to include in the same section, and with her kind permission, Mrs Gloria Siggins's illuminating account – sent in response to my own less than adequate first draft – of the postwar career and attitudes of her father, Major Alfred Bundy.

Two others whose generous help I would like to acknowledge are my French colleagues Dr Maurice Larès and Christophe Leclerc, for an investigation on my behalf which reached a largely negative conclusion. I asked them if they could trace the comment on the Versailles treaty famously attributed to Marshal Foch: 'This is not Peace. It is an Armistice for twenty years.' An intensive search through a substantial number of scholarly works in several institutions in Paris, including the library of the École Militaire, failed to find it. The general verdict was that it was arguably something which Foch said rather than wrote, and that the statement became known, or possibly was even made, to Winston Churchill, whose book *The Gathering Storm* (Volume I of his History of the Second World War) would appear to be its prime source in English. Since it expresses what with hindsight can be seen as an indisputable fact, I have retained it in my narrative (see page 345), if with the addition of the cautious adverb 'allegedly'; a further comment on this subject will be found on page 366.

The author and publishers would like to make due acknowledgement to a number of published works of autobiography or history which are specifically quoted at various points in the book. A detailed note on this subject will be found at the end of the Bibliography.

The General Index could not have been in better hands than those of Sarah Ereira; an index by her is far from routine or perfunctory, it is more in the nature of a comprehensive reader's guide.

Finally, and most importantly of all, I must make special acknowledgement to those whose vivid and memorable accounts – mainly letters and diaries, though here and there I have, selectively, used later memoirs – from which I have drawn the new, in the sense of hitherto unpublished, evidence used throughout this history. Their names (there are a good hundred of them), and the names of the copyright holders who have kindly allowed me to quote from their writings, appear in the Index of Contributors at the end of the book. They are honoured in the book's dedication and are also given a special word of gratitude in the Foreword, but here it might be appropriate to mention one distinguished former combatant whom I quoted at some length in my *Imperial War Museum Book of the Somme* and whom I again quote here, who died at the age of 102 as the book went into production. I refer to the well-known German soldier and writer, Ernst Jünger, an enemy in 1918 but certainly no longer so for many decades now. He gave his personal imprimatur to the quotations I used in my earlier book; in this case his German publishers have kindly given me permission on his behalf. With his name I wish to couple that of Herbert Sulzbach, also quoted here, if more briefly. He too was an enemy in 1918, but, being Jewish, was *persona non grata* in Germany during the Second World War and therefore saw fit to offer his help to the Allied cause. Thereafter he devoted the rest of his life to the self-imposed mission of improving relations between Britain and Germany. As the recipient of both the Iron Cross and the Order of the British Empire he was admirably positioned to do so. I recall the privilege of being present, in February 1985, at a ninetieth birthday lunch in his honour at the Embassy of the German Federal Republic in London. This book is about war, but its emphasis in its last sentences is on his favourite theme: reconciliation. I believe this is exactly as it should be; that is surely the note that should be struck in a book of this kind published as a century which saw so many dark times in its earlier years approaches what promises, in Europe at least, to be a more benign conclusion.

THE WESTERN FRONT 1918: THE GERMAN OFFENSIVES

NORTH SEA

HOLLAND

BELGIUM

Zeebrugge

Ostend

Bruges

Ghent

Nieuport

Dunkirk

Brussels

Liège

Calais

Passchendaele

FOURTH ARMY

Ypres

St Omer

Messines

Hazebrouck

Lille

Armentières

Laventie

SECOND GERMAN OFFENSIVE 'GEORGETTE'

Namur

MEUSE

Boulogne

Charleroi

FIRST ARMY

La Bassée

Lens

Douai

Mons

Valenciennes

SAMBRE

Etaples

Montreuil-sur-Mer

Vimy

Maubeuge

THIRD ARMY

Arras

Cambrai

Landrecies

Le Cateau

OISE

Abbeville

Bapaume

Albert

Péronne

FIRST GERMAN OFFENSIVE 'MICHAEL'

Mézières

Sedan

Longwy

SOMME

Villers-Bretonneux

St Quentin

Amiens

FIFTH ARMY

THIRD GERMAN OFFENSIVE 'BLÜCHER'

Montdidier

Noyon

La Fère

Laon

AISNE

Compiègne

Chemin des Dames

Soissons

VESLE

Verdun

FRANCE

FOURTH GERMAN OFFENSIVE 'GNEISENAU'

Rheims

Épernay

FIFTH GERMAN OFFENSIVE 'REIMS - MARNESCHUTZ'

St Mihiel

OISE

MARNE

Château-Thierry

Meaux

SEINE

Paris

30 miles

50 kilometres

Disposition of British Armies as on the eve of the first (21 March) offensive (NB: Second Army in Italy at this period)

■ ■ ■   Approximate line of the Front before the first offensive

ııııııııı   Approximate limit of the German advance, March to July

THE WESTERN FRONT 1918: THE ALLIED ADVANCE

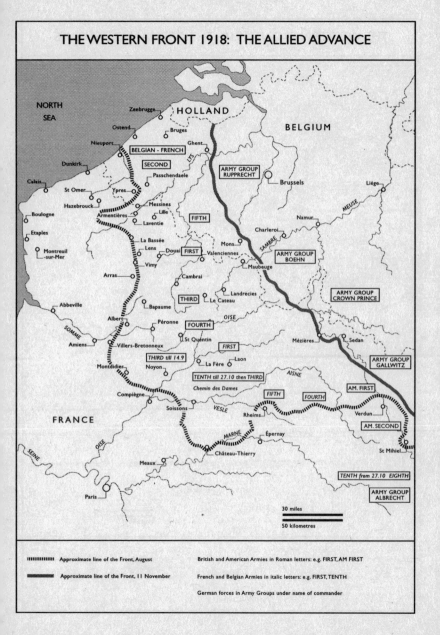

FOREWORD

A YEAR OF DARKNESS AND LIGHT

'WHEN IS THIS AWFUL NIGHTMARE TO END?' an English middle-class civilian wrote in his diary on 1 January 1918. Frederick Arthur Robinson, of Cobham, Surrey, who had recorded the progress of hostilities daily ever since 4 August 1914, felt that the outlook had never seemed so black. 'The country is getting tired out, people no longer talk of the war, they are saturated with it, they live with it, they sleep with it, it enters into their every thought and action, it is part of their flesh and of their bone. When are we again to live our proper lives? Shall we ever do so again?'

These were questions in countless people's minds at the beginning of the fifth year of a seemingly interminable war.

Yet a little over eleven months later, Frederick 'Fen' Noakes, a Private of the Coldstream Guards serving in France, could write in a letter home: 'I feel as if a great black cloud has been lifted from the world, and that the sun is shining again for the first time for years.'

The series of events that produced the astonishing change reflected in these quotations marks out 1918 as one of the most dramatic years of the century. Yet among aficionados of the Great War, and among the generality of readers, it is a year which – apart from its famous, regularly commemorated denouement in November – has been been very largely ignored. It is, of course, understandable that so much interest should have been focused on its notorious predecessors: 1916, the year of the Somme; 1917, the year of Passchendaele. These set-piece battles were, for the British, the epics, the great tragic sagas almost, of the war. Yet the casualty lists were massive on all sides in 1918, and never was there a year with more remarkable twists of fortune. Indeed at one time there was a serious fear that Britain might have to evacuate her troops from the continent and that the war might be lost. Yet only a matter of a hundred days or so later Germany's armies were retreating in disarray and her leaders were suing for peace. In a phrase that crystallized the feelings of millions, Queen Mary was to salute 11 November 1918, the day the Armistice was signed and the guns fell silent, as 'the greatest day in the world's history'.

This was also the day when, in what could be seen as a powerful metaphor of the suddenly changed times, town and city streets so long darkened could again be illuminated; the lights which had famously gone out over Europe in 1914 were restored at last.

Sadly the peace so long awaited and so hard fought for was to prove illusory, and a generation later a second war would replay, to a substantial extent, the scenario of the first. However, the shadow of subsequent events should not cloud the outstanding achievements of the men who brought the so-called 'Great War' to a brilliantly successful conclusion in 1918.

For undoubtedly, in military terms, the war ended well for the Allies. There was indeed a famous victory. As a senior British general, Sir Henry Horne, wrote to his wife on Armistice Day: 'Now the mighty German nation is completely humbled and the great German Army, which regarded itself as the most powerful fighting machine in the world, is in retreat to its own frontiers, broken and defeated!' Significantly he wrote this letter from the Belgian town of Mons, from which the British had retreated in the course of their first action of the war and which had just been retaken in the last.

Two symbols of the great 1918 success are perhaps worth mentioning here: a well-known photograph, and a hitherto unpublished letter.

The photograph (cover photograph to this book, while a variant is included in the first set of illustrations) was taken shortly after troops of the 46th (North Midland) Division, in a daring and brilliantly planned action carried out on 29 September, had seized the St Quentin Canal and pierced that mighty German bastion of defence, the Hindenburg Line. A mass of Tommies crowd the almost vertical bank of the canal near the bridge at Riqueval from which a Brigadier-General is making a speech of congratulation. Appropriately, a British official photographer, David McClellan, was present to record this historic occasion. McClellan had taken on board a legitimate criticism that official photography had frequently failed to reflect the colossal scale of the operations then in progress, and this photograph represented a worthy response. The division's own historian would later claim of the event thus being celebrated: 'The breaking of the Hindenburg Line marked a definite stage in the history of the war, for it opened the way to a war of movement which could end in only one way.' The verdict of one of the First World War's most rigorous students, John Terraine, in his 1978 volume *To Win a War*, was even more emphatic: 'There are really no words for what the 46th Division had achieved. . . . And the price of this scarcely believable triumph was less than 800 casualties.' In a war notorious for massive casualty lists, this was a modest price indeed.

The second symbol of 1918, the letter, has been preserved for many years in one of the 'Miscellaneous' files of the Imperial War Museum's Department of Documents. Its provenance is uncertain and there are no details available about the background, or fate, of its writer. From its contents the following likely pattern of events can be deduced.

On Friday 4 October (five days after the remarkable action just discussed) Corporal James Murrell of the 2/4th York and Lancasters, 62nd Division, found himself in the deserted house, or perhaps the office, of an agricultural merchant in the vicinity of Cambrai. He had been heavily engaged in the recent fighting but now his battalion was out on rest and he had evidently decided to occupy his brief respite with a bit of exploring. He also felt the obligation to make use of his free time to write an overdue letter to his parents. Having left his writing materials behind with his pack, he 'borrowed' several leaves from a memorandum pad belonging to his absentee host, doubtless assuming that in the circumstances the latter would have no objection. By any standards the letter he wrote on these elegantly printed pages is a potent document of 1918.

In its later paragraphs Murrell mentioned almost casually that he had just been recommended for an extra stripe and a Military Medal, following the successful taking out of a German machine-gun post that had been causing a great deal of trouble. But it is what he wrote on his letter's first page that has a particular resonance. He clearly felt that a great and well-merited success was about to be achieved and he was proud of the way it was being delivered:

> No doubt you have been wondering how I have got on during this big push we are in the midst of just now. Well so far everything is alright [sic], I have been in the thick of the fighting from the commencement and am now out for a rest which we well deserve. It has been a hard task of endurance as well as the fighting and really wants a strong will to carry one through it all but thank God *we are made of the right stuff*, Jerry is now beginning to realise that we are the master, and before many more weeks he will cry out for mercy.

The italics are mine, to highlight the keynote claim in this fascinating document; the statement 'we are made of the right stuff'. It is as significant as it is striking to find a phrase now usually associated with American astronauts being so confidently used by a British corporal in 1918! (For a fuller version of Murrell's text see pp. 257–8; for more on the phrase 'the right stuff' see pp. 351–2 under Notes and References.)

Apart from its intrinsic linguistic interest, however, Murrell's statement carries an important implication. Undoubtedly there was much disenchantment and loathing of war by this time, but it is part of the necessary truth of this conflict that after more than four years of sacrificial warfare there were many, possibly a substantial majority, among the fighting men who were as committed to the goal of defeating the enemy as any of the eager volunteers who had flocked to enlist in 1914. They might be a good deal wiser, they were undoubtedly battle-worn, but they would almost certainly have agreed with the axiom enunciated by a Tommy of the Queen Victoria's Rifles as far back as 1915, shortly after he arrived for the first time in the region of the Somme: 'We all have one great ambition, to see Germany smashed, and then have the time of our lives upon our return home.'

This, surely, is the message implicit both in the eloquent letter written by Corporal Murrell and in the cheerful if weary faces of the soldiers photographed on the canal bank. The task they had set their hands to was at last approaching completion. They had signed the contract and the consequent obligations were one by one being fulfilled. I am reminded of the simple, moving words of a former Company Quarter Sergeant-Major of the Honourable Artillery Company, W.E Bates, from the Foreword he contributed to R.H. Mottram's book commemorating the Armistice, *Ten Years Ago*, published in 1928: 'We did not argue, even in our own minds, for or against war. Most of us tried to do the job thoroughly, not because we liked it, or even because we had to, but because we were perfectly sure it was being done finally.' It was perhaps as well that they could not know that (as already acknowledged) the job was not being done finally, but in their terms it was, and the outcome they had long laboured for would be delivered within weeks.

However, one cannot quite leave the subject like that. The events of 1918 showed the Allies had 'the right stuff' and a victory was duly secured, but the cost was an especially high one. As far as the British were concerned, they not only suffered more casualties in 1918 than in any other year of the war, but also, remarkably, than in the whole of the second war.

This too, more than any other, was the year of the young conscripts, as lads still in their teens, who could never have dreamed when hostilities began that they would ever be called to the colours, took their place in ranks depleted by so many losses over so long a time. It was the fact of those losses, and of the intensity with which the war was being fought, that had made Britain abandon its cherished principle of relying on volunteers for its armed forces, with the result that 'conscription' had been in operation ever since the first half of 1916. Now the military machine was combing out the country's tenderest youth, and demanding of it the same commitment and courage that had been offered with such innocent enthusiasm by the first recruits of 1914. Thus if the 'symbols' just discussed are significant mementoes of this final year of the war, equally significant in its way is the small collection of letters and documents under the name of Private E.J. 'Ted' Poole, who trained in England with the 19th Reserve Battalion, London Regiment, and served in France as a member of the regiment's 1/2nd (City of London) Battalion (Royal Fusiliers).

The younger brother of a soldier killed on the first day of the Third Battle of Ypres in 1917, Ted Poole was conscripted in May

1918 and began his training at Aldershot. His letters largely consisted of answers to the persistent, caring enquiries of his father, who, having already lost one son, was naturally deeply concerned about the progress of his next in line. 'Yes, I have got used to the puttees, as they have got shaped to my legs by now,' he wrote in one letter. 'And I am getting used to my other things now, as I have been dished out with a rifle and bayonet, and now, when I go on parade, I have got to wear my belt, bayonet and cartridge pouch, and also take the rifle. They have been teaching us bayonet fighting today, and I can tell you it makes your arms ache when you make a point, that is when you lunge at an imaginary enemy with the rifle at arm's length. I think with this hard training, they will either make a man of me, or kill me.'

Sadly, in a sense they did both, in that Poole went out to France in August priding himself on being a fully capable soldier, but by mid-October he had joined the ever-growing lists of the year's fatalities. Preserved with his letters are three photographs. One is a group picture of his Company at Aldershot; the ranks of young soldiers all in their new uniform, eyes to the front, smart as paint for the occasion, cap-badges gleaming. The second is of a standard, wooden, wartime cross, with the inscription 'Killed in Action, 13.10.18. R.I.P.' (reproduced as illustration 27). The third is of his postwar headstone, giving his age at death – eighteen – and with the inscription, added at his family's request: 'Out of the stress of the doing into the peace of the done.' The British Official History records that on 13 October, in an action to the north of Cambrai, Poole's battalion captured ten machine-guns and 207 prisoners, but it also lost 117 men: statistics which show both sides of the mastery the British sensed they had achieved at this time.

Such 'brief lives' are also part of the fabric of this landmark year. Anyone visiting those parts of the Western Front specifically associated with the events of 1918 will find innumerable headstones in the military cemeteries bearing the poignant inscription 'Aged 18', 'Aged 19'. Nor are the young men buried beneath these headstones just from Britain; almost every part of the then Empire is represented too.

It is perhaps important to add that this was also a year of considerable carnage among senior officers, numerous battalion commanders perishing with their men, while as many as twenty generals lost their lives: eighteen brigadier-generals and two major-generals. In the ferocious cut and thrust of the war's final campaigns no automatic immunity was conferred by high rank.

* * *

This is the fourth volume I have produced under the name of the Imperial War Museum, using as a main source the Museum's rich reserves of personal writings about the First World War. I have been sustained throughout by the confidence that such material offers a valuable and legitimate way of getting under the skin of the past and of presenting worthwhile historical works to the general reader: works of which the principal claim for notice is that they aim to present the authentic voice of the period under review. It was thus extremely reassuring, while researching the present book, to find a statement by a former fighting soldier which offered, or so it seemed, a powerful and convincing justification for this method of approach. The soldier in question, after earlier attempts to enlist had failed owing to asthma, finally got to France in the second half of 1917, was wounded twice in 1918, once during the March retreat and again during the final advance, and continued to serve until his belated demobilization in October 1919. In 1934 he decided to type out for possible publication the full text of the letters he had written to his family during his years in uniform. By way of introduction he wrote what he called an 'Antescript' in which he referred to the mass of books of all kinds about the war that had appeared since the Armistice – novels, reminiscences, essays, criticisms – and offered an eloquent plea on behalf of the contemporary letter. Of his own he wrote, with unnecessary modesty:

> As examples of the art of Chesterfield and Junius, the letters are of course worthless; their possible value lies in their unpretentious authenticity as a means of showing how an ordinary civilian-soldier reacted to the stresses of the times, and how the world-shaking events of the Great War appeared to an insignificant cog in the machine. I have often thought how interesting it would be to read the actual letters of, say, a Roman Legionary in Caesar's 'British Expeditionary Force', or those of a sailor in Columbus's

first voyage to America – always supposing that such men were able to write at all! The war of 1914–18 will perhaps bulk as largely in future histories as either of these two events, and it may well be that personal documents such as these letters will be more highly prized by historians, as sources of those intimate, insignificant details that reveal the actual texture of the past, than the formal and often biased 'memoirs' of more practised contemporary writers.

The writer was the same Frederick 'Fen' Noakes of the Coldstream Guards whose exultant post-Armistice letter of 13 November 1918 is quoted on the first page of this Foreword. Noakes never achieved the publication he sought, though he did include a number of extracts from his letters in a memoir he had privately printed in 1952. This present book allows an opportunity of which I am pleased to take advantage to give wider currency to the writings of a soldier whom I believe to be one of the finest contemporary chroniclers of wartime events and attitudes I have come across in many years of research in this field. There is perhaps an extra virtue in that these are letters not by some highly educated subaltern, but by someone who never rose above the Army's lowliest rank (though it should be added that not every private soldier spent his convalescence after being wounded reading *Barchester Towers* and *Pride and Prejudice*, or felt driven to complain that a shortage of decent books in the YMCA library meant that he would have to read *Oliver Twist* for the two-thousandth time!).

Noakes is represented in a number of the book's chapters, but one of his most memorable letters might best be quoted here, because of the light it sheds on the mixed texture of the year 1918. In it he describes an episode of mid-October (an 'intimate, insignificant detail', he might have called it), of a kind which would never find its way into a formal history, but which is surely standard fare for a book such as this. The piece is the worthier of inclusion because it jolts one's almost automatic assumption that this last phase of the war must have been a time filled with anger, recrimination and the desire for vengeance, with scant opportunity for such moments of humanity between enemies as had occurred from time to time in earlier years. Noakes himself introduced it to his family as an incident 'which shows a pleasing and, I hope, a characteristic trait in the British Army's way of waging war':

> On Tuesday we had a long and tiring march towards the line to take up our position for the following morning's attack, and at one time we halted for an hour or two in an old trench just across the Schelde Canal. Here we found the body of a dead German – quite a boy he was – and our officer, with our own approval, gave orders to bury him. The funeral, such as it was, was just such as we might have given to one of our men. The padre read the funeral service over him, while the men stood around with bared heads. It was a small matter in itself, but I think showed a very chivalrous spirit. Everyone concerned was profoundly affected by this burial of an unknown boy by his 'enemies' in an alien land; one of the men who dug the grave cried like a child. (Of course, we were all more or less overwrought by this time.) The dead man's 'identity disks' were preserved, and will be, if possible, sent to his relatives in Germany.

Echoing the sentiments of the late Charles Carrington when discussing certain chivalrous moments on the Somme in 1916, one can fairly say that the historian of the Western Front rarely has anything so benign to record.

* * *

From the preceding sentence, and from almost all the evidence so far cited, it will be correctly inferred that this book's main emphasis is on the war of the Western Front. This is by deliberate choice. The British Official History devotes no fewer than five sturdy volumes to the 1918 Western Front campaigns. Put together these make a work substantially longer than the Bible. Additionally, the Imperial War Museum is especially rich in first-hand documentary material relating to this key theatre. These considerations made the decision to concentrate on this aspect virtually inevitable. To adopt too large a remit would result in telling too thin a story. But this clearly could not be the only theme. It seemed important to include, if not in great detail, something of the experience of the domestic fronts and of the so-called sideshows, the 'plots' of which necessarily reached their conclusions in 1918. It also seemed both necessary and fair to give substantial space to the contribution of the Americans, for this is the year in which they began seriously to undertake the world role which, if with notable interruptions, they have fulfilled ever since. It was clearly important too that the Germans should have a sufficient number of representatives, to show how the year seemed to those on the opposite side.

In the light of such decisions, some omissions became inevitable. Apart from a brief reference to the St George's day attack on Ostend and Zeebrugge, there is little mention of the role of the Royal Navy. By way of less than adequate compensation, some statement as to the nature of the Naval contribution to the victory of 1918 might therefore be attempted here. There was no set-piece battle of the kind constantly sought by the British Grand Fleet, but that fleet's very existence ensured that Germany's treasured and much vaunted High Seas Fleet was rendered virtually impotent; it became, in effect, a sword unsheathed. Additionally, the Navy put severe, indeed crucial, pressure on the enemy in a number of more positive ways. They ensured that troop hospital and leave ships crossed the Channel with almost total immunity from enemy attack; had German U-boats or surface ships achieved success in this area they might have posed a serious threat to the British Expeditionary Force's vital lifelines. The massed soldiery of the American Expeditionary Force was brought to Europe under the Royal Navy's protection; thus the successful introduction of the convoy system back in 1917 became a major factor in tipping the balance against the enemy in 1918. Meanwhile, the naval blockade was a prime force in reducing the living standards and the morale of the German populace, and ultimately in bringing about Germany's political collapse.

A major reason for leaving out such material is that it is clearly a study on its own. The same can be said of another subject deliberately underplayed in these pages; the war in the air. A strong incentive for so doing is the recent publication of a successful book on this very subject based almost entirely on Imperial War Museum sources (see Notes and References p. 353). So far as the story told here is concerned, it is perhaps enough to know that this was the year when the Royal Air Force was born out of the conjunction of the Royal Naval Air Service and the Royal Flying Corps (the date of this important change being 1 April); that aircraft were now playing a much more integrated role than had been the case earlier, working in close co-operation with ground forces in both defence and attack; and that this was also the prime period of the gallant heroes of the air – on both sides – who jousted with each other in the clouds and frequently died in so doing. Aces such as Von Richthofen, McCudden and Mannock were among the famous, tragic casualties of this final year of war.

Given (even with the omissions described) so large a canvas, for the sake of the sanity of the author as well as the reader, I have sketched in the strategic and political background relatively lightly, providing, it is hoped, just sufficient colour and shade so that the actions and attitudes of the characters in the foreground can be appreciated and understood. It is on them, after all, that the focus should concentrate, for they are the true heroes and heroines, and also in some cases the victims, of this story.

They are also, as already stated, the prime justification for the book. As in the case of the preceding volumes the number of 'contributors' included has reached three figures, thus producing a total for my four Imperial War Museum books so far published of almost five hundred, most of them appearing in public print for the first time. It is fitting therefore that I should take advantage of this Foreword to express my deep gratitude to my fellow-chroniclers (and indeed, in a very real sense my companions) in an enterprise that has so far taken the best part of a decade.

* * *

A final, personal word. Normally historical works are not seen as appropriate media for the display of an author's own sentiments, but this is essentially a work of personal history and therefore I hope I might be forgiven for claiming an exception to the usual rules. There is perhaps an extra legitimacy in this case in that the modest story which follows was a potent element in arousing my interest in the year under scrutiny in this volume.

Sometime late in the winter of 1917–18, a small group of people waited on a platform of the principal station of the city of Cardiff, then known as Cardiff General. They were there to meet a train coming from Swansea, which would halt for a few minutes before continuing its journey to London. The train would have on board a considerable number of soldiers on their way back to France after leave, among them a member of the family on the station, Private Ernest Vivian Radcliffe, of the 16th Royal Welsh Fusiliers. He knew he was expected and he would come off the train to talk with his relatives until the whistle blew for departure. A married man approaching his mid-thirties, he was one of two brothers who had taken the decision back in 1914 that one of them would volunteer in response to the nation's call while the other would stay to take care of the family business. No natural soldier, he had never achieved, or possibly might never have sought, promotion.

The train duly arrived and the group huddled together on the platform in conversation. Among them was a young woman of twenty-four, a first cousin of the soldier and herself the fiancée of a private of the RAMC, by this time also serving in France. As a stalwart supporter of the Temperance cause (in fact an active member of the well-known anti-drink organization 'The Band of Hope'), she could not help noticing that some of the soldiers on the train had clearly been taking alcohol and were rather the worse for wear. Instinctively she showed disapproval, at which – as she told the story herself years later, with deep emotion – her cousin laid his hand on her arm and said to her quietly: *'If you knew what they were going back to, you wouldn't say anything.'*

Sadly Private Radcliffe, whose wife was pregnant at that time with a daughter he would never see, did not survive to describe what it was that he and his comrades had gone back to, and he was to become one of the many thousands of the fallen of that war for whom there is no known grave. He is commemorated on the Memorial to the Missing of 1918 at Pozières, by the side of the old Roman road that runs between Albert and Bapaume across the former battlefield of the Somme. The young woman in the story was to become my mother, and her RAMC fiancé my father. My mother never forgot or ceased to mourn her favourite, much admired 'Cousin Ernie', and it was family lore such as the incident described which, early in my life, helped to stimulate in me an interest in that war which has never gone away.

Readers of my *Imperial War Museum Book of the Somme* might recall that I dedicated that volume to the memory of my father, Private W.G. Brown, who (by definition) survived the war, and of

Private Ernest Vivian Radcliffe, who did not. I stated that little or nothing was known of the circumstances of the latter's death. Since then further research has established a clearer context for that event, and so I have included a reference to the attack of 22 April following which he was among those pronounced missing, presumed killed, in the appropriate chapter of this book. This minor episode in the Somme region, at a time when the main focus was on the so-called 'Battle of the Lys' still being fought out to the north, is also part of the complex fabric of 1918. Indeed, in a sense, since my own father served in France only in that year, this volume could be said to be as much dedicated to his memory and that of Private Radcliffe as was its predecessor; except that I would like to link with their names all those others whom I have been privileged to include in my four Imperial War Museum books relating to the Great War of 1914–1918.

MALCOLM BROWN

March 1998

1

THE UNENDING WAR

VIOLENT GALES LASHED the coast of southern England on New Year's Day, 1918. Some damage to shipping was matched by sporadic damage on land, with many trees being denuded of their branches. Much snow had fallen, and though in some places skaters emerged to celebrate their seasonal skills, in London a bitter wind under leaden skies drove most people to seek sanctuary indoors. 'Casualties' from colds were reported as being heavy, while some of the nation's innumerable allotment holders, who kept rabbits to eke out increasingly slender food supplies, found their tiny charges frozen to death in their pens. Because of ice on the Serpentine in London's Hyde Park, the race for the Peter Pan Cup, already postponed from Christmas Eve, was cancelled, though several members of the Serpentine Swimming Club were able to take their traditional plunge close to the bank where the ice had been broken. By contrast Scotland's Hogmanay was favoured with ideal weather. Huge crowds thronged Glasgow's streets and every place of entertainment was open, some giving up to four performances, all of which were crowded out. Football matches also played to packed grounds. Remarkably there was a distinct decrease in drunkenness, only nine cases giving rise to charges at the Central Court.

Despite the inclement weather in the capital, there were cheerful reports that Cupid had been especially busy, there being a healthy crop of fashionable weddings, including six between what were described as 'well-known families'. Also causing pleasing ripples among the worthy and famous, the New Year's Honours List named five new peers, twenty baronets and fifty-two knights. Most of those thus elevated are now long forgotten, but two among those named as knights have retained their reputation: John Galsworthy, the creator of *The Forsyte Saga* (at this time with most of its constituent novels yet to be written); and Anthony Hope Hawkins, better known as Anthony Hope, author of that much admired, and much filmed, classic of nineteenth-century European romanticism, *The Prisoner of Zenda*, first published in 1894. In the circumstances of January 1918, that novel's gallant hero, Rudolf Rassendyll, far from being welcomed in the German-speaking world, would doubtless have found himself kicking his heels in some dreary internment camp rather than passing himself off as a king or winning the heart of a beautiful princess. In the case of Galsworthy the elevation was distinctly short-lived; there were hurried postscripts in the next day's newspapers, stating that the author's letter intimating his wish to be allowed to decline the honour was received too late for his name to be deleted from the list.

Meanwhile, news stories of more immediate concern to the general British public included warnings of meatless days to come, and an announcement that the Food Controller had now forbidden the making of ice-cream. One newspaper carried a photograph showing a vendor doing good business with a group of soldiers, while adding that such vendors 'will now have to find a new occupation as theirs is now "agin the law".'

On the matter of the prosecution of the war, certain news items offered some cause for hope. Under the headline 'TRUST IN OUR TROOPS', a recent speech by Lord Derby, the Secretary of State for War, delivered expressly for the consumption of the French, was given considerable prominence. The kernel of his message had been as follows: 'We hope and believe that during the coming year we shall see all the troops back home, having ensured for the world the triumph of right over force, a peace which will last not only during our time, but during that also of our children and grandchildren.' Less encouragingly, there were reports that the Kaiser had been visiting the area of the Western Front and that German troops in Flanders were being considerably reinforced. A delayed news story emanating from Rome, originally filed on 24 December, carried an even more sombre message. At a great council of war held at German General Headquarters the programme of action for the winter and spring had been thoroughly debated. Possible peace propositions had been rejected for a harder course of action 'favouring the vigorous continuations of operations without any direct efforts for peace'.

Chief of the General Staff Von Hindenburg was stated to have guaranteed that the initiative in operations would not be lost again either in Italy or on the Western Front. More specifically, he had intimated that an offensive in France might be undertaken towards the end of February, at about the same date as that of the launch of the historic German attack on Verdun in 1916. Austrian troops had already been chosen to support the proposed action. Perhaps most menacing of all was the statement with which the news item concluded: 'Germany is extremely anxious to finish the war before the American armies can make their weight felt.'

Parallel royal utterances to coincide with the New Year might be said to cancel each other out. Kaiser Wilhelm urged on his troops with the injunction; 'Forward with God to Fresh Deeds and Victories!', while King George V expressed to the French President Poincaré his 'Unshakeable Belief in Victory'.

News from elsewhere over the following days suggested that other belligerent countries were also making an austere start to the New Year. A report dated 1 January stated that Germany's canal transport was paralysed by ice, with forty-five fully laden coal ships frozen in the Rhine–Weser–Leine Canal. Ice-breakers had been sent in from both ends to make a channel and keep it open. In the USA snow had fallen in semi-tropical Miami, while New York's Hudson and East Rivers were reported as being 'wrapped in driving mist'. The city's Director-General of Railways was seriously considering suspending passenger traffic to let the coal-trains through. Because of the cold large numbers of New York's well-to-do were loading their cars with coal from their own cellars to deliver basketfuls to the poor. Meanwhile under the heading 'Making Ready for a Long War', *The Times* reported a speech by a representative of the French High Commission to a meeting of the American Historical Association in Philadelphia. Assuring his audience that France was as strong and confident as ever, he spoke warmly of America's commitment to the common struggle, foreseeing for her, within two or three years, great military power. At the same time he warned of a more immediate danger, in that 'the common enemy was preparing an offensive stronger than any previous one'. Should this succeed, he added, the war would be brought to an end – 'an end disastrous for

France, Great Britain, Italy and America'. His observations can only have left his audience in a sober and anxious mood.

* * *

Such was the beginning of 1918 as portrayed in the contemporary media, the newspapers of London's Fleet Street. There was a different perspective not so many miles to the south and east, on Europe's crucial battleground, the Western Front, where the soldiers on whom the outcome of the crisis facing the nation, the continent and the world, depended, stamped up and down and blew on their hands to keep warm in cold and comfortless trenches. In the 'civvy' streets of Blighty, 'the War' might seem remote and other issues might engage the mind, but here it was close, possessive and overwhelming. It was also, or so it could seem, devoid of any prospect of conclusion. Looking back on this period, a former officer of the 8th King's Royal Rifle Corps, Desmond Allhusen, would write:

> The future seemed to be an endless vista of battles, each one worse than the last. We still felt that we would win, but had stopped saying so. The war was the only real and permanent thing, thriving and increasing in a world that was going to ruin. All our discussions ended by complete agreement on one point: that whatever might be the need for the nations, our destinies were clear enough. We would be hit, and if we recovered we would return and be hit again, and so on until we were either dead or permanently disabled.... The morale of the army had settled on to a rock-bottom of fatalistic despair, in which the majority carried on mechanically, waiting for their next wound, while the weaker members went under, either to lunacy, desertion, or self-inflicted wounds.

The war seemed equally all-pervading to a young adjutant of a Northamptonshire battalion in 8th Division, Hubert Essame, who would later become an historian of this remarkable year. For him the main characteristic of those holding the line as 1918 began was a kind of numbed, patient, unique kind of doggedness:

> The mood of these men in their forward posts on this bitter New Year's Day could be summed up as stoical endurance combined with bewilderment. Any desire they had ever had to attack the

Germans had long since vanished: now they counted the minutes and hours still to be endured before relief came. Of hatred for their enemies there was no apparent evidence. . . . Fifty years later the impression which remained of them was above all one of immense mutual loyalty and good nature. Order them to go forward and they would stolidly advance, however intense the fire; order them to stand fast and they would stay till told to go or to the end. . . . The link with their regimental officers was very close; common exposure to hardship and danger had welded them into an association, an alliance from which were excluded the Higher Command and the civilians at home. In a dim way they felt they were a race apart, morally superior to men who lacked their experience, as indeed they were, and that henceforth, if they survived, they would continue to be.

Varied as these two descriptions might be, almost in places contradictory, what they undoubtedly confirm is that this was a time of low ebb in a war that seemed endless. The trouble was that 1917 had been a bad year, a year of which few mourned the passing.

Above all it had been a year of disappointments, of hopes raised, and then dashed.

On the crucial stage of the Western Front there had been notable successes: the seizure of Vimy Ridge in April in the first phase of the Battle of Arras; the recapture of Messines Ridge in June following the explosion of nineteen huge mines under the German trenches; the first-day breakthrough of the tanks at Cambrai in November – a triumph so dramatic and astonishing that it had been hailed in Britain by the ringing of church bells. Yet in each case after initial success progress had been minimal. The Allied lines had moved forward only to congeal, so swiftly indeed that the maps eagerly conned by politicians and civilians back home scarcely needed alteration. In the case of Cambrai there had been ultimately hardly any change at all, in that the enemy stormed back within days and reclaimed virtually all the areas he had lost. Yet ironically enough new ground had been gained overall to create the need to build and secure numerous new trench lines, almost all the hard labour required falling inevitably on the hard pressed 'poor bloody infantry'.

In Belgium, in the Ypres Salient (immortal or notorious according to one's point of view), some progress had been made, and for the moment maintained. Yet the slow slog towards Passchendaele over the long weeks from 31 July to November had become in effect a second Somme: an almost yard-by-yard advance at an enormous cost in casualties. It was the Canadians who finally fought their way up the barely perceptible ridge to take that aptly named village. Their achievement so etched itself into the consciousness of the young, emergent dominion that it would later be seen not just as a military gain but also as a symbolic act of sacrifice recalling a more famous example of almost two thousand years earlier. In the words of a Canadian soldier-historian, Captain Harwood Steele MC, writing in 1919: 'It is not too much to compare the Canadian troops struggling forward, the pangs of hell racking their bodies, up the Ridge, their dying eyes set upon the summit, with a Man who once crept up another hill, with agony in soul and body, to redeem the world and give Passchendaele its glorious name.' A battle which could produce such a response was scarcely one to gladden the heart and to reassure those hoping for some great leap forward in the progress of the war. Even here, however, there were gains, if at the time largely hidden ones, in that whereas the Third Battle of Ypres (to give this campaign its official name) had been hard for the attackers, the defenders too had suffered heavily in both casualties and morale; in the dour arithmetic of attrition, it had been a minus for the Germans, while not obviously being a plus for the Allies. More, out of its mud and squalor a better, wiser Army would emerge, to fight in better and wiser ways in 1918. The battle had its positive side too, in the context of Allied strategy; vitally, it had drawn the fire of the Germans at a time when the French desperately needed breathing space after a bad time in early 1917.

Meanwhile the year had offered the Allies little or no encouragement elsewhere.

The collapse and defection of Russia had been a slowly evolving saga throughout the year. First the Tsar had been dethroned, to be succeeded in a situation of flux and chaos by moderate politicians who attempted to establish some form of democracy in a country where that concept had never been part of the culture. These were themselves ousted by ruthless activists determined to found their own modern, ideologically motivated form of autocracy. Back from exile in Switzerland, given assisted passage by a Germany which saw him as a fireship sent into a hostile port, Lenin became the new all-powerful Russian ruler, establishing a so-called 'dictatorship of the proletariat' in which the latter instantly became that which was dictated to as opposed to dictating. In effect the long-established systems of Tsarist repression merely changed their labels, replacing old priest with new presbyter, Romanov with Bolshevik, except that the latter term spread an almost neurotic anxiety, not unlike the fear of Jacobinism which followed the French Revolution, across the democratic world, engendering a widespread social and political unease that would last for decades.

The instinct of the Russian Empire's new masters was to make peace with Germany, however punitive the terms; the process which would lead to the humiliating treaty of Brest-Litovsk was soon in motion. Such a move would relieve the Germans of the requirement to maintain their second front in the east, with the result that they could release a mass of their soldiery to prosecute the war in the west. To meet this threat the French, chief partner in the Anglo-French alliance from 1914, were now seriously ill-equipped, their numbers heavily reduced by the long battle for Verdun in 1916, and their morale sapped by the catastrophic failure of the Nivelle offensive in April 1917 – a failure the more devastating because the prospect of its success had been so extravagantly trumpeted. Defeat had been followed by mutinies, to which the authorities had responded with a policy of harshness to the ringleaders and concessions to the rest. It was this combination of events that caused the trauma from which the French needed time to recover and which the British were in part able to provide by their fighting on at Ypres almost to the beginning of winter.

The situation in Italy had also deteriorated badly in 1917. To the British a remote and barely understood theatre of war, where an ally with no great military reputation fought the armies of Austria–Hungary – an enemy seen by the British very much as second string to their principal opponent, the Germans – Italy had suffered a massive defeat at Caporetto in October, followed by a major retreat from the line of the River Isonzo to that of the Piave. (The name Isonzo still creates few ripples of interest among British aficionados of the First World War, but it is noteworthy that before abandoning it in 1917 the Italians had fought no fewer than eleven battles in that sector, in repeated, sacrificial attempts to force the Austrians out of their territory.) In consequence French and British forces had been rushed out to assist in the task of stabilization. General Sir Herbert Plumer, to his dismay and that of his commander-in-chief, Field Marshal Sir Douglas Haig, had been despatched there to take command even while the Passchendaele campaign, in which Plumer had been deeply involved, was still in progress. That this was a not insignificant task, however, becomes evident when one realizes that the withdrawal to the line of the Piave had brought Italy's enemies to within twenty miles of Venice. There was a political motive too, in that, with Russia arguably setting a fashion for withdrawing from the war, there was anxiety that Italy might be tempted to follow suit.

There had been little change in 1917 in the Macedonian theatre, where the British and French, from their base in Salonika, confronted the Bulgars in a curious campaign at times so peaceful that men played cricket in No Man's Land. However, further off, in Palestine, Jerusalem had been taken from the Turks in December, an event hailed by Lloyd George as a Christmas gift to the nation. Yet for those engaged in the 'big war' (as T.E. Lawrence, himself a player in the Palestine/Arabian campaign, described the theatre of the Western Front), such coups were merely matters of propaganda. Certainly they cut little ice in the trenches of France and Flanders.

A major plus in 1917 had been that, thanks above all to the institution of the convoy system, the Allies, in particular the British, were at last successfully grappling with the German U-boat menace. The figures of shipping losses had steadily declined from an alarming high-water mark in April, though even as late as September the British Admiralty believed that, unless they could be further reduced, defeat was still possible. Summing up the year's progress, the historian Cyril Falls would write: 'A victory had been gained, one in which the active and important part had been done by Britain, but she was not yet certain of it. She had, however, good cause to feel encouraged.'

By one of the war's greatest ironies the earlier success of Germany's 'unrestricted' submarine campaign contributed significantly to what was undoubtedly the greatest gain for the Allies in

1917: the entry into the lists of the United States on their side. This had happened in April, thus putting a happier gloss on the month which (as referred to above) would become notorious for its appalling losses at sea. The hope that the potentially massive resources of the great power across the Atlantic would be able to effect a turning of the tide was widely shared, but clearly it would take time. Among those directing the British war effort it was not yet a serious part of the equation. The situation was pointedly summed up by the distinguished and influential Secretary to the War Cabinet, Colonel Sir Maurice Hankey, in a diary note of 16 December. Describing 'the whole position', as he called it, as 'very difficult', he summed up the balance sheet at that time: 'Russia practically out of the war; Italy very much under the weather after defeat; France unreliable; the U.S.A. not really ready; our own man-power much exhausted by the senseless hammerings of the last three years; . . . labour in a disgruntled state and unwilling to make concessions for combing out even those few men who can be spared.'

Meanwhile the homeland of Britain had continued to suffer attacks from the skies. There had been twenty-nine air raids in 1917, almost all of them targeted at London, the south-east and East Anglia, though there had also been two minor incursions as far north as Yorkshire. A total of 696 dead and 1,597 injured resulting from those raids might seem puny compared with the figures that would accrue in the 1939–45 war, but from now forwards civilians remote from the fighting fronts could no longer consider themselves exempt from the realities of war

Overall, a few positive pointers apart, the balance sheet did not bode well for the coming year. In fact, the Prime Minister, David Lloyd George, had conceded weeks before that there was no hope of a victory in 1918. Hankey's diary for 15 October had recorded that, in a heated argument over war policy, Lloyd George had 'committed himself to the view that we could only win in 1919 and that we must conserve our strength for this.' The assumption that 1918 would be at best a holding year, with hope deferred until the following one, would persist for many months. As would the nagging fear that somehow the conflict might become so endemic that it might prove incurable. As late as September of that year Lord

Northcliffe, the famous newspaper proprietor would say to one of his subordinates: 'None of us will see the end of the war.'

* * *

At the level of those committed to the fighting, reactions to the continuing war at this time were many and various. The views of Allhusen and Essame already quoted were, by definition, hindsight ones; what of those expressed at the time?

As has already been stressed in the Foreword, in spite of all that had happened through three and a half years of warfare, there was still a high proportion of soldiers who had no intention of weakening their determination to bring the war to its required conclusion. There were many too who remained resolutely buoyant and high-spirited. Thus Lieutenant Alex Wilkinson, 2nd Coldstream Guards, recuperating in a French hospital after being wounded at Cambrai, could write home on 12 December: 'If once one begins to treat this war on its merits, and believe that it is a really awful life, one is done.... I insist on the privilege of trying to extract what fun I may out of it.' Similarly Captain Richard Stokes, 83rd Brigade, Royal Field Artillery, could write on 20 December to his father: 'You say something must crack – it won't be the British Army! whatever else it is!!' Equally positive and determined was the view of Second Lieutenant Gordon Hassell, 8th Battalion, Tank Corps, in his letter of New Year's Eve: 'We all certainly long for a really *peaceful* year, but I should never be happy in coming back a minute before my duty here was done.... No, if need be, dear ones, we *must* continue to suffer if needed for the permanent peace of the future – we should be cowards else.'

However, for a thoughtful new arrival, Corporal Tom Houghton, 211 Siege Battery, Royal Garrison Artillery, the prospect facing him when he was posted to the Ypres Salient in the last weeks of 1917 proved utterly dispiriting. In a letter to his mother dated 10 December (written in billets at, of all places, Hell Fire Corner, a place of extreme danger in earlier times), he offered her a vivid description of that much-fought-over Belgian territory:

This is a hopeless country. You remember the house in S. which had been struck by a Zeppelin bomb? Imagine streets and streets of buildings all about three times worse than that and you have a faint idea of a town I have been in today. Outside, as far as the eye can see the ground is honeycombed with shell holes full of water and strewed with every imaginable kind of rubbish left by both armies. Every tree has had its branches torn off as if it had been struck by lightning. The whole is a scene of absolute desolation, amidst which thousands of men are moving and working as part of the great war machine.

And the key element in this scene, the object of an intense, obsessive loathing by virtually all those thousands of men, was – mud. 'When I last wrote to you,' Houghton told his mother, 'I think I mentioned that we were having a keen frost. The thaw set in a few days ago, and yesterday we had rain all day with the result that the mud is worse than ever. We get mud here in every form, from the thick variety which sticks to our boots in thick clods to the liquid state which splashes over us every time a lorry passes.'

Nor was mud a product of the autumnal end of the 1917 Ypres campaign; thanks to a unusually wet summer it had dominated from the start. The diary of a Gunner, James Bennett – like Houghton a member of the Royal Garrison Artillery – contains the following lines of unattributed satiric verse under the title 'Reminiscences of Pilckem Ridge, August 1917' (Pilckem Ridge had given its name to the first stage of the Third Ypres battle):

> It wasn't the foe we feared,
> It wasn't the bullets that whined,
> It wasn't the business career
> Of a shell, or the burst of a mine.
> It wasn't the sniper who sought
> To rip our young hopes in the bud.
> No it wasn't the guns
> And it wasn't the Huns
> It was the MUD – MUD – MUD.

But mud was no subject even for astringent humour as the Third Battle of Ypres moved into its final 'Passchendaele' stage. The following remarkable description is from a letter written to his sister on 2 November by a young private of the Artists' Rifles, Mark

Yewdall, after an attack which gained no advantage at a very high price:

> Thank God I'm alive to write to you. ... Oh, it was horrible, horrible. And the hopeless folly of it all. The newspaper says today we advanced slightly at heavy cost. My dear, we hardly exist now. Only 156 of us left – all others mown down and blown up before my eyes. Poor Mr Williams is killed, so is our dear Chaplain and our captain – but I needn't (and can't) go on – only to say that *six* have come back in my platoon, I being mercifully among them. For miles and miles the enemy shells cover every *inch* of ground. You are in a shell hole one minute, the next moment it has gone and another almost in its place. One can only rage at the system that employs infantry in a war of shells. And people that can say that *any*thing is worth it can only be devils. Every step took one over the knees in gripping slime. I saw many sucked down and drowned and I had near escapes myself. A shell blew my section into a shell hole – all wounded but me. For hours we lay there with thousands and thousands of shells all over and round us and covering us with debris, but none came right in. Why, I daren't ask. I had a terrible time with the wounded – they kept sinking into the slime and I had to pile rifles and haversacks and equipment – anything – under them to save them. In desperation we struggled out at last, and wallowed and struggled in the open to the aid-post and eventually to the dressing station. It was a fearful distance and shells covered it all.
>
> If we have another stunt of this sort, I can't possibly hope to survive again. I do hope we shan't – it is too much to ask of a human being.

When Plumer left the Salient for Italy, he was succeeded by General Sir Henry Rawlinson, who as commander of the Fourth Army in 1916 would always be linked with the hard-fought campaign on the Somme. After having spent some months chafing in comparative obscurity, he was ordered to take command of the last actions of the Passchendaele campaign. He had little hesitation in awarding the palm in the matter of mud to the Salient. 'There is no cover for the men in the forward areas,' he noted in his diary on 12 November, 'and the low lying parts of the mud and shell holes are appalling – it is worse than the Somme was last year and we shall have heavy losses from sickness.' In a vivid comment two weeks later, on the 27th, he stated: 'Ypres was one huge pool of liquid coffee.' Quoting this description, his recent biographers added that he had written it 'a few days before sending two divisions into a quite futile attack'. It was this combination of squalor and apparent or real futility that would turn this, the greatest battle of 1917, into arguably the worst of the whole war. Certainly it offered no happy portent for the year to come.

For the newly arrived Corporal Houghton the bleak scene to the eye in the dying weeks of 1917 was reflected in a similar bleakness of attitude, a response that was inevitably exacerbated as December moved towards its routine festive climax. Christmas, for the soldiers of the Western Front, had always been a time for focusing their thoughts on the incongruity of the message of the season and the inhuman task in which they were employed. (An awareness of that incongruity and a determination despite all the hazards to celebrate the season had been one of the prime impulses behind the famous, and remarkably widespread, Christmas Truce of 1914.) Houghton wrote to his mother on Christmas Eve:

Tomorrow, the day of peace and goodwill towards men (what a farce it all seems!) I shall be sending 100lb high explosive shells to remind Fritz that Mr Asquith has not yet sheathed the sword and that Mr Lloyd George is as bellicose as ever (with his tongue of course). I shall be on the guns from 10 o'clock tomorrow morning until 10 o'clock on Boxing Day. Rather a strange way of spending Xmas. Nearly all our institutions seem to me to be so utterly inconsistent with the hard facts of everyday life as to be utterly ridiculous. Tomorrow all over Eng[land] people will be singing Peace on Earth, Goodwill towards men; the parson will pray for victory over our enemies, and on Boxing Day morning there will be more big headlines in the papers saying that more and still more men are wanted for the Army. The same thing struck me the other day when the Chaplain came round and said a few prayers in one of our gun-pits. There was the well-known phrase about 'not leading us into any kind of danger'! And the very next morning Fritz sent us a few of his usual greetings just to show us that he had not gone to sleep. And yet I am quite sure that our chaplain has never noticed the inconsistency of that phrase, any more than the clergymen at home who profess a religion that teaches that all men should be brothers and yet pray weekly for victory over our enemies. I am quite convinced that a large percentage of the men who 'hold positions', as the saying is, are either madmen, fools or hypocrites; and I have a suspicion that the proportion of Pecksniffs is not small.

All this was a far cry from the mood with which his predecessors had first gone to war; something of which Houghton was almost certainly aware, in that the statement he referred to by H.H. Asquith, the former Prime Minister, that Britain should not sheath the sword until the enemy had been finally crushed, was a product of the heady, hopeful days of 1914. Such statements could seem mere dead rhetoric in the atmosphere of the last days of 1917, when it was quite clear that there would be much more carnage, and many more casualties, before, *or indeed if*, the sword was sheathed.

Casualties there were, indeed, even before those last days expired. The 63rd (Royal Naval) Division had been released from the Salient following the end of the Third Ypres battle, and was now in the Third Army sector further south – in the area which was to become the first focus of the major actions of 1918. On 30 December its entire frontage of 6,800 yards was subjected to a ferocious dawn bombardment. Even the approaches, tracks and back areas were heavily pounded. The division was under further attack on 31 December: to mention just one of its constituent units, the Hood Battalion lost thirty men of its D Company being killed or wounded; it was finally relieved at 3.10 a.m. on New Year's Day.

One other event that took place on the night of 31st December/ 1st January near Arras was recorded in a Third Army intelligence report: 'North-east of Monchy the enemy attempted to fraternise but were fired on.' Captain A.E. Hodgkin, an expert in gas warfare whose post was that of Chemical Adviser at Third Army HQ, cut out the item and pasted it into his diary, endorsing the British response with the ironic comment 'with best wishes for a Happy New Year'. He also noted, with no fond retrospective glance, the passing of the old year: 'End of 1917 and a good job too.'

* * *

So the year 1918 began.

Private Arthur Wrench, a Seaforth Highlander of 51st (Highland) Division, approached the start of the New Year feeling miserable and unwell. In late November while on leave in Glasgow he had heard the 'terrible news, and official too' that his brother Bill had been killed at Passchendaele, just one week after arriving at the Front. When the time came for him to return to France he had hated the prospect as never before. 'I shudder at what I have already survived and must surely suffer again,' he stated in his diary. New Year's Eve found his battalion moving up into the line at Beaumetz near Arras: 'The going was good coming in but the roads were very slippery and now tonight I feel so wretchedly ill that I would much rather be dead. What a happy New Year *I* am going to have. I don't think.' But New Year's Day showed him climbing back out of his Slough of Despond, largely thanks to the determined attentions of one of his comrades:

A Happy New Year! What? Well, I am certainly not dead yet anyway. When I went to bunk last night I hardly expected to see this morning, and I didn't care either. But I went to bunk almost in a state of collapse and Wincholl insisted that he was going to make me take my rum which I have never done yet. So he persuaded the quartie to give him my issue then got some hot water and sugar from Willie Drysdale and against my protests poured a whole pint of the concoction down my throat. So it must have been that that put me to sleep, and if it is 'sweet and fitting to die for one's country' (like fun it is!) I still think it far more so to live for your country, and the old fellow who spun that tale is far from the truth. And much as I detest the rum I am thankful for that dose.

I have spent the day on office duty from 9 a.m. to 9 p.m. and now I am tired as a dog. But I hope for an easy time for the next two weeks or so since Charlie File has gone off to the rest camp and I am detailed in his place as General's orderly. So I'll get a chance to rest up too.

For Private William Sharpe, a thoughtful, reluctant soldier of the 2/8th Lancashire Fusiliers, 66th Division, New Year's Day signalled a return to the Ypres Salient. He had joined the Army under the so-called Derby scheme, a process initiated back in October 1915 under the Asquith government by Lord Derby, then Director-General of Recruiting, whereby men of military age 'attested' their willingness to serve if or when called upon to do so. In effect this was a midway system devised at a time when the flow of volunteers of the first phase of the war had subsided and before the nation was ready to accept the concept of conscription. The 'Derby Scheme' to its devisers, it was soon by those combed out by it dubbed the 'Derby Snare'. For though in theory it conveyed a hint of free will, in practice it could be very close to compulsion. August 1915 had seen the launch of a 'National Register', to which all citizens, male and female, had been obliged to supply details of age, sex and occupation, while at the same time being given the opportunity to state whether they could or would undertake work of national importance. Under the Derby Scheme, the recruiting authorities, using the National Register as a basis, picked out the names of men of military age not in essential work and invited them to attest. Sharpe, married with a young son, had been caught by this process, and, despite protracted wrangles with exemption tribunals, had finally donned khaki in June 1916, accepting that it was 'my duty to go', and claiming 'I was not afraid when the time DID come'. He was at first graded C1 and posted to Northumberland, but on 31 August 1917, 'after little or no examination', he was passed A1 and pronounced fit for overseas service. In October Sharpe sailed for France – noting that 'there were a good number aboard returning from leave and could tell, by the expression on their faces, that they were not very happy' – and by the second week of November he was in the Salient. The Christmas season, however, had found him undergoing further training at Étaples, a place normally hated by the troops but which Sharpe found relatively enjoyable after the dubious pleasures of Ypres. The 25th itself had been not been an occasion for celebration: 'The real Xmas day found us marching about with full pack, a punishment for some man who had committed a nuisance whilst the worse for drink and would not confess, so the whole of the Company was punished all day.' But he was to write in his account of his numerous adventures: 'We left Étaples after what might be called a happy time, for it had given us the evenings free, and of course it was so far away from the front line, that we nearly forgot there was a war on.' He and his fellow Fusiliers would be unlikely to do that when back in the Salient.

Second Lieutenant Frank Warren, like Private Sharpe, had attested under the Derby scheme. He had joined up in May 1916 at the age of thirty-eight, and was now serving in the 17th Battalion of the King's Royal Rifles, 39th Division. A married man with three young children, public-school educated, editor of a local county newspaper, a non-smoker, teetotaller and an idealistic practising Christian, he was no natural soldier, but he had felt the obligation to answer the nation's call. New Year's Day 1918 found him in the Ypres Salient, and in a quiet, almost benign mood, as he confided to his diary:

> A New Year, again in France! I wonder what it will bring for me! But a few days at a time are sufficient nowadays. Go up with CSM Foxwell and Sergt Williams and Randall to reconnoitre the line. A fine keen morning and good going. See many tank relics near the St. Julien road. A daring Boche chaser pursues one of our observer planes. Clever diving alone saves our man who gets away within 100 feet of the ground. The Boche flies off, along our support lines. A good sporting performance on both sides!

His senior in rank though greatly his junior in age, nineteen-year-old Lieutenant Douglas McMurtrie, 7th Somerset Light Infantry, 20th (Light) Division, was not far from Second Lieutenant Warren that day. Because of the number of officer casualties in the battalion he now found himself an acting Company Commander. He had first crossed to France the previous August and had been initiated in the hard fighting at Langemarck during the Third Battle of Ypres, but this was the first time he saw the remarkable city from which that battle had taken its name. Christmas had been spent in the vicinity of Hazebrouck – the occasion being much improved through the success of the mess waiter in acquiring a seven-pound turkey from the market at Aire-sur-la-Lys – but now they were to return to serious business in the Salient. In an account written some months later in circumstances which, as will be seen, provided him with far more free time than he could ever have wanted, he described the process of events:

On Jan 1st 1918 all the Coy Commanders had to meet at the
cross roads at La Belle Hostesse [the site of a well-known
estaminet] at 7 a.m. to go up the line. We left La Belle Hostesse
in an open bus, with overcoats and scarves and carrying tin hats
and respirator. We picked up the Kings and Cornwalls at Wallon-
Cappel and then began a very cold journey through Hazebrouck
and Poperinghe to Ypres. We saw the remains of the famous
Cloth Hall. Ypres was one scene of desolation, all the houses had
been destroyed, a few isolated walls were still standing and
dugouts and shelters, occupied by troops, were everywhere.

The city, however, was merely a curiosity to be noted and wondered
at as they passed through to the Salient's southern sector, where they
would be much engaged in the weeks that followed.

In a society thickly populated with young officers not long out
of school, it was unlikely that the New Year would arrive without
some attempts at horseplay. Lieutenant C.H. Dudley Ward recorded
a modest example among his fellow officers of the 1st Welsh Guards,
at this time in billets in a small town somewhere near Arras, and
behind trenches distinctly more 'cushy' than those of Ypres:

1st Jan 1918. I did not see the new year in – I was asleep – maybe
the noise of a piper that came to me in the night was the New
Year – I don't know. I however gave a dinner party to Broncho
and Arthur Gibbs at the pub. After dinner – and they turn you
out at nine – I believe Broncho and Mick went round and
wrecked everybody's room, but as they could not find my billet
I escaped. D.G., of course, opened the door, turned his money,
crossed his fingers, cursed in Scotch and goodness knows what
else.

This morning we moved up into the line. This is a quaint bit
of front and is held in a different way to most. We are in reserve
and live in excellent trenches. There is a YMCA dugout and all
sorts of little comforts and if there were only more deep dugouts
for the men it would be perfect.

Captain Vere Cotton, Royal Field Artillery, now serving as
Trench Mortar Officer, 23rd Division, celebrated the New Year in
Italy. Plumer and Haig might have been reluctant to see good British
troops sent to the Italian front, but among those so posted there had

been fewer objections. 'We are all in great spirits at being down here out of the mud of Flanders,' Cotton had written in a letter home on arriving there in November. 'It's like starting the war afresh with new enthusiasm and new experience.' In December, in the Montello sector, he had found himself to his delight in scenery he described as 'superb': 'One can see from the Alps on one side to Venice on the other. The latter I could see quite plainly yesterday (a clear day) through glasses, could even distinguish individual buildings and I hope that some day I may set foot in the promised land.' But in the matter of their purpose in being there, they had had little serious contact with their Austro-Hungarian enemies: 'It is deliciously amusing to read the daily newspaper reports about "intense artillery activity all along the Italian front". I was watching about twelve miles of front yesterday for two hours and didn't see a shell burst the whole time.' There was more to report following a move to Montebelluna towards the end of the month, with 'great aerial activity in this neighbourhood during which the Boche lost heavily' (it is noteworthy that the standard term for the enemy in France translated effortlessly to Italy, as also did the Tommy's favourite name 'Fritz'), while the French recorded a successful attack on a strong point called Monte Tomba. New Year's Eve had, however, concentrated his thoughts on home. He wrote next morning: 'Last night I and one other observed the time honoured ritual and opened the door at midnight and I wondered if you were doing the same.' Thoughts of home also brought up the matter of leave, but that did not present the easy option of a break in Blighty as normally available on the Western Front: 'There are rumours that leave will open again shortly (ours has been stopped since before we left France) but even if it does open it will be very slow and of course that means it will be months before my turn comes round. Even then I don't fancy it will be all jam as one will spend at least a day travelling for every day in England and I shall be very inclined to stay out here and see Rome or Florence now I am out here. Perhaps, however, I shall have different view when the chance comes.'

Blighty leave was hardly an option at all in those theatres generally known as the 'sideshows', so far from the mother country that men stationed there had little if any prospect of seeing their

homes or loved ones until – whenever that might be – the end of
hostilities.

Private William Knott, of 32nd Field Ambulance, 10th (Irish)
Division, began 1918 in southern Palestine. He had been in the
Middle East for two and a half years, having landed at Suvla Bay,
Gallipoli, in August 1915 and subsequently endured many tedious
months in Salonika. In September 1917 his division had moved to
Egypt and had then been involved in the advance towards Jerusalem.
That city's capture in December had provided him, as a keen
evangelical Christian, with the best moments of his military career,
as he found himself able to make regular visits there, though he had
been thwarted at Christmas owing to his having spent several days
in hospital. The first day of January found him in thoughtful, even
sombre mood – yet he was also, underneath, prayerfully hopeful, as
he contemplated the possibility of what he saw as the ultimate and
greatest deliverance of all: 'The new year has commenced badly, all
night it has been raining in torrents, at reveille the thunder-clouds
hung low over the valley of Ajalon, the mud is ankle deep and I am
afraid most hearts are damped at having to enter another year with
the world's conflict still raging. "How long, O Lord?" is the cry,
"when wilt Thou return for Thy waiting church?" If the call comes
this year may I be found watching and waiting.'

Palestine had at least seen recent positive action, but elsewhere in
some of the sideshows a tedious stalemate had set in during which
nothing seemed to happen and little seemed to matter. Major Alfred
Bundy of the Middlesex Regiment had experienced the traumatic
first day on the Somme in July 1916, and had also endured that
battle's most rigorous phase in October. Now, attached to 2nd
Battalion of the King's Own Royal Lancaster Regiment, 28th Division, he was in Salonika, not at the front but at the base, where he
found himself celebrating the New Year in a manner unthinkable in
more dangerous theatres: ·

1st Jan. Had a merry evening at the Cercle Français – the French
Officers Club. It is amazing how the French manage to get such
an abundance and variety of food. We had soup, oysters, salmon.
chicken, ices and fruit and cigars all served as well as in a first
class Parisian restaurant. The British Officers Club is in striking

contrast and one can obtain there very little more than the ordinary rations. All four of us had to walk back to camp with drawn revolvers because of the murderous thieves that frequent the roads. Nothing exciting happened, however, and we got back about 2 a.m.

But such idle enjoyment had its negative side. He had been profoundly relieved to leave the Somme, but all this kicking of heels far from the centre stage seemed too unrelated to the war's realities to be endured indefinitely. It was certainly doing nothing to end the war. If there was serious soldiering to be found even in Salonika, he would opt for it. Summing up his feelings over the following weeks he wrote: '*2nd Jan to 1st March*. Am getting tired of the humdrum monotony of life here. Had talk with the C.O. and cautiously sounded him of the possibility of a spell up the line. He was not at all pleased and after expressing the view that I was doing invaluable work plainly told me he would refuse to let me go.' Bundy was disappointed, 'but not shaken from my determination to get away as soon as possible'.

The further from home the more alluring the prospect of return to it seemed to be; certainly this was the experience of Captain Tom Sherwood of the South Persia Rifles, writing to his young pregnant wife as the last moments of 1917 ticked away: 'And here we are on the threshold of a new year and your birthday. 1918, think of it, 3½ years of War, no sign of it being over yet, wonder what the year holds for us, *apart of course* from our Baby, just imagine if you can my return to you both! indescribable joy! a honeymoon all over again, you treasure wife of mine.'

Gunner Ernest Barnett was in Mesopotamia. A regular for some years before the war, he had rejoined in 1916 and now found himself in a country for which he had no affection and where he would be – though fortunately he did not then know it – until well after the end of the war. His wife, Elsie, wrote long and informative letters which he faithfully kept and eventually brought home. A constant subject in them was the progress of their young daughter, often referred to as 'the dear little nip'. The following extracts are from a long New Year letter written from the family home in Walthamstow, East London:

Just another letter to help you keep going and it's the first day of the New Year and I wish you all you wish yourself. Pray God this year will see the end to this terrible war and so bring peace perfect peace to our dear ones safely and speedily. . . .

I am waiting another letter from you as it's now over 3 weeks since the last and am wondering if you are up the lines by now. Oh how I do long to see you again, I cannot express on paper my feelings dear, it seems years since I heard your voice and saw your dear face and some days I feel my heart will break and then I try and buck up for dear little nip's sake as I promised you I would but I do feel so lonely, even now I sit and write this letter all alone everyone is in bed and it's just 11ᵒᶜ but I felt I must write this letter I started yesterday to catch the mail. So I must cheer up for your dear sake in the hope that our dear little girl's and my prayers will be answered.

She concluded with a touching postscript, offering her hoped-for summary of her husband's wartime career:

> 1916 on 17 August joined up
> 1917 ”   ”   ”   sailed
> 1918 ”   ”   ”   come home to me please God.

A letter of a few days later indicated how bad civilian conditions had become by this stage of the war:

Here we are once more and things still seem much about the same, and no nearer the end of this terrible war, or our dear ones home, in fact I think things are much worse as we are slowly being starved out, we have to line up for everything, tea, sugar, marg., and a joint of meat is a thing of the past. Last week I was 2½ hours lined up for meat and only a few had any, hundreds had no joint or chops, only sausage meat or tinned stuff, all the butchers shops were closed down Friday afternoon, what a life to think we should ever come to this dearest, that we should have to line up in this bitter cold weather, inches thick with snow, we shouldn't mind so much if we could see any prospect of the end.

The faintest prospect of an end to the nightmare *was* perceived about this time by a woman of a very different stamp writing in her diary in the principal enemy's capital, Berlin. Princess Evelyn Blü-

cher, an Englishwoman who had married into a German family of
considerable distinction – one with some resonance in British history
in that it was a Blücher who had come famously to Wellington's aid
at Waterloo in 1815 – lived in Germany throughout the war. Torn
by a cruel conflict of loyalties, she was nevertheless as eager for
peace as her far-off compatriot, Mrs Elsie Burnett. She wrote in the
first days of 1918:

> The days come and go, and we have already crossed the border-
> land and have left the gloom of the old year, only to enter the
> darkness of a new one.... Christmas was, of course, but a sorry
> season, although the unexpectedly and seemingly successful peace
> movement in Russia undoubtedly created a brighter atmosphere
> for people here than they have known since the war began. Brest-
> Litovsk, mingled with the divine proclamation of 'Peace upon
> earth and goodwill amongst men' moved our hearts to a new
> throb of hope. It remains to be seen how far people are justified
> in believing this to be the first weak wavelet of the great peace-
> tide which is gradually but surely going to inundate Europe.

At the front, on the German side, prospects of peace, however,
were distinctly not on the immediate agenda. On the contrary, as
well as pride in the fact that Germany had held her enemies at bay
for so long, there was a also a sensation of excitement at the prospect
of a major thrust to come. An artillery officer, Herbert Sulzbach,
noted in his diary under '*New Year's Eve, 1917–18*': 'Once more a
year reaches its end, in which we can really be proud of each other,
since what we have stood firm against on this Western Front can
never be described in words; in fact, it will perhaps be understood
even less by the people at home.' As to the future: 'People are talking
a lot just now about a big offensive which is supposed to be coming
off in France; we are already keyed up, and hardly dare hope for it.
But there are so many preparations to be completed for an operation
like that, it obviously can't be launched just yet.'

The conviction that such an offensive was shortly to take place,
while it might create a positive response among soldiers eager for
decisive action after so many months of stalemate, struck only gloom
into the heart of the distinguished German writer Hermann Hesse,
at that time in exile in Switzerland. An opponent of the war from its

inception, he now looked forward in gloomy anticipation to what the year 1918 might bring. In an article dated December 1917 entitled 'Shall There Be Peace?' – to which question he could only give a negative answer – he wrote:

> For many days now the eyes of the world have been focused upon two places. In those two places, it is widely felt, the destinies of nations are coming to a head, the future beckoning, and disaster threatening. With bated breath the world is looking eastwards, to the peace negotiations in Brest-Litovsk. And at the same time it is watching the western front in dire anguish, for everyone feels, everyone knows that, short of a miracle, the most dreadful disaster that has ever befallen men is there impending: the bitterest, bloodiest, most ruthless and appalling battle of all time.

At a somewhat different level of expectation, that most famous of British Western Front trench journals *The Wipers Times* (by now, strictly, entitled: *The B.E.F. Times, with which are incorporated The Wipers Times, The 'New Church' Times, The Kemmel Times & The Somme Times*), was on the whole much more optimistic than might have been expected in the circumstances. Its first editorial of the New Year, entitled '1918', began jauntily: 'Seconds out of the Ring. Last round coming up. We have it on the best authority that William Hohenzollern has a little boat ready, with steam up, to cut it to Sweden. . . . We have heard so many tales from Hunland about what he's going to do now that he has fixed Russia, that it makes us think he is trying to forget what WE are going to do to HIM.'

The editorial's conclusion was almost up-beat, though not without that realistic and reflective tone which balanced the journal's wit and humour throughout its existence: 'So here's to 1918, a speedy finish and a job well done. Here's the best of luck to you all in the New Year, and a quiet thought and salutation to the memory of those stout lads who fell in the old.'

It was under such auguries that the world moved into the final year of the war.

2

WAITING FOR THE INFERNO

'THERE IS AN OMINOUS FEELING ABOUT, as if something is about
to happen.' So wrote Gunner J.W. Gore, of Z66 Trench Mortar
Battery, 66th Division, in his diary in mid-March 1918. It was a
sensation shared by many in the curious doldrum time that preceded
the first German offensive. A variant sensation was that of the
menacing pause that can precede some cataclysm of the weather.
Thus such phrases as 'Calm before the Storm', 'The Eve of the
Storm', 'Before the Storm' have appeared as chapter titles in historical works dealing with this tense and nervous period. Yet another
historian, seeing the approaching threat in quasi-Biblical terms, chose
the title 'The Wrath to Come'.

The ever eloquent diarist Private Arthur Wrench, in 51st
(Highland) Division, writing on the day before Gunner Gore made
the comment quoted above, chose similarly striking metaphors in his
speculations about the imminent attack. He did so in a reflective
entry, inspired by the incongruous peacefulness of a late winter day
in a zone likely at any moment to be pounded by the shells of a
massive bombardment:

> It is a beautiful evening with a cloudless azure sky and the
> thinnest streak of a new moon, pale but very visible because of
> the contrast. Like yesterday, it is very quiet again today and all
> that I hear is a single gun far away to the right while its solitary
> shell hums in the distance like the droning of a bee. Now all is
> serene again and the chirping of a few birds make me imagine
> this war is only a dream and all is well with the old world. These
> birds, poor little innocent things, have their own struggle for life
> but are free to go whither they will untrammelled by rules and
> regulations and discipline. Here and right into No Man's Land
> they hop around without sensing the danger that surrounds us
> and I wonder if a shell has ever hit a bird at all? It must be

wonderful not to have any dread of the future and certainly it's God's blessing that we cannot tell what even the next moment has in store for us. If it were always as quiet as it is here now I wonder how many ages would this war drag on?

But what will this same spot be when the Germans attack? A bloody inferno and it may happen at any moment, a sudden jump from this stillness into Hell, yet at this time I feel I haven't a care in all the world.

'A bloody inferno'; 'a sudden jump into hell': these concepts would indeed be fairly realized when the action began, and Wrench would not be the only one to resort to or echo such or similar descriptions.

What was the condition and mood of the British forces in France and Belgium at this time, as they prepared themselves for the ordeal to come? A useful 'official' snapshot survives in an important memorandum submitted to the War Cabinet at the end of January by the redoubtable General J.C. Smuts, former Boer commander in the Boer War, now a close ally of the Prime Minister and himself a distinguished War Cabinet member. It was the product of a six days' visit to France and Belgium by Smuts and the Cabinet Secretary, Colonel Sir Maurice Hankey, who in fact drafted the text of the paper, though it was released under his senior partner's name. It is praised in the Official History as summing up 'admirably' the then state of affairs on the Western Front. It is worth quoting at some length:

> I am satisfied that the morale of the Army is good. The bearing of the troops coming in and out of the line and in the large working parties all along the front is in every way satisfactory. The Army is well found and in good fettle. There is, however, no question that the men are tired. This applies more especially to the infantry. To a considerable extent the personnel of the artillery has been rested after the great fatigues of the Flanders battle. The infantry, on the other had, is not yet sufficiently rested. All the divisions were actively engaged in exhausting offensive operations during the whole of 1917. Much new ground has been wrested from the enemy, with the result that entirely new defences have had to be created on a large proportion of the

front, and the tired divisions had not during 1917 maintained even the old defences at the highest level. The change in the strategical situation, due to the collapse of Russia, has necessitated the construction of a great new system of defences in depth, the fronts of which, on most parts of the front, do not correspond with the first line trenches. A defensive system that amply sufficed for an Army continually on the offensive, does not meet the defensive needs of the existing situation, and behind the elaborate system of the main battle zone, reserve defences are being constructed.

The preparation of this vast but absolutely essential scheme of defence requires an immense amount of labour. As the greater part of the work has to be done within the zone of artillery fire, native and prisoner labour cannot be employed to any considerable extent. The burden falls in the main on the infantry. Consequently, divisions which have completed their term in the defensive line have, almost immediately, to be turned on to the construction of defence works. The result is that they suffer in regard both to rest and training. In the circumstances, the surprising feature is not that that they are fatigued but that their spirits are so good.

A matter of major importance, and interest, in this document is that it makes clear that a crucial shift of emphasis had taken place in regard to British Western Front strategy. Hitherto the prime focus had always been on the offensive: the ball was always to be at the feet of the Allies; they were to dictate the play. Now the focus was to be on the defensive. In effect this meant that the initiative had been passed to the enemy; it was the Germans who were expected to make the next move. The defection of Russia is adduced as one of the causes leading to the new concept; the vast amount of labour devolving on the poor long-suffering infantry, in order to build the new defence systems required, is seen as one of its unavoidable consequences.

In practice, the new dispensation required a complete overhaul of the system by which the British had organized their defences (a reorganization which, it should be added, was at least partly based on concepts of 'defence in depth' devised by the Germans). There were to be, in theory at least, three zones. The first, to be known as the 'Forward Zone', was basically to be an outpost line, held in sufficient numbers to offer the enemy some resistance but from which its defenders, after inflicting maximum damage at minimum cost, would rapidly redeploy to the main line of defence. This main defence area was to be known as the 'Battle Zone'; it would be 2,000 to 3,000 yards behind the Forward Zone, and would be a similar distance in depth. Being thus far back it would, it was hoped, be spared the first impact of any German attack. It too would not be fully manned, though the troops required to defend it would be sufficiently near to occupy it immediately when necessary. Reserves would also be at hand to move to any area under threat, or to mount counter-attacks. A third set of defences, to be known as the 'Corps Line' was to be set up behind the Battle Zone, but this part of the new scheme would remain theoretical only.

The Army itself was undergoing a major reorganization of another kind at this time, under the impact of the losses incurred in 1917 and of the shortage of available manpower in France. The ten Empire divisions were receiving sufficient reinforcements to continue unchanged, but the situation of the forty-seven United Kingdom divisions was such that it was decided that each of them was to be diminished by three battalions. Since the War Office, which ordered this remake of the BEF, insisted that Regular and First-Line Territorial battalions were to be spared, the axe fell heavily on the 'New Army' units formed in response to Kitchener's appeal of 1914 and on the wartime-raised Second-Line Territorials. Thirty-eight battalions avoided extinction by being amalgamated, seven others became 'pioneers' (i.e. principally labour battalions), but over a hundred disappeared altogether. The new scheme was put through quickly and without warning, beginning in January and finishing in early March. One Territorial battalion staged a mock funeral on the day of its disbandment, burying an empty coffin and marking the grave by a wooden cross inscribed 'BURIAL PLACE OF 1/7th LONDONS'. As a result of this change Infantry brigades, which had traditionally consisted of four battalions, were reduced to three, but, to no one's surprise, the three were still expected to do the work of four.

All this put much pressure on the men on the ground, quite apart from any damage inflicted by the inevitable blow to morale in those units which had suffered the *coup de grâce*. 'Working parties' had been the bane of the infantrymen's life throughout the war; they were particularly frequent, onerous and demanding at this time. So much is clear from the account of Private Sharpe, which bears out with remarkable precision the situation as described in the Smuts memorandum, though there is little to support (except perhaps in relation to one unusual occasion) the alleged prevalence of 'good spirits'.

Sharpe and his fellow 2/8th Lancashire Fusiliers, returning from Étaples, had only got as far as the hinterland of the Ypres Salient when they were given their first assignment:

> Reveille next morning was at 4.30 a.m. and we were informed that we were a working party. It was some 2½ hours journey by train from Brandhoek to Gordon House, Ypres, and then a long march along duckboards over the shell-holed ground and the work set to us was to make a strong line of reinforced trenches some two miles behind the firing line and to utilise some German 'Pill Boxes'. These were solid concrete fortresses about 15 yards square and 9 yards high and the concrete was all interlaced with steel tubes and practically indestructible. Along the sector where we were working there were about five of these.

This was a task that required numerous visits and it was certainly (in Smuts's phrase) 'within the zone of artillery fire': 'The German artillery found the range several times and on these occasions we took what cover we could beside the old pill boxes.' The routine was to work until 10 a.m., then make their way back to their camp, where they would arrive about 2.30, after which, apart from a rifle inspection, they would be off-duty for rest of the day. However, the men had little energy left to make much use of their free time: 'These working parties with always the same early start and long march to reach the work were very tiring and I was pretty well ready to lie on the boards of the hut with my three blankets, after of course writing a letter home.'

The irony was that, as had always been the case, the battalions provided such working parties when officially 'out on rest'. When not on rest they took their turn in the front line trenches, to reach which, as always in the Salient, entailed a journey that was not only arduous, it was also extremely dangerous, and not just from the attentions of the enemy. During one journey to relieve a battalion of the Manchesters in the area of the Passchendaele railway cutting, Sharpe encountered what he called 'the most awful conditions I ever ran into. The mud was thigh deep and we lost two men, who had to be left to die in the mud as it was impossible to extricate them.'

But the Tommy was ever resilient if there was the slightest chance of bending or outwitting the system. Even so conscientious a soldier as Sharpe was happy to snatch a little light relief if the opportunity offered, the more easily of course when not in the trenches: 'I had the unusual experience whilst on these working parties of playing a piano within 2½ miles of the front line amongst all the shell holes and bare country. It was in a very small Artillery canteen – just a ramshackle hut. It was a great novelty and one day I dodged duty with the Sgt-Major's instructions and he, together with three sergeants and myself stopped there whilst duty lasted, singing and playing.'

On the matter of morale, Second Lieutenant Frank Warren's diary for this period makes it clear that the one definite moment of 'good spirits' for his 17th Battalion, King's Royal Rifle Corps, while taking turn and turn about in the Salient was the moment of leaving it: 'We make our way with the traditional duckboard "crawl" to the soup kitchen, where we have a tiresome wait of two hours for the train. But of men coming out of the line nothing damps the spirits. They form up in groups and circles and sing and dance literally in ecstatic mood, so great is the reaction to the strain of shell fire.'

For Lieutenant Douglas McMurtrie of the 7th Somerset Light Infantry, morale became a disturbingly serious problem at this time; had he been aware of Smuts's claim that 'the Army is well found and in good fettle' he might have found some cause to demur. He had begun the year in a particularly unpleasant area of the Salient, the vicinity of Dumbarton Wood, a notably unhealthy spot just off the notorious Menin Road, of which he would write: 'It was a bestial trench system. Only in a few places could one stand up in a trench and not show miles above it. The communication trench did not get as far as my Coy HQ, so that if the enemy attacked I should have to rush up over the open and risk getting shot.' But it was after the battalion had been withdrawn from the Salient and moved to a safer area further south that the problems began to surface, producing a kind of grumbling disaffection and lack of commitment which had not been evident hitherto:

> During this period and for the next month it was one long struggle to get my officers and men to work really hard. All their work was only half done and the discipline was slack. I had great difficulty in getting the men to turn out on parade really clean and smart. I had a platoon inspection by Platoon Commanders every morning and then I went on parade and inspected the Company myself. One man would have his ammunition filthy, another his buttons or boots dirty and another mud on his putties. I provided cleaning material for buttons, dubbin was provided for boots and brushes were issued, so that there was no excuse whatever for any man turning up dirty. Yet it went on, they were not checked by their section or platoon commanders so I took matters in hand and they soon began to get better. Any man that turned up on parade dirty was immediately hauled up to Coy office and I gave him a pretty severe punishment.

Carrot as well as stick could be effective in such situations, and McMurtrie set himself to do everything he could to improve the men's morale, a task made easier when he was appointed battalion sports' officer. He carried out his new role with his customary enthusiasm. Indeed, as the time of the offensive approached, he was almost more concerned with organizing games for his troops than preparing for that other sport, the game of war.

Normally a time of waiting such as this would have inspired those in authority to attempt to scotch any slackness or lack of spirit among the troops by demanding the carrying out of raids; 'minor enterprises' in the language of the time, though some were relatively major and all were productive of casualties. As it happened there had been a general mandate to reduce this form of activity during the winter period. The Germans, however, had their own ideas: the Official History records as many as 225 raids between 8 December and 21 March (naming the 30/31 December attack on the 63rd (Royal Naval) Division, as described in Chapter 1, as the 'most formidable' of them). Inevitably, this created the need for retaliation.

Lieutenant C.H. Dudley Ward of the 1st Welsh Guards, in the front north of Arras, recorded several raids in this period, though he did so with considerably less enthusiasm than that of those who requested them, believing them ill-thought-out and largely futile. 'Our raid early tomorrow morning worries me,' he wrote on 9 March. 'We are so very obvious and clumsy in our methods and the Boche knows very well we are coming and if he cared to do so he could give our party beans. These minor operations are not conducted with any imagination at all.' In the event there was confusion as to the time when the raid was to be launched, the enemy was poised and waiting, a German prisoner sent back for interrogation never reached the British lines, and though on the positive side most of those wounded were successfully retrieved, the final tally included two men missing, believed killed.

While Dudley Ward was assessing the meagre results of this dispiriting effort, the Brigadier-General who had ordered it came to visit the battalion: 'I thought he was looking pretty blue, so much so that when he asked me what mistakes had been made to guard against in the future I did not like to tell him what I really thought.' Unnoticed by the Germans a wounded man managed to crawl in about 11 a.m. It had not been a significant contribution to the prosecution of the war.

* * *

The Guards' Division was not part of the southward move towards the Somme region that was a principal element in the disposition of British forces in the early weeks of 1918. Sharpe's 66th (2nd East Lancs) Division and McMurtrie's 20th (Light) Division were, as was Warren's 39th Division. The 20th and 66th Divisions went down in early March; the 39th had arrived by the end of January. They were sent there to become part of the Fifth Army, which was to take over a substantial part of the line hitherto occupied by the French. In effect this would put them in the forefront of the coming battle. They, of course, were happily without such knowledge, and generally reacted favourably to their new situation.

Clearly glad to be away from the dreary country of the Ypres Salient, Warren wrote on 28 January: 'Reach Corbie at 7.30 a.m. and breakfasted there. Wait until 11 a.m. for motor lorries, and then drive over rolling uplands away to Bray-en-Somme. It is fine country and the sun is warm and cheering. From one height we look down on a fine château with the Somme spreading itself as a wide lake in front of it. On all sides are steep hills, and in summer the whole place must be full of delight.'

For him, as it would also be for Sharpe and McMurtrie, this was a first sighting of a territory which, while it might appear delightful in its untouched areas, had elsewhere been transformed into a very different landscape. This was the product partly of the great Somme battle of 1916, partly of a deliberate policy of destruction by the Germans when they subsequently withdrew to new positions further east. The desolate zone thus created had lain fallow during most of 1917, and had even in part mutated into a place of strange beauty, with areas of grey mud turned to swathes of dazzling whiteness and wild flowers growing in abundance among the rusting wrecks of guns and tanks and the ruins of shattered villages. Now it was to be fought over again, though this year it would only be part of a much larger battleground, with the focus at first some way to the east of it.

Cambrai, St Quentin and La Fère were the key towns of the coming campaign on the German side, with the German lines running roughly north and south just to the west of them. Opposite, the British lines laced through or near a skein of small townships and villages – such as Havrincourt, Gouzeaucourt, Épehy, Villers-Carbonnel, Hargicourt – with, behind them, key towns such as Péronne, Bapaume and (at the extreme northern end) Arras.

If the soldiers reacted well to their novel situation – in another letter Warren would describe the warfare down south as a picnic compared to the 'shell-holes war' of the Salient – their commanders assumed responsibility for the new sector with no great enthusiasm. For the change in the disposition of Allied forces of which their move was a part was not the result of decisions made on strictly military grounds, but was part of a new military/political dispensation the elements of which had been decided during weeks of argument and acrimony in high places in both England and France.

This is not the place for a detailed discussion of this controversial subject, but some hint of its complexities might be gathered from a listing of some of the key players involved. These included: a British commander-in-chief, Field Marshal Haig, who wanted more men and a free hand for what he unshakeably deemed to be the central and decisive theatre of the war, the Western Front; a British Prime Minister, Lloyd George, who was anxious to avoid a repetition of the holocaust casualty figures on that Front in 1916 and 1917, and had therefore held back in Britain troops Haig wanted in France (thus being partly responsible for the reshaping of the BEF as earlier described); and a French Prime Minister, Clemenceau, who was one with Haig in wishing to concentrate on the Western Front, but was also determined to make the British take over more of it than they felt they could reasonably defend. (By way of footnote it might be added that the visit by Smuts and Hankey recorded earlier had had a second, undeclared purpose; to assess if there was any possible successor to Haig as British Commander-in-Chief, this being a product of a long-running hostility between Haig and Lloyd George which had been part of the sub-text of the Western Front war ever since the latter became Prime Minister. In the end it would be decided that there was no acceptable alternative, so Haig would stay and the armed neutrality between the two men would continue.)

Other roles, beneficial or Machiavellian according to one's point of view, were played by General Sir Henry Wilson, who intrigued constantly against Haig and replaced Haig's preferred Chief of the Imperial General Staff, Sir William Robertson, in February; the Chief of the French General Staff, General Foch, who was ever ready to accuse the British of not playing their full part (to which Lloyd George's retort was that since the Somme they had undertaken most of the fighting and suffered more of the casualties); and the French Commander-in-Chief, General Pétain, whose promise of French support if the British were attacked in the area they were now to take over was crucial in Haig's acceptance of his new responsibilities. The availability of such support depended on a concept elaborated at a Supreme War Council sitting at Versailles of which neither the British nor the French commanders-in-chief were members; the creation of a general reserve ready to be moved instantly to any weak spot on the front. At the time in question this was little more than an idea on paper.

Summing up the situation in early 1918 from the point of view of the British troops now settling into their new positions, the historian

Martin Middlebrook has written: 'Pity the poor British Expedition-ary Force – worn out by three major battles in the last year, five of its divisions sent to Italy, dissension between its commander and those at home and kept short of men thereby, having just taken over twenty-five more miles of new front line and forced for its safety to depend on the charity of the French and a Central Allied reserve that did not exist.'

In the event, two British armies would bear the brunt of the coming attack, but they would not be in the same state of readiness when it began. The Third Army, under General Hon. Sir Julian Byng, occupying some twenty-eight miles of front from to the north of Arras to the south-east of Bapaume, would be able to make substantial progress in implementing the new defence schemes. By contrast the Fifth Army, under General Sir Hubert Gough, occupy-ing overall some forty-two miles from its junction with the British Third Army to its junction with the French Sixth Army opposite La Fère, would always be several steps behind, so that in places alleged lines of defence would remain little more than preliminary scratch-ings in the ground.

* * *

On the other side of No Man's Land wire were the Germans, still a most formidable force despite their own very considerable sufferings in earlier campaigns, and now substantially reinforced from the east following the end of the war on the Russian front. That statement, however, does not tell the whole story.

What is now known but could not have been known at the time was that there were portents suggesting that the apparently implac-able will of the German Army to carry on the struggle was being significantly eroded. The transfer of troops from the Eastern Front to the Western was not a simple matter of adding to one war zone that which had been taken from another. There was a considerable amount of wastage on the way. Soldiers who had witnessed the collapse of the Russian war effort, and who in some cases had openly fraternized with their Russian counterparts, had hoped that the close down on their front might be, in effect, an end to their front-line service. They did not view it as a happy opportunity to transfer to the notoriously sacrificial fighting in the west. Many of the railway wagons they boarded for the journey from Russia carried the slogan *Schlachtvieh für Flandern* – literally 'fat stock for Flanders'; in other words, the troops herded into them saw themselves as cattle destined for slaughter.

The German railway system had been crucial to the launching of the war in 1914 by getting the troops so quickly to the frontiers. Now in a kind of ironic revenge it contributed to Germany's dissolution, as railway stations became the focus for political agitation and subversion. A substantial number of soldiers who took the long journey westward failed to complete it, yielding to the persuasions of certain societies established to aid men prepared to desert. These societies were active in a number of key cities across the nation, such as Berlin, Hamburg, Cologne, Stuttgart and Munich. Estimates suggest that some ten per cent of those being moved from east to west were diverted in this way. Offered forged papers, ration cards and money, they let themselves be spirited away, many of them to end up in the neutral states of Switzerland and Holland. Those who resisted such temptations were more likely to have done so out of instinctive loyalty and fear of reprisal than out of any enthusiasm for further fighting.

Prisoners of war held by the Russians and now released offered another potential source of supply for the German Army in the west, but many of these had converted to the socialist philosophy of their captors. They returned not so much as reliable reinforcements as potential troublemakers. Special camps were set up to reindoctrinate and re-enthuse them, but even in the difficult circumstances of the summer of 1918 some German commanders would find it preferable to fight with smaller units on whose loyalty they could rely absolutely rather than larger ones containing such men.

Dissidence was spreading in the civilian world as well, with potentially unhappy consequences for the military. January 1918, for example, saw a strike in Berlin aimed at achieving peace and constitutional reform. Many of the most militant strikers were immediately conscripted, but this had the effect of adding another element of disaffection to an already simmering cauldron.

Yet all this did not mean that the forces massing in the Kaiser's name in the west in early 1918 were not capable of delivering a powerful, possibly a knock-out, blow to their enemies. Any argument that they no longer constituted the mailed fist of power with which Germany had launched her war must challenge the evidence of such as Ernst Jünger, who would write of the great attack to come: 'After forty-four months of hard fighting they threw themselves upon the enemy with all the enthusiasm of August 1914. No wonder it needed a world in arms to bring such a storm-flood to a standstill.'

But there was also undoubtedly a sense that this would have to be an all-or-nothing throw. They were ready, if circumstances went well, for one or more further attempts to force a rapid outright win; but if these failed, and if the Americans were able to deploy in the strength of which they were known to be capable, who knew what consequences might then ensue?

* * *

Although the initiative was now clearly with the Germans, their High Command had prevaricated for several weeks before deciding on its strategic plan.

First ideas for 1918 had been discussed some months earlier on a notable date and at a notable location: 11 November, at Mons. Strong arguments had been put by one adviser, General von Kuhl, for an attack on the British at Ypres; equally strongly another, Colonel von der Schulenberg, had argued for an attack on the French on Verdun. Ludendorff favoured an attack on the British, but further south than Ypres. 'In particular an attack near St. Quentin appeared promising,' he had stated. 'After gaining the Somme line, Ham-Péronne, operations could be carried further in a north-westerly direction, with the left flank resting on the Somme, and lead to the rolling up of the British front.' This was in essence what was ultimately attempted, but there was much more argument before a final choice was made. On 27 December at a further conference Ludendorff ordered that planning and preparation should go forward for attacks in a number of areas: an offensive towards Hazebrouck, to be code-named 'George', with a subsidiary attack towards Ypres, 'George Two'; the St Quentin attack, code-named 'Michael', with a subsidiary attack, 'Mars', towards Arras, while other possible schemes were to be prepared for the French zone, either side of Verdun or in the Vosges. As Correlli Barnett has written: 'It was a jeweller's tray of glittering possibilities from which it was clear that Ludendorff could not bring himself to choose. Since the great battle must begin in only about ten weeks' time, it indicated a dangerous lack of clear strategic thought.' In fact it was not until 21 January that Ludendorff made his decision, following a tour of the front and a series of staff conferences. 'Michael' was selected, with 'Mars' as supplementary option. Vigorous preparations then began.

These were carried out with remarkable success, in large part owing to the fact that the Germans were now cleverly using a weapon that had been all too rarely in evidence during almost four years of campaigning on the Western Front: surprise. They would employ every possible ruse to make their strike come like a bolt from the blue. The British would be equally adept at surprise later in 1918, but first honour must go to Germany for her preparations for their March attack. Discussing some of the measures adopted, a German Medical Officer, Stephen Westman, would later write:

> The deception practised on the enemy artillery observers as to the appearance of new German batteries of large or small calibre was worked out to perfection. Our batteries had half their guns constantly on the move, appearing here, there and everywhere, firing at night a few shots into enemy territory: and when next morning British or French reconnaissance aircraft flew over to take photographs of the new battery position, there it apparently was, but actually consisting of wheels of farm carts with a wooden beam, all scarcely camouflaged. The British artillery fired fiercely on these dummies and the next night, a few hundred yards away, a new 'battery' popped up.
>
> And this deception manoeuvre went on for weeks from north to south, and especially on those parts of the front where no attack was intended to take place.

And the Germans had another card to play. The first infantry attack would be in the hands of specially trained storm troopers who would infiltrate the Allied lines at speed, leaving others to mop up any pockets of resistance. These constituted an élite, on whose fighting spirit and skill the Germans knew they could rely. Westman wrote of them, admiringly:

The men of the storm battalions were treated like football stars. They lived in comfortable quarters, they travelled to the 'playing grounds' in buses, they did their jobs and disappeared again, and left it to the poor footsloggers to dig in, to deal with counter-attacks and to endure the avenging artillery fire of the enemy. They were so well trained and had developed such a high standard of team work that their casualties were almost nil. They moved like snakes over the ground, camouflaged, and making use of every bit of cover, so that they did not offer any targets for artillery fire. And when they reached the barbed-wire entanglements of the positions opposite they had special torpedoes with which they blew up the defences – dangerous people to come up against.

Evidence of the success of the German preparation lies in the fact that, even after the offensive began, there was some uncertainty in the Third and Fifth Armies as to whether they were facing a real attack or a feint while the major thrust was elsewhere. The trench grapevine, arguably more fecund than ever in times of crisis, spread a range of alternative scenarios. As Second Lieutenant Warren would put it: 'There are big rumours of British Offensives at Passchendaele, at Lens, and where not? The French have made a big push at Verdun! So does rumour feed the tired Tommy!'

Also playing into German hands was the fact that the British awaited the enemy attack with a certain amount of complacency. It having been now decided to put the emphasis not on attack but defence, the prevailing view was that this would be the easier option. On 2 March after inspecting the defences along the fronts of three armies Field Marshal Haig spoke to his Army commanders in terms that suggested he was not only willing but even eager that the attack should take place. He underlined the necessity for being ready as soon as possible to meet 'a big hostile offensive of prolonged duration', yet, as he wrote in his diary that day, summarizing the content of his address: 'Plans were sound and thorough, and very much work had already been done. I was only afraid that the enemy would find our front so very strong that he will hesitate to commit his Army to the attack with the almost certainty of losing very heavily.'

This attitude would persist, so much so that on 20 March, on the eve of the launch of 'Operation Michael', Haig could write: 'Everyone is in good spirits and only anxious that the enemy should attack.' This was in a letter to his wife, who had been delivered of a son on the 15th. Paternal instinct obviously made him wish to hurry home, but this did not seem the right course of action: 'The enemy is rather threatening for the moment, I therefore think it will be better for me to delay coming over to see you for a week.... [U]nder the circumstances, it is right that I should do so.... [I]f he did attack on Saturday, and I was in England, it might lead to "talk".'

In fact the enemy attacked on Thursday and it would be some considerable time before the Field Marshal saw his wife and son. Meanwhile, in the words of the historian David French: 'When the offensive began on 21 March, the War Cabinet literally did not know what had hit them. The CIGS told ministers that "there was the possibility that it might only develop into a big raid or demonstration" and that the real German attack might develop further north. The force of the German thrust against Gough's army came as a most unpleasant surprise to both GHQ and the War Office, both of whom more than half expected the initial offensive to be but a preliminary to a more dangerous thrust towards the Channel ports.'

* * *

A matter of days before the great attack, Lieutenant-Colonel Walter Vignoles, CO of the 9th Northumberland Fusiliers, 34th Division, Third Army, noted the irony of the situation in which so many young men, of both armies, now found themselves. He wrote to his family on 11 March: 'Just a line to let you know I am well but very busy. It is pretty quiet and the weather is absolutely topping. Bright sun all day and a sharp frost at night. The larks get up at "Stand to" and it seems impossible that we are waiting on each side to kill one another.'

Yet waiting they were, with a mixture of apprehension and confidence. Lieutenant George Havard Thomas, 7th Sherwood Foresters, 59th (North Midland) Division, Third Army, was of the latter persuasion. He wrote on the 13th: 'Everybody is fussing about this coming offensive. We are preparing for them [the Germans] a quite warm though inhospitable welcome.'

Private Arthur Wrench was also convinced that if the enemy attacked he would find it no walk-over. 'Should he make the attempt, it certainly will be at tremendous cost,' he had commented in his diary on 6 March. Wrench had fought in the Battle of the Ancre in 1916 and for him attack was synonymous with high casualties, only this time it would be the Germans whose turn it would be to advance into the usual withering fire.

Yet he was experienced enough to realize it would be no picnic on the British side either and over the following days he chronicled an increasingly edgy, volatile mood in the British lines. On the 7th: 'There is still plenty of "breeze" about this offensive but tonight everything is as quiet as a funeral.' On the 11th: 'Still nothing doing but the suspense is getting on our nerves while the "breeze" is assuming hurricane proportions.' Again, on the 13th: 'Our guns were going at it hammer and tongs and God help Fritz venturing out beneath such fire. But he never came altho' *his* guns were going hard at it too, probably cutting the wire in No Man's Land.'

He was still speculating about the prospect of an offensive on the 20th: 'There's some breeze around here now that the attack is coming in the morning. Which might only be another rumour after all. Tonight Charlie File is off on leave so I am detailed for General's orderly in the morning. Here's hoping I'll have another good easy time as before.'

On the Fifth Army front, among the units of Lieutenant Frank Warren's 39th Division, false alarms had become so frequent that, as he recorded in an account written some weeks later in hospital in England, less importance rather than more was being attached to warnings of an imminent offensive as the last days before the attack slipped by.

On the 20th the statement of a German prisoner revived the notion that the enemy was poised to strike on their sector, but Warren and his fellow officers of the 17th King's Royal Rifles were not unduly perturbed. The battalion was temporarily out of the line in a hutted encampment near the village of Gouzeaucourt, some ten miles south-west of Cambrai, and its main function that day, as on several previous days, was to supply working parties – those working parties again – to dig new trenches; trenches of which Fifth Army was in very considerable need. Certain distinguished visitors appeared who clearly took the greatest interest in the proceedings: Mr Winston Churchill, then Minister of Munitions, the Duke of Westminster, and General Tudor, the GOC of the 9th (Scottish) Division – the division in which Churchill had served earlier in the war as a battalion commander. Using the historic-present narrative style he adopted for most of his account, Warren commented: 'Winston, who can never be like other mortals, wears a French helmet with a khaki cover; the Duke of Westminster is content with a cloth cap, though well within the area where a "tin hat" is compulsory.' The presence of such illustrious figures failed, however, to impinge on the generally relaxed atmosphere; Warren recorded that he and his fellow officers retired 'after a jovial evening in the mess, with a dim notion of the possibilities of the morrow, but with no special preparations for a "stand to".'

Meanwhile McMurtrie's 7th Somersets had had a very relaxed and enjoyable day. As described by the battalion's Chaplain, Revd T.L.B. Westerdale, in an account of the first spring offensive written immediately after its conclusion: 'On Wednesday the 20th the CO arranged a grand paper-chase on horseback. Every available officer turned out. Some who had never been in the saddle before soon found themselves in ditches. One horse preferred to go home and the officer on board found himself very quickly at the halt in the Transport lines, far from the quarry. Conversation that night was more lively than ever as funny episodes of the paper-chase were recounted again and again.'

There was no sleep that night for Acting Lance-Corporal (as he now was) William Sharpe. He was in charge of a company wiring party, as he had been every night from 15 March, working out in No Man's Land. As he described his unenviable task:

Each night when dark, 12 nice lads and myself got gingerly over the parapet and took iron stakes and spools of barbed wire and constructed nervously and as quietly as possible barbed-wire fences, getting into all sorts of tangles, dropping down when the 'zip-zip-zip' of machine-gun bullets came too close (i.e. when one 'felt' the whistle), and standing stock still like tree trunks when the firework display (Very lights) went up. This was quite a heart-thumping operation, what with the darkness, the uncertainty of whether it was 'our blokes' firing or 't'others', and just how far 't'others' were away, and what we might expect if some fool rattled a bundle of iron stakes together.

But this was not all we had to do, each morning at sunrise came 2 hours 'standing to', in other words waiting, fully prepared, for the enemy to come, and again at sunset. In addition to my wiring party I was also sent out on patrol nightly between 1 a.m. and 3 a.m. This consisted (with a party of six) of crawling, walking, lying in shell holes and listening to anything that might be happening in Jerry's lines, to which we had to get as near as possible, with the stars (if any) to guide us back to our lines, another heart thumping job, and one was devoutly glad when the 2 hours were up and one could get back to the comparative safety and comfort of a trench.

Again, our little lot were lucky and nothing untoward happened. Another patrol party of our company was not so lucky as, meeting a Jerry patrol of double strength, they suffered four casualties, a nice fellow, Clapperton by name, being killed. Information was given by the 2 survivors of this party that 4 Germans had been killed, and I touched for the job, with my patrol, of getting these men into our lines, but on reaching the spot, we were too late, a party of 20 Germans being there before us, and I will honestly admit on this job I was not comfortable, seeing we were outnumbered. I could not see what chance we had and went back, only to be severely reprimanded for not attacking, but I still think 'discretion is the better part of valour', and 6 men's lives and my own were of value to someone, if not to the Army.

On the 20th Sharpe had relaxed, enjoying the spring sunshine and counting, as he had done for several days, what few shells the enemy sent over: 'These did not average more than 10 per day – in fact it was really peaceful compared to the Ypres sector and one could hardly imagine a war was on.' But that afternoon he had felt a sudden unease: 'I sat on the top step of our dugout writing home to my wife and although it may be that one can be wise after the event, I had a premonition that something was going to happen, having quite an unsettled feeling, not a bit in keeping with the beautiful day.'

Later, after dark, he again led his small band of men over the parapet and resumed his work of wiring and patrol.

Away to the east, on a night of still weather which would culminate in widespread fog, the enemy was poised to strike. Private Wrench's 'bloody inferno' was about to begin.

3

SPRING OFFENSIVE: MARCH

PRIVATE WRENCH'S HOPES of an easy time as orderly to the General were not to be realized. When at the end of Thursday 21 March he found a moment to write up his diary, he began with the simple statement: 'We're getting it now all right.' Twenty-four hours later he would resort to more eloquent description: 'It is absolute Hell here. Cold-blooded murder and mass slaughter. The Germans in their mass formation get it from our Lewis and machine-guns while they give it to us unmercifully with their artillery. The fatigue is awful and the strain of holding on tremendous, and God knows how long it will go on. Our line is getting thin while the Germans seem to be coming on in inexhaustible numbers and must surely get through.'

Second Lieutenant Warren's had been an equally rude awakening on that unforgettable Thursday morning:

> It is 4.40 a.m. on the 21st when we are awoken by a crashing bombardment, and its intensity leaves no room for doubting its purpose. With a feeling of suppressed excitement we are out of bed and dressing quickly, amid a round of chaff and banter in our officers' huts.
>
> Shrapnel is already bursting heavily over the village and the word is passed to assemble in the valley on the football field, which is almost dead ground. Here we fall in by platoons in the darkness, only to find that fourteen of our men have been hit in the huts by shrapnel. My No.4 Platoon of our 'A' Company is reduced to a Lewis-Gun team of seven men.
>
> We avoid the village and go direct through the mist across the Downs, making for the valley edge of the wood. 'A' Company is there first, without any mishap, but with the uncomfortable feeling that we may walk into gas at any moment.
>
> 'C' and 'D' Companies are just arriving. There is a whizz of heavy shells, and two or three fall among the approaching platoon

groups. When the smoke clears, several men lie dotted on the slopes amid the mist, and the repeated call for 'Stretcher Bearers' tells its tale.

But these witnesses were behind the lines. Acting Lance-Corporal William Sharpe was in the Forward Zone, and thus at the heart of the storm now breaking over the front held by Third and Fifth Army. Overnight he and his working party of the 2/8th Lancashire Fusiliers, 66th Division, had been again out wiring and patrolling, and at 4.30 a.m. had taken their usual places in the front-line trenches for 'Stand To'. Looking back on what would be his last day of active warfare, Sharpe recalled that it was 'a thick misty morning, following the very hot previous day, with what could be likened to a heavy Scottish mist, so it was impossible to see above 5 or 6 yards.' At 5.30 a.m. there was a distinctive chlorine smell, which they assumed to be gas, prompting a hurried putting on of gas helmets, though finding this made the visibility still worse, many removed them, some to their later regret. Meanwhile: 'A terrific barrage had started – a succession of falling shells dropping increasingly nearer with each successive round. We who had been at Ypres began to compare, saying it was as bad, but it continued to get worse and came to a pitch when it seemed impossible that anything could live in it, and personally I prayed with every reverence.'

One memory that would remain indelible for Lance-Corporal Sharpe was of the terrified reactions of some of the young conscripts who had recently been sent to the battalion as replacements:

My section included four youths just turned 18 years, who had only been with our company three weeks and whose first experience of shell fire it was and WHAT an experience. They cried and one kept calling 'mother!' and who could blame him, such HELL makes weaklings of the strongest and no human's nerves or body were ever built to stand such torture, noise, horror and mental pain.

The barrage was now on top of us and our trench was blown in. I missed these four youths, and I never saw them again, despite searching among the debris for some time.

Notwithstanding their precarious situation Sharpe and his section were ordered to stay where they were, a jar of rum being sent forward to help maintain their morale. As they waited, stragglers from other sections of their company, who had been 'literally blown out of their cover', passed by heading for the rear. 'At 9 o'clock the mist was even worse and one could barely see a yard and still we waited, the barrage now being well past us.' There were soon indications, audible rather than visible, that the Germans were poised for the second stage of their offensive:

> A few minutes before 10, we heard signs of the wire in front of us being cut and we opened out with rapid fire, firing some 50 yards into the mist, without seeing anything. We followed this with bombs for some ten minutes and still with no attack. Not knowing exactly what to do, we decided to go for instructions to the command dugout, and made our way through what had been trenches to the sunken road though even this could hardly be recognized. The fog was now lifting and the sun breaking through. No sooner had we got into the road when we ran into 'Jerries', who opened fire with revolvers. A few of the lads bolted up the edges of the road and the remainder of us stood still, simply amazed, and were again fired at by a German officer. Directly afterwards a shell burst (one of ours we presumed) just a few yards away and this I am sure saved our lives. We were then told to put up our hands – or actions to that effect – and of course there was no help for it, for the whole road was occupied by Germans. They quickly relieved us of rifles, bombs, equipment, etc., and we were simply left.
>
> Thinking there might be some chance of getting away, I helped to attend the German wounded and there were some hundreds and some most awful wounds too. They all seemed to be quite decent fellows, as far as we could make ourselves understood, and pressed their cigarettes and food on to me.

Among the Germans was a soldier who spoke perfect English, having once worked as a waiter in London; he informed Sharpe that this was no mere decoy assault but his country's 'big push', and that they were 'miles behind our lines by now'. Sharpe shortly seized an opportunity to find out for himself: 'Gaining the sunken road again, I climbed the bank and what the German had told me was true. As far as the eye could see, on what a day ago were flat green fields scarcely pitted with shell holes, was nothing but the blue grey uniforms of German troops advancing in well ordered company formation.'

Now out of the fight along with thousands of others as a prisoner of war, Sharpe was made dramatically aware of his own side's determination to fight back: 'Our batteries now had begun to retaliate with a barrage and I was forced to take cover from this, after seeing a German service waggon and horses blown 30 ft high with a direct hit.'

* * *

The opening on 21 March 1918 of the German spring offensive was undoubtedly one of the towering moments of the war. Comparisons to huge storms, or (perhaps more tempting) to the beginning of some thunderous Wagnerian opera, can convey no adequate understanding. What it was in fact was the greatest concerted utterance of modern industrialized warfare to that date, as over six and a half thousand guns and three and a half thousand trench mortars fired virtually simultaneously along seventy miles of front in the area of the principal attack, while in three other sectors, Flanders, Champagne and Verdun, more massed guns fired by way of diversion. The Fifth Army commander, Sir Hubert Gough, would recall that he was awakened by 'a bombardment so sustained and steady that it at once gave me the impression of some crushing, smashing power'. Lying awake in a night of total silence at Nurlu – a village south-east of Cambrai which would be in German hands before nightfall – Winston Churchill leaped out of bed as the crescendo of noise began. As he described it: 'Exactly as a pianist runs his hands across the keyboard from treble to bass, there rose in less than a minute the most tremendous cannonade I have ever heard.'

Having dressed quickly Churchill hurried to the Headquarters Mess of 9th Division, meeting his host, General Tudor, on the duckboards outside. 'This is *it*,' said Tudor. 'I have ordered all our batteries to open. You will hear them in a minute.' Yet when they did open fire they added little to the tremendous cacophony already in being. 'The crash of the German shells bursting on our trenches eight thousand yards away,' wrote Churchill, 'was so overpowering that the accession to the tumult of nearly two hundred guns firing from much nearer could not be even distinguished.'

The bombardment, meticulously planned, and so precisely registered that it could go ahead in any kind of visibility, was aimed at a whole range of targets: artillery positions, unit headquarters, even divisional headquarters, telephone exchanges, telegraph cables, wireless stations, railway stations, every kind of strong point, dumps, key roads. It was thus much more than just an awesome demonstration of military strength; it was an attempt to destroy an enemy's capacity and will to resist. Gas shells added to the mayhem, rendering whole areas untenable, and forcing men into the clumsiness and visual impairment of gas-masks – or to the risk of trying to cope without them. Horses too had to be similarly equipped, adding their inevitable stress to that of gun-teams doing their best to calm and control them.

The initial impact was such that in certain sectors the entire force in the British 'Forward' and 'Battle' zones was eliminated. Some battalions were virtually annihilated, a few straggling survivors or scattered handfuls of prisoners in German cages the only indication that they had ever been there. The war diary entry of the 9th King's Royal Rifle Corps recorded: 'By the evening of the 21st, the battalion ceased to exist.' That of the 12th Royal Irish Rifles stated: 'The Diary now deals with the movement of battalion details. . . . The battalion itself was gone, killed, wounded and prisoner.' The 15th Royal Irish Rifles' diary was even more succinct: 'Battalion surrounded. 22 officers and 566 men missing.' Significantly, these were units of the Fifth Army, whose capacity for resistance was inevitably weaker than that of its better prepared neighbour, the Third. But the Third Army also had its disaster stories. In the Forward Zone of the sector held by 153rd Brigade of 51st Division were two and a half companies of the 1/6th and 1/7th Black Watch. The Official History would write of these troops that they were 'mostly killed, buried by the bombardment, or taken prisoner; the few survivors were not capable of much resistance, and none returned to tell the tale.'

For the Germans the sensation of success was instant and overwhelming. Of the opening bombardment, their most famous participant on the day, Ernst Jünger, wrote: 'This gigantic roar of annihilation from countless guns behind us was so terrific that, compared with it, all preceding battles were child's play. What we had not dared to hope came true. The enemy artillery was silenced, put out of action by one giant blow. We could not stay any longer in the dugouts. We got out on top and looked with wonder at the wall of fire towering over the English lines and the swaying blood-red clouds that hung above it.'

Fog, as Lance-Corporal Sharpe's account makes clear, came greatly to the Germans' aid that morning, and when five hours after the opening of the bombardment their infantry went into action fog assisted their tactic of infiltration in a manner they could barely have imagined. One of the best hopes of the Fifth Army had been that a mutually supporting line of machine-gun posts might score heavily against the German infantry; but to do so they needed to work in concert and to see at what they were firing. With communications cut by the bombardment and visibility reduced to a matter of yards by the fog, they found themselves virtually impotent. The unimaginable was happening; a Western Front line was being seriously breached, and in an incredibly brief time. The Germans were through, and on the British side, particularly on the front of the Fifth Army, defence began to mutate to the unthinkable: retreat. As Lieutenant-Colonel Rowland Feilding of the 6th Connaught Rangers, 16th (Irish) Division, Fifth Army, put it in a letter of 24 March: 'A retreat was the one possibility that had never occurred to us.' Now it became the unavoidable option.

The names by which the campaign thus initiated was to become known are significant. For the Germans this was, as we have seen, 'Operation Michael', or, alternatively the *Kaiserschlacht*: the 'Kaiser's Battle'. For the British it was the 'March Retreat'.

The respective size of the forces involved show good reason why this should have been the case. Forty-three divisions of the German Second and Eighteenth Armies attacked the front held by Gough's Fifth Army of thirteen divisions, plus three cavalry divisions; while nineteen divisions of the German Seventeenth Army attacked the front held by Byng's Third Army of twelve divisions.

The casualty figures for 21 March are also illuminating. It has been calculated that the British suffered 38,500 casualties, while the German count was nearer 40,000. However, two-thirds of the German casualties were wounded, and a substantial number of these would fight again. By contrast 28,000 of the British would not return; 7,000 were dead and 21,000 had become prisoners.

For another index of success: a standard aim of any attack was to reach the enemy's gun-line. On 21 March the Germans did so almost with ease, with the result that Fifth Army lost 383 guns that day, while the Third lost 150.

* * *

The lust for battle in the storm troopers who formed the spearhead of the German attack has been classically described by Ernst Jünger:

> The great moment had come. The fire lifted over the first trenches. We advanced. . . .
>
> I was far in front of the company, followed by my batman and a man of one year's service called Haake. In my right hand I gripped my revolver, in my left a bamboo riding-cane. I was boiling with a fury now utterly inconceivable to me. The overpowering desire to kill winged my feet. Rage squeezed bitter tears from my eyes.
>
> The tremendous force of destruction that bent over the field of battle was concentrated in our brains. So may men of the Renaissance have been locked in their passions, so may a Cellini have raged or werewolves have howled and hunted through the night on the track of blood. We crossed a battered tangle of wire without difficulty and at a jump were over the front line. The attacking waves of infantry bobbed up and down in ghostly lines in the white rolling smoke. . . .
>
> The English jumped out of their trenches and fled by battalions across the open. They stumbled over each other as they fled, and in a few seconds the ground was strewn with dead. Only a few got away. . . .
>
> The spirit of the attack had been kindled by success to a white heat of recklessness in every single man. There was no question of leading the several units. Nevertheless, one cry was on everybody's lips: 'On!' Every man went straight ahead.

At the humbler level of an ordinary German infantryman commenting on his country's success on the actual day, the diary of a soldier from Saxony, Max Walter Weber, is illuminating on a number of levels. His laconic yet triumphant entry reads:

> Today, 21 March, the German offensive began. Awakened at 3 a.m. by a deafening cannonade. Infantry attack began at 9.40, after a preliminary release of gas. It is now 12 o'clock. We have received good news of our advance. Allied prisoners have told us that the attack was expected but not at the places chosen. Herr Tommy has therefore been brilliantly outwitted.

However, this was Weber's last entry in a diary he had kept intermittently since 1915. The inside cover carries the later message: *'Please return to Capt. Saxon, 3rd N.Z.R.B. c/o 10 N.Z. DIV'*. The likely assumption is that it was found on Weber's dead body, himself, if this were the case, a victim of his country's outstandingly successful attack.

* * *

There are many accounts from the British side about the opening of the German Spring Offensive. Of the contemporary ones those in letters tend to be somewhat breathless assurances to inevitably worried families that the writer has survived, stronger therefore on atmosphere than on description. (By contrast, there must have been many families for whom there would never be any proper information at all, except the ultimate, formal admission of 'missing, believed killed'.) Hence the tone of this letter by Private Thomas Benson of the 7th Sherwood Foresters, 59th (2nd North Midland) Division, written to his wife as soon as he was able to put pencil to paper:

> Just getting my breath after 8 days with Old Fritz on our heels. Me and another and the Sergeant are the only three left out of our platoon of 36, 33 missing wounded and prisoners and dead so you see it was luck wasn't it dear for me? When we could hold Fritz no longer he came over in thousands to take us or kill us and I thought about you, I would not let them take me prisoner and had to run for my life under shell fire and machine-gun fire. But we got out with luck. Anyhow don't worry. If we go in again I hope it is a nice Blighty and can walk back so I can

see you. We may be out for a month and we may be only out for a few days. We have to be reorganized.

He ended with a statement which, though somewhat optimistic at the time of writing, would indeed ultimately prove true: 'But we have scotched Mr Fritz I believe.'

Lieutenant-Colonel Walter Vignoles despatched a hurried letter to his family on the 25th. 'I expect you will have been very anxious about us,' he began, 'but I hope you will have received my Field Postcard to say I was well.' (It was occasions such as this that made that tiny, universal postcard so invaluable; all a soldier had to do was to delete everything except 'I am quite well' and 'Letter follows at first opportunity', sign, date and address it and send it on its way.) His 9th Northumberland Fusiliers were in 34th Division, in the region of Bullecourt, where the defence had been sufficiently resilient for the tone of his letter to be generally upbeat and confident:

> I got an order to hold a certain position in front of a small wood on a hill and managed to get the Battn into position in the nick of time. We stopped the enemy's attack and drove him back a little way. Next morning he brought up a great many mounted infantry or cavalry and attacked again, but again we beat him off.
>
> At 1 p.m. he made another desperate attack, and bombarded Bn HQs and our position generally more heavily than anything I have ever seen. He used all sizes of shells, but mostly 8 inch and 9 inch; it was terrific and he kept it up until 5 p.m., the whole time sending forward wave after wave of fresh troops. Our men stuck in splendidly, but were driven out of the front line. I got our guns turned on to this line, and to our great relief the enemy began to retreat, our men shooting large numbers as they ran away.
>
> It was a great fight; I am sure we held up at least two Brigades during the two days' fighting.
>
> I will write again soon; I am O.K. and nerves sound notwithstanding the tremendous barrage.

But both these letters were written by soldiers of the Third Army, which, though it suffered massive casualties, was the less hard hit of the two armies involved. Inevitably there could be a more harrowing tone in accounts by men of the Fifth Army, of which it should be said, however, that though undoubtedly it bent, it did not break.

Gunner J.W. Gore of Z/66 Trench Mortar Battery was in the same division, the 66th, as Lance-Corporal Sharpe (by now a prisoner of war). His diary's somewhat staccato entries speak for themselves:

Mar. 21st. Got up and found the attack had started with thousands of gas shells. About mid-day we were told to get all maps and papers ready for burning. The road full of walking wounded and ambulances coming down the line. We made plenty of tea for the poor chaps on the road. Met a Captain with blackened face, torn tunic, one puttee gone and trouser leg in ribbons. He said 'It's all right, we are pushing Jerry back.' Later Bombardier Cartwright came down. He had his jaw tied up and tried to mumble to us as best he could with what seemed to be a broken jaw that Jerry was advancing and that all our Battery except four were killed or captured. Cpl Dakin was taken prisoner. The Divisional losses were very heavy. After tea Clarke and self burnt all the maps and papers behind the barn. Later Jerry started to shell Herville. All the huts were shelled and set on fire, including officers' huts and mess. Somebody got a GS waggon and we put on it our kits and one blanket per man and marched back behind the waggon to Nobescourt, where we slept in a large hut by an ammunition dump. We felt lost and homeless, most of our pals gone and all the stores left behind for Jerry to loot. He was advancing rapidly.

Mar. 22nd. Reinforcements were brought up from somewhere but it was hopeless. The Fifth Army was well whacked, with a German division facing one Battalion of our lads. Hopelessly outnumbered. Had to keep on retiring. Reached Brie where we slept in a chalk pit. On the river Somme the REs were mining bridges.

Mar. 23rd. Jerry advancing in massed formation. Had to skip it again. That night dead tired we slept in the open field and about 4 a.m. had to get going again. Marched back for miles through Barleux to Faye. There was an ammunition dump here and we were on fatigues loading up limbers with ammo.

And so on until, some days later, he and his comrades were able to put some distance between himself and the battlefield:

Mar. 26th. Jerry still advancing, had to buzz off very quickly and managed to get an ammunition lorry to Villers-Bretonneux.

For Captain Douglas McMurtrie of 7th Somerset Light Infantry these first days of the retreat had been a time of almost continuous action. The battalion had been out of the line when the attack began, but once it was engaged it had been like being involved in one long dogfight. Worst of all, he had had to endure the devastating experience of seeing the company on which he had lavished such enthusiastic concern and affection suffering virtual extinction. 'I think one of the most bitter moments I have ever had,' he would write soon afterwards, 'was to see my Coy being killed and wounded, broken up and nothing to remain of four months' hard work, except dead, dying, wounded and maimed.' Subsequently he found himself in command of one of several groups of survivors, including a number from the battalion's headquarters company, trying to retreat in some kind of order, while becoming increasingly aware of the high chance of being surrounded. The 24th began miserably: 'a hopeless dawn with thick fog and very cold weather', he called it. Then:

> As soon as the fog lifted the enemy, who under cover of darkness had moved up on the high ground to the right, started machine-gunning us and shells were exploding everywhere. We stuck this out till about 11 a.m. when ammunition and bombs began to run out. We were all very, very hungry having had no rations the night before. At about this time I received a verbal message by a runner from the Colonel to the effect that my party was to cover the withdrawal of the rest and then was also to withdraw. Almost immediately the rest started withdrawing and after they had got clear, I gave orders to withdraw too.
>
> I was determined not to let the men start running for once they did in such a situation it was impossible to hold them. I had my revolver out and anyone who tried to run I immediately threatened to shoot. This stopped all running but it was the worst hour I have ever had with the only exception perhaps of the Cambrai counter-attack on Nov 30th. The enemy was lining the right ridge and pouring a deadly fire into us, shells and shrapnel were bursting everywhere. German aeroplanes started flying over us and firing into our midst. Men were dropping everywhere,

some were wounded and calling out for help, others were dying and groaning in their pain. It was a ghastly situation. 2nd Lt Butler was killed. The Colonel had given me no place where we were to withdraw and so I steered a straight course to our rear.

The end was very near and soon we ran bang into a huge number of German artillery and transport and we were captured.

By this time McMurtrie's party was reduced to nine men, including just one NCO, a sergeant, from his Company. They were soon got on the move and marched to the neighbouring town of Ham on the first stage of their journey to captivity. Writing his account of his wartime career from enlistment to capture would be one way of passing the time during his nine months as a prisoner of war in a camp in Germany.

*   *   *

There were innumerable such actions at this time, as scattered groups of men attempted to fight their way out of the clutches of the advancing enemy, some successfully, some less so. But for vast numbers of the units of Fifth Army the only course was, in brief, to live to fight another day. On 28 March Lieutenant Philip Ledward, staff captain in 23rd Brigade, 8th Division, riding out with a fellow staff officer, Lieutenant Thompson, came upon what he would describe in an eloquent later account as 'a memorable sight, the Fifth Army in full retreat':

> The troops were walking down a main road. They were in no formation and units were mixed up in strange confusion. Officers and men were together and it was just a rabble, but there was no panic, no hurry, not much talking, no shouting – just a dogged steady slogging towards the rear. Shortly our Divisional Artillery Commander came up. We spoke to him and he told us to stop the rabble and make a line. You might as well have tried to stop the sea. We did get a line of sorts but it melted away the moment your back was turned.

Suddenly, in all this untidy confusion, Ledward was confronted with what seemed, in the circumstances, an oddly incongruous spectacle: a battery of the Royal Horse Artillery coming into action. 'They came along at a gallop, swung round in a clear space just off the road, unlimbered and stood ready. It was a pretty sight, exactly like a Military Tournament. My recollection is that they didn't fire a shot but waited ten minutes and then limbered up and galloped away.'

While he and his fellow officer were still trying to bring some order out of the prevailing chaos, Brigadier-General Coffin VC, an officer of a thrusting reputation currently commanding another brigade in 8th Division, the 25th, appeared on the scene. 'He was on horseback,' Ledward recorded, 'hard and sphinx-like as usual. He told us to abandon the line and allow the retreat to continue towards Moreuil. I recall his figure as he rode away; he looked the personification of fatigue and yet, as always, appeared to have a clear grasp of the situation and to be wholly intent on the military problem presented and to be quite without emotion of any personal kind.'

But this was one encouraging sign in a rapidly deteriorating situation. Separating from his fellow officer, Ledward got a lift on the running board of a staff car. He soon saw evidence the British were not the only Allied force in disarray: 'Before we reached Moreuil the stream of Fifth Army had been joined by a stream of French troops, and as we crossed the river going into the village I saw French soldiers chucking their rifles over the parapet of the bridge and heard them shouting *"tout est perdu"* – "all is lost".' Later in the town itself he and several other officers stood about waiting for orders 'watching the Rembrandtesque picture presented by the crowded square and main street lit up by a flare or two'. He commented, wryly: 'It was lucky that the Germans had no guns available.' Eventually he found a small body of composite troops from his division, Weekes, a fellow staff officer, arrived and they were able to march the men away about midnight:

It was about 96 hours since I had rejoined the Division from leave and I hadn't had much sleep and on that march I had the queer experience of falling asleep as I walked. I didn't feel particularly leg-weary but I kept cannoning into my neighbour and being forcibly pulled back into line. Eventually Weekes took my arm. It was a dark still night and we marched I believe about eight miles. At the end of our march I remember that we officers filed into a room that had a large table in it set round with wooden kitchen chairs and we just sat down around the table and went to sleep instantly.

Yet remarkably, even on the Fifth Army front, taking the brunt of the attack, morale was not the casualty it might have been. The 6th Battalion of the Northamptonshire Regiment was a unit of the 18th (Eastern) Division, a division rigorously trained by the redoubtable Ivor Maxse, now a Lieutenant-General, knighted, and in command of Fifth Army's XVIIIth Corps. His favourite division had been far from routed, but it inevitably had to join in the general retreat. The Northamptonshires' chaplain, Revd Carl Parry Okeden, who would be awarded the MC for his part in the care of the wounded and his support of the men at this time, got off a brief but breezy letter to his wife at the first convenient moment in the action:

> Only time for a line as we're fighting hard. We've had 2 days with the Boche within a mile of us and the Bn has lost heavily. I got my first sleep last night for 4 nights.
>
> I wouldn't have missed these days for anything in the world: and the men fought like heroes: I've never seen anything as ripping as the way they went for him [the enemy]. I'm awfully well and fit so don't worry about me.
>
> The Boche has my hairbrushes so please order me another pair to be sent out at once. Flat, stiff camp brushes the best.

Some days later Parry Okeden wrote again, on a notable date of the church calendar that would have normally seen him engaged in very different duties. He was still in a remarkably cheerful mood:

> Good Friday and what a day for us – we are still as men in a dream – still weighed down with sleep – still trying to recover from a shattering blow, and nearly all sense of time and date have gone. I can scarcely believe I am the same man as wrote to you last week: and yet what can I tell you? First of all I thoroughly enjoyed it! to watch the Boche coming on as we could with the naked eye, to see the guns, what were left, scattering him, to know and feel the tremendous courage of the men, to know above all that nothing else really matters but duty and helping one another and self is nowhere – all this was tremendously uplifting: and somehow I felt the joy and vigour of life as never before.

Parry Okeden's efforts to help his soldiers combined assistance with the wounded, as required, with frequent forays in search of food and other vital comforts. Thus on the second day of the retreat:

> I went off to try and get cigarettes and chocolate for the men and got back to find that our headquarters had been greeted with a salvo of shells and the occupants had only just got out in time. We spent the night very cold in a railway cutting and I was helping the wounded as best I could. The next morning we had to fall back; the 6th NN's would never have done so I believe, but we were outflanked and had to go. I spent the morning carrying wounded in a fearfully hot sun, lifting them on to carts and lorries. Unfortunately hundreds had to be left behind as the retirement was so rapid.
>
> Next day Sunday saw us taking up a line by a village we'd slept in. We stayed there all day and I went and caught three chickens and stewed them and got some fat and fried potato chips and we had an A1 dinner. I also got barrels of cider and gave the men drinks.

This clergyman's breezy ransacking of the localities they retreated through continued until the remnants of the battalion were finally taken out of action. He confessed to his wife: 'your once fairly high principled Hubs has become a looter of the most outrageous description.' But he also told her:

> Just a bit to comfort you: one officer said to me: 'What you're doing Padre ought to be written in letters of gold', and Stewart and the others all said that they didn't know what they'd have done without me and how I'd been the greatest help and value: and indeed they said too much as I simply acted naturally all the time and never thought about anything at all except helping in every way I could – and really I enjoyed it all the time. Only now as we begin to realize the extent of the disaster to England and the greatness of the blow and the loss of friends and all that, we begin to feel how great the strain was and what a tremendous time we went through. Still here I am safe and sound and awfully well feeling very un-Good Friday like. We can still hardly realize time, and the ordinary run of everyday life seems quite remote.

He nevertheless managed an appropriate greeting for the season with which to conclude: 'Well my angel darling a happy and blessed Easter Day to you and much joy of the risen promise and hope.'

* * *

Forcing back the Fifth Army was a major German triumph, but it led to a major German misjudgement. The commander of the Eighteenth Army, General Oskar von Hutier, owed his appointment to a notable tactical success at Riga, on the Eastern Front, in September 1917. Now he was showing a similar talent on the Western Front. In two days his forces had driven the Fifth Army back over twelve miles and were on the point of crossing the Crozat Canal and the River Somme. (It was his artillery commander at Riga, Colonel Bruchmüller, who had masterminded the massive opening bombardment on the 21st, thus giving von Hutier even greater credit.) This success dazzled the German supremo. As the historian, Peter Simkins, has written: 'At this point Ludendorff allowed the tactical opportunity presented by von Hutier's impressive progress to deflect him from his declared strategy – a tendency which bedevilled the German high command throughout the war. Instead of strengthening his right to ensure the success of his wheel to the north-west, Ludendorff reinforced his left.' The intention had been to concentrate his forces, in effect, in one potent thrust; now, writes Simkins, 'the armies would be advancing in divergent directions, like a hand with the fingers spread wide'.

It was a potentially fatal weakening, but there were still important successes to come and the outcome would be in the balance for days. Péronne fell on the 23rd, Bapaume on the 24th, Albert, 'capital' of the old Somme battlefield, on the 26th. The Third Army held firm near Arras, but had to swing back its right hand forces to maintain contact with the retreating Fifth. As it did so, it too was involved in some extremely fierce and sacrificial fighting.

* * *

Private Arthur Wrench of the 4th Seaforths in 51st (Highland) Division, Third Army, had found 21 March and the following days extremely tough going. Although one of its Brigades had lost heavily in the first stage of the action, it had nevertheless stood firm, with the aid of effective artillery and machine-gun fire, against the enemy's further efforts on the 21st, and the British Official Historian quotes the history of the German 24th Reserve Division as describing the 51st's artillery fire on the village of Boursies, after the Germans had seized it, as 'unbearable'.

A newspaper extract quoted in the papers of an orderly Corporal of the 1/5th Seaforths, present in March though not in the line, confirms that the Germans had the highest respect, even a kind of rival's affection, for this tough and determined division, which among other things had seized the prime fortress of Beaumont Hamel from them in the Ancre fighting on the Somme back in 1916. The relevant part of the press story reads:

> Yet there is a sporting element in the German Army. During the thick of the first clash on 21 March, a small balloon came floating down to where our men were making a splendid resistance. On being captured it was found to contain the following message:

> > *Good old Fifty-first*
> > *Sticking it still,*
> > *Good luck.*

Nevertheless even for the 51st retreat became unavoidable, the toll was inevitably very high and at the level of Private Wrench's personal experience the situation rapidly became one of shock, bewilderment and sheer wind-up. On Sunday 24 March, however, there came a sudden relief. As always this soldier's instant confidant was his diary: 'Praise God from whom all blessings flow! I'm wounded.'

On the 23rd he had spent the last hours of daylight directing stragglers to Frémicourt on the Bapaume–Péronne road, and then found his own way across country – 'tripping over old barbed wire, probably German stuff from before our 1916 push' – to huts occupied by some of his fellow Seaforths, where the cooks gave him some hot stew: 'and wasn't that just great?' He was also plied with the latest news:

> Now I hear that the roll call of the units hardly averages 100 men each so that it has been an awful massacre. The 152 and 153 brigade batts have about sixty men left while in the Black Watch I am told ten answered the roll call. Ten men. My God, so the

battalion is almost wiped out, but there must be many stragglers lost in the confusion who will turn up yet. Anyway, I do hope so. The Germans have not yet broken our line, and it might seem that the Highland Division is hanging on, as it were, to the very last shreds of its reputation. But who could withstand such a bloody onslaught of, they say, seven or eight German divisions pouring over en masse against our one?

Next day he was reunited with the Brigadier-General to whom he was attached as orderly: 'He took me out round all the posts the brigade is holding over on the ridge in front. We were shelled to hell, some bursting only a few yards away while aeroplanes were showering down their bullets like hail. Our tanks too were crawling back amid a bombardment.' Later it became impossible for them to remain in their present position so they left for a new one near Riencourt: 'The general went off in a hurry somewhere and called to me to follow and then a shell burst about 200 yards away. It seemed safe enough but a bit got me on the right arm near my shoulder. I got quite excited with the surprise of it more than anything but a vision of getting quit of it all for a time sent me happily back across the field with the signal officer shouting to me to "Get the Hell out of this".'

Across the road Wrench saw a red cross flying among some tents: 'a Casualty Clearing Station no doubt, but it was absolutely deserted so I trudged wearily on. Then I met Sergt Green (HQ mess) and he bandaged up my arm for me. It was so stiff and sore I could hardly get my coat and tunic off while the mess of congealed blood almost scared me, yet it was a small wound. So Sgt Green called me a lucky something or other and sent me on my way smiling.'

Wrench set off for Grévillers, a village west of Bapaume almost on the edge of the old Somme battlefield, where a padre escorted him to another Casualty Clearing Station. But because of the speed of the German advance this too was about to be abandoned, being no longer in safe ground: 'Field guns were blazing away out in front of the group of marquees while German shells were also bursting around and puncturing holes in the tents. I was the last man to receive attention here, and I got a seat on top of the last bus to leave.'

A thirty-seven-hour train journey to cover thirty miles – the line had been bombed and had to be repaired, giving rise to the delay – got Wrench to Amiens, from where he was moved to Abbeville and then to Camiers near Étaples, where he found himself in No. 18 General Hospital, staffed and run by Americans. At last he was able to look back on the situation from which he had so fortunately escaped: 'Now that I can give the poor boys up the line a thought, I will say, "God help them as He has helped me!" for it is the bloodiest Hell of an inferno imaginable and I am certainly lucky at this moment to be out of it.'

* * *

Private Frederick 'Fen' Noakes of the 3rd Coldstream Guards also underwent the experience of trying to get away from the battlefield after being wounded. He had not been present for the start of the offensive but had been part of the reinforcements rushed forward to attempt to bolster resistance on the Third Army front. For this purpose his 3rd Coldstream, together with the 2nd Irish Guards and the 4th Grenadiers, had been detached from the Guards Division to serve with the 31st Division. He wrote his account in hospital, in a series of episodes spread over several letters, not giving his family too much to absorb in any one instalment, and clearly wishing to pace his own recollections of what had been a very harrowing time. His story is not just a vivid account of dramatic events; it takes one into the mind-set of a soldier so caught up in the trauma of battle that he almost loses all interest in surviving.

When he began recounting his experiences, he told his mother (always his prime correspondent): 'I have had a taste of real war at last, compared with which all my previous experiences were almost peaceful. I consider myself very fortunate indeed in getting through so lightly – indeed it is the veriest miracle that I escaped with my life.' In his next letter he described his arrival in the battle-zone late on 23 March: 'Behind all seemed peace and serenity, as the last faint flush of the sunset faded: but in front! I can give no truer or less exaggerated idea of the scene than that it was like looking into the gates of Hell. In continued and never ceasing roar and bellow the guns thundered, the darkness was perpetually illuminated with the lightning-like flash of their explosion, accompanied by the intermittent crackle of machine gun and rifle fire. On our right, three or four buildings were burning furiously, and clouds of lurid smoke were rolling across the scene. Even Dante could imagine no scene more terrible and grand for the staging of his *Inferno*.'

The moment of truth for him was not then, however, but three days later, on the 26th, when the Germans began a sudden attack, of which Noakes and his fellow Coldstreamers, then in a trench some way in front of the main British line – virtually in a kind of salient – were only coincidentally a target. He described the pattern of events in his next and longest letter:

> We were in a curious position. Although we were surrounded on three sides, Fritz had *apparently* not discovered our trench, since for some time not a shell fell anywhere near us. At the same time, owing to our position on a rise in the ground, we could see everything that went on, as if we were in the circle of a theatre. Of course, bullets in plenty were whistling about, but as long as we kept fairly well under cover we were safe from them.
>
> From where we were, we could see the Germans swarming over the ridge opposite, and pouring towards us in an endless torrent. There seemed to be countless thousands of them, and in their grey uniforms they looked like an army of ants. They were not in their old 'mass' formation, but in 'open order', which is so much more difficult to stop by artillery fire. Everyone could see now that a retreat was inevitable. But we had to hang on as long as possible.
>
> The enemy attacked fiercely, despite a stern resistance, during which our aeroplanes, flying only a few feet from the ground, poured machine-gun volleys into the advancing foe. They had before long crept round our rear to such an extent as to leave us only one road by which a retreat could be effected.
>
> Then the British commenced a counter-attack, but I could not follow the progress of the battle after that, since just then the artillery found the range of our trench and opened a barrage on us from the rear. How we – any of us – came out of it, I don't know! Shells, the biggest kind, were falling like hailstones on all sides. I personally was convinced there was no escape. I remember wondering what it would feel like to die, and how you would take the news. I felt anxious to get it over. At no time did I feel

the slightest fear for what might happen after death. On that score I was quite confident. It was only the physical act of death I was apprehensive of. Like a man having a tooth out, I knew the operation would mean comfort and peace for me, but there was a temporary pang to be faced.

Well, contrary to my expectations, the shell that was to end things for me did not arrive, and presently the order came through to retreat. There was no possibility of holding our ground in that fire, so we moved down the trench for some distance, and then, finding the barrage seemed to follow us, we emerged into the open and ran. It sounds ignominious, but here we were facing, not men, but devilish mechanical monsters of steel, fired from miles away, which no amount of defiance would drive back. We ran across the open, with shells falling among us, on all sides of us, with a deafening roar and crash, and fragments were whizzing past in all directions. It was almost impossible to avoid being hit. I ran for some distance with the rest, and then, with a feeling of disgust for the whole job which I can hardly describe, I slowed down to a walk. I really didn't care which way things went. There was a deafening crash – and then I found myself in a shell hole and a stretcher-bearer was pouring brandy into my mouth and rubbing it into my forehead. Finding that I was not badly hurt, and able to walk, he hurried on to attend the serious cases, after giving me instructions how to reach the dressing station.

Further letters told how, after meeting other 'walking wounded', and travelling on by motor ambulance and train, Noakes eventually reached No. 7 Convalescent Camp, Boulogne. His wound, to the wrist, was not severe enough to take him to Blighty, but it still kept him out of action for several months. He was fortunate, as he himself admitted, to survive the incident just described; in it his Company had lost as many as thirty killed in ten minutes.

* * *

The area over which this double tide of men and weapons was flowing, without apparent regard to any of the elements or amenities of normal civilization, from crops and animals to real estate, was not heavily populated, but there were enough local inhabitants to produce a mass of refugees. Roads already clogged with trudging troops and heavily laden vehicles were also the only arteries of escape available to them. As they made their way west they left behind their homes like so many miniature *Mary Celestes*, the evidence of ordinary life still in place. Second Lieutenant Frank Warren, on the Fifth Army front, noted the results of one hurried evacuation in what he called 'a pretty village untouched by war'; untouched, that is, until that moment:

> A number of cottages open on to the winding street. Here is a table, neat and ready laid – with coffee pot, loaf and butter, as if for *déjeuner*. Next door perhaps, there is the sewing machine with a garment or piece of work spread out on it.
>
> One family bolder than the rest is but now setting out westwards on its journey to safety. Madame with firm, careworn face, framed with silvery hair, takes command, while Monsieur jabbers vociferously but ineffectually. A pretty girl of sixteen has a rope over her shoulder hitched to a handcart bearing the treasured feather-bed and a few household goods, and another rope is tied to the collar of a faithful dog. The front door is left open, as is the custom all along the road we travel.

Abandoned houses could also provide food and sanctuary for soldiers, who – as could easily happen in such confused circumstances – managed to lose contact with their comrades. Tired, hungry, and ignorant of what was actually happening anywhere but in their own immediate circle, they themselves became refugees, scavenging the homes of other refugees.

At first all had gone well for Bombardier Arthur Ellis, a signaller serving with B Battery, 106th Brigade RFA in 24th Division, Fifth Army; the battery's morale had even been significantly boosted by an unexpected distribution of mail and cigarettes. 'We felt a lot more cheery after that,' Ellis noted in his diary, being especially pleased about the 'cigs' – 'a godsend as we had been without for days.' But suddenly things went awry; this was at Beaucourt-en-Santerre, on the same route of retirement – Rosières, Caix, Beaucourt, Moreuil – as that followed by Lieutenant Ledward:

> Just as we got through Beaucourt I and another signaller lost the rest of the battery owing to the crush of traffic on the roads.

They were simply packed with infantry, infantry transport, French artillery and our own all going the same way and we could only get along a few yards at a time. The officer in charge of our lot took a side turning to get out of it and while we were going along Fritz suddenly opened up on the road causing them to go off at a trot while us two who were walking were too dog tired to run after them so let them go thinking we would catch them again further on as they would get caught in the traffic, but alas for our hopes nothing of the sort happened. I after tramping four or five kilos came to the conclusion we were lost.

After asking numerous fruitless questions we began to search round for food as we were ravenously hungry and we searched a house which had just been left by civilians. I could not but help feeling sorry for the people to whom it had belonged. It was a beautifully furnished house and they had been forced to leave almost everything. Here we found some chipped potatoes, evidently the remains of their last meal, and also some crusts of bread and some fruit jelly. We then explored the cellars and here we found a big jar of cream and two bowls of fresh milk and it was absolutely it! I had not realized before that cream and milk could taste as delicious.

Having satisfied our hunger a bit we then set out to find the battery. After three or four hours vain searching during which night had fallen and it had been pouring with rain, we decided to postpone our efforts and get into a deserted house in Moreuil, where with some infantry stragglers we passed the night. We were up at daylight and after a drink of hot tea made with some tea and sugar we found we set out again on our journey. After asking innumerable questions and wandering all over the country we finally obtained the information that our Divn HQ was in Castel about 3 kilos distant. We set out with light hearts as we thought we were on the right track at last, but to our dismay we were informed that they could not tell us where the divisional artillery were and told us to report to the D.A.C. [Divisional Ammunition Column] at Cottenchy 12 kilos distant and stay with them until we could rejoin the battery. We set off in a very downhearted mood but had not got more than 200 yards when we banged into one of our cooks on the search for water and he informed us that the battery was only 500 yards away. When we found them we were just in time for hot tea and biscuits and a couple of hours of much needed sleep.

*　*　*

As the month drew to an end, the Fifth Army, while still retreating, was also showing considerable spirit in fighting back. Captain Frank Parker, 5th West Yorkshire Regiment, 150th Brigade, 50th Division, had been away from the front when the crisis began and was not involved until the 29th, when he took up a small draft of reinforcements to assist whatever resistance there might be against the general tide. Writing some weeks later to his godfather, a retired major-general, he told him:

> When I found the battalion our line had been forced back about a mile to the River Luce between Hangard and Moreuil but we were forming up for the counter-attack. The Brigade had been made up into a composite battalion about 400 strong under our CO. Of the original battalion the CO and Adjutant were the only two officers who had been through the whole show though we had several other officers who had come up as reinforcements. The other two battalions were in the same way.
>
> I stayed at Bn Hqrs that morning, the 29th, and watched the attack which was very successful and advanced our line a mile, though we had very few or no supports at all. The Cavalry, Canadians, did awfully well both mounted and dismounted and one mounted squadron did a fine charge through a wood which bucked up the infantry very much. I'm afraid they suffered heavily as they were hindered by the trees and the whole wood was alive with Boche, but they seemed very pleased with themselves and said they killed any amount. The French also attacked on our right and did well.

Revd T.L.B. Westerdale, Chaplain of the 7th Somerset Light Infantry, recorded a similar heroic action:

> You might imagine from the rapidity of the German advance that we ran from St. Quentin to Amiens but the extraordinary courage of our troops cannot be better illustrated by the story of the deeds of our brigade at Le Quesnoy. Here at this village was

fought a fight that should make all Englishmen the wide world over thrill with pride.

Captain Coombes, our Brigade Major, and Captain F. Stoker found themselves holding this village during the retirement with fifty men of the 7th Somersets, 12th Kings and 7th D.C.L.I. Twelve hundred Germans poured out of the woods to attack this little band. It was one o'clock in the afternoon, and until five that night this mighty horde of Huns was held up by two British officers, a few trusty N.C.O.s and a handful of stalwart warriors.

Eventually the enemy got into one end of the village, and succeeded in knocking out our Lewis guns and their teams. Still the heroic band fought on, until at last only two or three rifles were left to crack. At 5 p.m. the two officers and nine men alone remained, and most of these were wounded. In the gathering dusk this little company of eleven got away to the main body of troops behind, having held up the German Army in this sector for four precious hours! Who knows but that those four precious hours saved Amiens and perhaps the British Army itself! When the list of honours comes to be issued the names of those eleven Englishmen should stand high on the record of immortal fame.

Westerdale later added to his account the fact that Captain Coombes had subsequently received a bar to his Military Cross.

* * *

Meanwhile the ripples emanating from the Germans' throwing of so massive a stone into the pond were spreading far and wide. From the perspective of many closely involved in the campaign the issue had largely become (as for example in the extract just quoted) that of whether or not the Germans would reach the Picardy capital, Amiens. From a greater distance the issue could seem that of whether or not the Germans might be on the point of taking control of the war. Ludendorff's wavering conduct of the March offensive might be a legitimate subject for criticism, but he nevertheless came very close to achieving one of his objectives, the splitting of the British and French Armies. Even the threat of such a possibility was enough to raise vital questions which would hover over this part of 1918 for weeks; namely might the British have to face the prospect of fighting

on alone, or even *in extremis* have to summon her Expeditionary
Force back home?

To avoid such a possibility, the Prime Minister, Lloyd George,
took swift and determined action. There were 170,000 troops in
Britain in late March in a more or less reasonable state of readiness;
these were instantly made available for France, while during April
another 52,000, not all in the prime of condition, were assembled
from various sources. Up to a third of the 170,000 were under
nineteen and thus, officially, not to be sent on active service except
in an emergency; but clearly that is precisely what this was and a
near-desperate situation required near-desperate remedies. Additionally, two divisions were called back from Palestine and one from
Italy. Next, the age of conscription was reduced to 17½ at one end
of the scale and raised to 50 (or if need be 55) at the other. These
measures produced, in combination with the obviously serious news
from the front, a notable surge in patriotism, even among the ranks
of organized labour, though difficulties in this area would again
surface later in the year.

The second string to Lloyd George's bow was an appeal to the
Americans, of the war but not yet fully in it. They agreed to send
more men, though they required more British shipping to get them
to France. Lloyd George accepted their terms, even though this
might mean delaying the delivery of urgent foodstuffs and raw
materials.

At the same time important changes were taking place in the
matter of organizing the Allies' response to the new German strategy
in the field.

On 26 March in the Hotel de Ville at Doullens, just behind the
area of the 1916 Somme battlefront, a milestone conference was held,
the result of which was to establish unified command on the Western
Front. Largely initiated by Haig even though he knew the outcome
would be his own subordination to a Frenchman, this crucial meeting
resulted in the appointment of General Foch as senior soldier on the
Allied side. The text of the agreement read: 'General Foch is charged
by the British and French Governments with the co-ordination of
the action of the Allied Armies on the Western Front. He will make
arrangements to this effect with the two Generals-in-Chief, who are
invited to furnish him with the necessary information.' The two

Generals-in-Chief were Haig and Pétain. After his appointment as co-ordinator, it was virtually inevitable that Foch would soon take the next step and become effectual generalissimo. On 3 April, at a second conference, this time at Beauvais, he was formally entrusted with 'the strategic direction of military operations', with responsibility to Britain as well as to France.

This was no immediate magic solution but it certainly led to a better awareness of mutual problems and created an agreed framework of collaboration which had hitherto barely existed. An early consequence was that Pétain was soon moving divisions which he had held for a possible defence of Paris to the British sector, at that time clearly the point of greatest danger. Importantly, the Beauvais agreement was signed by the Americans, who had not been present at Doullens.

If these were positive responses to the crisis, a less happy one was the sacking of the GOC of the Fifth Army, General Gough. A scapegoat was required and it was Gough who found himself on the lonely journey home. General Sir Henry Rawlinson took over an Army which, having changed its commander, also shortly changed its number and became the Fourth; the title of the Army he had commanded, with mixed fortunes, two years earlier on the Somme.

On a copy of papers handed to him by the departing Gough Rawlinson later noted: 'It was a difficult task to stay the hostile advance and save Amiens but by superhuman efforts we managed to do it.' But this was a somewhat disingenuous comment. As Rawlinson's biographers, Robin Prior and Trevor Wilson, have stated: '[T]he truth was that there was virtually no relationship between his accession to the direction of the Fifth Army sector and the halting of the German advance. Rather, events on the German side were determining that in the last days of March the drive towards Amiens would grind to a halt.'

For the German offensive was losing momentum not only because of the forthright rearguard fighting of the British or the increasing helpfulness of the French. Casualties were mounting massively, fatigue was causing the Germans literally to drag their feet, and another factor was having its effect for which they had no one to blame but themselves. At first their attack had made fine headway because it was over relatively unbroken ground. But then they had struck the zone which they had deliberately 'scorched' when withdrawing to their new defence lines early the previous year. As the Official History comments: 'It was a strange but fitting Nemesis that the devastations of 1917, a mere exhibition of spite and "frightfulness" which had not perceptibly delayed the British advance, should distinctly contribute to the German failure in 1918.' (Indeed, the rubble of buildings the Germans had destroyed had provided the British with admirable road building material when they took over the territory the Germans had left.) For the Germans, now coming at speed the other way, the ground they had ravaged, compounded by the even worse state of the former Somme battle-field, with its trenches, craters and entanglements of barbed wire, acted as a major, indeed a crucial, brake on their advance. As a German commentator, admitting the fact of this virtual 'self-inflicted wound', would later put it: 'The Somme desert had spoken its last inexorable and mighty word.'

And there was yet another factor which might be described as a direct if somewhat bizarre consequence of the long-standing Allied blockade. German troops accustomed to meagre rations at the front and conditioned by stories of severe shortages back home found themselves unable to resist the temptation provided by the rich pickings suddenly available to them in the territory now falling into their hands. When Captain McMurtrie of the 7th Somersets, after being taken prisoner, reached Ham, he was confronted by a remark-able sight: 'All the streets were full of Huns, looting the houses, nearly every man I saw was carrying a bottle or so of wine, some had biscuits, cigarettes, tobacco and chocolates, which they had taken from the large canteen in Ham.' His prime reaction was to envy them because they had food, since he and his fellow prisoners would clearly have to wait for theirs and it would no doubt be very basic when it came. But the significant item in his list was the wine, for the generous availability of alcohol to troops who found it there for the taking would become a further brake on the carrying out of Operation Michael.

Notably when the German advance across the old Somme battle-field front reached Albert, there would be an abrupt halt to its progress precisely for that reason. A well-known chronicler of the war from the German side, Captain Rudolf Binding, a staff-officer, would write in his book *A Fatalist at War*:

> When I got into the town the streets were running with wine. Out of a cellar came a lieutenant of the Second Marine Division, helpless and in despair. I asked him, 'What is going to happen?' It was essential to get them forward immediately. He replied, solemnly and emphatically, 'I cannot get my men out of this cellar without bloodshed.' When I insisted ... he invited me to try my hand, but it was no business of mine, and I saw, too, that I could have done no more than he. I drove back to Divisional HQ with a fearful impression of the situation.

The Official History puts these developments in a somewhat more sober, though equally telling perspective. The policy of the retreating British had been to clear or destroy all dumps of ordnance and other military supplies, and to do the same with respect to Expeditionary Force Canteens and officers' and other clubs. After the salvaging of everything that could be moved 'passing [British] troops were invited to help themselves, so that some lucky units found themselves enjoying corona cigars and other such luxuries'. But this still left much for the enemy: 'In spite of it all, the Germans were still able to discover a mass of food and to them many unheard of "delikatessen". Seeing that they had been informed the British were starving as a result of the submarine blockade, such windfalls, in the end, contributed to depress their already waning morale.'

* * *

Reading between these lines from the Official History would seem to suggest that it was now open house on both sides for the serious looter. The British had numerous adept practitioners in this art. One such was Private Robert Cude of the 'Buffs', the 7th East Kents, 18th Division, a soldier whose talent for survival had been honed by many months of service during which an eye to the main chance had been a constant characteristic. Attached as a messenger to 55th Brigade Headquarters, he had been with a party headed by Brigadier-General E.A. Wood, which had become separated from the bulk of the Division and was making its escape as best it could. This was after some fierce resistance which had prompted Cude to note: 'I have never seen such a glorious attack', and which had been followed by a swift despatch of German wounded and prisoners on the grounds that there was no way of feeding them while the British, short of food themselves, were in retreat.

Foraging for his party had started with the local livestock: 'Get some of the lads to milk a cow or two, and so we had a good drink of tea or two, and incidentally this was a kindness towards the dumb animals that were walking about the town bellowing pitifully.' Rabbits also served to keep Cude and his comrades in appropriate fettle: 'We kill off some beautiful ones, and have *some spread*, and after skinning some more, we make up a parcel for a future boil-up. I invite General Wood to have a good dinner with us, although it is rough and ready, and he does so with gusto.' (Cude did not lightly give honour to his superiors in rank, but when he did so, his approval could verge on hero-worship: 'Here is an English gentleman, and as long as he stops at Brigade, I shall not mind going through Hell itself.')

On the 31st they reached Villers-Bretonneux; with a comrade attached from the artillery Cude explored the local possibilities, which included an abandoned château, always a mouth-watering temptation to the practised hand: 'The Gunner and I are soon on a prospect around, and note that we have a loft full of pigeons to fall back on in the grounds of the château.' But there were better rewards to be found in the town itself, which they now proceeded to visit, if warily, for the line was only a thousand yards away: 'Jerry is shelling this place like fury but necessity demands that we get something to eat, etc. This is well known to us as a very high class place, so we reckon that there must be a decent bit worth taking. I chalk up "Bde HQ" on a billet just off the boulevard, and after telling the chaps of the place, we continue our voyage of discovery.' They spared a thought for the 'poor devils [i.e. the local inhabitants] who must have pushed off very hurriedly', but that was no deterrent to their enjoying what was now to fall into their laps as a result of the fortunes of war:

My first stunt was a bath in a shop which apparently thrived as a Perfumery, and the bath that I have is half full of Eau-de-

Cologne, and I take ½ dozen bottles to be sent home as soon as I can get a chance. After this we wend our way to the Bonded Stores, which we knew to be in the town, and although we expected to find a drink or two, I had the surprise of my life, for tons of canned fruit, meat, and game were stacked up ready to be eaten. In the drinking line, we have our choice of wines of all qualities and age, but our attention was drawn to the champagne that is present in large number. Case after case, and 20 bottles to a case. We have soon reinforcements down with stretchers, and for myself a pass signed by the General to bring away anything that I salvage. Journey after journey I make, and we have enough to last out a siege of a few weeks very soon, and then we turn our attention to the other shops and houses. What a harvest, for there is everything that one could need, and we soon have new underclothes, and nice light boots, for our others have got quite hard, owing to not taking them off and not cleaning them since we started.

Cude's breezy descriptions could cover more commitment and courage than he sometimes owned to. It is a matter of record that he was awarded a Bar to his Military Medal for his 'gallant conduct and devotion to duty in the field' in the period 21 to 25 March.

* * *

Thursday 21 March had seen the beginning of the main theme of Ludendorff's spring offensive 'Michael'; Thursday the 28th – the day on which Captain Binding was reduced to near despair in Albert – saw its variation, 'Mars'. In a secondary attack notable for its remarkable ambition he threw his troops north of the River Scarpe towards that Gibraltar of the northern plains, Vimy Ridge. His final objective, seventy-two miles from Arras, was the port of Boulogne. As Cyril Falls has commented: 'If this had gone as well as the attack of 21 March the war might have been nearly as good as won. Unfortunately for the gambler Ludendorff, his nine divisions ... struck four British as good as Britain could show and of all types of her Army: regular, New Army, and Territorial.' These were the 3rd and 4th Divisions of regular troops; 56th (London), Territorial Force; and the 15th (Scottish), a division of the New Army. Again quoting Falls: 'The Germans attacked with sparkling vigour and skill. They were fought to a finish by a defence at once elastic and resolute. Ludendorff stopped the fight that very night.'

But that, of course, was not the whole story since even successes have their sacrifices and victims.

Private Thomas Bickerton had volunteered in 1915 when only sixteen, and had fought with the 11th Royal Sussex during the Battle of the Somme – notably taking part in the attack on the Stuff Redoubt – until being sent home to England in November 1916 as under age. Back again the following year he had been involved in the later stages of Third Ypres and was now with the 2nd Essex, 4th Division, Third Army, in the Fampoux sector near Arras. His role in the March fighting was a brief one, in that, like Captain McMurtrie, he was one of the thousands of British soldiers who would find themselves heading eastwards not as victorious conquerors but as prisoners of war.

Ever since the 21st he and his comrades had been very aware of the 'terrific' bombardment away to the south, but, as he stated, in a postwar account written for his family, 'still we were quiet in our sector'. At 3 a.m. on 28 March, however, their moment came:

> We were bombarded with everything the Germans had got. At daybreak we could see the Germans advancing down the valley. We immediately let loose with everything we had got. We had a system of Very lights to send up immediately we were attacked and this would call for artillery fire on no-man's-land. We sent up our Very lights but no artillery fire came. The artillery had been withdrawn and it appeared to us that we were going to be sacrificed. We sent back runners to Battalion Headquarters for instructions. The first two runners were either killed or taken prisoner; the third runner came back to tell us the Germans were cooking breakfast in our Battalion Headquarters kitchen.

Bickerton was a member of a Lewis gun team, whose members took over one after another as the non-stop firing continued. But their chances of escape were clearly diminishing by the minute, and their efforts left them 'mentally and physically exhausted and wondering what the end would be'. Missing the platoon commander, Bickerton went into the next bay to look for him: 'He was sitting on the fire step in the corner with a revolver in his hand. I think he had shot himself rather than be taken prisoner.'

By now the Germans were almost upon them: 'A Corporal tied his white handkerchief to his bayonet and stuck it over the trench. Those of us who were gunners had torn our Lewis badges off our jackets as we were afraid of what might happen to us. All arms had to be abandoned and we were instructed to run with our hands up towards the German rear.' This was the abrupt and brusque conclusion to their fighting war.

A second participant in this action was Lieutenant R.J. Blackadder, 151 Siege Battery, Royal Garrison Artillery, whose account is of most value in relation to the light it casts on the elasticity praised in the description by Cyril Falls. One man's elasticity can seem like another man's retreat, for Blackadder was distinctly less than pleased with the orders he received on 28 March. Instructed to withdraw, he commented in some dismay: 'On my front I could see no reason for this sudden change of tactics, as only last night I had been informed that there was to be no retiral – a fight to the finish!'

But withdrawal from action, hazardous enough with the requirement of six substantial caterpillar engines and eleven lorries to pull his battery along a badly cratered road, did not mean withdrawal from danger. 'Nothing of value was left,' Blackadder wrote, in an unusually emotional comment for a normally terse diary, 'but the price was paid in human lives. In all this my Officers worked splendidly and the men like heroes, but poor Lt. Howe was killed, four gunners too gave their lives and about 15 were wounded. Again I was spared – why, I cannot say.'

* * *

It was on Saturday 30 March that Second Lieutenant Frank Warren received the wound that would send him to hospital in England. This was not long after he had been greatly distressed by the death of his servant, Private Marden, who had rashly been caught in a sniper's sights while helping to dig some scratch trenches during their retreat. Marden's example flashed through his mind as he was hit:

> Suddenly I am knocked spinning by a numbing blow on the back of the head. I fall, instinctively rather than by the force of the blow, and my first thought is that all is over and I am dead. I

think at once of my servant who was shot through and killed only three days earlier! Then I hear someone calling 'Warren's hit! Warren's down!'

Several men come running round me, including Sergt Page of C Company who asks me if I have a shell dressing. I tell him 'No' and beg him not to let a crowd assemble, or it will draw fire and someone else will be shot.

Sergt Page dabs a shell dressing to the back of my head and secures it into position. I sit up and unbuckle my equipment which with revolver, ammunition, pouch, glasses, compass, haversack and water bottle is no mean weight.

I find I can now stand well, so wishing the men 'Cheerio', and with the parting words 'Give them one for me!' I begin my journey off the field.

As Warren and countless others like him fell out of the action, by death, wounding or capture, a stream of reinforcements was coming the other way. But this was no organized force primed and ready to take over the task of holding back the German onslaught. On the contrary, there was much confusion, even chaos, as efforts were made to sort out a mass of troops into some semblance of military order.

Captain Geoffrey Christie-Miller of the 2/5th Gloucesters had been away from his 61st Division at a Senior Officers' course in Aldershot and was on an end-of-term leave when the attack began. On Easter Sunday, 31 March, he and most of his former colleagues from the course met at the boat train and headed for France. He was concerned about his own prospects through being separated from his battalion, and understandably anxious about the fate of the many friends he had left in the line, but the problem of finding the necessary men for the present emergency worried him most of all: 'Where were reserves to be found? One saw thousands of boys being poured across the Channel. Were they fit to be plunged straight into one of the severest battles of history?'

Once in France he witnessed the desperate attempts being made to cobble together more or less coherent units from the mixed bag of available personnel: the newly arrived conscripts, men turned back from the leave boats, soldiers of various trades who had never imagined that they would ever be called on to wield a weapon in anger. Christie-Miller himself recorded the case of a Sergeant shoe-maker who by virtue of his rank was soon to command a section in action. But he also noted a sombre side to these strenuous efforts:

> Countless tragedies arose over the improvisation of these units for the line. They were sent up to the fighting line and pushed right into the battle. Their nominal roles were incomplete and sometimes non-existent. Thousands went missing and it is not known to this day to what units they were sent, or in what part of the line they were fighting.
>
> Captain Badcock, one of the best Company Commanders the Gloucesters ever had, was put in command of such a Company and sent up to a unit of 24th Division, but no information could be obtained as to his fate. The unit to which he was sent was traced, but as his Command had been put straight into the fight there was no one left with the unit who knew him by sight or could say what became of him.

*   *   *

On Monday 1 April, on an afternoon of pouring rain, a Captain of the 13th Middlesex, Cosmo Clark, noticed a handful of cars driving down the road from Amiens to Bertaucourt, near where his company, exhausted after many days of retreat, had dug themselves in. The cars stopped and a number of civilians and French and British officers got out and walked towards Clark's command post. Winston Churchill had been at the front at the start of the spring offensive and here he was once more as it moved towards its final stage, this time not in 'a French helmet with a khaki cover', as described by Second Lieutenant Warren on 20 March, but in a more modest trilby. Hailing the officer as 'my boy' he asked his name, and when Clark answered he continued: 'Here is Monsieur Clemenceau. Come along and I will introduce you to him.' Thus Captain Clark met two of the titans among the leading politicians of the Allies, the ever forthright and ardent Churchill, and the Frenchman whose embodiment of the patriotic fervour and determination of his country had earned him the nickname 'Tiger'.

Clark would always remember the brilliant shining eyes of the French Prime Minister, as he assured him and the others gathered around that thousands of French troops were behind them, while thousands of British were coming out of England. His repeated affirmation 'They will never get Amiens' rang in the ears of his audience as he and Churchill left after a general handshake all round.

Clemenceau's prophecy would be proved correct, but this was by no means assured at the time. That same morning Churchill had telegraphed to the British Prime Minister, Lloyd George: 'It is considered certain here that the Germans will pursue this struggle to a final decision all through the summer and their resources are larger than ours. It would be fatal to be lulled by the talk of depression in Germany leading to peace. Every effort must be made to avoid destruction. . . .' But it was the German resolve which gave way first. On 4–5 April the threat to Amiens was decisively parried ten miles to the east at Villers-Bretonneux, by the determined resistance of the British 14th and 18th Divisions and the 9th Australian Brigade. On Friday 5 April – a day and date as significant in their way as that Thursday 21 March, just over a fortnight earlier, on which the great attack had begun – Ludendorff took one of the hardest decisions of his career and closed down his offensive. His troops were exhausted and they had outrun their artillery and much of their transport. More, they had suffered casualties on a scale that Germany simply could not afford, in contrast to the (potentially, given the mass of soldiery regularly arriving from America) limitless bank balance of manpower on the Allied side. Though he could not know it, the German supremo had started a pattern of initial success and subsequent failure that would be repeated several times more before the spring of 1918 was over. And after each effort his own more modest bank account would be crucially eroded.

On Saturday 6 April, Churchill, recognizing the change of fortune but also aware how close had been the call, memorably wrote: 'It has been touch and go on the front. We stood for some days within an ace of destruction.'

*   *   *

How can one assess the balance sheet of this first German offensive? A recent historian, J.H. Johnson, seeing it in relation to the long sequence of indecisive battles that preceded it from Neuve Chapelle to Cambrai, offers this illuminating perspective: 'It was the Germans . . . who broke the long stalemate on the Western Front. . . .

The depth of penetration exceeded by far anything yet achieved by the Allies and appeared to indicate that the key to opening the door on the Western Front had at last been found. It was not, however, to be. The Germans had won a tactical, but not a strategic, victory. . . .'

In the circumstances, of course, a strategic victory was the only one that would count; effectually, as its authors acknowledged by halting their campaign, a tactical victory was no victory at all. Admitting that this was 'an operation that had shaken Britain to its foundations', and that what the enemy had accomplished 'was, from the viewpoint of the BEF's own offensives in 1916 and 1917, unimaginable', the Australian historian Trevor Wilson has stated: 'Yet, on a wider perspective, the Germans had purchased a tactical success at the price of a strategic calamity. They had sustained irreplaceable casualties to the tune of 250,000 men. And they had overrun territory that, a year before, they had gone to great trouble to abandon. . . . In the course of acquiring it they had learned that the process of defeating the British simply could not be accomplished – least of all before the arrival of the Americans. This meant for Germany that the war could not be won.'

This did not mean of course that she would not try again; there was not the slightest chance of her leaders accepting such an interpretation at this time.

What of the emotional, psychological balance? One possible answer for the British is that though retreat might have brought disarray, it had also brought resilience, and it brought pride. It could even produce a kind of St. Crispin's day mentality; a young Lieutenant of the Royal Field Artillery, Leonard Tansley, writing home well before the outcome was known, on 31 March, clearly saw things that way: 'The more I think of it the more I feel that people of my age ought to be here in it – it is the only possible way of carrying on, and bringing the war to some sort of conclusion. Some say that this tremendous blow has again delayed the end of the war – but I think that on the contrary it has not – that actually it will be beneficial in letting the British nation see what it is really up against.'

Bombardier Ellis, who had added several more orthodox adventures subsequent to his forty-eight hours of separation from his battery, was also able to sum up his experience in positive terms; he was particularly proud that the British had shown that, whatever the setbacks they faced, they could 'stick it':

> That period between March the 21st and April 7th [he dated the end of his involvement at the point of his brigade's going out for 'a very much needed rest'] is indelibly printed on my memory. To begin with, the scarcity of food, exposure to the weather and the tremendous nervous strain was enough to break down the strongest constitution and how everyone stuck it I do not know but stick they did, from the Major down to the lowest rank, and not anybody showed more to advantage than did our Major. His coolness and resource again and again pulled us through a tight corner. Not only our battery but the whole brigade. His first thought was for the men and he never told anyone to do what he would not do himself, and many of the men who disliked him before had nothing but praise for him. He has since been decorated with the D.S.O. and a bar to his M.C. and good luck to him, he deserved it.

In early April Lieutenant-Colonel Walter Vignoles, now recuperating away from the area of the March offensive, sent via his wife a cheerful, up-beat message to entertain and reassure his young sons: 'Tell the boys the battle was just like the pictures; artillery galloping into action, guns working at top rate of fire, shooting at the masses of enemy they could see coming over the hill, in many cases only a few hundred yards away. The Boche is a plucky fellow, but he fails at the final assault; he does not like cold steel. We kept him off for hours though he must have outnumbered us very largely.'

He added: 'We are in a quiet sector now, and having a fairly decent time.' His 'quiet sector' was near the town of Armentières; what he could not know was that his division had been moved to an area which would be a prime target of the second great German offensive of 1918.

4

SPRING OFFENSIVE: APRIL

ARMENTIÈRES – 'Armenteers' to the men in the trenches – had had a relatively quiet war. It had been briefly occupied by the Germans in 1914 before being recaptured by General Pulteney's Third Corps in October. Over the years it had suffered sufficient bombing and shelling for it to be described by the Official History as 'much battered', but, unlike Ypres, a mere twenty kilometres to the north, it had not been reduced to a ruin.

Now it was suddenly in the firing line, and – also unlike Ypres, which the British were able to hold throughout 1918 – it found itself under German occupation. It would remain so until General Plumer's Second Army liberated it on 2 October. By that time it would have joined the distinguished list of cities and towns of France and Belgium to be almost completely erased during the Great War.

It was the second of Germany's 1918 initiatives which sealed the fate of the town. The first strike having failed, Ludendorff was in no mood to throw in the towel. The next in his short list of possible offensives was rapidly turned from plan to practice and what would become known to the British as the Battle of the Lys was opened on 9 April. As in the case of the 'Michael' operation, it had a powerful initial impact. There was, however, a significant factor suggesting that it was not quite in the same league as Michael in that, in acknowledgement of the strains and wastage of that operation, the Germans changed its code name from 'George' to 'Georgette'.

Yet it was this second German offensive which was to produce the greater political repercussions. There had been much jangling of Allied nerves during the weeks since 21 March, but, as viewed from the British standpoint, the fighting had taken place, relatively, deep inside France. Now it suddenly seemed quite possible that the unthinkable might happen and that the war might be lost, as the maps being studied daily on the breakfast tables of the nation showed enemy lines advancing far too close for comfort to the BEF's main bases and the Channel ports. Within three days of the launch of the attack, Major J.D. Wyatt, appointed second-in-command of the 2/6th Royal Warwickshires in 61st Division because two of his senior officers had become casualties, was writing in almost distraught terms in his diary: 'We have lost all the old forward area which I knew so well both in 1914–15 and again in 1916. Armentières, Estaires, Sailly and even Merville have all fallen into the hands of the Boches. We are now required to hang on to the fringes of what used to be our back areas.' It was not very far from those fringes to the coast.

The offensive began, as with its predecessor, with that prime weapon of 1918: surprise. This was especially effective in the case of the area now chosen because it had acquired the reputation of not being suitable for serious fighting until later in the year. Traditionally this whole sector from La Bassée to the Belgian border – a region of flat agricultural land intersected by numerous dykes and drainage ditches – had been waterlogged throughout the winter. 'The experience of three years', comments the Official History, 'had shown that the ground did not permit of an attack on a large scale before the month of May.' This year, however, there was a difference, of which arguably insufficient notice was taken: 'Against all precedent, the ground of the Lys plain began to dry in February and March.'

There was enough anxiety for it to be thought advisable to remove from the front, or at least reduce the area held by, the weakest link in the chain of defence: the 2nd Portuguese Division in the vicinity of Laventie. Least committed of the Allies, sent to fight a war in which they had little or no interest, less than fully trained and slow to acquire Western Front expertise, the so-called 'Pork and Beans' were seen as highly vulnerable in the event of an attack.

They were seen in precisely the same light by Ludendorff. He would later write that, once 'Georgette' had been decided on, 'the sooner it could take place the more likely it was to surprise the Portuguese in the plain of the Lys'.

When the attack was launched, its timing was even better than Ludendorff could have hoped in that it caught the Portuguese in the act of being relieved. They broke and fled in confusion. Something of the shock of the German onslaught can be sensed in the diary account of a British Liaison Officer, attached to the Portuguese, Captain R.G.C. Dartford; his account, of which the following are brief extracts, also suggests that among those who did not retreat, including some of the attached British, there were many casualties:

> 9 *April Tues.* Woke at 4.10 a.m. very heavy shelling. Guessed from the start it meant an attack. Phoned to brigade – every communication cut already. Next 3 hours we could do nothing, but nearly got asphyxiated by lack of oxygen owing to having to keep gas blankets down. Heavy fog on and everybody seemed isolated from others.
>
> I think the Boche must have taken our front line about 8.30 and the B line 8.45 and was up to batt H.Q. by 9.15 or so. One message from X. de Costa (CO 29th Batt.) said he no longer had any command and that it was now a question of individuals fighting out. He was killed we learnt after. So was Captain Montenegro, OC 20th Batt. (right) and nothing is known of Montalvao (left) and Woodrow and Sgt Ransdale.

As the Portuguese broke, the British division to their immediate north – one that had been severely mauled in March and was in process of rebuilding itself – was 'hustled back' (the Official History's phrase) with them, though on their southern flank a well-rested division, the 55th, offered a stubborn resistance. Indeed, it was able to turn the tables on the enemy, so that one young company commander, Captain C.L. Overton of the 1/4th King's Own Royal Lancasters, could claim in a letter written on the 10th: 'We drove him right out again and hold the original line, 6 of us captured 85, they simply gave themselves up, I think our battalion captured over 400.'

The Division seriously destabilized by the Portuguese failure was the 40th, which had 119th and 121st Brigades in the front line. The commander of 119th Brigade, Brigadier-General F.P. Crozier, a senior officer of Irish extraction and doughty reputation, has left a terse but vivid description of the state of affairs on the eve of the German attack, and of the opening of the attack itself:

> On the night of 7th–8th April we arrive in the line south of Armentières. On the right are the Portuguese. I don't like the feel of things – all is quiet – too quiet. I go down to the Portuguese front with a colonel. We walk seven hundred yards and scarcely

see a sentry. We examine rifles and ammunition lying about. All are rusty and useless. 'Where are the men?' I ask my companion. A snore gives me my answer. Practically all the front line sleeps heavily and bootless in cubby holes covered with waterproof sheets, while their equipment hangs carelessly about. . . .

'Our communication trenches are fearfully bad,' says the colonel, 'stretchers can't move with ease in them!' 'I know,' I say, 'I'll see what can be done about them, but from what I can see,' I reply, 'I should think we'll be shot out of this at dawn, *via* the rear!' I go back to my headquarters in a farm, and report what I have seen. 'They're always like that,' says a member of the British Mission attached to the Portuguese, on the telephone. 'They shouldn't be there,' I say, 'that's the crime.'

In the early morning of 9th April, a deafening bombardment wakes me up. Before long my batman Starrett arrives. 'Put this on', he orders, holding out my gas respirator, 'and get dressed at once. You'll be wanted. I'll pack the kit. Get you to the telephone place, it's strong.' I obey!

All is mystery and gas.

The Portuguese bolt and leave the way open to the Germans.

Crozier's batman, Private David Starrett, himself an Irishman of lively and volatile character, has also given an account of the occasion, one characterized by a distinct admiration for the forth-right and determined commander he was proud to serve – 'my man', as he sometimes chose to describe him:

The noise of battle had lost its power to keep me awake, but that night Fritz certainly got me up, and a good job too, for gas was coming over and being stirred with shell of the same order. It took a lot to convince some of the boys, as it is always, for most get some way to coma before they're warned, but at last we were all staring at each other's ugly mugs made hideous by the War Office contraptions reckoned by the London Staff to keep out gas. If they'd been forced to wear them in the conditions we did they would not have been so cock-a-hoop about them.

Just as I rushed my man's mask to him a shell wrecked the kitchen, and as soon as he'd disfigured his face with his mask down came another stinker, pulling the walls down on our heads. It was time to get out, but having to salvage all the new kit, and there seemed tons of it [Crozier had lost all his previous kit in the March retreat and it had just been replaced], made the going not over quick. By the time I got to the signallers the general was away, and the linesman told me the Boche had broken through the Portuguese and flanked us beautifully.

Back came Crozier, swearing dreadfully, to lead us or drive us once more in hurried retreat to Bac-St-Maur on the other side of the Lys. Our reserve battalion did its best to put some guts into the Portuguese defence, and how the general managed to be with them and with us at the same time passes my understanding to this day. But there he was whipping us into some sort of order and there he was steadying the reserve, with every bit of ground he trod torn to pieces by heavy stuff. My! his charmed life was being proved just then.

The GOC of 40th Division, himself an officer of high reputation, was Major-General John Ponsonby. When, soon after 5 a.m., the news came through that the Portuguese were retiring, Ponsonby 'ordered the 120th (Highland) Brigade, which was in reserve under Brigadier-General Hobkirk, to move forward to Laventie railway station, where it could strengthen the now exposed right flank of the Division; and next despatched Captain Harry Graham, of the divisional staff, by car to the headquarters of the 2nd Portuguese Division to ascertain the situation there'.

Thus the cool words of the 40th Division's official history. Captain Graham, writing to his wife some days later, described in vivid detail what turned out to be far from a routine mission, promising to maintain 'a discreet reticence' only on the question of Britain's oldest ally – a reference to the role of the Portuguese. His letter conveys strikingly the chaotic conditions behind the lines in the immediate aftermath of this massive German attack:

On the 9th of April we were peacefully asleep at 4 a.m. at a little place called Croix-du-Bac, near Armentières and close to Sailly and Bac-St-Maur and Steenwerk, when an intense bombardment began on our right. General John at once sent me post haste in an open motor to visit the Goose [i.e. the Portuguese], who were on our right flank, and from whom no telephone message could be obtained, to find out what was up. I started gaily out at 4.45

a.m., but when I reached the outskirts of the village (or town) of Estaires I found it being very heavily shelled. We managed to get through it somehow, though it was most unpleasant – a shell hit one house just as we were passing it, and it came down with a crash into the streets, scratching a lot of paint off the car and frightening the driver and myself quite a lot.

With a sigh of relief we reached open country beyond, but at the next village (La Gorgue) we found that the Hun was gassing it as well as shelling it, and our adventures were even more alarming! However, we arrived at last at Lustrem, the Goose's HQ, just as two shells fell through the roof of the Château where the old bird lived. Needless to say (it was about 5.30 a.m. by this time) the only people left were three *British* officers and the old P. General himself, a pale but dignified figure, much shaken by the fact that one shell had fallen into his room just as he was leaving the door. Not another soul anywhere to be found, for every bird had flown at the commencement of the bombardment, and no chance of discovering what was happening in the front line.

I must not tell you what happened *there*, but knowing our oldest Allies as I do, you can well imagine. Enough to know that the right flank became exposed to the furious onslaught of a great number of Hun divisions at 5.30 a.m. but that *we* clung on, as thank God, the 40th always do, for six more hours, and only retired when we had to about noon. Meanwhile, as I was talking to the pathetic remnant at the Goose's HQ, another British officer arrived, and told me that the 40th was being heavily attacked and our HQ at Croix-du-Bac shelled – and I thought it time to go home and see what was happening.

Graham's return was even more difficult than his outward journey, but they at last managed to get back to HQ at about 10 a.m., 'very hungry and somewhat alarmed!' Ponsonby had had news of the shelling of Estaires and other places just after he had left, 'and had spent anxious hours thinking that I must have been done in. His joy at seeing me again was really touching and I was quite moved by the rest of the staff's relief at my return.'

* * *

Some hint of the overpowering impact of the offensive on units caught up in the throes of it survives in the diary account by a gunner NCO, Sergeant James Sanderson, whose 'A' Battery, 121st Brigade RFA, 38th (Welsh) Division, was at Erquinghem, just to the west of Armentières on the banks of the River Lys, when the crisis began. Feeding the general state of confusion was the rule, apparently known only to some of those involved, that there was to be no use of the keynote term – the 'r' word as it would be called now – when there was any possibility that the intention to withdraw might become known to the enemy. Thus Sanderson would write of the first stage of the attack: 'Before long bullets were coming unpleasantly near and Lt. Clark ("Nobby") phoned to the Major for instructions. *"Don't retreat, but get out of it"*, came the reply. Poor Clark could not understand – he did not know that the word "retreat" was not to be used on the phone, and it was only with difficulty that I managed to persuade him that it would be perfectly in order for us to pack up.'

Even when explicit orders were delivered by word of mouth, the roar and din surrounding all verbal exchanges in such circumstances could hamper speedy execution. More, the withdrawal itself was an operation fraught with immediate and frightening danger:

Our infantry were now retreating behind us, and officers were galloping madly across fields and ditches. The Major ordered 'Limber Up' – we obeyed and were beginning to leave when our section officer, who had not heard the order, made us drop into action again. The order was repeated and this time we left at the gallop, for with no infantry support it was useless to remain. Not a shot seemed to have been fired in the infantry's retreat, excepting by our own Lewis gunners.

We were obliged to lie right over the off-side of our horses to avoid machine-gun bullets. Fortunately a high hedge screened us from Fritz but even so Sergeant Evans's charger immediately in front of me was shot dead, a lead driver was killed and several Gunners were wounded. The latter were nearly all toppled into the water-logged ditch on the right of the road, being hit just as their gun-team swerved to avoid a dead horse.

Yet attempts to hold up the German advance had not been entirely abandoned, as Sanderson and his comrades shortly discovered: 'On we went until we came to a railway crossing, where Staff Officers of high rank were stopping all and sundry and ordering them to make a stand.' Within minutes the Battery was once more firing, its target being the nearby roads along which the Germans were advancing. Hurriedly pulled into position in a ploughed field, 'A' Battery's guns fired round after round of shells through clouds of smoke and flame rising from blazing dumps of timber and stores lining the railway. There had been no time to organize normal procedures, so the Battery Commander, having stationed himself at a point on the embankment where he could get a better view of the action, 'observed the effect of our fire, passing his corrections to us, not by telephone, but by means of semaphore – flags – the signaller taking shelter behind a stack of timber. This was the only occasion on which I saw orders transmitted in this manner.' Yet the effectiveness of their firing was rapidly diminished by the condition of their hastily chosen position: 'In the soft ground our trails soon became buried, and we had great difficulty in swinging our guns on to new targets.'

Such improvised stands were merely gestures against an impossible tide; they were very soon once again in full retreat.

*   *   *

By the end of 9 April at the maximum point the Germans had made an advance of three and a half miles. They were satisfied enough to extend the battle north of Armentières on the 10th. Now other even more famous prizes were to fall to the Germans. The Messines Ridge, spectacularly gained in June the previous year following the explosion of nineteen mines under the German positions, was rapidly overrun. More potentially damaging to British morale, however, was the withdrawal by the British from the Ypres Salient. For Plumer, back from Italy and again in command of his much loved Second Army, this was a bitter decision, but, after an initial reluctance and under pressure from Haig and his own Chief of Staff, Harington, he accepted that there was no alternative. The story is told that on being advised by Harington that he would have to quit the Passchendaele Ridge, Plumer at first refused point blank, walking out of the room.

A few minutes later he returned, saying: 'You are right. Issue the orders.' On the positive side there is no doubt that these orders were carried out with great efficiency, frustrating an attack the Germans were preparing against the Ridge. By dawn on 16 April, Plumer's Second Army was defending a tight perimeter around Ypres, with its 'Battle Zone' along the ramparts and the Yser Canal. This was as far back as they could go without yielding the city itself, but then that was being held on to with the kind of *'Ils ne passeront'* intensity and passion that the French had displayed in 1916 at Verdun.

What effect the news had on those earlier quoted who had struggled so sacrificially to hold the Salient in the first months of the year is difficult to gauge, for Warren was recovering from wounds in England, while McMurtrie and Sharpe were undergoing the rigours of captivity in Germany.

* * *

It would not be long, however, before the Lys offensive began to lose its energy, as had been the case of its predecessor in the previous month. How did this second German attempt seem to those involved, when at last they were able to take a longer perspective?

Two days before the attack, on 7 April, Lieutenant-Colonel Vignoles, 9th Northumberland Fusiliers, 34th Division, in the line near Armentières, had written home in buoyant mood: 'We are in trenches but things are fairly quiet and we are not having a bad time so far; also we look forward to being relieved.' His next letter was written on the 19th, by which time the division was out of the action and recuperating near Poperinghe in Belgium. He acknowledged that he and his battalion had come through an extremely bruising experience, but he also claimed some success in holding up the German advance:

> We have seen war in real earnest now. It has been a terrible time; but we remain unbeaten though exhausted, and the men are extraordinarily cheerful. They will be awfully bucked when I tell them what I have just heard, that the Battn. has been reported to the Corps as having done exceptionally well.
>
> We are in reserve, fairly close up, at present, but hope to go right out of it tomorrow for a rest, and we jolly well deserve it.

It is heartbreaking to think of the fine fellows who have gone under, but luckily the proportion of wounded to killed is high and many have only slight wounds.

Major C.E.L. 'John' Lyne, like Sanderson of the Royal Field Artillery – his brigade and division at this time are uncertain – was not far from Vignoles in the vicinity of Armentières when the attack came. 'Everything so far fairly peaceful,' he had reported in a letter of 1 April, after returning from leave to a position his battery had held for some time and where he had struck up cordial relations with the local people: 'Had a big welcome from the family here, they all had lots to show me round the farm, new lambs and cows, etc. It's a very good life at present.' His next letter, however, written over a fortnight later, showed clear evidence of the shock he and his unit had experienced, but there was also pride in the way they had hung on:

> You'll surely be wondering how things are with me of late. My word, what a business, I never expected or hoped for such a campaign. As for rest or sleep, nothing doing in that line.
>
> A most fearfully exciting time. I got the battery away four times under machine-gun and rifle fire at close range. The Boche only got one of my guns, they surrounded it on three sides at a range of about 200 yards.
>
> We are holding them now, but the going was great while it lasted.

He amplified his story in a series of letters written over the following days. This on the 20th:

> All organisation went by the board, rations and forage were hard enough to get, and for days we lived on the country, as the saying goes. It's been a hard time for everybody, but it's been jolly fine and good training for all of us. The Brigade did exceedingly well, time after time we pulled out by the skin of our teeth under rifle and machine-gun fire and this battery generally seemed to pull out last.
>
> I've kept wonderfully fit throughout, bar the second night. I was out forward by myself in the early morning to try and find out the position of the infantry, or whether there were any at all,

and ran into some gas, was all right till the evening then got it very bad, and the night was a nightmare of horror. I was rather bad next morning and thought I'd have to be a casualty but cleared up a bit, and have been going strong ever since.

Yet he also carried a burden of anger and distress which he desperately needed to declare. As one who had made a point of friendship with his French neighbours he commented movingly, even passionately, about their appalling plight when caught up in a lightning, all-out offensive. He wrote this on 28 April:

I have seen the civilian population streaming out of bombarded Ypres, old men and women with barrows and bundles, I have seen civilian towns under German bombs, but nowhere have I seen anything to compare with the bitter pathos of those first five days' retreat.

The reddest horror of the battlefield grows smaller by comparison with what war brings to these poor inhabitants. People in England imagine that all the terrors of war are theirs when an air raid comes, and feel brave when they endure the discomfort of a night underground, but they have never seen the stark misery we saw a fortnight ago. Things were so sudden, so hopelessly unexpected, and those who should have given warning had none themselves. Even in our first position, people would come weeping to us to know if they should go or stay, and we couldn't tell them.

They looked to us for help we couldn't give them, they looked to us to stay the attack while they collected their few belongings and we couldn't do it.

He was especially saddened by the fate of the family close to his original wagon-lines:

Early in the war the Hun had overrun their once prosperous farm, driven off their cattle, killed all their stock and left them destitute. Then the tide flowed back; for 3½ years they had scraped and toiled till twelve fine cows stood in the stall, pigs, poultry, etc; their crops were all in and the old man had just put down 1000 francs worth of artificial manures. Every penny in the world was in that farm, and suddenly the crash came. Father, mother and eleven children, they had to leave everything. Poor old Grandpère of 80 was left behind. 24 hours later that farm was given as one of my targets, but I never fired on it.

What I've been telling you is such a pitiably incomplete fragment, just a glimpse here and there of the tragedy of it all, impossible to describe, but never to be forgotten.

And so much of it is our fault, more than they will ever realize, I hope.

That there were serious faults on the Allied side in the matter of the sufferings of the local French inhabitants was also the view of the 40th Division Staff Officer, Captain Harry Graham. In addition, there was the crucial extra disadvantage that when it became militar-ily imperative to withdraw retiring units had a civilian problem on their hands as well. In the letter of 18 April already quoted, Graham wrote in some heat of the morning of the attack:

All this time the battle was increasing in activity, and it was obvious that we couldn't remain longer where we were, unless we wished to be cut off and surrounded. But alas! by the idiotic policy of the past four years, all the neighbourhood was still crowded with French civilians, some of whom had lived in perfect security close to the front line for so long that they couldn't see the necessity of forsaking their homes. Also, there was the difficulty of moving them away, many of them (indeed most) being very old people or children. The General sent his motor off with a load, and we filled up some ambulances and so on. But by afternoon the Hun machine-gun bullets were whizzing down the street and we were forced to shift ourselves.

One of the most terrible things about this battle, to my mind, as compared with our other shows, is the awful casualties among civilians. Even the Hun must have felt stirred to loathing when he reached Bac-St-Maur and Estaires and other places and found the bodies of women and children and poor old people lying about the streets – but I *do* think it is the fault of the French or even our authorities for not clearing the inhabitants away just as they did in the south.

* * *

In spite of the hazards and the horrors of those dramatic April days, Major Lyne's overall tone was one of confidence; but he was also ready to admit that there were moments when the situation appeared to be one of the greatest danger. 'Five days ago I thought the war was over,' he wrote on 20 April, 'however the line holds now.' He returned to the same theme on the 23rd: 'I am afraid the papers give a very misleading account of the present show, but it's hard to minimise the severity of the break which brought us back from one of the most strongly fortified sectors of the whole British line, a line which has been strengthened and improved for 3½ years, line after line of trenches, mile after mile of defences.' As he saw it, press stories of high gallantry in defence or of inflicting huge losses on the enemy while yielding twelve miles of front entirely missed the point, by 'quite losing sight of the fact that the Boche ought never to have advanced so much as half a mile'. (Strictly, it might be commented that at a time when defence-in-depth – or 'elastic defence', to give it a variant description – was the order of the day, a loss of half a mile was of no great significance, indeed was well within the accepted rules; but Lyne's focus was of course not so much on British tactics as on the antics of the British press.)

Captain Graham was equally disparaging of what he saw as the ludicrous boastfulness of the newspapers. He wrote, also on the 23rd: 'I see the English press is beginning to talk as though we had won a great victory, or at any rate as though all danger were over. Oh Fools and Blind; the Hun offensive is only just begun, and we must be prepared for many another equally violent offensive. The *Morning Post*, I think, had a heading: 'German *Defeat* on the Lys', which is really about the limit!'

* * *

That the situation was seen as one of extreme gravity elsewhere than among the fighting troops is evident from the fact that the third day of the Lys offensive, Thursday 11 April, was the occasion of a most unusual, indeed a sensational, event in the history of the Western Front. This was the issuing of a 'Special Order' addressed 'To All Ranks of the British Army in France and Flanders' by Field Marshal Sir Douglas Haig couched in the most ominous terms. Noting that it was three weeks since the enemy began his 'terrific attacks', and that 106 German divisions had been thrown into the battle with a reckless regard for human life, the Commander-in-Chief continued:

Words fail me to express the admiration which I feel for the splendid resistance offered by all ranks of our Army under the most trying circumstances.

Many amongst us now are tired. To those I would say that Victory will belong to the side which holds out the longest. . . .

There is no course open to us but to fight it out. Every position must be held to the last man: there must be no retirement. With our backs to the wall and believing in the justice of our cause we must fight on to the end. The safety of our homes and the Freedom of mankind alike depend upon the conduct of each one of us at this critical moment.

Those who lived through the Second World War might well find a Churchillian ring in these memorable sentences; there are, surely, recognizable resonances of the promise of 'blood, toil, tears and sweat' which galvanized a shocked and anxious nation in the dark days of 1940. Undoubtedly there were many who at the time read the C.-in-C.'s 'special order' in such a light; there were even suggestions that it ranked with Nelson's last message before Trafalgar. Vera Brittain, serving as a VAD nurse (see Notes and References p. 357) not far from the focus of action, saw it as invigorating and inspiring, encouraging a renewed determination to devote maximum energy to the pursuit of the nation's cause. For three weeks following the first German attack the exhausted doctors, nurses and VADs of 24 General Hospital had endeavoured to cope with the stream of convoys, each bringing a new supply of wounded – 'to be despatched, [as she would describe in her celebrated postwar account *Testament of Youth*] a few hours later, to England after a hasty wash and change of dressing, or to the cemetery after a laying-out too hurried to be reverent'. And meanwhile, 'into our minds had crept for the first time the secret, incredible fear that we might lose the War'. Now, suddenly, 'there was a braver spirit in the hospital that afternoon, and though we only referred briefly and brusquely to Haig's message, each one of us had made up her mind that, though enemy airmen blew up our huts and the Germans advanced upon us from Abbeville, so long as wounded men remained in Étaples, there would be "no retirement".'

Undoubtedly the 'Special Order' represented a remarkable departure for a commander not normally associated with eloquent public pronouncements. As the soldier-historian Cyril Falls put it in his one-volume account *The First World War*: 'He was a man not given to fighting with words. Now he resorted to them.' Clearly endorsing Haig's gesture Charles Carrington, in his autobiographical history *Soldier from the Wars Returning*, described it as 'the only appeal of that kind he ever made, and by that the more effective'. By contrast, Lieutenant-General Alexander Godley, former commander of II ANZAC Corps and now GOC of XXII Corps, recorded that he treated the message with considerable amusement, knowing that they had had 'their backs to the wall since March, and did not need to be told'. Even more dismissively, the naval historian Stephen Roskill would see the order in a distinctly less heroic light; his verdict, in his biography of the secretary to the War Cabinet, Colonel Sir Maurice Hankey, was that it was 'almost panic-stricken'.

How was it seen among those for whom it was principally intended, the soldiers in the field desperately trying to hold the line? Evidence is patchy in that it would seem that most officers and men when writing home cared more about reassuring their families than discussing the overall thrust of the campaign – indeed one suspects that many were not even aware the order had been issued – but nevertheless some interesting reactions have survived which show that attitudes were far from being uniform, and in some cases were extremely critical.

Lieutenant Philip Ledward, who had witnessed some of the results of the attack on the Somme front three weeks earlier, later wrote of this period: 'At this time we were taking a gloomy view of the prospects of the war. Those of us who had seen the Fifth Army retreating on March 28 and knew that only ignorance and fatigue, and the fact that guns could not keep pace with men, had prevented the Germans from marching unopposed to the coast, felt grimly sceptical about the future.' In such a context Haig's message was less than welcome; indeed, stated Ledward, 'this famous and much praised order had a very depressing effect on the fighting soldiers. The end of the war was not a thing that the troops envisaged clearly or thought much about, but I am sure I am right in saying that the majority of us interpreted Sir Douglas Haig's order to mean that the game was, if not quite "up", at least a forlorn hope. Fresh from our hammering on the Somme, with news coming through of the tremendous offensive in the North, we envisaged a long-drawn-out "die-in-the-last-ditch" affair with an ultimate German victory.'

Indicative that such a view existed at the level of an ordinary soldier is the terse comment in the diary of W.R. Acklam, a signaller in 190 Brigade, Royal Field Artillery, in 41st Division, writing on 16 April: 'Heard bad news again about German advance and about him being near Bailleul [it had in fact fallen the previous day]. I have given up hope altogether of our winning and think that the sooner we make peace the better.' If not quite so despairing, the chemical warfare expert Captain A.E. Hodgkin wrote in terms of extreme anxiety on 12 April: 'I have never before felt quite so much as if I were living on the edge of a precipice as I do at present.'

The sense of pessimism inspired at this time would also, in Ledward's view, have unforeseen consequences when several months later the tone of the reports from the front changed, suggesting that now it was the enemy who was showing signs of being seriously 'on the run'. He noted: 'I remember very clearly the incredulity and sarcasm with which we used to comment on the early bulletins recording the Allied advance when the tide finally began to turn.'

Sarcasm was, of course, a standard reaction among the fighting men after so many years of war, and high-flown pronouncements, whether valid or otherwise, were far more likely to be given the two-finger treatment by the Tommies than hand-on-heart approval. A Lieutenant of 8th Division, then adjutant of a Northamptonshire battalion, Hubert Essame, who would later become a distinguished chronicler of the events of 1918, wrote of Haig's message: 'Naturally these sentiments met with acclaim from the home press and the literal-minded not personally involved in the battle. In the front line only too often the men to whom it was read as ordered had only one comment and that a rude one. They did not expect from their commanders this sort of rabble-rouser's rant in which Welsh politicians and press lords of the day were wont to wallow.'

A typical Tommy's reaction was that of Private H. Baumber of the 10th Lincolns, also known as the 'Grimsby Chums', a Pals battalion with a long record of tough fighting from the first day of the Somme onwards:

An officer came along and read out a message from Haig for us to stand fast at this point and die if needs be. We veterans (for that's what we were now) took little heed of this claptrap as we had heard it all before, besides talk's cheap, especially if you are out of touch with conditions on the spot. It was stated that we now had to fight with our backs to the wall. The lads just treated it as a joke saying *there is no wall* so we will soon be back in Blighty having a drink. Of course there is no doubt that things were serious but we didn't need anyone to tell us that.

An even pithier response was that recorded in Captain J.C. Dunn's famous history of the 2nd Royal Welsh Fusiliers, *The War the Infantry Knew*. Under the date 13 April, he noted: 'The C.-in-C. tells us "our backs are to the wall." His men are asking, "Where's the ... wall?"'

Among officers identified with the world of the Staff as opposed to that of the combatants, two contrary reactions are perhaps worth noting. Brigadier-General John Charteris, Haig's former intelligence chief, commented in tones not dissimilar to those of Lieutenant Ledward: 'I wish D.H. had *not* issued his order. It will immensely hearten the Germans when they hear of it, as they must. I do not think our own men needed it to make them fight it out. If the French are really hurrying to our assistance, they should be here in a few days, almost as soon as the order will reach the front-line troops. If they are not, it may have a really bad effect to raise hopes in the troops' minds.'

For a strongly supportive view there could be nothing more positive than the comments of Guy Dawnay, at this time serving as Major-General, General Staff, at British GHQ at Montreuil. On 13 April he wrote in a a letter to his wife: 'Didn't you think the Chief's "Special Order" was very good indeed?' He supplemented his question with a distinctly upbeat view of the then military situation: 'The Germans have employed six-sevenths of their force against the English. On every method of calculation we have borne six-sevenths of the brunt. The German plan was to knock out *one* Ally – a very sound plan too. But they haven't done it – and the mere fact of the extent to which we have borne the brunt means that – someone else is fresh. . . . This is the greatest battle the world has ever seen – so you mustn't form any hasty judgements based on any local happenings.' This confidence was not misplaced, and though the crisis was by no means over when Dawnay wrote the above, the Lys offensive was doomed to peter out as had its larger predecessor.

The Official History, perhaps not surprisingly, gave the 'backs to the wall message' (as it was generally described) a ringing endorsement. 'To many officers and men at the front it was the first intimation that the situation was really serious; it aroused throughout the fighting troops a strong wave of determination not to be beaten, and they responded to it by giving of their best. It also had a most valuable effect in the United Kingdom, and on "resting" troops and men in the rearward services.' In support the History cited an order by a subaltern of the 1st Australian Division, found during a visit to the trenches by a liaison officer, of which these were the leading clauses:

(1) This position will be held, and the section will remain here until relieved.
(2) The enemy cannot be allowed to interfere with this programme.
(3) If the section cannot remain here alive it will remain here dead, but in any case it will remain here.

* * *

That the Lys offensive ultimately failed like its predecessor to the south was not entirely due to the brave resistance of the British. Enemy exhaustion and human frailty also played a part. The German medical officer Stephen Westman had not been present at the collapse of Operation Michael, but he was a witness of the breakdown of its successor. At the very moment that it seemed as if the road to the coast lay open, there was a sudden dearth of troops available to exploit the advances of the storm battalions:

A few units of the following-up divisions emerged on the northwestern edge of the forest [of Hazebrouck], but of the rest many did not appear, and others turned up in a state unfit for combat – in other words, they were dead drunk. They had found huge depots of wine and spirits, and each man had taken with him a bottle of whisky or the like, and had constantly sipped it as though it was lemonade or *ersatz* coffee.

Thus the German offensive, at least at our part of the front, came to a stop – not for lack of German fighting spirit, but on account of the abundance of Scottish drinking spirit! This was something Ludendorff and his staff officers had not foreseen.

Orders were hurriedly issued for wine barrels to be opened and their contents spilled on the ground, and for bottles of whisky or liqueurs to be smashed, but by then these deadly illicit weapons had already made their potent, if bizarre, contribution to the outcome of the 1918 war, as the alcohol effect witnessed in March by Captain Binding at Albert was replicated in April at Hazebrouck.

Westman does not date his report, so it is difficult to know whether this preceded or followed a significant German success of the last phase of the Lys offensive, the seizure of Kemmel Hill, just south of Ypres. Defended by battle-weary British divisions, the sector had been taken over by relatively fresh French ones. On 25 April, following a bombardment of colossal proportions, seven German divisions, newly thrown into the battle, stormed the hill and seized it. Foch reacted swiftly by shifting reserves north to prevent the capture of any more of the Flanders heights. A further thrust by the Germans on the 29th proved to be the last; they made small gains in two areas but against that there was the massive plus overall of a major onslaught determinedly repulsed. The second German offensive was over.

* * *

As was always the case at the time of a major campaign, whether launched by the Allies or by the enemy, other initiatives continued elsewhere. These were often, in effect, merely sideshows to the main action, sometimes achieving little more than pinching out a minor salient or seizing a local point of vantage, but nevertheless adding to the dreary total of casualties in killed, wounded, or missing.

When the 34th Division went north to Armentières to what would become a focal point of Ludendorff's April attack, it relieved the 38th (Welsh) Division, which, moving south, eventually took position in what had been the hinterland of the Somme front back in 1916. There some of its personnel found themselves within sight – just – of the Hanging Virgin of Albert: the gilded statue of the

Madonna and Child which, following a direct hit by a German shell back in January 1915, had ever since hung in a virtual high-dive configuration above the streets of that long-suffering Picardy township. At this time, it should be emphasized, Albert was in German hands. Thus it came about that an officer of the 2nd Battalion of the Royal Welsh Fusiliers, Captain Moody, chanced to observe a happening long predicted in that region, and one that was the subject of much soldierly superstition. It took place on 16 April, during what he described as an 'extra active shelling of Albert': 'I saw a direct hit on the already damaged tower of the cathedral, which brought the leaning Madonna crashing to the ground. It happened about 4 in the afternoon. The incident caused a certain amount of gloom among those who thought there might be something in the saying that when the Madonna fell the War would end soon in the defeat of the people who perpetrated the deed.' Captain J.C. Dunn, quoting this in the battalion's history, added his own contemporary comments on the event: 'One of our six-inchers did it. Our prestige with the French people has fallen so low that it would be worth hearing what they say about it. The stump of the modern Byzantine tower still rises above the Millencourt ridge.'

If the 38th (Welsh) could still see the truncated tower of Albert's basilica, the valley of the River Ancre to the north was not within their view and it was decided that the Division, or at least one Brigade of it, should remedy this by a specially mounted attack. They would be assisted by the Division on their left, the 35th. The Brigade selected for this operation was the 113th, consisting of the 13th, 14th and 16th Battalions, Royal Welsh Fusiliers; the time chosen was 7.30 p.m. on Monday 22 April.

The regimental history of the Royal Welsh Fusiliers offers the following laconic account of the subsequent action:

> There is nothing much to be said of this affair, except that it was gallantly carried out. . . . There was no preliminary bombardment, and the troops left the trenches with an ineffective barrage in front of them. The brigade suffered heavy casualties, but won a position from which the desired observation could be obtained. Eighty-six Germans were captured, and six machine-guns.

Our 13th Battalion, at a tremendous sacrifice, reached the

objective given, the shell-hole position, thanks to the gallant leadership of Captain C.B. Williams. But 2nd Lieutenants B.T. Evans, H.S. Heaton, F.C. Hutchins, J.F. Samuel, T.B. Winter, and D.J. Thomas (attached from the 15th Battalion), were killed, together with 62 other ranks; and 3 officers and 210 other ranks were wounded; 2 other ranks were missing.

The 16th Battalion, in the centre, only succeeded in advancing some 250 yards. All the officers of A, B, and C Companies were casualties. Lieutenants F.T. Linton, W.S. Goff, V.P. Williams, H. Bennet. S.E. Jenkins, and 46 other ranks were killed; 2nd Lieutenants B.O. Davies, A.O. Owens, and 20 other ranks were missing; 2nd Lieutenants A.B. Brodin, S.C. Skuse, and 159 other ranks were wounded.

With two companies assaulting, the 14th Battalion made no appreciable advance and lost Lieutenant J.G. Webb, 2nd Lieutenants J. Huxley, G.O. Richards, and 5 other ranks killed; 14 other ranks missing; and 95 other ranks wounded.

Counter-attacks on the 23rd and 24th April were beaten off.

The present writer's second cousin, Private Ernest Vivian Radcliffe, as referred to in this book's Foreword (see pp. xxxi–xxxiii), was a member of the 16th Battalion. It must be assumed that he was one of the battalion's unnamed '20 other ranks' missing following this brave if somewhat less than glorious minor episode of 1918.

The battalion's war diary adds the following details: 'Except on the left we failed to obtain the first objective, and it was found impossible to advance. This being so, Battalion dug in, and remained in this position until the night of the 25th, when it was relieved by 17th RWF. The Battalion went in with strength of 14 Officers and 450 ORs, and came out with 5 Officers and 225 ORs.' From later evidence it appears that the last that was known of Private Radcliffe was that he was heard calling, or crying, for help from a shell hole in No Man's Land. It would appear that this information, communicated at some point to my uncle, the late Thomas Archibald Radcliffe (himself a former soldier of that war), who died in 1946, was deliberately withheld from other members of the family as being too distressing, and only discovered by chance at a later date.

As stated in the Foreword, Ernest Radcliffe is commemorated on the Memorial to the Missing at Pozières; his is one of 14,690 names of men who died on the Somme in 1918 and who have no known grave.

* * *

Operation 'Georgette' might be over, yet Ludendorff had not entirely renounced his hopes of breaking through in the area of his first offensive, 'Michael'. There was to be, as it were, a postscript to it, constituting another, equally unsuccessful, attempt to seize that greatly valued prize: the Picardy capital, Amiens.

The town of Villers-Bretonneux lies some ten miles to the east of Amiens, on a road which runs straight as an arrow towards the city's outskirts. On 24 April the Germans took it from the British in another superbly orchestrated attack. This action was notable for the only tank battle of the war, with thirteen German against thirteen British, seven of the latter being light 'whippet' tanks (with a top road speed of 8 miles per hour as opposed to the 3.7 mph of the heavier Mark IV). On the following day General Rawlinson ordered that Villers-Bretonneux should be immediately recaptured. This was achieved with remarkable speed and dexterity by one brigade of the British 18th Division and two brigades of the 5th Australian division, and though the enemy held on to Moreuil, which had been taken from the French on the 24th, his progress on the Amiens front was halted for good.

But at a price. Lieutenant Ledward's 23rd Brigade in 8th Division, for example, suffered appallingly in the first stage of the action from the sudden, overpowering onslaught of the German guns. As he described it: 'At Villers-Bretonneux the battalions were decimated in six hours by the perfectly infernal bombardment. Very few prisoners were taken. The German tanks did serious execution too. They moved over our trenches and enfiladed them so that the wretched defenders were rendered defenceless and stood helplessly to be mown down. But it was the bombardment that did the worst damage. That was a truly ghastly business.'

Yet on the other side of the coin was the achievement of the Australians, for whom Villers-Bretonneux would become a famous battle honour, and where eventually they would build a national memorial. Summing up what he saw as the good and the bad of the Australian contribution to the Western Front war, Ledward stated:

It is my considered opinion that the Australians, in 1918, were better in a battle than any troops on either side. They were not popular. They had a contempt for Britishers to begin with – that is, some Australians voiced such a contempt. I myself heard the expression 'not bad for a Britisher' used by one about some successful feat of British arms. They were untidy, undisciplined, 'cocky', not 'nice' enough for the taste even of Thomas Atkins; but it seems to me indisputable that a greater number of them were personally indomitable, in the true sense of the word, than of any other race. I am glad they were on our side.

At Villers-Bretonneux the Australians had only been out of the line for four days and they had to march twelve miles to reach the battle area. The line of attack selected for them was oblique to their old front and through very thick country. The Germans opposed to them were shock troops and had had an easy passage and must have been in good fettle. The night was dark and the actual situation of the enemy was only known in places. Yet the attack was completely successful. Not only was Villers-Bretonneux retaken but the new line was established beyond where the old line had been, and a lot of prisoners and guns were captured. It was the most wonderful performance of which I had direct knowledge during my service. At their own request they had no barrage or support of any kind from the artillery. They just went forward, each man for himself, in the way that only they had mastered.

*   *   *

One important feature of these desperate weeks has not been sufficiently emphasized: the sheer size of the casualty toll. (If an attack as relatively minor as that of the 113th Brigade just described could produce such high figures as those listed, it is clear that fighting on the scale of the great March and April encounters must have been infinitely more expensive.) 'Terrible losses on both sides', was the concluding sentence of a diary entry for 21 March by Corporal A.H. Roberts of the 13th (Pioneer) Battalion Gloucestershire Regiment. It was a prophetic comment. Many thousands, particularly members of those battalions which disintegrated under the impact of the initial German attack, simply disappeared without trace. The same fate

befell some units during the Lys battle. For example, of two companies of the 20th Middlesex which took part in an early morning
raid on 9 April – by unlucky chance the very day on which the
Germans attacked – the Official History states: 'Most of the men of
these two companies were never heard of again.' The daily toll
during the forty days from the launching of 'Michael' to the end of
'Georgette' was approximately 6,000; this figure included the
wounded and missing as well as the dead but even so it is depress-
ingly high, the more when one realizes that it was at least matched
on the German side. And many among them were teenagers like
those with Lance-Corporal Sharpe in the forward trenches of 66th
Division on 21 March, or the young reinforcements whom Major
Christie-Miller had subsequently seen on the Channel transports in
late March, sent direct from UK training camp to the front, to do
battle in a country they barely glimpsed before they were buried or
went missing in it.

The principal symbols of this appalling slaughter available today
are the military cemeteries and memorials with their thousands of
names. Meaningful documentary evidence from a period of great
movement and activity is perhaps less easy to find. To offer an
example which, in its attempt to extract some kind of comfort out of
a situation of confusion and personal tragedy, must have been
paralleled many times: a letter written as late as 25 May to a Mrs Lill
describes how her husband, E.S. Lill, a driver serving in an unidentified unit of the Royal Horse Artillery, was fatally wounded in the
21 March attack. After apologizing for the long delay in making
contact, caused partly by uncertainty over her address but mainly by
a shortage of witnesses, the writer, Major A.W. Van Straubenzee,
informs her: 'Your husband's Sectional Officer was wounded and is
a prisoner, and all I can tell you is the story told by the one
remaining driver of the gun team.' He states that when Lill and his
leading driver were hit following a shell burst between the horses, he
was 'unconscious from the first', and, having been evacuated to a
Casualty Clearing Station, 'died there never having regained consciousness'; the implication, standard in almost all such letters, is that
the victim suffered no pain. He offers the prospect of further
information in due course: 'I have written to the other driver, to try
and get further details if possible, and I will let you know everything

he says. But it takes some time to find them in Hospital.' Clearly hoping to encourage and console by praising the dead soldier's courage, he continues: 'We had a very trying time on the 21st, and your husband together with all the other drivers twice drove through the barrage and gas, with ammunition for the guns, and they all behaved magnificently.' He adds, apologetically: 'I had not had the pleasure of meeting your husband as I had not long since joined the Battery, and we were very busy at the time.'

To offer another small but telling example: a postcard survives written on 23 April by a Private C. Smith of the 7th Bedfordshires beginning, 'Just a line to say that I am still in the pink and out of the line, hope you are all well.' Attached to it is the information that Private Smith was killed at Villers-Bretonneux the next day.

For a death caringly chronicled in the fallen soldier's family papers there could hardly be a more moving example than that of Captain Norman Austin Taylor, 1st Surrey Rifles, also known as the 1/21st Battalion, London Regiment, 47th (2nd London) Division. He was wounded on 24 March in fierce fighting on the Third Army front in the vicinity of High Wood, where his division had fought hard and bravely in the Somme battle in September 1916. He died two days later. A letter to Taylor's father from a fellow officer opened the correspondence:

> Your son was very badly wounded last Sunday – 24 inst. – a machine-gun bullet passing thro' the abdomen – he was at once carried away back for a distance of two miles and when I saw him was very cheery and not in any pain. Yesterday I heard that he passed away in the hospital train on the way down to Étaples.
>
> All of us here offer you our deepest sympathy and we shall miss him very much indeed – he was immensely popular and died a soldier's death which is the noblest ambition under these trying circumstances, which I am now able to say are well in hand.

A letter to Taylor's sister, Dorothea, from a close family friend, or perhaps a relative, working for the Ministry of Munitions, combined shocked sympathy with an attempt to take some comfort from the dead officer's fine record:

> I was most awfully sorry to hear from Mother this morning that Norman had been killed in this last great battle. I'm afraid it will

be a terrible blow to you all seeing that he was the only son and brother. It is a great thing to think how splendidly he had done before and must be somewhat of a consolation to you all.

Do you remember the words of the hymn 'We feebly struggle, they in glory shine'? I think they are very apposite at such times as you and I have both known.

But the most memorable expression of grief at Captain Taylor's death is surely that which survives in a letter by another sister, Joyce, written over a year later in April 1919. After informing her correspondent – with whom she had been out of contact for some long period – of the circumstances of her brother's death, she continued, in a passage which captures the deep and abiding sense of loss which so many must have known at that time:

Five foot ten of beautiful young Englishman under French soil. Never a joke, never a look, never a word more to add to my store of memories. The book is shut up for ever and as the years pass I shall remember less and less, till he becomes a vague personality; a stereotyped photograph. I was dancing at four o'clock on the morning of the 24th. My partner said to me 'whereabouts is your brother now?' I told him and he said, 'Good God, aren't you anxious?' Now I had been anxious to the verge of frenzy for four years and I believed in the goodness of God; but nevertheless I felt that icy hand on my heart which I shall never now feel again.

* * *

If there were thousands of fatalities during the great retreat, there were also many more thousands suffering from serious wounds, the numbers increasing substantially each day. The ambulance trains were never idle – nor, for that matter, were the ordinary troop trains, co-opted into an ambulance role for the more lightly wounded – while at the same time convoys of lorries loaded with reinforcements and supplies heading towards the front crossed the paths of countless motor ambulances going the other way. All this produced a situation of continuous emergency lasting for many weeks in the BEF's overworked hospitals.

Miss Dorothy Nina Seymour was a VAD nurse of considerable

seniority, having embarked for France as far back as November 1914. The daughter of a general and granddaughter of an Admiral of the Fleet, at one time a Woman of the Bedchamber to HRH Princess Christian, she was an adept both at the social round and at such pursuits as horse-riding, hunting and gardening; nevertheless, she took readily to nursing under the challenge of war. She spent several months of her five years of service in Petrograd, where she was posted to a hospital in the palace of a Grand Duke, becoming well known not only in the British diplomatic community but also to many members of the Russian aristocracy, including the Tsarina herself. In this way she was a close witness of the first Russian revolution in February 1917, but she escaped to England soon after the Tsar's dethronement and by early 1918 was back in France. Posted to the BEF's main base at Étaples, she was able to see at first hand some of the tragic human consequences of the German spring offensives; and though by definition she and her like were away from the fighting zone (if often within close earshot of it) they were not free from danger, as there was sporadic harassment from enemy air raids. Nor were they simply concerned with wounded *British* soldiers; Étaples at this time was a teeming crossroads with troops of several nations going to or from the front, while innumerable civilians and other refugees – such as HQ staff or WAACs fleeing from areas the Germans had overrun – also flocked there urgently seeking sanctuary and support. The following extracts from her diary account, which was written up from detailed notes shortly after the war, sketch a vivid picture of this most famous of bases at this most harrowing time:

March 24th. Bad air raid again last night, Germans flying low and circling over camp for about twenty minutes. Two bombs dropped in sand one each side of railway station – sounded as if it was at my door. Trains with troops going up incessant and ambulance trains down without number.

March 26th. Aeroplanes busy again. Wounded pouring in and drafts going up the line, train after train. Everyone from here cleared out and refilled with fresh men and thousands more than before. Wounded arriving in ambulances straight from the field stations, and also sitting cases coming down in cattle trucks.

March 30th. Place teeming with excitement. 1000s coming over from England, only stopping to do gas drill and then on up the line. Head Quarter Staff pouring in from Abbeville, Amiens, Doullens and Hesdin. Also WAACs from the same. Mostly sleeping on floor as beds have run out. Ambulance trains unceasing. Two trainloads of French boys just called up went off today just as three trains of New Zealand troops arrive. Noise deafening. Slight air raid last night.

April 4th. Hospital terribly busy. Such an awful lot of bad cases and deaths.

April 10th. Guns on front terrific all night. Troops going on through here without ceasing. Refugees fleeing from here every night by the one train civilians are allowed on. Women and children with bags and bundles fighting for a place and some have to be left behind every night.

April 11th. Laventie gone. Suppose it was that we heard last night. Hospitals busier than ever, lot of wounded who'd been left out lying some time. Hear that the casualty stations only had the last patients carried out as the Germans got in, machine-guns kept them off till then – but they've got all the stock, but staff escaped.

April 14th. Merville gone now. Last night could see star shells bursting quite distinctly towards Aire. Guns terrific again. Many people, women and children, among the wounded.

April 15th. Trainloads of refugees, French people, came into siding last night right below here. All more or less starving, some very old, lots of children. Soldiers all splendid, making tea for them and helping them to get warm and find a sleeping place. One woman then proceeded to have a baby, sympathetically attended by the nearest soldier! An ambulance that was sent for arrived too late to move her before it arrived. Forty WAACs arrived today having taken three days to get here from St. Omer. Allowed one night on the floor and then sent on to Rouen. Poor wretches.

There are no further entries for a fortnight, and then at last Miss Seymour had something amusing to record: '*April 30th*. A German balloon got astray and wandered over Étaples. Caught on a telegraph

1. German troops concentrating in St Quentin just before the 'Michael' offensive of 21 March 1918.

2. Fully equipped German storm troopers, 1918.

3. German Official Photograph, captioned 'German Infantry Assault, Western Front'. Although no doubt taken during training, it nevertheless gives some impression of what the British Third and Fifth Armies faced in March 1918.

4. German troops advancing south across the battlefield of the Chemin des Dames.

5. The fruits of success. German troops milking a cow and drinking the milk; near Soissons, late May

6. French and British wounded retreating together, 27 May, the first day of the Chemin des Dames attack.

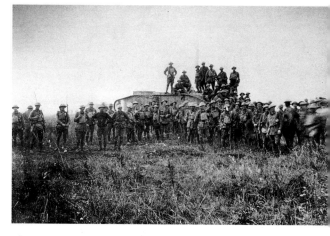

7. Australians celebrating their succesful advance, Battle of Amiens, 8 August.

8. A ruined street in Albert, recaptured, by the 18th (Eastern) Division, 22 August.

9. New Zealanders on a captured enemy howitzer, celebrating the capture of Grévillers, near Bapaume, 25 August.

10. American troops disembarking at Le Havre, 12 July.

11. American light artillery passing through a French village.

12. Battle of the St Quentin Canal: Brigadier-General J.V. Campbell, VC, CMG, DSO, on the bridge at Riqueval, congratulating soldiers of the 137th (Staffordshire) Brigade, 46th (North Midland) Division, following their successful crossing of the Canal on 29 September. Photograph by David McClellan (variant of dust-jacket photograph).

13. Massed German prisoners in a clearing depot, Abbeville, 2 October.
Photograph by David McClellan.

14. Canadian troops in Cambrai, liberated 9 October.

15. M. Georges Clemenceau, the French Premier, and Field Marshal Sir Douglas Haig during a visit to Cambrai on the day after its liberation.

16. Lille, liberated by the British, 17 October; the photograph records the enthusiastic welcome given by a crowd of women to the first French soldier to enter the city.

17. London, Armistice Day, 11 November; cheering crowds celebrating outside the gates of Buckingham Palace.

18. An official war-artist's retrospective comment on the Western Front war: 'After the battle'; inscribed 'Paul Nash 1918–1919'.

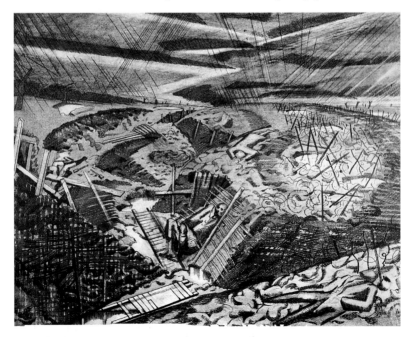

post, it wrenched itself free and then knocked a chimney over, then drifted over Paris Plage where I hear it came down.'

To Miss Joanna Anderson, a VAD attached in an administrative capacity to the 55th General Hospital, there fell the dispiriting but necessary task of sending letters of condolence to the families of men who had been brought to the hospital for treatment but had then died of their wounds. Writing to her predecessor in the post, in a letter continued over several days at the height of the crisis caused by the April offensive, she commented that she had found the work since arriving there 'delightful in most ways'. However, there was now a grim other side to the coin: 'The only trying part is the sense of horror of the suffering in the hospital as seen from the outside. There are so many deaths just now. My heart is ploughed into furrows when I visit these dying patients in the ward and then come back to the office and see their homes rise up before me and all the anguish that my letter will bring them. At times I feel as if I wanted to go away and howl.'

A touching tribute to the work of women of the calibre of Dorothy Seymour and Joanna Anderson survives in the 1918 pages of a scrapbook belonging to another of their number, herself a nurse who spent many months in France. Dated 10 April, and written by a soldier signing himself 'Sapper 70503 Frank Burchell, 3rd Corps Signals, BEF', it reads:

> Man's inhumanity to man
> Makes countless thousands mourn.
> > Robbie Burns

How true! But the good and devotional work of such noble women as our nurses has taught us that women at the least are doing their utmost to counteract man's inhumanity. With all homage due to one of these, Miss Kathleen Forrest, from a sincere friend.

* * *

The story of April 1918 cannot properly be told without referring, however briefly, to two important events, one of them on the Western Front, one elsewhere, which are essential if minor components of the fabric of this multifaceted year.

On the 21st the supreme German air ace, Baron Manfred von Richthofen – famous as 'the Red Baron' because of the colour of his Albatross aircraft – was shot down in the Somme region while attempting to claim his eighty-first victim. Who achieved the kill has long been a subject of dispute, but, in the words of the historian Trevor Wilson, 'what is plain is that, under the unrelenting pressure of aerial combat, the Red Baron on this occasion exercised less than the rigorous caution that had enabled him to survive so far.' His death can thus be interpreted as a symbol of the changing balance in air power, in which area the Allies, despite heavy losses in men and aircraft, could now be said generally to have gained the upper hand (though the Germans were still capable at times of achieving *local* superiority). The planes at least could be, and were, replaced rapidly by the Allies' factories – indeed, it has been estimated that in March the Royal Flying Corps requested 1,993 machines and were sent 2,259, whereas the Germans were beset by shortages, not only of aircraft, but also, crucially, of petrol. Thus their new pilots, with fewer flying hours during training than would normally have been deemed desirable, became easier targets when they found themselves in combat. Co-ordination between ground and air also suffered, with the Germans, reacting slowly to the new patterns of warfare, being notably laggard in moving their airfields close to the shifting battle-lines.

Two days after von Richthofen's death, on 23 April, the Royal Navy, with a mixed force of 'bluejackets' and Royal Marines, attacked the Belgian ports of Zeebrugge and Ostend. It being St George's Day this was clearly a case of the British attempting to engage the lion in his den. (This was not, however, the comparison used at the time: in a famous response to the signal of Vice Admiral Keyes 'St George for England', Captain Carpenter, commanding the chief warship in the action, HMS *Vindictive*, replied, 'May we give the dragon's tail a damned good twist'. It is told that the signalman, perhaps not wishing to swear at a Vice Admiral, substituted 'darned' for 'damned'; overruled by his captain, he salved his conscience by spelling dammed with two m's.)

The intention was to block the mouths of the canals which connected Zeebrugge and Ostend with the inland port of Bruges, site of the submarine pens which housed many of the German

Navy's U-boats; at this stage, virtually the enemy's only active maritime weapon. The attempt at Ostend was less successful than that at Zeebrugge, where, despite furious resistance which produced 700 British casualties, two out of the three blockships assigned to the operation were duly sunk in the canal mouth. Unfortunately, they failed to seal the exit completely and so the U-boats were still able to come and go and continue their predatory work. However, this was not evident for some time; what was clear immediately was that the sailors and marines involved had carried out a brave and bold deed under the enemy's nose, with unmistakable echoes of the old tradition of singeing the beard of the King of Spain, or of Nelson at Copenhagen and the Nile. The effect on the morale of the nation, with – for a change – a heroic and heart-warming *sea* story to pore over in its newspapers, was considerable. Above all the episode raised the spirits of the Navy, glad after months of frustration that at last its personnel had been offered a chance to show their fighting spirit and assist their comrades in khaki. But the latter gained too, their morale being undoubtedly lifted by the awareness that they were not alone in trying to show the Germans what for!

That despite its mixed results the Zeebrugge attack would retain its hold on the popular imagination, and its place in naval mythology, is evident from the curious fact that it was reproduced with realistic models at the Wembley British Empire Exhibition of 1924–25.

* * *

Although his first two strikes of March and April had failed, Ludendorff had not yet fired all the arrows in his quiver. He would make a further effort in May, while other plans were maturing for further efforts elsewhere. By an unfortunate irony, some British Divisions which had suffered heavily in the earlier fighting became victims of his next attempt, having been moved fortuitously to the point of attack on the assumption that this was a peaceable sector, a benign place in which to draw breath and recover. The 'sanatorium of the Western Front' was one description of it; 'home from home' was another; but these were descriptions that would shortly require serious revision.

The location in question was the 'Chemin des Dames', in the region of the Aisne; an area lying between Soissons to the west and

Reims to the east. One soldier who narrowly survived the German attack there would later write: 'The people at home know very little of this battle compared with their knowledge of the Somme and Ypres battles for the reason that few British units took part. Yet it was probably a greater disaster to British arms than any previous battle in the Great War.'

5

SPRING OFFENSIVE: MAY

'CHEMIN DES DAMES': the name consorts oddly with the other sectors of the Western Front associated with the British effort in the First World War. As indicated by the ex-soldier just quoted, former Private William Hall, names like Ypres, Loos, Arras or Somme all slip effortlessly into the vocabulary of the student, or the aficionado, of the Western Front, as they once slipped easily into that of the British Tommy. But *Chemin des Dames*? For one thing, it is a name defiantly French (if with a last syllable remarkably reminiscent of an English expletive) and one not particularly amenable to convincing translation. Strictly it means 'The Road of the Ladies' – 'The Ladies' Road': but which ladies and which road? In fact, it was a highway specially constructed in the eighteenth century so that the daughters of King Louis XV – father of the sixteenth of that name who married Marie Antoinette and came with her to an unhappy end in the Place de la Guillotine – could speed in comfort from the royal palace in Compiègne to the Château de la Bove, the residence of a highly favoured aristocrat, the Duchess of Nemours. Essentially, therefore, it was the product of the whim of an absolute monarch of the Bourbon, pre-Bastille, era, and so by definition utterly remote, culturally and historically, from the mind-set of the British soldiers travelling towards it in the spring of 1918. At least the name of the overall area to which they were moving was reasonably familiar: Champagne – though the vast majority of them, certainly among the other ranks, had little chance of sampling the world-famous product of that region. (Private Cude's acquaintance with that beverage, as described in Chapter 3, was the product of very exceptional circumstances indeed.)

The divisions caught up (though not all to the same extent) in the fighting that took place here were: the 8th, 19th, 21st, 25th and the 50th (Northumbrian), now constituted as the IXth Corps under

the command of Lieutenant-General Sir Alexander Hamilton
Gordon. They had been moved south in exchange for French
divisions now on the British front and they were to serve under
French command as part of the French Sixth Army. The irony of it
was that, instead of – as had been intended – quietly recovering from
their earlier ordeals, they found themselves at the heart of an offensive even more ruthless than its predecessors, which would bring the
Germans as near as they would ever get to Paris in 1918. But from
the British point of view this attack would also be, in the words of
one officer who fought there and subsequently wrote eloquently
about his experiences, 'the last of the ebb'. When it ran out of
energy, as it duly did, the stage was set for the magisterial return: the
great flow of the tide the other way. There would be other German
efforts before they finally conceded, but the BEF would not be
seriously involved. The battle fought here can thus be seen as, for
the British, a pivotal point of this last year of the war.

Strictly, the fighting which took place here would become officially known as the Battle of the Aisne. This at least would have a
familiar ring, because there had been a similarly named encounter in
1914 in which the original BEF under Sir John French had been
involved. However, the so-called 'Race to the Sea' of that now far-off
year had transferred the British far to the north, and for three and a
half years they had been engaged in other, less exotic sectors. Most of
those who had fought here thus early in the war were by now long
gone from the scene; dead, wounded, prisoners, or at any rate for one
reason or another not actively concerned in the agenda of 1918. For
the great majority, therefore, the area had an air of novelty, and, since
they came in May to a part of France notable for its natural beauty, it
was seen as balm to the eye and the spirit after the dour greyness of
the battlefields they had so recently vacated. As Sidney Rogerson, the
officer quoted above, would write: 'To battered, battle-weary troops,
whose only knowledge was based on the Northern front, the Champagne country in the full glory of spring was a revelation. . . . The
countryside basked contentedly in the blazing sunshine. Trim villages
nestled in quiet hollows beside lazy streams, and tired eyes were
refreshed by the sight of rolling hills, clad with great woods golden
with laburnum blossom; by the soft greenery of lush meadowland,
shrubby vineyards and fields of growing corn.'

The sector had had its significant moment of history a year before, in that it had been fought over in the disastrous, over-optimistic offensive of April 1917 associated with the name of the flamboyant French general Robert Nivelle. Far from producing the great leap forward Nivelle had so confidently promised, it had led to open mutiny, or rather, in the parlance of the time, 'collective indiscipline', of which 119 acts spread across fifty-four divisions were officially recorded over the following weeks. The sector had also witnessed, during that same battle, what has been described as 'a holocaust of tanks'. The wreckage of many of these, along with other pieces of military detritus, lay scattered about the area of the front; but, as had happened in 1917 in the territory of the Somme battle, nature had taken them over, mantling them with tall grass and surrounding them with wild flowers, so that they scarcely impinged on the general effect of rural calm. Also helping to relax any incipient tension was the fact that No Man's Land was so wide, in parts as much as 800 yards, as to put the enemy almost out of sight. It was perhaps all too easy therefore to put him out of mind. Thus the arriving British, in the words of the historian of one of the battalions involved, the 2nd Devons of 8th Division, found themselves in a line 'more comfortable than defensible'. 'Indeed,' he wrote, 'in some places in the trenches there were arbours covered with rambling roses.'

More pithily, the CO of another battalion in 8th Division, the 2nd Middlesex, told his officers as they were about to head south that they were going to an area where by constant improvement the trenches had become 'rather like the Savoy Hotel removed under-ground'. Recalling this the battalion's medical officer, Captain M.S. Esler, added ironically: 'He told us that we were really going on a glorious picnic where we would see the butterflies mating, hear the bees buzzing, and hear the song of the thrush at dawn.'

Even for the ordinary shilling-a-day soldier conditions were excellent, as the already quoted Private William Hall, of the 2nd East Lancashires, also in 8th Division, noted: 'The French had actually erected wire beds in the dugouts, and cookhouses were quite close to the front line.' Although only twenty-one Hall had fought on the Somme and at Passchendaele and also in the March Retreat of two months earlier, so that he was writing from experience when he

stated that 'the change of country after the devastated regions we
had for so long been accustomed to, was a revelation, one had
forgotten that such country, seemingly untouched by war, still
existed.' With fine and warm weather, the birds in full voice and
practically no enemy action, it was, he stated, 'hard to realize that
there was a war on in this part of the world'. There was, of course,
no cessation of hard labour for the Tommy, one particularly exhausting task – by special order of an over-enthusiastic officer – being
that of carrying ammunition boxes each weighing seventy pounds
up to the front with a single soldier to each box as opposed to the
usual two: 'This wonderful idea did not work out too well. Far more
men in the end were required, longer time was taken and a number
of men were *hors de combat* for a day or two.' But then the lot of
the ordinary infantryman was ever thus, however pleasing the part
of the line in which he found himself.

For Lieutenant Philip Ledward, fellow staff officer of Sidney
Rogerson's in 23rd Brigade, his first memory of the Chemin des
Dames front was also benign. He was billeted in the village of Roucy
in the Curé's house, 'where white and purple lilac trees in full flower
pushed their branches actually into my bedroom. At Brigade HQ
we had a splendid deep dugout *"en cas de bombardement"*, though
we lived in quite attractive little rooms on ground level.' Yet he soon
noted a certain change in the atmosphere of the place. 'The French
boasted they had had three casualties in two months and the trenches
were in wonderful condition. But the quietness of the sector ceased
as soon as we entered it, and the shelling became quite frequent. We
attributed it to the fact that our gunners, unlike the French, would
move about freely by day and give away their positions; but in fact
it was due not to this but to the fact that the Germans were busy
"registering" with a great number of new guns, brought up for the
coming attack.' Since it was not realized that this was the case, the
illusion of peacefulness continued.

To visit the Chemin des Dames today is to understand how easily
it was for British divisions released from the battlegrounds of the
March and April offensives to assume that this was not a likely place
for serious war. It is a gracious area, with pale pastel ridges receding
into the distance, each one paler than its predecessor; sleepy rivers
between the ridges (the largest one, the Aisne, so languid it occasion-

ally needs a stretch of canal to make it navigable); grey old villages straight out of the novels of Alexandre Dumas tucked around their church and château; well-tilled fields, swathes of lush woodland; and, on either side of the *chemin* itself, deep plunging valleys. For the soldiers arriving from the north by slow train, transport lorry or their own flat feet – and in full springtime – the rest of the war must have seemed a thousand miles off, on the dark side of the moon.

There had been warfare here before and there would be again. Napoleon, in his final desperate attempt to hold back the avenging allies in 1814, prior to his exile to Elba, clashed here with the German commander, Blücher, whom he would meet again at Waterloo one year later – aptly, 'Blücher' would be the German codename for the attack about to be launched here. Near Craonne a statue of the French Emperor, well over twice the original's height, broods formidably across a broad field. Opposite the entrance to a large farm called Hurtebise a striking double statue stands under trees, of a French and a German soldier knee to knee and eye to eye, with the tell-tale dates on the plinth beneath: 1814–1914. On a wall of the farm a plaque commemorates a clash of 1940 between the Germans and a certain Colonel Charles de Gaulle, proof that the Chemin des Dames also played its part in the Second World War. But the area's high point for action was the first war, although it seemed in early May 1918 that this year at least it might be spared and allowed to lie fallow.

However, largely unheeded by the British, and by the prime custodians of this region, the French, the Germans had been conducting discreet and thorough preparations for an attack for some time. A prominent participant in this was Major-General von Unruh, Chief of Staff of the 4th Reserve Corps. Summoned on 25 April to the Chief of the General Staff, German Seventh Army, he was instructed to undertake a discreet reconnaissance of the Allied positions, to ascertain whether an attack was feasible, and to estimate how many troops would be required. He set about his mission with alacrity:

> This was a task surely to delight the heart of any soldier. I asked to be allowed two or three days in which to do this, and this was granted. Walking alone, I spent the ensuing days and nights going

in scrupulous detail over the sector and noting with satisfaction the nature of the ground and some not inconsiderable disadvantages of the position from the point of view of the defence. When I came close to the enemy front line on the Aisne at night I was both hailed and shot at by the English. They even offered me cigarettes, but I did not trust this friendly gesture and preferred to keep still and rely upon the cover of the darkness whenever my presence was detected. This personal reconnaissance enabled me easily to get an exact idea of the front line and all its difficulties, and I was further helped by the knowledge, experience, and observations of our front-line patrol leaders and scouts.

The Chemin des Dames front ran over awkward, hilly ground, not best territory for defence, and not the easiest for the Germans to attack, since their positions were such that along most of the sector they would have to advance over the crown of the ridge. A distinctive feature of the high ground through which the 'Ladies' Road' was constructed is an eminence that was known to the Allies as the 'Californie Plateau', though to the Germans it was the 'Winterberg' – Winter Hill – so called because of its white chalk crest, which from a distance gave the impression of being permanently covered in snow. At first to von Unruh's observation it seemed curiously innocent, inactive, menacing more for its topography than for any military threat it might offer:

> But observing it and the Chemin des Dames with a good pair of glasses for hours on end and day after day, it was quite evident that both positions were very much alive. Orderlies could be seen coming and going. Here and there was an occupied observation post, and now and then steel helmets could be spotted moving along a trench. The trenches and wire looked to have been strengthened. It was not difficult for a trained observer to locate the enemy's strong points and indeed to trace the scheme on which the defences were based.

Von Unruh's report was positive and there would be no doubt that the attack would go ahead.

There was one special weakness of the Franco-British position which the Germans would not be slow to exploit. The bulk of the defenders were crammed into a relatively small area between the

Chemin des Dames heights and the northern bank of the River Aisne, with their artillery installations on that northern bank. The idea that such a dense compression of forces with a river impeding the line of retreat might constitute a possible hazard had even reached the ordinary Tommy. Private Hall commented: 'One heard gossip to the effect that the British position in this sector was very dangerous if Jerry broke through on our flanks, because with our backs to the River Aisne we would have little chance of getting away.' What applied to the British applied to the French in equal measure. The British GOC expressed his anxieties to the Sixth Army commander, General Duchêne. Duchêne's approach, it should be added, ran counter to the current philosophy of his commander-in-chief, Pétain, who was now a firm advocate of the concept of elastic defence. But Duchêne was of an earlier school of thought and so the situation remained unchanged. In a statement in the mode of Pontius Pilate, Duchêne replied to Lieutenant-General Gordon: '*J'ai dit*': 'I have spoken.' With a small British contingent among a larger French force, under a French commander of higher rank determined to defend every metre of sacred French soil, Gordon could do nothing except report the situation to GHQ, but his plea for guidance came far too late to have any effect. Yet by and large the soldiers whose fate would be greatly affected by Duchêne's obtuse strategy were not greatly concerned. As Hall put it: 'As everything was quiet, nobody seemed to worry.'

* * *

Sunday 26 May was the day when the shadow fell. Up to that point it had seemed to Captain Esler and his fellow officers of the 2nd Middlesex that their CO's prophecy had come true: 'The trenches were well made and dry, the weather was fine, I thought occasionally that I heard the buzzing of a bee, or it might have been the whine of a bullet, the noises are somewhat similar, and I certainly saw two butterflies mating.' Nightly before dinner he and three of his colleagues played bridge, while consuming a half bottle each of champagne, that commodity being both cheap and, if only for officers, easily obtainable. 'We were quite content', he commented nostalgically, 'to remain there, playing at soldiers, to the end of the war.' However, the dream was all too soon to be shattered:

We were sitting that evening about six o'clock, half a bottle of champagne inside us, on good terms with life, minding our own business, and just playing a rubber before dinner, when an orderly came in, saluted, and said to Hugh [Captain Hugh McIlwaine, a senior company commander], 'The Colonel's compliments, sir, and he would like to see you at once.' Hugh jumped up and went to the Colonel who told him news that very much altered our lives. A German prisoner had been taken in that afternoon and, after interrogation, had informed us that the Boche were attacking in great strength that very night. Hugh was ordered to go round all the Companies' defences and see that they were all prepared. I had to get to my aid post in readiness. It was situated about two hundred yards away behind the trenches in a wood.

In life I have found that one does things instinctively that alter conditions of life very much. The medical unit of a regiment, that is, the MO, his sergeant and stretcher bearers, whose duty it is to move about the dead and dying, are issued with arm bands, bearing the red cross which identifies them as non-combatants. The wearing of them was quite optional and I had never worn one in action before. My usual feeling is 'whatever will be, will be'. The evening was as peaceful as usual, in fact, I heard a nightingale singing in some distant trees; surely on a night like this it could not remain anything but peaceful. The prisoner had, probably, given false information – so ran my thoughts, yet a small voice within me suddenly prompted me to put on my armlet, and to tell the sergeant and stretcher bearers to put on theirs. This act, I think, almost certainly saved our lives.

* * *

For Private William Hall, whose battalion was out of the line on the 26th, the summons to prepare for a possible attack was equally sudden and unexpected: 'It had been a glorious day, the men were enjoying short strolls in the neighbourhood, or fraternizing with the French in the farmyards or the little estaminet. We had all been looking forward to a concert that had been arranged for the evening, when suddenly we received the order to "stand to".' They paraded in full battle order, but after an hour half of the men were sent to the front line, while the others, Hall included, were dismissed to their village billets, though ordered to be ready to move off at a moment's notice. 'There were the usual rumours flying around: we were going "over the top" that night, Jerry was going to start a "big push" at any minute, and there was the ever popular comment that the whole thing was just "wind up".' Eventually the conversation died down and men began dropping off to sleep:

I was on the point of falling asleep myself, when suddenly the silence was broken by the whistling and explosion of shells nearby. I sat up and almost immediately experienced a smarting sensation in my nose and eyes, the gas alarm was given, and with it came the order to put on masks. All the men were wide awake now, fumbling in the dark with their gas masks; some could not put their hands on this now very necessary article, having taken it off to lie down and there was much swearing. The gas-mask always seems for ever to be hanging around the neck when not required and regarded as an encumbrance, but it is extraordinary how it just happens to be put at one side on the few occasions it is wanted.

We paraded in quick time and formed in line. Shells began to fall fast on the village and the people were making hasty preparations for departure. One could hear the excited shouts and the wheeling of carts. Only a few hours previously we had seen the people happy in the company of the Tommies, in the quiet and tranquillity of a lovely Sunday evening. They were no doubt happy in the prospect of good crops of which we had seen good evidence all around, and now they were fleeing for their lives, leaving their homes and the rewards of their hard labour behind. It was all so sudden as to seem unreal, but one couldn't dream amidst the roar of the high explosive shells which crashed all around us.

Hall's account closely reflects the precise pattern of the German bombardment that night. The Official History quotes a German monograph on the attack: 'From 1 a.m. for the first ten minutes, all guns and trench mortars, using gas ammunition, simultaneously devoted themselves at the highest rate of fire to all targets within reach. This was designed to create at the very start irremediable confusion and moral effect among the enemy. After this, the mass of the batteries turned their fire for 65 minutes [1.10 to 2.15 a.m.], with gas and high explosive mixed on the Allied artillery, whilst the trench mortars set about the systematic destruction of the front defences and their wire.' The infantry was to go over at 3.40.

Against such an onslaught the Allied defences broke virtually along the whole front. The earlier attacks by the Germans in March and April had been stunning, but this one on the Chemin des Dames sector was even more shattering. The Official History states: 'For the second time in the War, the first having been at Messines in June 1917, what had been so often attempted in vain had been accomplished; so thorough had been the preliminary destruction that all resistance was crushed and the infantry had only to advance to take possession of the front position.' Messines had been a British victory, achieved by that most thorough and respected of British commanders, General Plumer, principally with mines though artillery had also played a notable part. The attack on the Chemin des Dames was the 'masterpiece' – the Official Historian's word – of the German artillery expert Colonel Bruchmüller, who had prepared the attacks against the Fifth Army and the Arras front in March. These were preludes to his outstanding achievement in May.

Confirmation of his success in destroying the guns of his opponent can be found in this succinct comment from the account by 8th Division's Lieutenant Philip Ledward: 'The Divisional Artillery never fired a shot. The Germans had ranged our gun positions so accurately that they overwhelmed them in the first few minutes of the bombardment. I remember being told that one of the guns received a direct hit from the very first shell that came over, and the whole of that battery was permanently out of action in five minutes.'

From a point to the south of the river to which brigade and divisional staff had now retired, Ledward was also able to see the consequences of the German success: the blue sky of a glorious summer morning full of German sausage balloons over what had been the British forward positions. And something else that imprinted itself in his mind almost like a sequence of film:

I feel as I should never forget the view of the plain up to and across the Aisne towards our old front line, for it was black with Germans. At that distance they looked like ants, small, busy and innumerable. All shelling had stopped except that a heavy howitzer was still directing a few shells at Roucy Château, where our Divisional Headquarters had been. Within quite a short time the field where I had sat and discussed the situation with the Brigadier-General and the road up which I had walked with my fellow officer Papworth were thick with Germans, and I personally directed a machine-gunner to open the ball by firing on the road below us, which he did, scattering the Germans hurriedly but hitting no one.

It is worth adding at this point that on the following day, 28 May, the opposite view to Ledward's would be enjoyed by none other than the German Emperor, Kaiser Wilhelm II, who, taken there to admire his soldiers' achievement, would look down on the smoking battlefield from the vantage point of the Californie Plateau; literally at that moment the monarch of all he surveyed.

Meanwhile those subjected to the effects of the masterly German bombardment, or overrun by that mass of advancing ants, had been dying, falling wounded, or, in huge numbers, had been taken prisoner. Others, often as it seemed miraculously, were somehow contriving to make their escape.

*   *   *

Captain Esler, MO of the 2nd Middlesex, would recall that the night of 27 May remained peaceful as they waited for zero hour and that, when the moment came, it was as if 'every gun left in the German Army had been moved up to the Champagne country and all opened fire together'. Esler had always looked askance at the often eccentric behaviour of his commanding officer, Lieutenant-Colonel Page, who combined an ambition to become a gentleman of the cloth with a distinct lust for warfare and a remarkable richness of vocabulary. On this occasion he did not disappoint:

> I was in a tunnel with the Colonel and Hugh. In the ordinary way the Colonel should have remained there and runners should have reported from companies every few minutes and he would have directed orders as circumstances required. But no. He must go out himself and visit every sector of his defence. I remember him saying 'I must go and see what all this bloody row is about',

and, turning to Hugh, he said 'You deal with reports as they come in, and I will deal with events as I find them.' As he made his exit from the tunnel his last words were 'Phew what a bloody smell of gas, look after yourself, Esler.' That is the last I ever saw of him.

The night wore on, to the accompaniment of falling shells and an intense cacophony of sound. Esler waited with his sergeant for casualties. Eventually the barrage eased. He became concerned:

I said to Sergeant Walsh: 'Curious thing, nobody has come in wounded, I will go out and see what is happening and will let you know whether the stretcher-bearers are needed.' As I emerged into the open I smelt the early morning smell of mist and vegetation, with a pervading scent of cordite superimposed. I have never experienced the exact smell again, but I have remembered it all my life.

As I came out, through the bushes emerged a few men with fixed bayonets, and an officer with a revolver in his hand. From their helmets I recognized that they were German, and that they were making a bee-line for me. When the enemy break through they are excited and out to kill: If they see a man opposing them they shoot or charge with a bayonet. If they see a dugout they chuck a hand grenade in first before they investigate. As they came running the thought crossed my mind 'the possibility of being exterminated by a shell has been present with me often, but I never thought of ending my life with a bayonet wound in my belly, and I don't like the idea one little bit'. All I could do was shrug my shoulders and point at my Red Cross armlet. The officer recognized this at once and told his men not to kill. I pointed to my dugout and said 'Red Cross', so they did not chuck in their usual grenades. Thus it was that my instinct to don our Red Cross armlets saved the lives of myself and my comrades in the aid post dugout.

In a mixture of broken English and sign language – 'which one understands better in a crisis' – the officer directed Esler to a trench that had been held by the battalion so that he could offer medical help to any casualties. Esler now understood why he had had no clients at his aid post. They had not been allowed the chance to get there; where they had been hit they had remained. 'I found the trench, as I expected, occupied by Germans, and in the bottom lay the dead and wounded and dying, some British and some German.' He noted that the fate he had so narrowly avoided himself had clearly been suffered by men on both sides. 'There must have been a lot of hand-to-hand fighting for many of them had bayonet wounds.'

He had slung his medical haversack over his shoulder when he left his aid post and so was able to dress wounds and administer morphine until all those he could help had been picked up and carried away by German stretcher bearers. As he worked he was joined by Sergeant Walsh: 'He had been winkled out of the aid post and sent down to help me.' But for two of the battalion's young officers there was no remedy. As he observed them lying dead, neither of them aged more than twenty-five, Esler found himself thinking: 'Well, worse could have happened to you, you have had a virile and, I hope, happy life up to date, you were killed instantly and so avoided all the possible troubles of an invalid life and, eventually, a failing old age.'

Among his many abiding impressions of that memorable May morning was a realization of the efficiency of the German Army. The field kitchens had followed up immediately and were cooking bacon and sausages which the men occupying the former British trenches were already enjoying: 'Like Napoleon, they believed that an army fights and travels on its stomach.'

When he and his sergeant had done all they could, they, along with any other British survivors, were rounded up and marched off in groups. 'My thought was "that is the end of the war for me, I am alive and shall not be shot at any more". My thoughts were a little premature for, as we proceeded to the rear we had to pass through a pretty heavy barrage by our own people on the German reinforcements coming up. A few were wounded and killed which was certainly a bit tough after escaping enemy action for so long, and then to be hit by our own side.' Eventually, however, they were clear and after being left to their own devices for most of the day – 'I could have done with a nice lunch but no picnic lunches were being provided' – they were herded into a barbed-wire enclosure about a mile from the lines. He was shortly joined by his friend Hugh McIlwaine, who had spent the day creeping through cornfields but had been found by some Germans bearing bayonets and had wisely decided to continue the struggle no more.

It was the beginning of several months of captivity which would form a considerable contrast to the comfortable life they had led on the Aisne before the attack. As Esler put it, nostalgically: 'We missed our champagne at night, one unripe gherkin had not the same kick.'

As for his Commanding Officer, Esler would receive news of him from a fellow officer when back in England after the war: 'I had a letter from Major Drew saying that he had seen the Colonel who was slowly recovering from the seven wounds he had received on the night he had been taken prisoner.' It was perhaps a suitable ordeal for the would-be cleric to undergo on the road to attaining his hoped-for goal. Many years later Esler would hear from his friend Hugh McIlwaine that he had seen someone of the Colonel's name and decorations – DSO, MC – listed on the board of a vestry of some small country church, where he had evidently officiated for the ten years from 1930–40. Esler commented: 'How I would have loved to hear him preach, that hard swearing and hard fighting brave soldier I had served under in 1918. He had achieved his two ambitions, to kill Germans during the war and to serve the souls of his parishioners during the temporary peace that followed.'

* * *

Major-General Henry Jackson, GOC of 50th Division, found the Chemin des Dames attack a shattering experience. Admitting the shock but trying to make the best of things, he wrote to his mother on 30 May: 'Just a line to say that I am alive and well. We have had rather a strenuous time – the Boche attack breaking in full force upon us. I have lost all my three Brigades and we are a poor affair at present, but given some men and a little time, we will be all right.'

Corporal Arthur Speight, 7th Durham Light Infantry, a soldier whose career stretched back to the Second Battle of Ypres in 1915, was at General Jackson's Divisional Headquarters when the attack began. The Division had taken over a most pleasant château, with garden attached, at a village called Beaurieux situated a mile or so north of the Aisne. Artillery Headquarters was installed in another large house, the garden of which adjoined that of the château. Speight was one of three Divisional draughtsmen, his other colleagues being a Corporal Tony Schaeffer of the 5th Northumberland Fusiliers and a young conscript named Garton – 'a lad' Speight would call him in the account he subsequently wrote of their joint adventures – who had arrived in France as recently as the beginning of May. (He was one of many such; by this time, wrote Speight, 'the Div. was mainly composed of lads of about 18 or 19 years of age with practically no military experience'.) They had set up their drawing office in an elegant octagon-shaped summerhouse in the château's garden, in good shape apart from a hole in the roof from a stray enemy shell; reassuringly, it had an under-section beneath a concrete floor which they could use for sleeping. 'In front we had a small verandah with a rail on which we used to sit at night and listen to the nightingales and signal to some nurses at a small French hospital – at least Tony did.' By virtue of either prior commitment or natural reserve, Corporal Speight clearly felt the need to dissociate himself from such questionable inter-Allied activities.

Their stay in the area seems not to have been quite as peaceful as was the case elsewhere, although it had certainly been quiet on their arrival: 'To keep Fritz on the hop, night raids became rather frequent and things were soon livened up.' Speight did not approve: 'It seems that the Brass-hats have an idea that a soldier loves to go round slaughtering the enemy but my opinion is that, if left alone, the armies would mix pretty freely and a lot of differences would be patched up.'

Suddenly, on that fateful Sunday, came the rumours of the expected attack. An early sign of its imminence was the oddly incongruous beat of military music on the still evening air. 'The night of the 26th saw all battalions who were not actually in the line moving up to battle positions with their bands playing them so far on the road.' At this point the bands sent their instruments back and carried on as stretcher bearers.

At 1 a.m. the bombardment began. 'Fritz put down a barrage like nothing I'd heard before. His name for this type of artillery fire was "Trommelfeuer", which means "drum-fire" and actually this was the best description. It was like a roll on a tremendous kettle-drum. All artillery positions were subjected to knock-out blows from concentrated fire and within half an hour hardly a gun in the Divisional area was left intact.'

On hearing of the forthcoming attack Divisional Headquarters had promptly vacated its château and established itself in a suite of dugouts near by. Speight and his two comrades elected to stay in their summerhouse, 'not out of bravado, but because a shell doesn't usually hit the same spot twice'; in any case they had their concrete floor for protection if they needed to snatch some sleep. When dawn began to break Garton went out in search of breakfast. He returned shortly after with the news that no rations had come up the night before. 'At about half past seven we had a visit from the Intelligence officer, a Captain Milne from some Scottish regiment; on being asked how things were doing he answered: "Bad enough! We've lost the Plateau so you'll know that something's on." I said: "Yes sir, when do we move out?" The IO said, "Oh! I'll send someone down to tell you when to clear out."' Speight had become used to abrupt retreats in March and April, so he knew what to do by way of preparation: 'We began to get together the things we should need most such as baccy, matches, iron rations, maps in rolls and boxes and as much stuff as we could think of that might come in handy during another trip to the back areas.' Meanwhile, somewhat disturbingly, they could see a number of khaki figures making their way down the road in the direction of the neighbouring village of Maizy, where there was a stalwart iron bridge across the Aisne. 'Shells of a small type kept dropping amongst them. I had not heard or seen shells quite so small as this and was rather curious but not altogether happy about them.' It was clearly time for them to be on their way:

> When all was ready I took two despatch cases of papers and maps up to the headquarters dugout and shouted down to the inhabitants, if any. There was no answer so I went below and found the place deserted. On all the wood work, tables etc, there were candles burning, evidently to burn the place out. I left my boxes of maps in the hope that Fritz would not get them. I returned again to the fresh air and hearing a clatter of horses' hooves turned and saw one of the French gendarmes who were attached to the Division coming along at full gallop with sword drawn and a grim look on his face. I howled out: 'Hola, Jacques! comment ça va?' He waved his sword, pointed up the road and shouted: 'Allez! Les Boches!' I 'allez-ed' and made my way down the street in the direction of the HQ château. I became aware of

sudden buzzing noises, accompanied by sharp cracks – rifle fire. This was rather too much for my shaky nerves so made for the château without any more ado.

As I entered the door a bullet hit the door post with a resounding crack so I did a swift side-step to the right and behind the wall. The rooms lately occupied by the clerks and other people were empty, the room occupied by the general and the staff officers was in a turmoil, the furniture etc being all piled up in the centre of the room and crowned with an overturned and flaming oil lamp. Not caring to endanger my valuable carcase any more I left via the French windows and wandered down the garden to the summerhouse. Here I spread the joyful news that we had been left stranded and we got our kit together, loaded our rifles and sallied forth.

Crossing the garden they were suddenly attacked by a low-flying German aeroplane; Speight noted its red body and dazzle-painted wings: 'We disappeared into the bushes until he cleared off, then got going once more.' He set course for a nearby farm, from which he knew there was a drainage ditch running down towards Maizy. To reach the farm they had to cross the road: 'When I reached the road I was astounded, on looking along towards the village, to see dozens of Germans standing at the cross roads. Luckily they all seemed to be gazing in the opposite direction, so I hopped quickly over the road behind the farm. I signalled to Tony to hurry and he and Garton joined me. Those beastly little shells began to drop a short distance from us so we got into the afore-mentioned trench and made our way along it at a good pace.' The trench led to a point where there was a cutting some four feet deep alongside:

I peeped into the cutting and then beat a rapid retreat up the trench again. There were only about sixty Germans in the cutting! Tony always had a fairly good vocabulary and he certainly said some strange things. We held a short council of war and decided that we couldn't put up any show against sixty and thought we would do well to clear off further up the trench to seek another way out. However Fritz stopped all argument by coming in on top of us with pointed rifles and waving bombs and with shouts of '*Hände auf! Engländer*'. [Hands up, Englishmen.] I had often thought that in a case like this I should be scared to death, but strange to say, fear didn't seem to come into the picture at all. Disappointment seemed to be the great thing. Here we were – captured without a chance of hitting back.

We had the satisfaction of knowing that our hands did NOT go up! They went into our trouser pockets instead. We were kicked, thumped, jabbed in the ribs with rifle butts and generally made to feel that we were, to say the least of it, superfluous!

As was the case with all prisoners of war, they were now the chattels of their enemy. For some days afterwards they were put to work filling shell holes, clearing streets and even pile-driving for a bridge across the Aisne. 'I happened mostly to get on the street clearing party but poor Tony was on the bridge party which was the worst. He expressed his dislike of pile-driving in no uncertain terms.'

Speight had one memorable moment of contact with his captors: 'While working one day I was greeted by a German corporal, a machine-gunner, who said: "Well, corporal, how goes it?" I said: "Bad enough, but where did you learn English?" It turned that he had been in British ships since he had been about thirteen years old. His father was a German and he had never been naturalized, and as he himself was in a German port when war broke out, he was on their side. He frankly admitted that had he been in an English port on August 4th he would most likely have been in the British Army!'

As a footnote to Speight's story, it should be recorded that the 50th Division's 'scorched earth' policy in respect of the Beaurieux château worked only too well; it was, it appears, totally destroyed by the fire started by the departing British. Now a new, incongruously modern building stands in its stead. A new summerhouse that Speight would not have recognized graces the adjacent garden.

* * *

For Private William Hall there was one overriding concern during the days following the Chemin des Dames attack, a determination to make his escape. He wanted to sacrifice neither his skin, nor his liberty. It would not be easy, and indeed his dash for freedom would turn into a one-man adventure story almost like something out of Stevenson or Henty, except that for him it was no fiction, but a long-drawn-out, hazardous ordeal, though one not without its moments of heroism and even of romance.

From the start he had been aware of the scale of the Allied setback: 'We passed some of our wounded going to the rear and they told us that the Germans had attacked with great force about 3 a.m. and almost completely wiped out our men on the north side of the Aisne. Few had been able to retreat across the river.' Sometime later there had been a distinct hint of panic: 'Suddenly there was a commotion down the trench, some men came running up shouting "Get out of here we are being surrounded!" I joined the hurrying throng and heard someone say that the Jerries had crossed the river on both flanks and were now working to the back of us.'

As they continued what was turning into more of a rout than an organized retreat he and an assortment of disorientated comrades – now to the south of the Aisne – found themselves facing a mass of German troops advancing menacingly towards them across their line of escape. These were Ledward's black ants in close-up, and the sight of them was awesome:

> They were all huge men, evidently Prussian Guards and they came forward in perfect order; all their actions were carried out with parade ground precision. They carried the rifle across the body, brought the muzzle down smartly, fired, and then carried back across the body. There was something inhuman about these smart parade-ground movements on the battlefield, the Germans looking like a horde of robots; no haste, no flurry, just cold and calculating human machines.
>
> It took but a brief glance to take it all in; I hesitated for just a fraction, and as if some unseen force had pushed me, I broke into a run and with my rifle at the hip I dashed clean through the encircling robots. My dash carried me to the edge of a wood, a fusillade of shots followed me, but I bore a charmed life and was not hit. I took refuge behind a large tree, unable for the moment to proceed further; I was taking breath in great gasps, my heart pounding furiously.
>
> I looked round the tree and saw the Germans throwing hand-grenades into a packed trench, and capturing men coming out of it. My impulse was to pick up my rifle and pick one or two

Germans off, but I couldn't keep my rifle steady, I was shaking
rather badly and taking aim was out of the question.

I turned away and walked slowly up the rising woodland
path, dodging behind trees. I saw only two others who had
dashed through the ring, and these had now disappeared and I
was quite alone.

He eventually reached a main road where he was glad to fall in
with a party of stragglers. These met others in similar disarray until
at last there was a party of about sixty men. But Hall could see no
military advantage in what was simply 'an isolated body of troops,
with not the slightest semblance of a line; no artillery supports, and
nobody apparently with any idea of the direction of Jerry's line of
advance.' Sensing no other option they continued a somewhat confused progress rearwards. Their morale was not improved by the
sight of line after line of Germans crossing some fields in the far
distance, clearly meeting no resistance. Then Hall suddenly became
aware of the beat of hooves and a Staff Officer came galloping up to
them on a very fine-looking horse:

> I stood close up to the horse and heard the rider appeal to the
> men to make a stand; one of the men drew his attention to the
> enemy advancing on our flank, but he did not seem to be
> impressed and again asked for a stand to be made on the hill. He
> glanced down at the various regimental badges and appealed to
> the honour of the units they represented and when he looked
> down at me and spoke of the glorious record of the East
> Lancashire Regiment, I felt as big as his horse, however, seeing I
> was the only representative of that regiment, the glorious record
> was not in very good hands. Nevertheless, I stood firm, being so
> near to the appealer I was probably too ashamed to move and
> would, I believe, have stayed to the end, had the Staff Officer
> remained.
>
> While some of the men were still hesitating, one of the men
> shouted that a Jerry tank was coming up on the other side of the
> hill and immediately there was a stampede to the cover of the
> woods below. I remained at the side of the horse watching the
> rider, who, standing up in his stirrups, was peering at the crest of
> the hill; he suddenly sat down, wheeled his horse and galloped
> full speed down the hill. From his lofty perch he had a view

denied to me, but as the sight was sufficient for him to retire in such indecent haste, it was sufficient inducement to speed me on my way. I ran full tilt down the hill, and as the German tank breasted the crest, its machine-gun blazing, I reached the bottom and crashed through some bushes into the cover of a wood.

The previous day when near a village called Bouvancourt, before it became dark, he had made a careful survey of the country to the rear, with an eye to future eventualities, and had seen a long line of transports disappearing over a hill many miles away: 'We were strangers to these parts and were not acquainted with the roads as we were with those behind the Somme lines or the Ypres Salient, so I marked well the direction of the hill over which I could see our transports moving.' Now, having escaped from the German tank he decided to wait no longer, 'making a bee-line for the hills in the distance which I knew from my previous night's observations led to the main line of retreat. In this way I found myself alone, which led to my strangest experience in the war.'

Increasingly unaware of time he made his way, foraging in empty houses where sometimes the coffee-pot was still warm, or exploring an empty château at which his former schoolboy anxieties about trespassing came back to him, though this time with the exhilarating feeling that the normal rules no longer applied: 'Here I was experiencing greater adventure than I ever had in my wildest dreams and this roving about without molestation was truly the happiest adventure I had ever had; I could wander along to my heart's delight and wished for no happier life.' Half-stripped he bronzed in the sun, barred by a river he swam across it, he improved his kit from an abandoned French valise he found in a wood, always trying overall to keep his intended direction: 'My appearance must have presented a real Robinson Crusoe effect; without tunic and shirt, wearing a French officer's hat, and a bundle tied to the end of my rifle which was slung across my shoulder, I must indeed have looked like the sole survivor.'

In one village he met a group of seven Tommies also keen to make their escape. But the village was suddenly targeted by German artillery fire and as they tried to get away all but he and one other were killed and he found himself yet again on the run, charging through a plantation as fast as he could with his one remaining companion following on behind him: 'I seemed to have lost all the lightness of heart and carefree spirit I had had before I met the men in the village and was beginning to feel depressed and hopeless. My spirits revived somewhat, however, when my companion pulled half a loaf of bread and some chocolate out of his haversack; we very soon ate it, I was ravenously hungry.'

They plodded on, the more quickly once Hall had persuaded his new companion to abandon the substantial pack of loot he had been carrying on his back:

> After a few miles we were relieved to come up with a long column of French transport and heavy guns intermingled with all kinds of refugees' vehicles. My companion soon found himself a seat behind one of the gun-carriages, and I proceeded up the line a bit looking for a suitable conveyance.
>
> What a sight met my eyes; vehicles of all descriptions, farmers' carts, handcarts, bassinettes and in fact everything on wheels, all loaded to capacity with every conceivable article of household goods. Sometimes perched on the top were children, tied on to prevent them falling. Some of them were pulled by horses, but many by hand, the old farmer pulling at the front with a rope around his waist, and poor madame pushing at the back.
>
> Some of the military lorries carried refugees, and perched on the back of one of these was a young French woman with three small children. Taking pity on my apparent weariness, she beckoned me to take a vacant place near her and her children, and feeling that I must relieve my leaden feet and legs, if only for a few minutes, I heaved myself on to the lorry. Madame's first words were 'pauvre petit, quel age avez-vous?' – 'poor boy, how old are you?' – and I didn't feel like a soldier any more.

The convoy was heading purposefully south but was not yet in safe ground, not least because of hostility from the air: 'I was just falling asleep when I heard the sound of aeroplanes, and four of the enemy's came into sight flying very low along the road, their machine-guns blazing away and the air was filled with whistling bullets. Madame hugged the children tight to her as the planes passed over.' Hall determined to be ready if the planes returned; he had been a battalion sniper and thought them a likely target if he could fire enough shots into them. At first he had no success, then:

> For the fourth time and what proved to be the last the pests came back. I took up my firing position, and close by were the four French soldiers who had been riding the wagon behind me. I took deliberate aim at the leading plane, my shots being accompanied by the cracking shots of the French rifles. To the great delight of myself and companions, we at last hit the plane or its pilot in a vital part, because it came to earth in sweeping circles and landed in a field close by.
>
> I started to dash across the field with a few others, when the other planes came flying down in circles around the fallen plane and used their machine-guns on us. I put my rifle to my shoulder and fired, getting in some good shots when I felt a sharp stab in my hand and heard a terrific crack, my rifle slipped from my grasp, and I put my hand under my armpit, as I had done at school after I had been caned.

It was a wound which would effectively end Private Hall's fighting war, though it had come following a notable blow at the enemy. It would not, however, put an end to his adventures. In spite of his damaged hand, he felt the need to secure a souvenir of his exploit, but before he could reach the crashed aircraft a French soldier carrying away an item of booty from the plane – 'an instrument like a clock, no doubt a gauge of some kind' – told him that there was nothing else left, also that there was a dead German in the plane, shot through the jaw. Hall turned away to find that the column, which had continued its journey during the recent fracas, was receding steadily out of sight: 'So I never saw Madame and the children again, but hoped that the Jerry planes would not trouble them again, and they would safely get through.'

He walked on in gathering darkness until he reached a cross-roads where he saw signs of activity. 'On reaching the corner I saw that a dressing-station had been set up in a long narrow wooden building. I entered, and saw that it was full of wounded. At the end of the building I saw a man in shirt sleeves attending to a badly wounded soldier.' Earlier Hall had seen an American doctor working almost single-handedly to treat any members of the retreating forces needing his help. He now recognized the same man: 'What devotion to duty! Here he was still attending the wounded after two days. It was probable that he had not yet had time to rest. He presented a real battle-stained appearance, his hair dishevelled, and his shirt well stained with blood, yet he had a cheery word for each of his patients. Eventually it was my turn: "And what can I do for you, sonny?" he said. I had always been prejudiced against Americans, but this doctor looked really great to me.'

His wound cleaned and treated, he shortly continued his journey as the last soldier to climb on board an overcrowded motor-ambulance, which rattled its slow and painful way south to Château-Thierry, on the northern bank of the Marne. Here he hoped for a hospital, but the Germans were too near for comfort, so with a mass of other wounded, including a handful of Tommies, he was put aboard a hospital train heading east. Sanctuary was at last found at the cathedral city of Vitry-le-François, on the upper Marne and no great distance from Bar-le-Duc, the town famous as the starting point of *La Voie Sacrée* – The Sacred Way – the road by which Verdun had been supplied and reinforced during the great siege-battle of 1916. Here, thanks to a smattering of French, rare among Tommies, Hall made numerous friends, among them a lonely Sene-galese recuperating after the amputation of a leg, and a French engineer who, as they both gradually recovered, became a friendly guide to the sights and entertainments of the town, and who also introduced him to a beautiful young French girl who was a student at a nearby convent school:

> She was learning English and was eager to speak to me; the eagerness was not all on one side. I met her the following afternoon and we strolled on the banks of the Marne. I was very happy but I am afraid embarrassed and awkward in her presence. I had the feeling of unreality that one gets after living a rough and dirty life over a long period, just as the wounded feel when they see a nurse in her spotless linen for the first time. She was charming and untouchable in her neatness, by comparison I felt I was still too tarnished with the grime and vermin of the trench-life to walk too close to her, although I was now cleaner than at any time since I arrived in France.

She suggested that I visit her at her home while I remained at Vitry, and help her to make progress with her English, and made an appointment with me for the following day. I couldn't imagine a more pleasant task, and looked forward to it with pleasurable anticipation. I left her at the gates of her home which was a large house on the outskirts of the town.

Alas for love's young dream; when I returned to the hospital in the late afternoon I was met by a hospital orderly who told me that the British were all being evacuated that night. I was of course eager to go forward on the next stage to home, but I had very mixed feelings as I was now beginning to enjoy myself and experience the only real happiness I had had in France. I was intensely disappointed at not being able to keep my appointment with the lively young French girl, though no doubt she would get to know soon enough that the British had left the hospital and would understand that the notice had been too short to permit me to say 'au revoir'. It was my misfortune to meet her only at the end of my stay here instead of at the beginning.

* * *

The fierce fighting occasioned by the May offensive added tragic battle honours to some of the battalions involved. One such was 8th Division's 2nd Devons, which put up a heroic defence for which they were cited in British Army orders and given a Corporate Croix de Guerre by the French. This took place at a point in the eastern sector of the battle zone, where the high ground of the Chemin des Dames yields to a gently undulating plain of fields, farms, tiny villages and woods. It was in one of these woods – the Bois des Buttes (literally the 'Wood of Knolls', perhaps best translated as the 'Wood of the Little Hills') – that the Devons faced the German onslaught. Trench lines, deep in the leaf mould of many decades, are still hauntingly visible in this now dense and thicketed woodland, while depressions here and there give evidence of the ferocious shelling to which the whole Allied front was subjected. If one penetrates deep into the wood the *buttes* which gave it its name become vaguely apparent through the thick screen of trees, their elevation modest enough to have little effect on the profile of the *bois* overall. Fighting in such a location must have been reminiscent of the terrible encounters that made notorious some of the woods of the Somme, such as Trônes, Mametz or Delville, or of the Ypres Salient, such as Polygon Wood or Inverness Copse. What made this feat of 1918 particularly remarkable was that, as Lieutenant Ledward described it, 'it was not a stand by the 2 Devon Regiment really, it was a stand by a mere handful. Most of the Devons were overwhelmed in their great tunnel [they had been in reserve at the start of the attack] and taken prisoner before they knew what was happening.' Ledward had the highest praise for the battalion's CO, Lieutenant-Colonel R.H. Anderson-Morshead: 'He deserved his fame. He could have got back over the Aisne, as we of the 23rd HQ staff got back, but he refused to do so. He collected what men he could find and refused to surrender and was duly killed.' A major of the Royal Artillery, himself attempting to make his escape with the remnants of his battery, caught a glimpse of Anderson-Morshead 'calmly writing his orders with a perfect hell of H.E. all round him. I spoke to him, and he told me nothing could be done. He refused all offer of help.' Another eye-witness described the Devons as 'merely an island in the midst of an innumerable and determined foe, fighting with perfect discipline, and by the steadiness of their fire, mowing down the enemy in large numbers'.

'Large numbers', of course, was inevitably a relative claim when put against the high casualty toll on the British side. Overall the enemy had suffered lightly. As Major-General von Unruh stated: 'Our losses were remarkably small. The enemy had no time to resist. The English, who could usually be relied upon to hold out in shell-holes, firing to their last cartridge, were given no opportunity ... to display their customary coolness. They were up against "force majeure".'

But the very success of this 'force majeure' was to create its own problem. The temptation to exploit it drew Ludendorff into pouring more effort into the advance from Chemin des Dames and thus delaying a further intended push, more important in terms of overall strategy, against the British in Flanders. Yet in spite of giving it more guns and men this third German onslaught followed the example of its two predecessors and ran out of energy. Physical exhaustion, overstretched supply lines, and a dwindling sense of purpose as the speed of advance slowed; all these played their part. By early June, as von Unruh would admit, 'in truth the brilliant offensive had petered out'.

Three attempts having failed, the Germans were, in effect, in considerable trouble. And now a new element was to enter the equation of 1918 which would help to tip the scales finally against them.

6

'OVER HERE': ENTER 'UNCLE SAM'

BY NOW THERE WERE CLEAR PORTENTS suggesting that Germany's hopes for 1918 were foundering. On 28 May, a critical day in the attack on the Aisne, the 28th Regiment of the US 1st Division went into action in the French region of the Somme. They attacked the German salient surrounding the village of Cantigny, four miles north-west of Montdidier, on a front of 1,700 yards, and captured it, penetrating over a mile. This was the first all-American action of the war. Soon the 'Doughboys' – their own name for themselves; they disliked being called 'Yanks' and 'Sammies' – were beginning to bring their 'force majeure' to bear elsewhere. On 1 June their 2nd Division took up a second-line position to support the defences of Château-Thierry, while on the 3rd a machine-gun battalion of the 3rd Division went into action in that sector. On 6 June the 2nd Division counter-attacked at Belleau Wood, to the west of Château-Thierry. They would continue to worry at this German strong point until they finally seized it on the 25th; the Aisne-Marne American cemetery at Belleau, with its 2,289 graves, shows that they had now joined the war not only in terms of commitment but also of its inevitable cost. These first actions were relatively small affairs, but, as John Terraine has written, 'they had a great significance: the United States was in the fight at last. . . . The Germans had lost their race against time.'

* * *

Whatever it is, it is up to me to be there, and I wouldn't be your son if I didn't. Now do not pray that I shall fail my physical test or be color blind or anything. It's the best thing that ever happened for the Kingdom of the Lord, the U.S.A. and to your son, who loves you very much and is proud of you.

The writer was a young American volunteer, Kenneth E. Walser, attempting to reassure his anxious parents that he had done the right thing in responding to the nation's call following America's entry into the war back in April 1917. Yet while seeking to encourage them he made no attempt to hide his belief that there would be a long and challenging road ahead: 'I don't see how people think the war will end soon; Germany has ten million men under arms at the present time, and is not divided. From a military standpoint it will take five years. The economic pressure will make it less, I am sure. But less than two years is out of the question.'

The United States was a late entrant into a conflict which, having been up to that point largely, though far from exclusively, a European war, could now be fairly labelled a 'World' war. An initially reluctant President and people had been persuaded by a series of events and pressures that they could not stand aside. Unrestricted submarine warfare by the Germans, adding to the shock of earlier, widely publicized events such as the sinking of the *Lusitania* and the introduction of poison gas; the impact of the infamous Zimmermann telegram which, intercepted and decoded by the British, appeared to show that the Germans were prepared to support Mexican military and territorial ambitions against those of the United States; the slow conversion of the strange aloof figure in the White House, Woodrow Wilson, from an instinctive pacificism to the belief that war could make the world safe for democracy – these were some of the elements that brought the future superpower across the Atlantic to take up the role which she would fulfil, with occasional interludes of isolationism, for the rest of the century.

Once committed, the American people took the cause to their heart. The enthusiasm, and also the animosities, of Europe in 1914 were now replicated across the Union in 1917. Walser's idealistic and patriotic sentiments precisely paralleled those of his British, German, French, and other European counterparts of three years earlier. Significantly, in 1916 one of the best-selling songs in sheet music and records had been 'I Didn't Raise My Boy to be a Soldier', while another hugely popular number, 'We Take off Our Hats to

You Mr. Wilson', had praised the president's commitment to isolationism. A year later these had given way to the new song for the times, 'Over There'. 'The boys are coming', it breezily proclaimed, and the country was now massively behind them as its boys prepared to go.

Winston Churchill famously slept content on the night following the news of the Japanese attack on Pearl Harbor in December 1941; America was now in the war – the 'Second World' war this time – and he saw her presence on the Allied side as the guarantee of ultimate victory. This was an echo of the sentiment, widely shared a generation earlier, that America's impact would in the end be crucial, would assure which way the balance would ultimately fall.

Yet, while she might have a substantial navy, America had no really modern army to send 'over there' to Europe. As a recent American historian has written: 'The cadre of professional soldiers was small, scattered over forts and garrisons in the United States and stationed in far-flung colonial posts such as the ones in the Philippine Islands. ... Divisions existed only on paper. ... [I]n 1917, most of the eager soldiers would train with wooden mock-ups for rifles, machine-guns, and mortars, and some would go to France without even the most rudimentary instruction in rifle assembly, care and cleaning, and marksmanship.' The much-valued American right to bear arms did not automatically guarantee the nation a mass of competent sharpshooters. Not unlike the British in 1914, America had to begin the process of reinventing herself as a twentieth-century belligerent, converting her industry to a war footing with few, if any, blueprints for expansion. Also like the British, she had to turn herself into a land power. In so doing she would face the difficult ordeal of joining a campaign in which the other players already had a three-year advantage in knowledge and experience. Guts and enthusiasm would clearly not be enough.

America set foot in France in June 1917, in the person of General John J. Pershing and his staff. Their entry into Paris on 4 July was triumphal: the citizens lined the streets and showered roses on the open cars in which they drove from the station to their hotels. France had just suffered the humiliation of the disastrous failure of the Nivelle offensive. Somewhere out of the limelight General Philippe Pétain – who would be caught up in France's troubled destiny for the next thirty years – was resolving the problems accruing from the mutinies that débâcle had inspired. Pershing, who had a distinct dramatic flare, looked every inch the saviour the French nation hoped to see.

The problem was that in French eyes the concept of ultimate victory was too hazy and distant a prospect; what they wanted was a miracle of immediate deliverance. But it would take many months before the Americans would undertake anything other than a secondary or supportive role. Also casting a question over their welcome was the fact that there was no generally accepted notion as to how in practice American troops might be used. Legions of fine tall men striding down gangplanks at the ports might make for encouraging statistics, but how were they to affect the outcome of the actual conflict? The generals and politicians who had already been long in the fighting had their ideas, but these would not be ones readily shared by the new arrivals. In particular those who surmised that, by virtue of being junior in the field, the American commander would fall in happily with the schemes of his seniors, would find a determined resistance in the strong-willed and self-confident personality of General John J. Pershing.

New to the warfare of the trenches, he was no novice in terms of more conventional military experience. He had commanded troops in Cuba in 1898, winning the Silver Star for gallantry, and later in the Philippines; he had also been an outstanding university professor of military science before making an equally distinctive mark as an instructor at West Point. Most recently in 1916 he had commanded the punitive expedition sent to Mexico by President Wilson to pursue Pancho Villa and his marauding army following their attacks on American border towns along the Rio Grande. He was thus a natural choice to command the newly raised American Expeditionary Force. However, with so important a responsibility, the last role Pershing saw for himself was that of a supplier of piecemeal reinforcements to British and French commanders long muddied in the three-year-long struggle, whose achievements had been, even on the best interpretation, and certainly in American eyes, distinctly ambiguous.

The second man ashore from the first convoy of American troops in June 1917 was the future leading American soldier of the Second

World War, George C. Marshall, then a senior staff officer of the US 1st Division. In a significant passage vigorously discussing the pressures on America at this time, his biographer would write of her European partners:

> From the moment of the declaration of war, when the French and British missions in Washington were urging the Americans to come quickly, the Allies had been arguing for the integration of American soldiers in French and British units. The generalship of the past three years had accomplished nothing more successfully than to kill off the young manhood of Europe. Now that the manpower reservoirs of Britain and France were so low that neither could any longer make good the losses of daily attrition in the trenches, much less build up for offensives, the Allies looked hungrily at America's untapped supply.... [T]hey thought it foolhardy to take the time to form a complete and self-sufficient national army.

Almost inevitably the press of France and Britain also clamoured for the immediate integration of the new arrivals in the Allied war effort. There were, however, those who demurred from this facile view, sensing precisely why the Americans were taking their particular line. Major-General Guy Dawnay, a senior Staff Officer at British GHQ at Montreuil, wrote to his wife on 9 April 1918 (significantly, when the British were under severe pressure during the Battle of the Lys): 'I think our newspapers are idiotic about the Americans. They only exasperate them by talking as if they were simply reinforcements for us.' He saw that their prime requirement was 'quick intensive training', to which the Allies could best contribute by helping to initiate them into the techniques of trench warfare 'till they are ready to stand alone'.

Dawnay's sentiments precisely interpreted the American commander's intentions. Pershing would not become a tool of the Europeans but would fight the war in his own way and on his own terms. Indeed, he had no alternative, because he had arrived with the clearest of orders from President Wilson and Secretary Baker. Empowered with 'all necessary authority to carry on the war vigorously ... towards a victorious conclusion', he was under specific instruction to co-operate with the Allies 'but in so doing the underlying idea must be kept in view that the forces of the United States are a separate and distinct component of the combined forces, the identity of which must be preserved.' There would be much lobbying over his head as French and British diplomats in Washington pleaded at various junctures for amalgamation with their own forces, but such requests were referred back to Pershing and, though often under extreme pressure, he determinedly held his ground.

Thus was the pattern set for the rest of 1917 and a major part of 1918. This is the context in which volunteers such as Kenneth Walser, and countless others like him, crossed to Europe and took their place on the politico-military chess-board. At first more waiting-game than war (though they as ordinary soldiers were not aware of all the arguments over their disposition and use), this was nevertheless a campaign to which they committed themselves with a remarkable eagerness and determination. So much is clearly evident from their letters, which also have the extra virtue of charting a remarkable, and on the whole extremely benign, mingling of cultures as the New World now came to the assistance of the Old.

* * *

Second Lieutenant Walser – he had been commissioned not long after his enlistment – arrived in France in October 1917, and served with the 101st Field Artillery, 26th Division, in the Soissons sector from February to August 1918, when there would be a sudden, and unexpected, end to his military career.

Private Sam Ross, a New Yorker serving with 165th Infantry Regiment (69th New York), 42nd 'Rainbow' Division, American Expeditionary Force, also arrived in France in October 1917. This famous division was so called because it was drawn from the National Guard units of twenty-six states; it included among its members such future luminaries as Douglas MacArthur and George S. Patton, whose presence helped to make it one of the best American divisions of the Great War. Ross would fight in several actions in 1918, including the St Mihiel offensive in September, and the Argonne offensive in October.

Major Leland B. Garretson served in France from June 1918, as commander first of the 314th and later of the 315th Machine Gun Battalions, 80th Division. He took part in a whole series of battles in the campaign's last hundred days, and was still fighting up to the last hours before the Armistice.

Walser's prime motivation, as is clear from his already quoted writings, was a strong sense of moral obligation. By contrast, Garretson approached the task ahead, at least in its initial stages, almost as a kind of romance. 'Here we are sailing merrily along over the bounding ocean in search of the Great Adventure,' he wrote breezily, two days into his transatlantic voyage in May 1918. He had no anxiety about the threat from enemy submarines, showing implicit faith in the method of protection now firmly in place, if after much hesitation and controversy: 'All I can say about this convoy business is that it is as safe as human ingenuity can make it, and it is taken care of by our thoroughly efficient friends the Navy.' He added: 'It is rather an odd sensation to go to sea without the slightest notion on earth as to where you are going, other than "somewhere", but after you get over the strangeness of that notion, it makes up into a very pleasant voyage.' As for his men: 'My hill billies are having the time of their lives. They are packed in moderately thick, they are very adaptable and every new event is a new sensation, so by and large they are having one grand time.'

'The whole thing so far has been fun', Private Ross had written in a similarly upbeat mood six months previously, on 23 November 1917, in a letter in which he described his reactions to the first sight of Garretson's 'somewhere'. Following their somewhat protracted voyage, frustratingly capped by their being held on board for seven days after it was over, Ross and his comrades 'were some happy crowd after three weeks of confinement to get our feet on dry land again'. A subsequent leisurely train ride across France in the general direction of the battle zone had been hugely enjoyed: 'Gee it was a great journey through a most wonderful country, all the prettiest gardens and queerest houses you can imagine, all hedges and trees in different colours, and this is November!'

Ross had been consigned to a carriage with soldiers from another company – 'I did not know any of them and figured I was in for a pretty bum time' – but they turned out to be 'pretty good fellows, except one'. He had also discovered an easy way of keeping in touch with his special chums: 'After the first day out (we were three days on the train) I found where Beckie and that bunch were and spent all my time with them, except when we were at mess and sleeping; we used to go up and down the running board on the side of the train.' Thanks to Private Beckie, who had some money and another comrade, Private Mattie, who spoke French, they achieved an early acquaintance with the local *patisseries* and wine, while dismissing the latter, perhaps to allay family anxieties back home, as 'nothing but grape juice'.

On the third day 'we stopped about three times in towns, and for the first time since we left New York it looked like war; up to this time things were just usual. The people came down to the train to see us and cheer us, they sure were glad to see the Americans. We saw a lot of German prisoners working along the railroad and passed one large prisoners' camp and later on went through two American camps. On Wednesday morning we arrived at our place.'

'Our place' was a town somewhere in the French sector about twelve miles from the trenches: 'we can hear the big guns all the time.' Twenty-four of them were billeted in an old house which at first 'looked rotten, but after a little work it was fine, a fireplace and everything and it looks better every hour'. There was an early meeting with the inhabitants: 'Each French town has a place for washing, a building especially for that purpose, and you can only wash there, so now you see fourteen or fifteen soldiers and a few French women washing and borrowing soap, the men trying to speak French and the women English.'

Ross concluded with a comment which at this time spoke more of national folklore and pride than of contemporary reality: 'They say the Yanks are knocking "Hell" out of the "Boches" the only trouble is getting them to stop. They take one trench and then keep on going and the Dutchmen [i.e. the Deutschers, meaning the Germans] are ready to quit.' What such comments do confirm, however, is the undoubted gusto and self-belief with which Ross and his kind approached the enterprise in which they were now engaged.

* * *

Meaningful contact with the enemy was, inevitably in the circumstances of the time, slow in coming. First there would be much military training, and then a period of introduction to the fighting zone, usually through attachment to some more experienced unit. Lieutenant Walser reached this stage in late January 1918. A month into it he wrote home, from an address chosen with deliberate emphasis and intent:

> Decidedly Somewhere
> Feb. 27, 1918

My darling Family

I don't see how you can help knowing sooner or later that I am at the Front and have been there for four weeks. I have been so tremendously busy that writing has been out of the question, and I wanted to wait until I get adjusted a bit. Our Division is undergoing 'instruction' in a quiet sector. You would never guess it (the latter, I mean). At this present writing, I am in an old Boche 'pillbox' with a metre of very good concrete around, except in one place where a French shell cracked the roof and the rain is dripping on my bed. I have a candle on my bed before me, and in the same room, so to speak, are three French telephonists and a French liaison officer. I am at the French Battalion Command Post, and the Boches are almost a kilometre away, and very quiet at this moment. Every couple of minutes the candle shudders as a shell falls more or less in the vicinity. I have been in the front line for three weeks as a Liaison Officer with the infantry and as a Forward Observation Officer. The most interesting work I ever did in my life. A narrow escape once in a while makes it all the more interesting.

I laughed till I cried when you said you were going to send me *The Glory of the Trenches*, for I was standing up to my knees in the stickiest mud that ever existed, watching a bombardment to our left and reading your letter at the same time. Believe me, the ground was a mass of shell holes and debris of battle and beside me were the remains of a Boche who shuffled off his mortal coil in October and left it ill concealed, stuck out of the side of the trench. *The Glory of the Trenches* – it is not the martial glory that is evident here.

The Glory of the Trenches was one of several popular books glamorizing war by an English soldier-writer who had lived in New York, Lieutenant Coningsby Dawson, who, after being wounded, devoted himself to preaching the Allied cause in both Britain and

America. Pithy, brief, pocketable and of good provenance – they were published in London under the imprint of John Lane, The Bodley Head – they were an instant success, especially in the USA. His first, *Khaki Courage*, sold 100,000 copies there under its American title *Carry On*; it was a book, said the *New York Times*, that every pacifist should be legally compelled to read. Later, under the auspices of the British Foreign Office and as the guest of the US military authorities, he produced a volume describing the aims and achievements of the Americans in France, under the title *Out To Win*. But it was *The Glory of the Trenches* that was making the clarion call to war at the time that the first American troops were being integrated into the actual fighting. Proclaiming the conflict in Europe as a great and noble adventure, it made little of the downside, such as the squalors of trench life now becoming manifest to Lieutenant Walser. Nevertheless, despite such drawbacks, Walser's enthusiasm remained high, as he made very clear in a further letter written on 4 March:

> The Poilus [i.e. the French soldiers] here, whom I have come to know quite well, are amazed at my happy state of mind. I tell them all the Americans feel the same way, and they shake their heads in pity, I guess, for our imbecility, but it is true that everybody is very happy all the time, taking the hardships as a sort of game. Obviously the novelty of everything wears off after three years of it, and I don't blame them. But you do feel like laughing when the enemy land a shell at your feet, and the darn thing fails to go off, as it did with me the other day. That is you laugh a few minutes afterwards, for a moment you are flat on the ground where your instinct told you to put yourself when you heard it coming. And a week ago when I was in the sector to the left, a 150 battery registered on the very spot where I was at my observation point, and quite successfully, for they broke the scissors telescope that I had in my hand.
>
> I am really enjoying myself immensely. The physical discomforts you experience are a part of the game, and you can stand anything for a while. The shells which you hear switching [*sic*] towards you in a great crescendo are fairly terrifying if they get close – but there is a splendid feeling when you see they missed you.

It was not until after the launch of the German spring offensive that Private Sam Ross was able to claim that he had been at the sharp edge of the war. He wrote to his mother on 24 March:

Sunday. Everything is quiet except the distant booming of the guns. I suppose by this time you know that we have been in the trenches and are out again and on our way back to our base; hiking – it seems very hard to make us foot it all the way – 130 miles, but this outfit seems to always get the worst end, but there is one good point, we can do our bit no matter how hard.

My company was in the front line trenches for nine days. We had only three men hurt and they had slight shrapnel wounds so you see we were very lucky, as some of the other outfits were hit pretty hard. Claud and Quack were gassed. They are all right now. They got their masks on in time and the gas did not have much effect. Whittie has been recommended for a war cross for the work he and some others did during a gas attack.

To a sister, Eva, he wrote a longer and more frank account in early April, including such episodes as a major raid carried out on his sector by the French with some sixty Americans in support: 'About two hours before the raid some batteries that were kept silent opened up and so did the trench mortars – it was just one continuous roar; when the raiding party reached the Huns' lines there was nothing left of the trench or dugouts and the ground was strewn with their dead.' Most vividly of all he described his own experience of one of the infantryman's essential roles in trench warfare, that of being on sentry duty – 'standing post' in American parlance – while his comrades took their rest:

Standing post at night is something – you see there is thirty feet of wire in front of our trench and the posts are put in very irregular. It is almost impossible to find a place where you could see clear through the wire, even in daylight, and at night every post or broken tree looks like a man and if you look long enough the object seems to move. The first night I stood post I imagined the trees were men and at times I saw them stoop and climb over the wire, but after that I was used to it and learned how to tell a man from a tree. If you give a false alarm it means that the fellows who are sleeping in the dugouts are awakened and have to come

up and 'stand to'; at the best the fellows get very little sleep, and
if there are any alarms they get none at all. So the wise Hun has
all kinds of ways to coax an alarm, cats are used, and they have
whistles which make moaning noises. You hear a cat on the wire
and one of these whistles is blown, and you look out and think
there is a man cutting the wire.

They had been spared one particular trench-hazard, for the absence
of which he was extremely thankful: 'We were very lucky as the
weather was very good. It rained only once while we were in and it
was bad enough in dry weather, but when you have to stand in the
mud, it must be hell.'

Ross had been discretion itself in the matter of avoiding naming
of places, but when Major Garretson made landfall in early June he
had no compunction in stating where he had disembarked: 'Here we
are "Somewhere in France", and as the censor has no objection I can
tell you that we are at Rest Camp near Bordeaux.' As with Ross, the
voyage had had its *longueurs* after its romantic beginning: 'Monotony is rampant,' he had stated after five days at sea; and he had also
found the wearing of 'life preservers', as he called them, extremely
tedious as they approached what was assumed to be a less secure
area of the Atlantic: 'Frankly I find no fun in having a sort of
chicken coop effect strapped round me all the time, although I admit
it is sensible to require them.'

Five days further on he had at last felt able to contemplate the
next phase of the adventure:

Another beautiful day! As I sit here rambling along I can look
out and see many painted ships upon a painted ocean. Our
voyage is coming to an end, and with luck we should pick up the
French coast tomorrow. It may be a day or more after that before
we actually set foot in poor old war-beaten France, but when we
do I will feel that the first great step of our mission has been
accomplished.

Soon the real work will begin. As for adventure it should be
full of it, as for respectability it is unquestioned, as for its end it
is righteous – what more could we ask?

Garretson arrived in the spring as compared with Ross's autumn,
yet he seems to have seen a different France from that about which

the latter had been so lyrical. The consequences of war had cast too great a shadow:

> We got to our Rest Camp Sunday, after a most interesting trip through the wine country, but my word you should see it.
>
> We passed village after village and château after château which were practically deserted, the shutters were up, and it made you weep to see the lawns going rank and the wonderful gardens overgrown with weeds. A few people are around, and then only old men, women, practically all of them in black, and children, with here and there a badly battered up soldier. It was not a cheery spectacle, they seemed very tired and looked very, very sad, but they were glad to see us, and 'Marching through Georgia' and 'God Help Kaiser Bill' were greeted with 'Vive l'Amerique'.
>
> Yesterday the men were cooped up but the officers went on a 'seeing Bordeaux'. The city is beautiful indeed but among the natives there is little joy, furthermore it has become thoroughly Americanized, American soldiers and sailors overrun the place but manage to have a pretty soft time doing it.

Six days later they were on the move, after a stay in the vicinity of Bordeaux from which he felt everyone, officers and men, had greatly benefited. It had had its amusing side too: 'Travelling with "Sammie" [clearly Garretson had no compunction in using the term about his men] is no end of fun, his French is a scream but he gets there, and along the line the poor tired natives give him a hand and are glad to see him. You cannot discourage him to save his life.'

From now forward, however, he wrote, while their train 'ambled along at an easy gait in the general direction of the scene of activities', he would revert to anonymity in the matter of French locations and destinations: 'While at Bordeaux it was unobjectionable to mention the fact, but from now on you need not expect many lessons in French geography.' In the matter of railway comfort his men did not have the good fortune that Ross and his comrades had enjoyed, but the primitive conditions of French travel did not deter them one whit: 'The officers are provided with first or second class carriages but my poor Army has drawn box cars to the tune of forty to the car.' These were the standard 'chevaux 8, hommes 40' cattle-trucks which the British Tommy had complained about ever since 1914. 'It sure is thick, but this morning the whole works were as happy as clams at high tide, and when they were let off for coffee, they fed and then beat it to the locomotive for hot water so they could shave.'

* * *

For all American troops in Europe 4 July 1918 was to be an Independence Day far from home, but for Major Garretson, now in the British sector of the Front at one of their numerous training establishments behind the lines, it was to become an occasion of international solidarity to cherish and remember. He wrote home three days later:

> On the Fourth of July the whole of France and England made a gala day of it, and it was indeed a curious privilege to be in a British Army Service School and hear British officers toasting the United States for the courage it showed a hundred and fifty years ago in insisting on personal liberty, and fighting a mad German Prince [i.e. King George III] to get it. It may be said to the Britons' credit, there was never a word of regret about lost territory or anything of the sort, which was quite remarkable when you think of the Britons' love for empires beyond the seas.

Imperial echoes of a more traditional kind, however, informed Garretson's somewhat amazed account, written a few weeks later, describing his dealings with one of the British Army's more elderly representatives:

> In all the towns near the trenches the British have what is called a Town Major, who is usually a retired officer who has come back into active service, and yet is too old for the strenuous work at the front. His job is to assign the billets, generally care for them, and act as go-between between the troops and property owners. The Town Major here is a dear old gentleman who retired as a Brigadier-General in 1914, on account of age, and came toddling back when war broke out and then came out here with the rank of Colonel. He has some sort of a title though it is camouflaged under his military handle, and is now serving in his 47th year in the British Army! He told me his service includes 18 years in India, and 11 years in South Africa. He sports all the campaign ribbons under the sun and also has a number of

decorations which he has gathered in his goings and comings. He has an old Major who is a sort of Man Friday to him, and they're a great pair. He has been extremely polite, and has had me and the Adjutant to dinner.

Inevitably the compliment had to be returned, though the event turned out to be not entirely without its cultural hazards:

The Adjutant and the mess officer arranged the details. The table was resplendent in a new piece of oil cloth. For dinner we had puree of beans (our old friend the army bean), poulêt roti, pomme de terre naturel, tomates au pot, lobster removed from the can and tastily draped on a bit of lettuce, pie made from issue strawberry jam, and a savory consisting of grilled sardines on toast. Under no consideration must one ever dine an Englishman and not give him a savory. But the said savory was almost the death of us, for they were new to our butlers from the hills of Virginia, and of course they managed to bring them in after the salad, instead of after the pie, in spite of written instructions, so it seemed as if we were almost having a canned fish dinner. Coffee, cigars and a bit of Scotch were also on hand, and we topped the entertainment off by producing a couple of mandolin players and a ventriloquist from the battalion to amuse the old gentleman. They were very polite, and I think had a good time.

Cultural differences of another kind became evident when his battalion moved nearer the front and found itself billeted in a series of French villages and townships. Of one such he wrote:

Again I am billeted chez M. le Curé. There seems to be something connected with the CO's job which results in his landing as a guest of the Curé's time after time. Of course the Curé is the spiritual CO of all these French towns, and generally runs the best establishment, and as the CO gets the best billet it is all very logical.

Another thing our wanderings have brought us to is to return us to an area where the manure pile is the most prominent of all the local 'lares and penates' [i.e. household gods]. As a matter of fact the present village can be smelt before it can be seen. They do keep the inside of their houses clean, but in spite of your ability to see that your bed chamber is spotless, when you climb a manure heap to get into it, you have your doubts as to the general sanitary condition.

What is more they are damned touchy about their manure. You know that you can engineer a fairly active '*affaire*' with a Frenchman's wife with very little risk, but if you cut down one of his trees, or fuss with his manure pile, he takes on something awful. Only yesterday afternoon an industrious Officer of the Day, looking for something for some idle prisoners to do, decided to turn up a couple of particularly messy piles in the town square, and the Mayor himself got on the loose and wouldn't be quiet for a second until the CO in person got out of bed and assured him we did not want a single pound of it.

*   *   *

While Garretson was enjoying his leisurely and ethnically illuminating progress towards the realities of war, Lieutenant Walser had seen enough of them for what he had earlier considered to be something of a game to acquire aspects of a nightmare. He had spent some time chafing in a staff appointment – 'here on the staff we play around with papers and reports and make new maps and get out orders and might as well be in a law office' – and had then at his own request gone out on liaison with the infantry. This was in May, but he clearly experienced more than he had anticipated over the following weeks, for his next surviving letter, written to a family friend on 2 August, struck a markedly new, disenchanted tone:

I am back with the wagon train for a couple of days rest, having had rather a rough time of it since we started on the push that you have been reading about. I spent a good deal of the time as a liaison officer with the infantry, and was roughly handled by some shells, with the result that I was in a fairly dazed and exhausted condition. I have now successfully completed a 36-hour nap and am ready for anything, or will be after I have had another like it.

The American infantry has proved itself unquestionably to be the best in the world – a little too brave perhaps. Every one of them ought to have a DSO. With us on the 75s [French guns of high reputation, which the Americans were now using], it is a question of following them closely, keeping awake all the time, and keeping enough horses alive and unwounded to pull the guns. It is quite like the movies in a way, with guns galloping into position in open fields and caissons [wagons] rushing about for ammunition.

The dead and wounded are harrowing sights, sometimes. Worst of all, the shell-shocked cases. Then as you go through a field you find a squad of Americans, lying as they fell, with faces and bayonets pointing towards the enemy. The last three days I spent at an OP [observation post] where I had to practically sit on three deceased German gentlemen, and a horse likewise deceased, but sometime previously, I think.

I wish that all America could follow us along the road of this advance; to see the way the Boche has filthied everything, pillaged everything – great châteaux with piles of picture frames, whole canvases have been cut out to be shipped back to Germany, with goodness knows what else – bullet holes in every mirror, and the finest places converted into the most abominable pig sties – so that they might feel at home, I suppose. It is the sight of things like that which makes me realize the Boche character, even more than the boys from home, who come in torn and groaning, and the others who are lucky enough to have gotten it clean and are covered up with blankets.

We were able to see the results of some of our work, and there is no doubt in our minds as to the murderous quality of the 75s, and yet the poor fools we hashed up were just as sure they were right as we are. It's a funny world.

The action in which Walser had been involved was that known to history as the Second Battle of the Marne, which took place between 18 July and 7 August. It was launched with a two-pronged attack by the Germans on either side of the cathedral city of Reims, and it ended with their being heavily rebuffed and thrown back. It was to be their last offensive of the war. They struck with a massive force consisting of fifty-two divisions, but they no longer could claim the virtue of surprise; and though they were confronted by a smaller force of thirty-four divisions, including nine American and two Italian, with two British just arriving, the state of preparedness on the Allied side stunned them, and they soon saw they were not to have it their own way. For those Allies who had been many months in the field it was one of a long sequence of encounters, going back even beyond the First Battle of the Marne in 1914, but for the Americans involved it was a serious blooding, a dramatic and costly initiation. It has been recorded that when a Scottish division relieved an American division in one sector its men were saddened by the sight of masses of dead in American uniforms lying in regular lines – precisely as described in Walser's moving account. In defence they had shown themselves determined not to yield whatever the cost, and now in attack they clearly meant either to get through or to perish. It was as though the new ally was learning for herself and by a hard way the grim lessons the British had learned at Loos, on the Somme or at Passchendaele, and that the French had learned in the long siege of Verdun or in the heroic but failed attempt under Nivelle in Champagne.

Just as those earlier battles produced their crop of mentally scarred and devastated men, so this 1918 battle wrought havoc on the psychology of some of those who took part, among them, clearly, Lieutenant Kenneth E. Walser. His expectation that he would shortly be 'ready for anything' was, unhappily, not realized. Sometime in the month in which he wrote the above letter – apparently his last of the war – he was given an honourable discharge from the US Army.

Yet though the Americans had suffered heavy casualties they had also convinced their allies that they were capable of unstinting commitment to the common cause. Private Sam Ross's claim quoted earlier that the Yanks were knocking the 'Hell' out of the Boche and that the only trouble was getting them to stop had now acquired a reasonable justification, except that getting enemies to stop was precisely what the Germans' rugged and professional systems of defence were most competent to achieve. Ross's own 42nd Division had also taken part in the Marne battle and he described his experiences in a letter clearly so unguarded in its references to the places and units involved that a section of it was completely erased by the censor. But its message was clear; there had been hard fighting (in which, as it happened, he and his comrades had been exceptionally fortunate) but, he claimed, they had 'done their bit, even more than their bit, towards getting the Huns back where they belonged'. In the uncensored sections of the letter he stated:

All our boys came through OK, with honors, except one. Poor Earle is still out on the fields. We advanced past our objective and had to retire; a couple of days after we pushed on again and when we did we found the remains of four of our men – the four who had advanced the furthest in the big battle, one of them was Earle.

He had been shot through the head, he died instantly, the bolt of his gun was open in one hand and he had a clip ready to insert into the breech.

If a fellow was allowed to choose his own finish he could not have picked a better or more heroic one than our little Earle's and one without pain, the position of his hands shows this.

So don't feel sad, but feel proud that he died a hero pushing ahead for right.

The Hun that killed him was also killed as some of Earle's papers were found in the pocket of a dead Dutchman later.

Claud distinguished himself – he killed four Huns with his bayonet, was cut in the cheek himself, had it sewn up and then went back into the fight with another company.

A later letter to his sister, Flossie, carried an even prouder message, on account of the recognition of the performance of the division as a whole:

We have been decorated: some honor for a National Guard division – and considered the Kid division on account of the average age of the fellows – to be put ahead of the crack Regular Army outfits, but believe me the bunch sure did some fighting. Father Duffey said that ours was the greatest American victory – the best the Huns had were against us, and we had a position to take that was almost impossible. He said never before had Americans faced such artillery fire or machine-gun fire, in any war.

It makes a fellow feel good that all our hard training and hiking was not lost.

But as well as the pride there was the sadness: 'Some of the best and bravest fellows I have known are still along that river and on the top of that hill, but their names will never be forgotten, they are part of our history.'

* * *

How were the Americans received by their fighting comrades in other uniforms? 'Good keen men. They are fresh and they are interested:' this was the verdict of Major C.H. Dudley Ward, writing in August after six platoons of the 1st Battalion, 320th American Infantry Regiment, had been attached to his 1st Welsh Guards for instruction purposes. 'They are very willing and good-tempered,' he added in a second letter, commenting that in spite of things going wrong, which at times they inevitably did, 'they keep their spirits well. They make our men laugh they are so green and nervous – but they are keen. Some of them went out on patrol last night and saw an army of Huns in every row of stakes. I ordered them to fire on everything they thought suspicious and the result was a ripple of shots all through the night.' He also recorded an amusing moment involving the major who was in command of the attached battalion: 'He was very American and thirsty. Without saying a word he clawed hold of a bottle of diluted peroxide which I use for my teeth and took a long drink. "Gee!" he said, "that's the strongest water I have had for some time." I hope it won't hurt him but I didn't tell him about it.' His only serious reservations were a complaint that they had shown a dangerous degree of incompetence during a relief (something which experience should soon cure), and an instinctively hostile response to the newcomers' addiction to lively, and therefore extremely noisy, band music. This was to prove a standard grievance among the British, but the Americans had brought their support and their manpower to Europe, and there was no way of stopping them from bringing their culture.

There were, almost inevitably, earthier attitudes among at least some of the British other ranks; Private William Hall's reservations mentioned in the previous chapter were not his alone. His views had been changed by contact, but meetings between Americans and British could be double-edged, for there were many hardy troopers among the latter, such as the irrepressible Cude, whose key motivations included an instinctive mistrust of every other nation involved in the war. Their particular target was, of course, the Germans, though their opprobrium could easily extend to any known ally. Significantly, Brophy and Partridge in their book of soldiers' songs and slang, *The Long Trail*, after defining 'Yank' as a term 'applied by the British to all Americans, not always politely', continued:

'Cf. Russki, Macaroni, Pork-and-Beans, Chink, Aussie, Froggie'. Clearly, a certain type of Tommy found much satisfaction in blithely denigrating his fellow labourers in the field.

By contrast, Sidney Edwards, a gun layer in D/306th Brigade RFA, 61st Division, had nothing but praise for an American attached for several weeks from the 317th Infantry Battalion. He noted on 12 July: 'At 11.15 a message was brought to "Sammy" (as he was nicknamed) telling him to return to his HQ. We were awfully sorry about this as he was an awfully nice fellow, who had always been more than ready to assist in anything although the battery had no claim on him, as he was only "lent" to us to enable him to learn what he could about RFA work in general. Many mornings he accompanied me to the gun-pit and I showed him the way to "take down" the breach and the easiest and quickest way of re-assembling it.' Their guest left next day: 'At 10. a.m. "Sammy", with full equipment strapped to bicycle, set off for his destination. He had a hearty send off, and we were all very sorry to see the last of him.'

Perhaps not surprisingly, the Australians took easily to the new arrivals, doubtless sensing in them a similarly oblique stance to the British, from whom the Americans had escaped politically a century or so earlier, while the Australian way of showing their independence lay in their individualistic, 'bushranging' style of conduct and combat. Hence the following enthusiastic reaction of an Australian infantry officer, Lieutenant Edwin 'Ted' Trundle, writing to his wife on 29 June: 'There are plenty Americans about the line and just in rear now. There has grown a wonderful mutual admiration and understanding between our boys and the Yanks. I'm sure the Yanks are going to prove excellent fighting troops.'

* * *

The American contribution to the 1918 war was largely one on the ground, but it also made its mark elsewhere. Whereas Pershing's policy dictated that his Army would not be fed piecemeal into the fighting in France, in other theatres such as that of the air individual Americans served with other nations' units without let or hindrance. Thus in the late spring of 1918, Ensign Kenneth B. Keyes, United States Navy, as a member of the crew of a Royal Air Force flying boat based on Felixstowe, on England's East Anglian coast, found himself in an episode of aerial combat which drew much publicity, being reported at length in such stalwart members of the British press as *The Times*, the *Daily Telegraph* and the *Daily Mail*. Writing about his adventures to his mother in Massachusetts, Ensign Keyes stated: 'The papers say that it was the greatest scrap ever held over the North Sea and I guess it was.' Five British aircraft had been involved, three from Felixstowe and two from the nearby base at Yarmouth.

The action had been fought to the north of the Dutch island of Vlieland, and had ended with some of the RAF flyers interned in neutral Holland, among them the only other American involved, Ensign Joe Eaton, a friend with whom Keyes had trained in Vermont. Indeed, it had been rumoured at the base that Keyes himself had either been killed or interned, and since the British force had lost two aircraft, while the second pilot of a third had been shot, the chances of returning unharmed and ready for immediate further service had not been high.

The odds were even higher in the actual combat in that they had been heavily outnumbered, finding themselves confronting a force of fifteen German seaplanes with their modest five:

> We steered straight for the middle of the fifteen. The fight lasted a half hour, longer than they usually last. In that time one of our boats had to descend on account of the engine being shot up, then we were cut off from our formation by seven enemy planes. We nose dived and put up a running fight in which we drove off the seven.
>
> I was in the front cockpit of our boats (we always call them boats for short, they really are flying boats carrying five or six men and mounting several machine-guns), firing the forward gun when I happened to look around and saw that Lieutenant Galvayne was in a stooping position with his arm over the seat. On looking closer I saw that his head was lying in a pool of blood. About the same time five or six shots passed through the wood about 3 to 9 inches back of me. I had to turn around and keep firing. When I had fired my last round of ammunition I crawled back to Galvayne, laid him out and took that seat myself. Just about the time we had driven off the last of the seven planes our engine gave out and we had to 'land' ten miles North West of

Vlieland. If we hadn't driven the Huns off they would have shot us up on the water or if our engine hadn't been fixed in a few minutes we would have had to set fire to it, get help from a Dutch trawler and we would have been interned in Holland for the rest of the war. But we were lucky enough to fix our engine, rose from the water, picked up our two other boats and flew back in formation to Yarmouth. We were in the air seven hours and a half.

I don't mind telling you that when I saw that we were cut off by those enemy planes I thought that I had seen home for the last time and everybody says who knows about the fight, it was just by the grace of God that we ever got back.

I might say that two enemy planes were shot down in flames.

Lieutenant Galvayne, whose place Keyes had taken in such dramatic circumstances, had been the flying boat's second pilot. Subsequent medical examination established that he had been killed instantly. Keyes commented: 'When we had that forced landing I loosened all his clothes and felt his heart and I could have sworn it was beating but perhaps I was mistaken. The bottom of the plane was covered with blood and when we got in my hands, face and clothes were smeared with it. On looking over the plane we found it was riddled with shots.'

They finally reached base at 2 a.m. The following morning 'the CO and the Warfight Captain [sic] came around to shake hands with Captain Barker and myself, the only two officers to get back to this station.' Later that day he was called to headquarters in London to write 'a report of our scrape, one copy of which will go to Washington'.

This was not the end of Ensign Keyes' high-risk adventures, as he confessed to his mother: 'The fight happened on June 4th. The next day, after getting back from London, I took some pupils up and when I started to glide down, the port motor refused to shut off. This threw us into a flat spin. Well, we crashed, the boat sank and we had to swim for it, the only one who was really hurt was the engineer who had to have six stitches in his head. We managed to get him through all right.'

He added, somewhat defensively: 'This was my first crash. Of course I lost that plane at Arbroath but that wasn't a crash.' He concluded by suggesting that, not having had any official leave since coming to Britain, he might apply for some in a few days' time.

* * *

As indicated, the episode just described took place in June. It was one piece of exciting news in a month which was to prove a time of considerable anxiety, even depression, in Britain, and which also saw the first upsurge in Europe of an alarming phenomenon which would cast a long shadow over a year which had had more than its fair share of dangers and disasters already.

7

UNEASY SUMMER

WITH THE BENEFIT OF HINDSIGHT the events of the spring of 1918 can seem to bear a hallmark of inevitability, as though every German offensive was bound to follow the pattern of the first and end in breakdown. There was a basic in-built fault in the design, they would all fail, and when they did the initiative would automatically pass to the Allies. In the anxious middle months of this extraordinary year matters did not seem so cut and dried. In particular they did not seem so from the point of view of the governments involved, nor of the capital cities.

The Chemin des Dames offensive had brought the Germans alarmingly close to Paris; when they took Château-Thierry they were barely sixty miles away. This added a psychological pressure to a military one which the city had been experiencing ever since 23 March, just two days into 'Operation Michael'. It was on that date that the specially built Krupp 210 mm cannon 'Long Max', so-named because of its 130-foot barrel, began its occasional, taunting bombardment of the French capital. Fired at 7.16 a.m., its first shell struck north-west Paris four minutes later, having traversed a distance of 74.12 miles. Overall, this new variant of the ancient siege gun would claim 256 Parisians killed and 620 injured. It would not significantly affect the functioning of the city and the government, but it had its notable consequences. In the words of a distinguished visitor to Paris at this period: 'The long-range German cannon, which threw its shells about every half hour, had effectually cleared away nearly all those who were not too busy nor too poor. The city was empty and agreeable by day, while at night there was nearly always the diversion of an air raid.' The sang-froid thus displayed was that of the ever resilient and high-spirited Winston Churchill, able to pluck something positive out of circumstances which filled countless others with nervous concern. Underlining his just quoted comment, he would also state: 'Paris was calm and even pleasant in these days of uncertainty.'

But Churchill had not gone there to see the sights: the nature of the business that occasioned his visit is an indication of the depth of the anxiety felt at this time. The British Air Force (officially the 'Royal Air Force' from 1 April) had come to rely on armaments produced by several factories in the Paris region. As Minister of Munitions Churchill needed to be present at discussions as to whether or when the work of these key factories might have to be continued elsewhere. For a brief time there was a genuine dilemma: 'If we moved without cause,' he would write in his book *The World Crisis*, 'we interrupted production. If we tarried too long, we should not be able to get our machinery away.'

Meanwhile London was still being reminded of its vulnerability to enemy attentions from the air. Along with parts of Essex and Kent, the capital had suffered a major raid as recently as the night of 19/20 May, during which 159 bombs had been dropped leaving forty-nine people killed and 177 injured. As it happened, this, the sixth on London in 1918, was also the last air raid of the war (there would be one more visit from Zeppelins in August, to Norfolk, during which no bombs would be dropped and so there would be no casualties), but such reassuring intelligence was not available at the time. It would take weeks for the climate of fear engendered by such enemy activity to evaporate, while the news from the battlefronts was at its best only partly reassuring and at sea German U-boats were still sinking too many ships. There was thus no mood of easy assurance that the war was moving steadily the Allies' way. On the contrary, there was still a nagging fear that, despite their setbacks, the Germans might somehow contrive to induce the catastrophic failure on the Allied side that had been their clear target throughout the year.

'I cannot exclude the possibility of a disaster', wrote the ever thoughtful Cabinet Secretary, Colonel Sir Maurice Hankey, on 4 June, after a visit to France which had done little to steady already badly frayed nerves. At the War Cabinet next day, there were two main subjects for discussion: the question of shortening the line by abandoning Dunkirk, strongly argued for by the British CIGS, Wilson, but anathema to Foch; and – an even more alarming prospect

– the possibility of the crisis becoming so acute as to require the withdrawal of the whole British Army from France. 'If the French crack' was the condition that would bring such a last-ditch eventuality to pass. Hankey's 5 June diary comment conveyed the dour mood of the occasion: 'It was', he wrote, 'a very gloomy meeting.'

The very mention in this context of an emotive name such as Dunkirk, and of the prospect of a British Army being forced to withdraw across the Channel, inevitably prompts memories of another uneasy summer a generation later, when that name and that prospect dramatically combined. It is oddly chilling to think that what actually happened in May–June 1940 was seen as a genuine possibility in June 1918.

Curiously, though perhaps not surprisingly, the situation gave rise to what might be fairly described as precursors of the Dunkirk spirit. Thus under the heading 'June 1918' Mrs Ethel Bilborough, of Chislehurst, wrote in her diary: 'Things look about as gloomy as they possibly can. The sinking of our ships (daily) by the German submarines continues in appalling numbers. The pent-up fury of the Huns is all being concentrated in their last "Great Offensive" and our lines are broken badly at the front, yet our brave boys remain undaunted, and continue the struggle valiantly against tremendous odds. Fortunately the thought of *England conquered* is *un*thinkable (which sounds rather a paradox!).'

A similar confidence in the face of adversity had been expressed by a British VAD nurse in France, Joanne Anderson, at the height of the 'Backs to the Wall' crisis some weeks earlier. She wrote to a fellow nurse: 'I refuse to pack up a single thing. If England should be beaten and we forced to evacuate I would pitch my extra belongings into the sea to sink with England.' Yet she still saw even that contingency, if it came to pass, as merely a temporary setback, concluding triumphantly: 'We shall be conquerors yet!'

*   *   *

June 1918 has another claim for attention; it was during it that the first news stories announcing the arrival of a mysterious new illness began to circulate. It was swiftly dubbed 'the Spanish Influenza', or, more poetically, the 'plague of the Spanish Lady', though there is no evidence that Spain was its point of origin. That country, however, gave it its first publicity, in that it seems to have been brought to the world's notice by two Reuters' cables from Madrid on 4 June, the first of them announcing that 'a strange form of disease of epidemic character' had appeared in the Spanish capital. What also helped to link it to Spain was that among the vast numbers of Spaniards who succumbed to it was their king, Alfonso XIII, though he was among those who were fortunate enough to survive.

The disease's first actual outbreak had occurred in the United States in March, at an army base, Camp Funston, in Kansas. American troops thus emerge as its probable carriers, though throughout its course it was surrounded by uncertainty as to its cause and ignorance as to any possible cure. The casualties of battle or bombing raids people could comprehend, but the 'Spanish Flu' descended like a pestilence of the Old Testament, a visitation of displeasure, as it were, from the Almighty. It was almost a twentieth-century version of the Black Death, punishing many nations, and not only those most deeply engaged in the contemporary struggle. In fact, its worst effects were in Asia, especially India, which suffered 12.5 million deaths out of a total, world wide, of 21.5 millions. Other countries which suffered heavily included the Dutch East Indies, Japan, Australia, Madagascar, Brazil, Mexico and the United States, where the figure of fatalities reached well over 500,000. In its visit to the States it wrought great havoc in sophisticated centres such as Chicago, Philadelphia, and the nation's capital, Washington DC, claiming 3,500 victims in that city alone; there was such widespread fear of infection that people moved about the streets in gauze masks. It struck the family of the future president, Franklin D. Roosevelt, though happily everyone in the Roosevelt home effected a recovery. Roosevelt himself, then Assistant Secretary of the US Navy, caught his bout aboard the British cruiser HMS *Leviathan*; he was spared to fall victim some years later to a plague of a different kind, polio. Other notable temporary sufferers included the actress Mary Pickford; a young volunteer Red Cross ambulance driver, training in Chicago with a view to going to France, named Walter Elias Disney, later to reduce his first name, memorably, to Walt; the French C.-in-C. of the war's early years, Marshal 'Papa' Joffre; and other such key players on the 1918 stage as General Pershing, Kaiser Wilhelm and the British Prime Minister, Lloyd George. The then US president,

Woodrow Wilson, also contracted the disease, late in the year; it has even been speculated that its after-effects might have distorted his judgement during the Paris Peace Conference in early 1919.

As for the countries of Europe which were, or had been, most heavily engaged in the war, the estimated figures were (in descending order): Russia 450,000, Britain 228,917, Germany 225,230, France 166,000. The numbers given are of fatalities; add to these the massive number of those who were attacked but survived and, it has been estimated, the total reached over a billion, more than half the global population. When looking back at 1918 and concentrating on the course of the military campaigns, it is all too easy to overlook this devastating phenomenon, which arrived without warning, surged, declined and surged again over the best part of a year, and then as mysteriously departed. It was one more blow for a world which had already had four years of trying to cope with the inexplicable.

Before June was out it was making its presence felt on the Western Front. Lieutenant Harold Horne of the 63rd (Royal Naval) Division caught it in the second half of the month. He noted in his diary: '*17–22 June*. At Hérissart; I developed "Spanish Flu". In bed 21st and 22nd. *23rd*: Battalion went into the line, Mesnil Sector, I went with rear HQ to Louvencourt Wood in tents. I still had 'flu.' But his was not a serious case; by the 25th he was back in harness prosecuting at a Field General Court Martial.

Similarly Wireless Operator A.R. Atkinson of the Royal Air Force was only briefly disabled by an attack in early July. 'Contracted Spanish Influenza at Squadron,' he noted on the 4th, adding on the 5th: 'Better but in bed all day.' His diary was soon at its routine business of laconically recording the normal round of RAF activity.

Another early sufferer was Lieutenant George Havard Thomas of the 7th Sherwood Foresters, 46th (North Midland) Division. He wrote home in late June from the Red Cross Hospital at Wimereux near Calais: 'I am down here for a few days with that new sort of influenza. I hope none of you will ever get it, it just sprang on me with a temperature of 104 one afternoon in the line, accompanied by all manner of things. It seemed to be spreading through the army like fire.' On 3 July he wrote again: 'The influenza is going for everybody and a great number come down daily, for about ten days one feels simply dead.' Fortunately he rapidly recovered and, after a week and a half's retraining at the Infantry Base Depot near Étaples, was back with his unit.

Havard Thomas's claim that influenza was 'going for everybody' was an exaggeration; nevertheless it has been estimated that over fifteen per cent of the British Army entered hospitals, though, as in the case of the examples quoted, most were quickly on their feet again. By contrast, in the German ranks, where the disease became known as 'Flanders fever', its effects were much worse, poor diet being widely assumed to be a significant contributory factor.

A reference which reflects more or less exactly the state of affairs on both sides occurs in the diary account of an Australian signaller, Private G.V. Rose. Under 17 July he wrote:

> A number of our men were taken bad with Spanish Flu and were sent back as far as Battalion HQ. In consequence the line was held very thinly. One day a Yankee general came over on a tour of inspection. He said to 'Achi' Barber – 'Waal, I guess it's marvellous.' Achi said, 'What's marvellous?' He answered: 'The bluff you are putting over on the Hun with your one man to every hundred yards or so of trench.' If the Hun *had* come over we would have had a very rough time. It's quite possible, though, that he was having the same trouble as we were.

(In explanation it should be added that 'Achi' Barber was Rose's CO, so nicknamed because of the Australian connection with Gallipoli, where Achi Baba was a famous and much-fought-over landmark.)

If the British Army fared reasonably well, the same could not be said of the Royal Navy. As early as 1 July the First Sea Lord, Admiral Sir Rosslyn Wemyss, told the Cabinet Secretary Sir Maurice Hankey (as the latter noted in his diary): 'the influenza is rife in the Navy [with the result that] many destroyers have been unable to go to sea, so that the loss of several merchant ships is directly attributed to this issue'.

Also during July in England the disease hit the coal-mining areas of Northumberland and Durham, and it began serious depredations in the capital, swiftly accounting for over 700 Londoners. On the 10th, writing from Walthamstow in London's East End, Mrs Elsie

Barnett (quoted in Chapter 2 above) described the situation to her soldier-husband in Mesopotamia, itself notoriously a disease-ridden country. After expressing the hope that he would keep his health in spite of the monstrous flies and intense heat of which he had been complaining, she told him of the even more frightening scourge nearer home: 'We have had a terrible doing from the Spanish Flu as they call it, but doctors are inclined to think it's malaria brought about by soldiers. Am thankful to say I've kept clear so far and we are warned to wear camphor about us as people are dying with it in a few hours if they don't lay up at once.'

It is noteworthy that, lacking awareness of the nature of the infliction which was creating such havoc, there was an instant recourse to such traditional means of rebutting disease as camphor – an odorous decongestant at one time highly popular but by now long unused in medicine. Its chances of doing anything to combat the new disease, other than as a psychological placebo, were nil. As the year wore on there would be numerous attempts by commercial organizations to offer their products as barriers against the disease. The makers of Oxo would claim that their product would fortify the system against influenza infection, as also did the manufacturers of Brand's Beef Essence. Advertisements for 'Formamint, The Germ-killing Throat Tablet' posed the question: 'Why catch that Influenza? Attack the germs before they attack you.' The manufacturers adduced support for their product from allegedly reliable medical sources: ' "Suck at least four or five a day" – so says Dr. Hopkirk in his standard work *Influenza* – for "in Formamint we possess the best means of preventing the infective process which, if neglected, may lead to serious complications".' [See illustration 35.]

If the disease's inroads on the Western Front were less widespread and virulent than elsewhere, it nevertheless had the power to shock and dismay, for it often seemed to have its greatest effect on the fittest and strongest. Thus Guy Chapman in his 1930s memoir *A Passionate Prodigality* would write of this period: 'Since March 1st we had lost over forty officers and well over a thousand men; but war had not quite let us go. An epidemic of influenza fell upon us. Half the Transport men went down with it, and in a week we learned that death had overtaken our good Corporal Andrews and with him our young boxer, Dale. The pity of it was painful enough for laughter.'

* * *

The first day of July inevitably brought back memories of the catastrophic opening day of the Battle of the Somme two years earlier. But in 1918 it produced its own special disaster, this time at home and with munition workers, not soldiers, as its victims. There were two huge explosions at Chilwell, Nottinghamshire, the site of Britain's largest shell-filling factory, claiming over 130 lives and leaving scores of wounded, some very seriously. The occasion moved the Parliamentary Secretary to the Ministry of Munitions, Mr Kellaway, to state, in a speech at the opening of an exhibition of women's work in the Midlands just eight days later, that it 'had been the occasion of a display of heroism on the part of the workers as fine as anything which had been recorded in the war'. Quoting the example of the French Government, which had conferred the highest honour in its power on the city of Verdun for its resistance to the great German offensive of 1916, he asked: 'Why should not the Victoria Cross be conferred on this brave factory?' The 'VC' Factory it duly became, in popular reputation if not in actual fact.

The analogy with the fighting fronts was not lost on Mr Kellaway's chief at the Ministry of Munitions, Winston Churchill. In a telegram to Lord Chetwynd, addressed to him at the Chilwell factory, Churchill stated: 'Those who have perished, have died at their stations on the field of duty, and those who have lost their dear ones, should fortify themselves with this thought. The courage and spirit shown by all concerned, both men and women, command our admiration, and the decision to which you have all come, to carry on without a break, is worthy of the spirit which animates our soldiers in the field.'

A poignant echo of what happened so often in 'the field' survives in some hand-written pages in the collection of documents relating to the disaster held in the Imperial War Museum. The explosions were so massive that they left a substantial number of dead who could not be identified. The recurring word 'Unknown' at the end of numerous entries in these pages serves as a reminder of what was happening on a far greater scale in the place where the shells filled with their dangerous contents at Chilwell were intended to be used.

There are other echoes in the citations describing the actions of those who were later given the OBE (the honour of Officer of the Order of the British Empire, a new order established as recently as January 1918) in the wake of the explosion. There were twelve in all, four of them women. Thus of Joan Welcome Clough, it is stated that 'although injured she worked in the Red Cross Station until all the other cases had been dealt with'; of Alison Evelyn McKenzie that 'although suffering from shock, she helped in the rescue work throughout the night'; of Dorothy Nicholls that she showed 'courage and devotion to duty on two occasions when explosions occurred'; and of Margaret Waller that 'she was severely cut by falling glass, but remained at work until she had to be taken to hospital'. The citation relating to the Chilwell chaplain has even more of a Western Front ring about it: 'For courageous devotion to duty. Injured in the head he continued to organise the work of rescue, proceeding with it all night.'

In view of the number of women among the casualties, there is perhaps an irony in that it was only in the previous month that women had at last been given the vote, at this time restricted to those aged over thirty. The right of women to stand for Parliament was also conceded in 1918, in the month in which the war came to an end.

* * *

The summer of 1918 saw the return of a phenomenon which had assumed menacing proportions in the early months of the war: an upsurge of xenophobia directed at all things German. This new epidemic of animosity was so nationalistic in tone that not even comrades-in-arms were exempt from the public's wrath. Thus the Press Bureau issued a so-called 'D notice' (i.e. a formal request to the newspapers to refrain from publishing material deemed not to be in the public interest) urging that the term 'alien' should not be applied to Belgian refugees. There were even complaints that the term was also being applied to citizens of Britain's chief ally, and senior partner through most of the war, France.

The main target, however, was, as before, anything remotely connected to or symbolic of the prime enemy, Germany. People of

German origin who had escaped the earlier comb-out because of their identification with the country now found themselves swept off to internment, including some who had lived long years in Britain, were married to British wives and had sons fighting in the British Army. Massed meetings of anti-German protest were held (including, on 23 July, the biggest demonstration witnessed in Trafalgar Square since the outbreak of war), while in August a monster petition bearing over a million names was carried to Downing Street. Street names with the slightest whiff of German about them were changed, though the royal family, originally named 'Saxe-Coburg-Gotha', was now secure from criticism by virtue of having switched to 'Windsor' the previous year.

That this upsurge of xenophobia could be viewed with favour at the front is evident from a letter of 24 July by an artillery officer, Captain Richard Stokes. 'I wish to goodness they'd intern all these alien blighters,' he told his mother in some vehemence. 'For myself I never wish to see, speak to, or have anything to do with any Hun after the war.' He ended his outburst with a comment which offers a powerful reason for his, and countless other people's, anger at this time; sheer frustration at a log-jammed conflict which seemed to offer no hope of an early positive outcome, in which context any target, token or real, could seem fair game. 'The war may, I suppose,' he wrote gloomily, 'end in a couple of years.'

* * *

There was another matter giving rise to Captain Stokes's anger in the early summer of 1918. 'What about the strikers?' he asked – also in his letter of 24 July – in a comment about protesting munition workers which showed how quickly sympathy engendered by the Chilwell disaster could evaporate: 'They are swine and I hope they ram them all in the Army and shoot one in ten straight away.'

The civilian diarist Frederick Robinson shared this viewpoint precisely. Writing just three days later, he referred approvingly to the current military efforts being made in France and then stated, in some heat:

> While the brave men at the front are doing all this, the munition
> workers at home are again causing trouble and are threatening to

strike en bloc, in fact some thousands in Coventry and Birmingham have already 'downed tools'.

The pity is that one cannot shoot some of these gentry, but that
would probably have the opposite effect to that desired and the
whole lot would probably come out on strike. But these munition
workers have been exempted from military duty because of the
importance of the work they are doing, and if they won't do the
work there is no reason why they should be exempted.

This attitude was becoming public policy even as Robinson was
writing his personal diatribe. He recorded with full approval the
terms of an official notice published that same day to come into
virtually immediate effect: 'It is now necessary for the Government
to declare that all men wilfully absent from their work on or after
Monday, July 29, will be deemed to have voluntarily placed themselves outside the area of munition industries. Their protection
certificates will cease to have effect from that date, and they will
become liable to the provisions of the Military Service Acts.'

The unrest in question was not simply a complaint about money
or conditions; there were certain aspects of the terms of employment
which made the protesting workers feel that they were being unfairly
treated despite their best endeavours. What Robinson does not
record was that the Government also offered a committee of inquiry
into their grievances. The combination of stick and carrot worked,
in that the strike ended but both sides felt they had gained from the
encounter. In the event, despite the ripples of dismay it had caused,
there was little interruption to the making of the necessary munitions
for the national cause.

* * *

What of the situation not in the British homeland, but the Fatherland, in Germany itself?

On 16 June a housewife in a village near Hanover called Grossen
Wieden wrote a letter to her soldier husband on the Western Front;
she was named Lena, her husband Fritz, surname and regiment
unknown. The assumption must be that the letter was either taken
from a prisoner or found on a German soldier's dead body, the latter
case being perhaps the more likely.

Nothing in the letter suggests anything in the way of German triumphalism; if anything the longing for peace is even greater than than evident in the letters of Mrs Elsie Barnett, largely arising from the very large number of fatalities in the writer's immediate area. It offers a moving insight into the mood of an ordinary German family and community in mid-1918:

Beloved Fritz,

Heartiest thanks for your dear letter of the 10th inst. which I received Friday last. I am sorry that I was unable to answer sooner as it always seems to get dark so soon. Hard work never seems to lessen with us but continues to get worse. We would all do it ever so willingly if only this cursed war would come to an end, which we hope will be soon. During the last few days there has been a spirited discussion about peace in the newspapers according to which peace will be declared in March 1919, but I cannot quite believe it; it is already high time but nothing is yet accomplished. We will all be able to realize it when an end is made to all this slaughter. I have already told you about Wilhelm Beisz from Kleiner Wieden; he was killed on June 1st and Henry Nautmeier on the 30th May. A week ago yesterday the Nautmeiers received news that their son Henry had fallen and just a week later a second telegram to the effect that their younger son Ludwig had been killed. What a dreadful blow to the parents to lose two sons in such a short time – scarcely ten days. Yet it seemed to make very little difference, the Lord hath such wondrous ways of comforting bereaved parents, that they bear it all with patient fortitude.

Man in his life is like grass in the fields, he blooms like a flower – but when the scorching winds pass over, he is no more and only once can his bloom be blighted.

Ah my dear Fritz how often I long for you in my soul – yet when the time comes when you are on leave and we are together, I look upon you as a free man and have never a thought of the regrets I had when you were not with me. Alas your leave goes past, and once again your name is at the bottom of the list.

The hay is almost all in store and harvest will be upon us soon and yet we have no rain. Fodder is very scarce, so much so that we can scarcely feed our cattle. Otherwise things are not so bad, except that tomorrow is our sad anniversary. It will be two years then since our beloved and only brother was killed, and what a number have fallen in those two years. We ourselves in this small area can count 33 and yet there is no end.

With heartfelt greetings and in the hope of seeing you soon.

Your own dear and faithful

Lena.

＊ ＊ ＊

At the level of the ordinary soldier on the Western Front the late spring and early summer of 1918 was a time of waiting and uncertainty. Clearly there would be a response to the series of German attacks but they did not know how, where or when.

For many it was back to the old routines of trench warfare as though nothing had changed, while for some it was a case of back to France after having been employed, sometimes dangerously, sometimes less so, in far-off sideshows. This was the fate of the 2nd Post Office Rifles, which had previously served in 60th Division in Palestine and Salonika, and now became part of 30th Division in the theatre where the outcome of the war would ultimately be decided.

Writing in early July, Private H.T. Pope described with a mixture of wit and resignation his return – having been there before he knew the score – to what he called 'this land of slime and slaughter'. 'March about 14 miles, via St Omer, to Nieppe.' he wrote in his diary on 8 July. 'Seems like old times to march over the cobbled roads crowded with military traffic. It has a certain fascination but we do not feel eager to know what the future has in store.'

The battalion's attachment to their new division officially took place on the 10th, on which day they were visited by the GOC of their new Army. Pope noted the event: 'Inspected by white whiskers (Plumer)'. It was not until the 25th that the battalion went up to the front; then on the following day they were ordered to pack and go forward to a point to the right of Mount Kemmel on the Bailleul–Locre road, near Locre Château. They did not like what they found. Pope commented:

What a re-introduction to the Western Front! Very uncomfortable – no trenches. Position very exposed and the only cover a few small shelters built into the side of the road. We stayed here for the day and in the evening took over the front 'line'. There was no line. Only a few shell holes 'improved'. Travers, Fullager, Hawley and I form one Lewis gun post. It was a fairly deep shell hole with a piece of corrugated iron over one side as a shelter – water at the bottom and the sides loose mud. Of course it rained all night. There was continuous shelling and machine-gun bullets flew very close every now and then. We were like shipwrecks on a lonely isle except that the platoon was *somewhere* about and we knew that there were more troops *somewhere* behind – about every hour or so an officer and man would come round to see if we were awake.

Pope's Lewis gun team was fortunate; a fellow team from his battalion was less so: 'In a heavy bombardment towards dawn Pibworth's gun team was knocked out and several were killed and I heard afterwards Pibworth had lost a leg. Eventually we were relieved from this post and went back to the roadside for 24 hours.' They would continue this dour, unproductive routine until well into August.

Elsewhere, however, there had been a notable development which showed that there were ways of discomfiting the enemy, and spreading alarm and despondency in his ranks, while incurring relatively little cost on the Allied side. With their tails up after their striking achievements at Villers-Bretonneux and elsewhere, the Australians, and also the New Zealanders, launched a kind of 'private war' on the Germans opposed to them. As the Australian official historian put it: 'Wherever the ground gave any freedom of movement, these Dominion troops began to pester the enemy, trying to waylay his patrols and cut out his posts. . . . This was supplemented by a series of set attacks, generally planned to capture sections of the new front line from the Germans before they had fully established it. . . . Recalling the methods by which German industry before the war was "capturing" the trade of most British countries, the Diggers called these tactics "Peaceful Penetration".' It might be commented that there was a touch of irony in the selection of the adjective 'peaceful', for often considerable force was used, though there was no doubt about the success of the penetration. In the words of a more recent Australian historian: 'For four months, between April and August, "peaceful penetration" was virtually the only activity on the British front. It suited Australian temperament, for its chief weapons were stealth, individual initiative, patience, and skilled bushcraft. . . . [Their tactics] terrorised the German divisions placed against them, some were disbanded after heavy loss, a few protested at having to re-enter the line opposite Australians, and most feared to face an Australian sector.'

Writing to his wife Lousia in Australia on 30 May, Lieutenant Edwin 'Ted' Trundle, of 26th Battalion, 2nd Australian Division, AIF, reported on some recent operations in this fashion in which he had taken part:

> The weather is beautiful now and the 'strafing' good. I spent all last night in our most advanced outposts fitting them up with fireworks – rockets, flares, etc., and incidentally gave some pals a hand in a little 'Hun-strafing' expedition they were carrying out on one of the Hun's most advanced posts. We crept up and threw about half a dozen bombs into it and then turned a machine-gun on to the Huns as they ran away. At the same time a few of the boys carried out a similar affair on another post a few hundred yards further along the line. In their case they rushed the post instead of using the machine-gun. In this way we are able to keep the Hun busy, killing and capturing a few each night, and of course it's good sport for the lads.

A further letter of 13 June showed clear evidence that the new tactics were having a distinct effect on German morale:

> On the night of the 10th we had another scrap with the Hun lasting for about three hours. During that time we advanced our line nearly half a mile, killed and wounded hundreds of Huns and caught about 300. I caught eight Huns myself. The incident was very funny although a little uncomfortable at the time. I saw these fellows about 10 o'clock running away. They were in some crops close to one of my advanced dumps. I immediately yelled after them whereon they halted and turned towards me. As soon as they saw me they threw up their hands and ran towards me in a mob. At the time I was standing at the door of a dugout and soon found myself inside and alone, confronted with eight big burly Boche. The first of them dropped his hands to his side,

perhaps to come to attention on seeing I was an officer, or to get to his pockets, I don't know which. Anyway it made me feel a bit uncomfortable for a while as I didn't even have a pork sausage to point at him. A pick was lying at my feet so I grabbed this up and threatened to stick it through his 'napper'. This had the effect of putting the wind up the mob and they all threw up their hands again and fell on their knees. The big chap nearest to me cried for mercy – which of course he got. By this time several of my men had rushed up so everything was OK. Well, dear, the whole stunt was most successful and we are all very 'bucked' about it.

The diary of the Australian signaller G.V. Rose confirms that this kind of warfare really did affect the Germans opposite with 'wind up'. Under 29 July he noted the results of a another effective piece of penetration, a distinctly less than peaceful one this time: 'The prisoners started to drift in. I think that some of them had been surprised in No Man's Land, they came in so quickly. The first ones were taken to our dugout and searched. I got a few souvenirs. One man remarked "English ver goot". I showed him my shoulder badge "AUSTRALIA" and he shut up. They did not like the Australians.'

Unconventional was a standard epithet for the Australians; the so-called 'Diggers' were forever marching to their own tune and not only in terms of actions of war. Private Rose recorded certain irregularities of dress at this time which might well have produced cardiac arrest among some of the staider senior officers from the motherland had they been aware of them. The virtually unavoidable depredations of lice, or 'chats' as they were often called, provided the cause. Earlier Rose had described his own reaction to the tedious business of combating these ever-present pests: 'I caught 60 and then knocked off because I was tired; also, as spring was approaching, I threw away my under-shirt and left numbers of them to a lingering death.' But there were others who resorted to much more extreme measures; under the date 26 May he stated:

There was a great shortage of shirts and underpants amongst the lads, and so, as the troops become more and more 'chatty', they took to wearing civilian underclothing, mostly women's. Bill Collins was wearing a chemise with lace at the throat, and ladies'

stockings. Several of the men had drawers on instead of underpants, and I believe that the nurses had many a laugh when some
of our wounded men began to take their clothes off.

Such behaviour no doubt raised a laugh and cheered the spirits,
but it did not affect the overall situation. For 'bucked' as Lieutenant
Trundle's energetic battalion might have been after its taunting of
the enemy, the enemy was still there, and Trundle himself would
acknowledge when looking back on this period from the vantage
point of the year's end how grim was the general mood and how
uncertain seemed the prospects, in spite of the failure of Germany's
series of attacks. 'I'm afraid, Lulu dear,' he would write, 'that the
endless-looking job that seemed to lie before us about the middle of
this year was beginning to tell on us all and making us careless and
dull, afraid to look forward.'

Lance-Corporal Robert Cude – 'much against the grain' he had
been compelled to take a stripe at the behest of his general some
weeks earlier – reacted in a similar way to the small-scale successes
of this period. His 18th Division was also indulging in such activities,
but clearly they were not enough:

> We try almost every night to take a prisoner, but all to no effect.
> We penetrate right into Albert, so incidentally we are sneaking
> ground. This is called 'Peaceful Penetration', but still, it is the
> infliction of very heavy casualties that will decide the time when
> Jerry is to throw up the sponge, and although we must not
> belittle the fact that we are steadily gaining ground, we must not
> lose sight of the fact that Jerry is not losing anything from the
> change [in tactics], except the lack of morale, and I do not think
> that his troops have much of that latter commodity anyway.

* * *

Curiously, at this uncertain time, anxieties of a different kind began
to stir among those who had committed themselves so long to the
cause that they now feared what might happen when that commitment was no longer required. The war had become so pervasive, so
possessive, that it was an essential part of the fabric of their lives. A
classic description of this condition is that of Guy Chapman in
A Passionate Prodigality (already quoted in this chapter). Despite

admitting that his predominant sensation throughout his years at the front had been one of 'shrivelling fear', he acknowledged the growth of 'a compelling fascination': '[And] in that fascination lies War's power. Once you have lain in her arms you can admit no other mistress. You may loathe, you may execrate, but you cannot deny her. No lover can offer you defter caresses, more exquisite tortures, such breaking delights. No wine gives fiercer intoxication, no drug more vivid exaltation. Every writer of imagination who has set down in honesty his experiences has confessed it. Even those who hate her most are prisoners to her spell.'

One who would have no quarrel with such sentiments was Captain Charles Carrington of the Warwickshire Regiment – himself to emerge as a writer of distinction about his experiences under arms – who had worn the King's uniform since volunteering in the summer of 1914. With all its dangers and drawbacks, soldiering had provided a way of life which offered the kind of fulfilment no peacetime occupation could possibly rival. But what would happen when the war ended? As the summer weeks of 1918 unrolled, Carrington viewed the future with increasing concern.

Throughout most of the year he was based in England. He had mixed responses to his situation. Writing on 7 July and looking back on the recent dramatic events in France, he wrote to his most constant correspondent, his mother in far off New Zealand: 'It hurts me to think that such momentous things are happening and I'm not there.' Yet he was also honest enough to accept that his period of active service had had its problems as well as its successes. Though he had emerged with honour and some glory from the Somme campaign, he had had to admit to himself that he had been more or less played out by the time it ended. Nineteen seventeen had been a far less satisfying year than its predecessor, and he had not been entirely unhappy at being sent in December to the less stressful climate of Italy. On leave in England in January 1918 but distinctly out of sorts, he had been persuaded to visit a doctor. Physically there appeared to be nothing wrong with him, but as he put it in the letter already quoted: 'I was glad to stay in England for a spell as my nerves were rotten after last autumn's fighting.'

Remaining for any length of time in hospital, however, seemed to him merely 'masquerading as an invalid', so he persuaded a medical board to pass him fit. It did so, but not yet for service abroad. After a further spell of leave, he found himself in Northumberland with the 5th Reserve battalion of his regiment, engaged in the training of new recruits.

His posting led to a remix of familiar emotions: relief that his nerves were not yet to be challenged by the prospect of combat; frustration at being reduced to a spectator role. But now there was a third element; a sense almost of panic at the thought that the life that had owned him man and boy since 1914 was inexorably approaching its dissolution. A future offering an indefinite peace – the standard aspiration of most men involved in uniform – seemed to him not so much desirable as daunting. It was like contemplating the ending of a long affair. He told his mother, in that same letter of 7 July: 'I'm sorry to say I've got a positive dread of the end of the war, when we shall all drift away from each other, and these enormous bachelor parties will stop. All the younger ones of us will have to make new friendships and professions and interests. I, for one, shall be lost.'

One recurring ordeal Carrington was spared by his home posting was that of returning to the front after leave. It was the unavoidable other side of that much longed-for 'ticket to Blighty' of which most serving soldiers dreamed, whether officer or man, or, it might be added, even senior general. The following extracts are from a letter written on 11 July (just four days after Charles Carrington's musings quoted above) by the 40th Division staff officer, Captain Harry Graham, to his much loved wife Dorothy: his sentiments must have been shared by thousands throughout the war, though they might not always have been expressed with Graham's moving eloquence:

> Shakespeare was an ass when he said that parting was such sweet sorrow: it is the bitterest sorrow in the world. I think that days like yesterday and Tuesday shorten life; one feels older at the end. . . .
>
> Who could have prophesied 4 years ago that at 12 o'clock one morning I should be kissing you under Charing Cross Bridge, and within ten hours be listening to our guns in the Forest of— [Nieppe]. I had a very rough crossing, but bribed a steward to give me his cabin, and lay down and so survived. At Boulogne the rain came down in torrents, an absolute downpour, and I

could find no car. It turned up at 7 p.m. and I got here 3 hours later.

What a perfect leave I did have. Everything about it was wonderful, and there was just the perfect mixture of all the ingredients, moral, physical and meterological, that go to make complete happiness. I thought of you as I sat in the train to Folkestone, and I felt I knew something of what you must be feeling. I know what a sad night you will have had, for I had it myself. Oh, the futile waste of time, the waste of companionship, of all that is most priceless in life – it makes me mad to realize it. . . .

* * *

The recruits whose training Carrington was helping to supervise were mostly teenagers: the men of eighteen of 1918, on whom the nation now increasingly had to rely as the fighting continued without sign of abatement.

That not all went willingly to an ordeal which they knew would be formidable and might very easily be fatal is evident from a letter by Private E.J. 'Ted' Poole, 19th Reserve Battalion, London Regiment (the story of whose brief service and early death is told in the Foreword; see pp. xxv–xxvi). Himself a 1918 conscript, he accepted his new situation philosophically and tried hard to become a competent soldier. But he was aware of others in his camp at Aldershot who were not so minded. He wrote on 5 June: 'We have got a lot of prisoners in the next room to us (when I say prisoners, I mean boys who have run away and have been caught) and you ought to see how they guard them. When they have their meals, there are two or three soldiers round them with fixed bayonets, and if one of them wants to go to the WC, a soldier goes with him, and there are two soldiers outside the door of our block, with fixed bayonets, day and night.'

Yet 1918 still had its quota of eager, even ardent warriors. One such was Private, later Lance-Corporal, Frank Earley, from Derby, who had already started a career as a journalist before joining up in June 1917. His very first letter from his training camp (to 'my dear Father and all') set a breezy, optimistic tone that would characterize all his correspondence, excepting only his last letter of all: 'I think we are all going to be happy, or most of us. I think I am; I am sure, in fact. The life is wonderfully healthy, and when once my feet are better I shall enjoy it wonderfully.'

His enthusiasm continued despite the unfortunate example set by some of his comrades. Thus on 24 November 1917: 'I can say with truth that the months I have spent at this camp have been ones in which I have had the best health I have had in my life. The air, the food, everything seems to suit me. I sleep well, eat well, I am well in every way. This has been a great blessing to me, thanks be to God; because the life here has made absolute wrecks of some poor fellows.'

His first letter of 1918, on 25 January, contained no heart-searching thoughts about the war or the prospects ahead. Snow had fallen on the camp and he was happy to report a benign, almost Dickensian response to it in which all ranks seem to have joined: 'There was continuous snow-balling; and, after the surface had frozen, snow sports of all kinds. You should have seen the toboggan-ing down the slopes of the valley opposite our last huts! Colonels and privates, WAACs and Barrack Wardens were snow-balling each other impartially, sliding and riding the snow in the sleighs! Such whizzings and shoutings, such shouts and laughings, never were, I think.'

Earley was not among those sent as reinforcements during the German spring offensives. In fact it was not until 18 July that he could send a letter from 'somewhere in France'. He reported his arrival with relish:

Our ship was escorted by destroyers and airships. The sea was calm, and the boat so steady that no one felt any qualm. At last we saw the coast. We drew nearer. I looked and looked, it seemed so strange to see France! Soon we entered a harbour filled with fishing smacks. We drew alongside a wondrous pier, overgrown with sea-moss, dark and green. On it stood a strange crowd – smart French soldiers in their blue uniforms, officers and grinning Chinese coolies. Soon the gangway was secured. I crossed it. My foot trod French soil for the first time in my life. I will never forget how I felt.

Thro' the sunshine we marched, under the lee of a big hill where was the old church with its church tower. With a band in front we set off under the trees. Little children ran screeching by us. A man threw off his hat with fine gesture – *Vive l'Angleterre!* Then on, by an orphanage of the Sisters of St. Vincent de Paul, by a fine church, and up a tremendous hill between quaint – and dirty – houses. Women offered beer at a shilling a bottle. All the way it was *'Bière*, sair?' At last the big hill was surmounted and we came to our camp.

Concluding his account he told his family: 'Well, as you see I have started the great adventure. The first act is over. What the others may be I cannot yet say.'

Nine days later he wrote to say that he had been posted to a battalion of the King's Own Yorkshire Light Infantry, the 1/5th. There was no diminution in his high spirits: 'As you see, I am still alive and well, and as usual enjoying life to the full.' This in spite of, or indeed because of, his now being close enough to the line to be within enemy artillery range:

Last night, the guns were firing as they are now. Every now and then would come a whistle and a crash. This meant that Fritz had sent over a shell to remind us of him. They kept whistling over the barn all the night thro', but at long intervals. I think Jerry is getting a hot time here, and the worst of things.

I cannot tell you where I am, but I think I can say that I am well in the heart of France, and in a famous front.

Send me news of how you all are at home, and rest assured that I am enjoying myself – in spite of straw beds and Boche shells. This is an adventurous life anyway.

Sadly for Frank Earley it would not be an adventurous life for long.

* * *

Politically and militarily, the summer of 1918 was a time for much serious reflection on the Allied side. Rogerson's 'Last of the Ebb' – the Chemin des Dames campaign of May–June – had ended, just to their advantage, but the shock of the Germans' near success had brought them, in particular the French, to a new sense of reality. They had had to yield more of their heartland to the enemy and to do so with some ignominy. Their Prime Minister, Georges

Clemenceau, was to call that campaign a 'lamentable rout'. In so defining it he caught a swing of mood among many French people who had tended to assume that the setbacks of March and April could not happen to them but were due to a lack of fibre or commitment on the part of the British. They now recognized that they too were vulnerable and the Alliance was the stronger for this new understanding.

A second consequence was the abandonment of the Duchêne concept of keeping massed forces close to the line and stubbornly refusing to give ground: a strategy that had signalled its weakness with particular clarity in the Battle of the Aisne. Pétain's 'prudent policy in defence' – to quote the Australian official historian, C.E.W. Bean – was now the dominant philosophy. The French C.-in-C. believed that as a result of his schemes of 'defence in depth', the enemy's bombardment of forward areas would be largely wasted, while attacking enemy infantry, harassed and divided by strongly defended French outposts, would lose cohesion and impetus before they ever got near the real line of resistance. The effect of this new policy was seen in mid-July when the Germans made what really would be their final throw of 1918.

This action has been described in outline in the previous chapter, with special emphasis on the contribution of the Americans. It only remains here to note the outcome and the consequences. When the German attacks faltered after their less than successful launch on the 14th, the French drew breath and, on the 18th, delivered a stunning counter-blow which shocked the enemy as much as it surprised him. Ludendorff was caught far off in Flanders, preparing yet another attack which would now never take place. He had no alternative but to order troops which he had been deploying to the north to return at once to the south. But this would all be in vain. At last the time had come for him to acknowledge that his best efforts had been thwarted and, in effect, to throw in the towel. The Germans instructed their forces in the Marne salient to withdraw. In the words of the Australian official historian: 'Their 1918 offensive had failed. Ludendorff, like Micawber, could only hope for something to turn up.'

Private Earley's comment just quoted – 'I think Jerry is getting a hot time here, and the worst of things' – had in fact registered an important truth. The 'possibility of a disaster' as seriously contemplated by Colonel Hankey in early June was no longer on the agenda by the end of July. The initiative had now, at last, passed decidedly to the Allies.

8

ALLIED ADVANCE: AUGUST AND AFTER

FOR GERMANY IN 1918, August, not April, was the cruellest month. Before it was over even so stalwart a warrior as Leutnant Ernst Jünger – signalled out for special praise in a Divisional Order issued on the 12th, and destined in September to receive Germany's highest military honour, *Pour le Mérite* – was forced to recognize that his country would lose the war, though there was pride as well as grief in the admission: 'By this time there was not a man who did not know that we were on a precipitous descent, and the fact was accepted with an equanimity that only the moral force which in every army accompanies its armed force can explain. Every man knew that victory could no longer be ours. But the enemy should know that he fought against men of honour.'

Yet the month began with no presentiment of disaster on the German side. On the 4th Ludendorff issued an order of the day which began with a stern rebuke to any who feared or suspected that the Allies were about to seize the initiative: 'I am under the impression that, in many quarters, the possibility of an enemy offensive is viewed with a certain degree of apprehension. There is nothing to justify this apprehension, provided our troops are vigilant and do their duty.'

Four days later, on a date to become infamous in German military history, Ludendorff's confidence was blown away by an offensive of such overwhelming authority that it can be claimed that it marked the beginning of the end of the First World War. 'The black day of the German Army' was Ludendorff's own description of what would be recorded in the histories as the first day of the Battle of Amiens. For the Allies it was the breakthrough that had been dreamed of for so long. It produced such a swing of mood that it

would stand high for those involved among the war's most unforgettable experiences. Thus one participant officer, Captain Oliver
Woodward, of the 1st Australian Tunnelling Company, could later
write (in a comment understandably concentrating on the outstanding contribution of his own countrymen, though equally high praise
was due elsewhere):

> Only those present can understand the great feeling of relief
> which followed this glorious attack of the Australian Corps. For
> some months we had seemed to be living under the fear that the
> enemy might at any moment launch another great attack, which
> possibly might be as successful as his early one. We were up and
> about before zero hour on the 8th, wondering what success
> would be ours in the coming attack. We were to measure swords
> with the enemy. Failure might mean anything. Yet, at 9 a.m., we
> felt that once again we were on top, and that we would eventually
> win the War. How and when this end would be reached did not
> concern the individual. The essential fact was that one; and all
> recognized that we had the game well in hand and eventually the
> winning goal would be kicked. Our whole viewpoint had been
> changed in a few hours.
>
> Early next morning I inspected a great portion of the area
> which had been so brilliantly captured, and it may be difficult to
> believe that except for the sound of the guns ahead, I walked over
> this area unable to imagine that 24 hours earlier it was in the
> hands of the enemy.

A potent element in the production of this outstanding success
had been surprise. Surprise had been a strong weapon in the German
offensives earlier in the year and now it was used with telling effect
by the Allies. Added to that was a soundly based confidence, a sense
of assurance that the deed could be done, and a professionalism that
was a world away from the clumsy techniques which had prevailed
in this same area of France just over two years earlier. Such professionalism was not just a matter of attitude and focus, it was a product
of practical concepts carefully evolved and rigorously employed.
Wireless was beginning to be used in battlefield communications, a
notable if at this stage far from universal advance in an area where
hitherto reliance had been placed on vulnerable overland lines or

even more vulnerable runners. Aircraft now combined their standard reconnaissance role with the new aggressive one of ground attack. The new Mark V tank was available in such numbers – there were 342 of them – as to make their contribution (at least in the first phase) central rather than marginal. There were also 120 supply tanks, plus seventy-two of the lighter 'Whippet' tanks poised to work with the cavalry in exploiting any Allied success. In infantry fighting the new-style, self-contained, highly trained platoons, complete with bombers, grenadiers and Lewis gunners, were ready to prove their worth. Integration of effort and the close collaboration of all arms involved were now the standard policy, enforced with emphatic determination by General Rawlinson, who, as GOC of the British Fourth Army, was back in the region of his former, controversial efforts of 1916 but was now controlling his campaign with a distinctly surer touch. Meanwhile, ready to launch a surprise bombardment were over 2,000 guns, organized by Major-General C.E.D. Budworth, who has been described as the Fourth Army's answer to the German master-artillerist Colonel Bruchmüller. This time an advance across the landscape of the Somme region would be markedly different from the sacrificial, attritional grind of two years earlier; it would have vigour, style, even panache, though it would have numerous local setbacks and would still, inevitably, exact a massive toll in casualties. And a hundred days later, there would at last be silence on the Western Front.

Deception of the enemy as to the Allies' intentions played a vital part in producing the necessary surprise. The Canadians, like the Australians a force of formidable reputation, were required for the attack, but they had been for some time attached to Plumer's Second Army in Flanders. Two battalions were left there with instructions to keep up a steady flow of false signals traffic, while the remainder of the Canadian Corps was brought to the Amiens sector in a series of deft nocturnal moves which left little or no evidence for the German spotter planes.

Early in the following year, while recovering from wounds in the Canadian hospital at Taplow, Berkshire, Herbert L. Witherby, an NCO of the 20th Lethbridge Battery, Canadian Field Artillery, wrote a striking description of this phase of the 1918 campaign. At thirty-eight somewhat older than many of his fellow soldiers, by trade a farmer from Alberta with a great love of horses, he had inevitably been drawn to an arm where the horse was crucial; a compassion for the animals he served with clearly underlies his whole approach to war:

The night marches were most fearfully hard on us, especially towards morning, it was so hard to keep awake. I was in charge of 'A' Sub-section, consisting of one Gun with a six horse team, and two Ammunition Wagons each with six horse teams on them. I had to keep riding up and down, shaking the drivers and gunners to keep them awake, and this helped me to keep awake myself.

We would draw into some tree-lined field about 5 o'clock in the morning, and pulling the vehicles well into the hedges, etc., would lie the horses up under cover, already watered and fed. And then for our breakfast. How hungry we would be, how good the fried bacon smelt, how delicious the tea tasted; then for sleep, blessed sleep. I would take a blanket off my saddle and dive into a cool shady spot, and sleep. Whistles and shouts would get us together some hours later, to feed and water up, and have dinner, then we would lie around, smoke and talk until early evening, when we would water and feed up for the last time and have supper, then orders would come round for the night's march.

Everyone starts getting ready, the drivers harness up, the gunners repack the ammunition wagons and gun limbers, and see that everything is secure. At dusk the whistle goes and the drivers 'hook in' their teams, the Section Officer rides round and looks over everything, asking me if all is ready for the road. At last the Major rides on to the scene and we get orders to 'Stand to our horses', then to 'Mount', and once again we go off into the night. Already the dry choking dust is thick everywhere, everywhere are big guns pulled by tractors, lesser guns pulled by lorries, and countless field guns, all going the same way.

We had about three nights and days like this, then we arrived at some large woods before it was light early one morning. We pulled all vehicles right up into the underbush, and then as a further precaution cut branches and covered them over, the horses were tied close into the bush, and we were cautioned to keep under cover during daylight.

Up to now, we knew nothing whatever of what was expected of us. On the morning of the 6th August the NCOs were got together and told for the first time of the work we were going to do.

To reach their intended staging point they went through Amiens itself – a 'fine well built city,' Witherby recalled, 'we must have driven through some of the best parts, because I saw one building evidently a fine theatre, and several other very fine buildings.' In normal circumstances to take such a route would have been unwise, since such large population centres would almost certainly have their spies and informants, but as a deliberate policy the Picardy capital had been emptied of its civilians and so presented no hazard in the matter of the betrayal of intelligence. On the night of the 6th the 20th Lethbridge Battery took up its assigned position for the advance, in woods near Villers-Bretonneux.

We drove away from the camp, on to one of those wonderful, straight, pavéd, tree-lined roads running from Amiens, the star shells becoming plainer, and the gun fire clearer all the time. We soon turned off this 'Route Nationale' and went down a sunken road, with all the evidences of war, trees knocked about, shell holes, broken wagons, etc. Shelling was going on just ahead of us, eventually we got through, and got our guns into the woods, losing one man, Bombardier Pearson, who was killed. We were very close to the line and had to be careful to cover up the guns and equipment against enemy observing planes.

The woods were shelled all night, stopping about daybreak, but no one else was hit; all day of the 7th we rested well, had the last orders and lay low. This was all we had to do; keep out of sight.

* * *

The main thrust of the coming offensive was to be shared between the Canadians and the Australians, while the substantial British contribution would include no fewer than twelve tank battalions. The French First Army under General Debeney would attack further south. A vivid chronicle of the Australian effort during the Amiens

battle survives in the diary of Major Donald Dunbar Coutts, of the
Australian Army Medical Corps, then serving with the 24th Battalion, 6th Brigade, 2nd Australian Division. Having been involved
in the Third Battle of Ypres from the previous September, he was no
novice at war, and though his 1918 diary records numerous successes
he is far from triumphalist and is always ready to acknowledge
setbacks and difficulties or his own times of fear and anxiety. Thus
his account of Tuesday 6 August includes the admission: 'Felt very
"windy" this morning for some reason or other. Didn't like getting
out of the sap at all.' Once out and about he observed the evidence
of preparations for the attack which he had only realized was
imminent from the previous Friday, 2 August, when he had noted:
'Rumours of Stunt in a few days. New guns coming up every day.
Camouflaged dumps of ammunition lying about everywhere.' Now
the process was rapidly intensifying: 'Saw a lot of new 18-pounder
batteries in position about Bn. Hdqrs. There are small dumps of
ammunition scattered about ready for the guns to come up to them
after the barrage opens. Saw a lot of artillerymen from all divisions –
also lines of ammunition wagons and guns coming up.' His own
special responsibilities in the matter of maintaining the battalion's
health and well-being briefly demanded attention: 'I met Colonel
and he complained about the sanitation – asked me to go round with
the Adjutant and improve matters.'

Later he reported to his senior medical officer at Brigade who
took him into his confidence about the time of the expected attack:
'Ellis told me as a secret that the hop-over was to be on the 8th in
the morning. Saw barrage maps, objectives, etc. Colonel had Company Commanders at the dugout – he read the operation orders to
us, and told us all our parts in the show.' The plans thus disclosed
showed with what precision and foresight the offensive had been
planned: 'The battalion was to be withdrawn from the front line, to
leave it free from troops, 10 minutes before zero. Everybody was
to keep in the trenches, because our guns at first would be firing at
such short range that the shells would be skimming the ground.'
Reacting to this he and Ellis went to the Regimental Aid Post and
arranged to get a party of men from one of the battalion companies
to deepen the trench adjacent to it, 'so that we could do dressings in
the open during the stunt. Party turned up about 3 p.m. and worked

till 5 p.m. – drained the trench and deepened it about a foot. Heavy shelling all night.'

There was sporadic shelling all next day. One missile landed on top of the Signal Office next to the RAP and fatally buried five men. The shelling continued into the evening until about 11.30 p.m., then suddenly stopped: 'It was a very anxious time, as we were expecting a shell to get us at any minute. The nearest one landed on the parapet of the trench in front of the RAP door, and the concussion shook us up pretty badly.' About midnight they caught a distinctive sound slowly approaching from the rear: 'We could hear the tanks coming up for the hop over. One crossed the trench near the RAP.' But there was also another sound, a louder one, mingling with the tanks' unmistakable growl: 'A few of our aeroplanes were flying overhead with the throttles open, to make as much noise as possible, so that the Hun could not hear the tanks.'

This, it should be interposed, was just one part of a sophisticated plan devised by the RAF commander, Major-General Salmond, to give the Allies air superiority at the start of the attack. He would follow up this initial contribution by delivering, at first light, a concentrated assault with his bombers and fighters on all nearby German airfields. More, by keeping air activity at a normal level in the build-up to the battle, he had achieved another coup in the matter of deceiving the enemy, with the result that the Germans still had their main air concentration many miles away, in the vicinity of Reims.

More and more officers and men crowded into the Aid Post, Coutts noted, among them twenty stretcher-bearers who arrived about 12.30. The tension rose, but so did the sense of anticipation: 'Everybody was excited and very optimistic about the possibilities of the stunt.' When the time came for the forward troops to go back to the old front line, 'a good many of the men refused to go back, because they wanted to have a good view of the stunt.'

At last the waiting was over, and at 4.20 a.m. on Thursday 8 August the Battle of Amiens began. 'The battery of 18-pounders just behind us,' Coutts observed, 'which had been firing intermittently all night, opened with a burst, and immediately afterwards we could hear every gun on our front open up.'

An eloquent description of this defining moment appears in the account by the Australian Corps Commander, Lieutenant-General Sir John Monash:

> And suddenly, with a mighty roar, more than a thousand guns begin the symphony. A great illumination lights up the Eastern Horizon: and instantly the whole complex organisation, extending far back to areas almost beyond earshot of the guns, begins to move forward; every man, every unit, every vehicle and every tank on the appointed tasks and to their designated goals, sweeping on relentlessly and irresistibly. Viewed from a high vantage point and in the glimmer of the breaking day, a great artillery barrage surely surpasses in dynamic splendour any other manifestation of collective human effort.

* * *

Captain Henry Smeddle was to command a section of three Mark V Star tanks in the Amiens battle. He had enlisted in June 1915 in the Army Service Corps, from which he had been formally discharged in July 1917, with the modest rank of Lance-Corporal, to take up a commission in the recently formed Tank Corps. The fact that he had been an engineer in civilian life was no doubt crucial in allowing him to make the step from a single stripe on the arm to three stars on the shoulder, though his having been for two years at a public school, Dulwich College, might also have assisted the transition. He had been posted to the Tank Corps' 15th Battalion. Late in 1918 he would write a detailed description of his experiences of the previous summer. His account is of particular interest in that it shows some of the ways in which tanks and foot soldiers collaborated at this very early stage in the development of armoured warfare. He explained his battalion's proposed role in the action:

> On this occasion we were not actually what might be termed 'shock troops', but were intended to start from a point about 1500 yards behind the front line at ZERO+1, (which in plain English means one hour after the commencement of the attack), and to follow the advancing infantry and tanks, until a point known as the red line had been reached and consolidated. This was the second objective. Here the leading infantry would stop, and it was our duty to pass through them and proceed to another

line, the blue line, a line of old trenches intended for the defence
of Amiens prior to the German advance in the spring. In these
trenches our 'passengers' were to be dropped; they consisted of
twelve machine-gunners with ammunition and guns in each tank.
Afterwards the ground in front for a distance of 250 to 500 yards
was to be patrolled by our tanks which in the event of a counter-
attack would be able to deal with most things which might come
along in the shape of German infantry.

Smeddle's account also offers abundant evidence of the meticulous attention to detail and the elaborate efforts to achieve surprise
which have already been seen as being an essential part of the Amiens
offensive. As was the case with the Canadian guns, careful conceal-
ment was the rule in the case of the British tanks. A few days before
the attack, in the early hours of the morning, the battalion had been
discreetly concealed in deep country some ten miles to the north-
east of Amiens: 'Our Tankodrome consisted of a long line of elms
on the banks of a canal; their leafy foliage aided by our camouflage
nets amply protected our tanks from the prying of any scouting
aeroplane.' Following a conference of section commanders at Company headquarters, at which details and plans of the forthcoming
operations were discussed, Smeddle returned to his section to give
his men a rough outline of the proposed action 'excepting the actual
date, time and location, which would only be given at the last
moment'.

Smeddle spent the day before the attack in careful professional
preparations, supervising the laying of tapes – 'this was done without
undue exposure, as we were well within view of enemy observation
posts' – and, through the circumspect use of communication trenches
giving access to the front line, making sure that he obtained 'a good
look over the ground which we were to pass with our tanks on the
following day'.

The effort to achieve surprise was also evident in the precise rules
as to what could or could not be done during the approach to the
start line: 'There was to be no smoking, or flashing of electric
torches, and no shouting, whistling, or unnecessary noise during the
march. Only tank commanders would be allowed to smoke; the
glow of their cigarettes was to be the method by which they would

guide their tanks whilst walking in front without undue attention.'
Anticipating questions that might arise in the mind of anyone
reading his account, Smeddle commented: 'One might think that all
these precautions were superfluous and unnecessary when the noise
of the tanks alone is sufficient to drown any lesser sound like talking
or shouting, but it is astonishing how a single human voice when
raised will carry far beyond the dull mechanical roar of the tanks,
which from a distance would not be distinct enough to give the
unaccustomed ear any idea that tanks were in the vicinity.'

As they began their move forward at 1.30 a.m. on the 8th, the
tanks proceeded at no more than a slow walking pace – again, in
order to produce minimal noise – while the distance between tanks
was kept at twenty-five yards, the speed of the column being
regulated by the speed of its slowest vehicle. Thanks to the well-laid
tapes they were soon in their assigned positions. Smeddle recalled
that, as zero hour approached, 'the silence seemed like that preceding
a storm, the occasional crackle of machine-guns in the distance or a
far-off boom of heavy artillery being the only sounds that met the
ear, yet there were only minutes to go before the commencement of
one of the greatest battles of the war'.

When the barrage started, 'it broke the silence with a terrific
crashing roar, flashes were spurting up from all round where we
were standing. It was still dark, but the flashes of the guns gave out
sufficient light to distinguish the forms of the gunners and guns, the
nearest of which was twenty-five yards from where I was standing,
and so quietly had everything been prepared that I was not aware of
its presence until it started firing.'

* * *

Some twenty minutes after the start of the bombardment, Major
Coutts stepped out from his Aid Post, to find that a phenomenon
which had aided the Germans back in March was now in turn
assisting the Allies: 'It was just getting light, but there was a heavy
fog, so thick that you could not see more than ten yards in front of
you.'

Fog and smoke might confuse the enemy, but they also had
disadvantage for the Allies, particularly those whose forte was
advancing at speed. Visibility was so restricted that when Sergeant

Witherby's 20th Lethbridge Battery went into action he could at first hardly distinguish the two officers walking just ahead of him. He was aware that they were heading eastwards not over open country but along some kind of road, though there was no visual clue as to where precisely they were going. Soon their pace of advance began to quicken, and the attack became a series of impressions, some heroic, some horrific, that would stay with him the more vividly for the strain and tension of the battle and the increasingly hectic pace at which they were now charging into it:

> We were travelling fast, the sweat was rolling down my face, the shells were bursting everywhere, some of them very low, only just seeming to skim our heads and to burst not far from the road that we were travelling on. Machine-gun bullets also whistled over us from the left flank, where the advance had been held up for a while. We had not gone far up this road before out of the smoke came a team of horses alone, trotting down the road with their harness on. I knew them at once, for one of the teams had gone ahead of us; I knew by this that things were happening somewhere ahead, through that awful smoke. Soon after, one of the gunners of 'E' Sub-section came walking down the road holding his left arm which had been hit. No one spoke to him; you just had to get ahead on these occasions, regardless of what was happening around you. Then we came upon the other section. The first thing I saw was one of the drivers lying face down in the dust, dead. Some horses were lying in a heap, where the shell had landed. On the left, I saw someone pulling one of the other drivers, also dead, out of the way into a shell hole. A man's feelings get blunted at these sights, and his mind being fully occupied by the work in hand, he has no time to consider such things in the sad and awful light of what they really are. All I remember was that I turned round and shouted to the lead driver of my gun to swing out, so as to avoid the man in the road and the dead horses. It's strange how small details on such occasions remain riveted in one's mind; I can well remember how well this man's spurs seemed to stand out from the dust and grime, bright and shining. But there was no time to consider anything at such a time, all one thought of was 'to get on' and through with the job.

The mist and smoke were lifting fast now, and we could see further around us – on our right was a shallow trench, used by the Germans that morning, and some dead Germans lying there. Bunches of prisoners were coming across country, in some cases absolutely unattended, only too glad to get out of battle. We halted. We soon got our range and angle, and then started firing, the orders coming through by phone from our Observing Officer ahead who was in touch with the Battery.

The sun was getting high in the heavens now, and the day was becoming quite hot, the mist and smoke had practically all lifted, and we could see a great distance on all sides. Just then a large fleet of tanks came up and passed us; I think they must have been spotted by a Hun aeroplane or observation balloon, because they drew a heavy fire just ahead of us, some of the shells came quite close, and the Major shouted for us all to take cover in the shallow trench to our right. We were glad to to do this for a time, because the shells were coming over thick and fast, as if the Germans were firing their guns for all they were worth before they lost them. When things quieted down we went on with our firing; we soon however got orders that we were out of range and so stopped. While we waited for further orders, we had the first rest since we had started out in the early morning. We had some bully beef and drank water from our bottles, and then had a chance to look round, and there was a great sight of tanks, infantry, cavalry, transport, all going forward, a wonderful sight.

Amidst all the evidence of a massive European war, a memory came to him of the great plains of Canada from which he had come to help to fight it:

It was now about 9 a.m. and the sun was well up. It was fine hot day, a typical August morning, just such a day that in Western Canada puts the finishing touch to the ripening wheat.

*　*　*

Seeing precisely where he was going had been a problem for Captain Henry Smeddle and his tanks when they began their advance at the appointed hour of zero plus one. 'The first part of our route was down a steep incline at the bottom of which were the trenches forming the British front line, but owing to the thick mist it was very difficult to keep the sense of direction.' Making good use of his pocket compass, however, he guided his section to the trenches, to find them virtually empty as the infantry and the first wave of tanks had already gone forward. Soon they were meeting batches of wounded and German prisoners coming the other way: 'From information I got from some of the wounded things were going splendidly and very little infantry opposition was being met with; from the number of dead lying about I judged this to be correct.' That the enemy was not entirely inactive, however, became evident when, in improving visibility, they halted at a refuelling point in Warfusée valley to fill up with oil and petrol: 'Several German planes came over machine-gunning our advancing infantry, but from what I could see not inflicting many casualties. Unfortunately one of my runners who was standing near me received a bullet in his stomach. We did what we could and sent him back on a stretcher, but the poor fellow died before reaching the dressing station.'

They then proceeded to their first objective, where as they approached they found themselves the focus of an unfamiliar but already potent weapon of war: 'At this point one of the official cinema operators came along and filmed my tanks as they were moving along.'

Shortly afterwards the shell fire became more intense, and the young captain had a very near escape: 'A nose cap from a shell struck the tank two feet from my face and ricocheted off into the air with a bizzzzs.' Nevertheless the opposition they encountered as they moved forward was, on the whole, surprisingly small; indeed they soon discovered that the Germans were in such disarray following the shock of the Allied attack that they were offering the easiest of targets:

> The enemy were evidently quite unaware of the rapidity of our advance, for just as we were about opposite Harbonnières we saw an ammunition train steaming into the station as if nothing was the matter. It was immediately shelled by all the 6-pdr guns of the approaching tanks. One shell must have struck a powder van for suddenly the whole train burst into one great sheet of flame, reaching to a height of not less than 150 feet. Needless to say that train was stopped.

It was followed by another one, a passenger train rushing up fresh troops; this was running on another track and ran right into our lines where it was captured, complete with personnel.

* * *

All this suggested a scale of advance well beyond the dreams of most of those taking part, and the euphoria would continue, though there would inevitably be setbacks and difficulties as the campaign continued. Something of the excitement engendered by the success of this August push survives in a letter by the Australian infantry officer, Lieutenant Edwin 'Ted' Trundle, written to his wife, when he was finally able to put pen to paper, on the 12th. The start of the month had found him engaged in a four-weeks training course at a 'most delightful spot right on the coast', where he had been entirely unaware of the prospect of the stirring events to come. The weather had been ideal and in spite of it being what he dubbed 'a pretty strenuous course' he had found ample time for sea-bathing. Indeed he pronounced himself as having been restored to the pink of condition; since he had been the unfortunate sufferer of several minor wounds this was no mean claim. However: 'It all came to an end very suddenly after just one week. About 11 a.m. last Monday I received an urgent wire through Army HQ to return to Bde HQ at once and a motor car turned up to take me back. I got back to HQ about midnight the same night to find it was the eve of this huge battle you have been reading about during the last few days. From then on I have been on the go day and night until today.'

He had been summoned by his General to take charge of the Brigade's ammunition supplies during the attack, and his new responsibilities had been recognized by being given what he described as 'a new "pip"'. Having made clear to his wife that this meant that next time she should write to him as 'Captain E.F. Trundle', he summed up the gains of the Allied offensive so far:

> During the last few days we have advanced over twelve miles and captured a huge number of prisoners and much booty, so you can guess we have been kept on the move. It is no small job to keep a whole Brigade supplied with ammunition during a continuous battle like this one, particularly when they are moving the

whole time. However up to the present everything has gone excellently and everyone is in high spirits.

The attack completely surprised the Hun. I followed the attacking infantry with a team of thirty-six pack-mules carrying ammunition forward and had a dump established within a couple of hundred yards of the most advanced troops within half an hour of the objectives being reached which was about seven miles into the Hun defences. Ever since then we have kept continually moving forward until now we are over twelve miles ahead of our starting position.

Writing on the same day, 12 August, Acting Captain Gordon Hassell, now adjutant of his 8th Battalion, the Tank Corps (the same who had written so stalwartly on the last day of 1917 of the need to keep up the struggle, asserting 'we would be cowards else'), praised the Allied achievement in a cheerful letter to his family:

Organisation was perfect; as for advancing the speed was terrific. Within a few moments of the Huns running from our Tanks and Infantry, groups of men were repairing the roads for traffic, guns were coming up into new forward positions, and *we* were going down into Warfusée-Abancourt to establish a HQ. There we found that the barrage had absolutely left no house standing – everything was demolished, and so we set up the flag in the open (near some dugouts), and I remained to receive reports from the Companies while the CO went ahead with our Reconnaissance Officer to see the progress of our 'busses' [i.e. tanks.]

It was glorious once again to be in the rush of an advance. So different from March, when *we* were the ones on the backward trail.

Hassell took particular satisfaction from the fact that the Picardy capital had been largely spared and, with its environs, was already showing signs of returning to some kind of normality:

Amiens will very quickly become populated again. Already (and indeed it was on the night of the 8th that it began) trains are puffing about what has been for three and a half months a deserted city; and in this village (on its outskirts) I have already seen several people coming back. The advance has liberated hundreds of acres of crops and today bands of French and Aus. soldiers are reaping.

It is a glorious thing to feel that thousands and thousands of homes (intact with all furniture etc.) will once again open. The cathedral has only suffered one or two slight hits, and although it is true that there are a great many wreckages of houses and shops, the city is really habitable and has literally been saved.

As for the contribution made, and the cost paid, by his own service arm: 'Some of my friends are unfortunately wounded; as a Battalion we did four days fighting, and so suffered somewhat severely; but the Corps and Fourth Army acknowledge that we were instrumental in *saving* thousands of casualties among the infantry, which is our role in life.'

The Battle of Amiens was undoubtedly proving a tremendous success. So much had already been claimed by General Rawlinson himself, writing on the 9th to his fellow general, Sir Henry Wilson. He told him, in evident satisfaction: 'I think we have given the Boche a pretty good bump this time.'

* * *

There was 'another black day' for Ludendorff – admitted as such – on the 20th, when General Mangin launched the French Tenth Army against the German Ninth Army in the region of the River Oise. Although they had expected the attack, the Germans nevertheless were forced back some two to three miles. For Foch this was a further sign that the enemy, already discomfited on the Marne and now hit hard opposite Amiens, was severely shaken along the whole Front, thus making it vital that every opportunity of sustaining pressure on him must be eagerly seized. He said as much in a message to Haig, praising him for the 'moral ascendancy' he had now gained over the Germans, and urging further effort without timidity and 'with violence'. Haig responded by urging, in regard to his own troops, 'the necessity for all ranks to act with the utmost boldness and resolution in order to get full advantage from the present favourable position'. Significantly, he added: 'Risks which a month ago would have been criminal to incur, ought now to be incurred as a duty. It is no longer necessary to advance in regular lines step by step. . . . A vigorous offensive . . . will cost us much less than if we attempted to deal with the present situation in a half-hearted manner.'

Quoting this forceful message, a distinguished historian of 1918, Gregory Blaxland, has commented: 'Appeals of this nature had been made before. Indeed, Allenby had issued one very similar in wording after his Third Army had successfully broken into the Hindenburg Line at the opening of the Battle of Arras [in 1917]. It had caused death and derision, little else. But now at last there was real justification for a more daring approach. . . . The enemy's morale was low and his defences were shoddy, and Haig had the guns and the tanks to spread his offensive over a wide frontage, thus enabling him to retain the initiative by making frequent switches of pressure.'

It is worth adding that another sign of the grasp and confidence with which Haig was marshalling his forces at this time was his willingness for his commanders, at all levels, to make their own judgement and use their own initiative. This campaign was being run on a much looser rein than had previously been the case, and it showed.

The advance was soon claiming notable trophies. Albert fell to the British 18th (Eastern) Division of Fourth Army on the 22nd. Of sentimental memory to thousands of British who had marched through it when going to or from the great Somme battle of 1916, this was a particularly important prize, except that by now after four years of continuous warfare it had almost ceased to exist. Major C.H. Lemmon of the Royal Field Artillery, ordered to march his battery to and billet in Albert immediately after its liberation, found his instructions extremely difficult to carry out:

Our maps showed that we were approaching Albert, but in the evening light no town could be seen at all, and I realised all at once that we could not *billet* in Albert, because, for all practical purposes, there was no such place. A jumbled mass of stone and iron-work on our left was identified with difficulty as a cemetery, and then we entered a street, represented by two rows of brick heaps, in which there was hardly a cellar intact.

A guide met us, and soon afterwards, my billeting officer, Westrop. He had hardly found any ground where horse-lines could be put up, as the whole place was a mass of builder's rubbish and barbed wire. He had only found one or two cellars as possible accommodation.

Darkness fell as we were pulling headquarters' wagons into the allotted patch of ground. The acting R.S.M. was in a grumbling mood, and things were not too cheerful. By dint of poking about in the rubbish, we found a wood-house [sic], and a loose-box. The wood-house was constituted as the mess. Underneath was an old dugout, where two officers elected to sleep, and the other three of us slept in the mess. The men had another dugout, a shattered cottage, and a few holes in the ground.

Nor was there the consoling sight of that totem of the war's earlier years, the tall tower of the Albert basilica, with its famous hanging statue of the Virgin and Child. That (as has been described in Chapter 4) was now long gone, while the smashed basilica was now just one larger, more contorted heap of ruins amid the general desolation.

* * *

Meanwhile Sir Julian Byng's Third Army, whose earlier, more halting progress had in part prompted the vehemence of Haig's message as quoted above, was showing its paces to the north of Albert, and in a way only possible in 1918. German intelligence forwarded to the local commander offered – in the words of another distinguished historian of 1918, Barrie Pitt – 'the curious, and to him heartening discovery: fifty per cent of Byng's infantry could well be described as "boys" – and undernourished ones at that, for they consisted largely of those troops hastily rushed out to France after a most inadequate training, in response to the emergencies created by the St Quentin and Lys Battles. For many of them this was, in fact, their first taste of action.' Pitt's account continues:

> Thus encouraged, the Germans brought up close reserves and launched one of their more aggressive counter-attacks – which ran into point-blank fire from the field artillery, then arriving on the scene with a fortunate but unusual timeliness. Despite heavy casualties, the counter-attack was pressed until it was finally broken – and indeed, flung back – by the unyielding defence of

the 'boys', who had had time by now to dig themselves in and who were armed, not only with an adequate supply of machine-guns, but also with their own ignorance augmented by an as yet unshaken faith in their leaders. By nightfall the Germans were back in their own lines, leaving their dead to litter the battlefield, and feelings of considerable satisfaction to hearten their enemies.

The 'Byng Boys' was the name these young men took for themselves, and they wore the title like a badge of pride. Claiming rather more expertise and sophistication than the description above allows them, one of them would later write: 'We were young; we were very fit; we had been trained and now we were quite acclimatised in spirit to a war in which death was a general expectation and the loss of a limb was counted a lucky escape.' They had also acquired very rapidly the standard 'Tommy' attitude to what was generally known as 'a Blighty one': 'A wound that would take one back to dear old Blighty was always an occasion for congratulations from one's comrades.' The author of these comments, then Corporal F.J. Hedges of the 10th Lancashire Fusiliers – in a book published seventy years later under the apt title *Men of 18 in 1918* – would quote with obvious satisfaction the verdict of an official account of this action: 'The "Boys" having been now "blooded" fought like veterans.'

Also with the Third Army at this time, newly moved to its IV Corps, were the veterans of the 63rd (Royal Naval) Division. Captain Harold Horne, Royal Marines, noted the following in his diary on 25 August (in an entry showing how near they had now got to the next prime target-town of Bapaume):

5.30 a.m. Battalion attacked enemy positions in front of and in the village of Le Barque, 2 miles S.W. of Bapaume, on the main Bapaume-Albert road. The final objective was reached at 6.50 a.m. and the position immediately consolidated. This operation resulted in the capture of 150 prisoners, 2 trench mortars, 60 machine-guns and much material. Two enemy counter-attacks were repulsed.

The Third Army continued its hard-fought but powerful advance, Bapaume being pocketed by the highly competent New Zealand Division (also part of IV Corps) on the 29th.

Meanwhile the Fourth Army was picking its way one by one through the famous, or infamous, villages and woods of the Somme. In the diary of Lance-Corporal Robert Cude of the 7th Buffs, 18th Division, the familiar names stand out: Bécourt, Mametz Wood, Trônes Wood, Bernafay Wood, Combles. The last named was attacked on 1 September: 'We go over with the E. Surreys, and so rapid was the advance that we bagged a German Red Cross Ambulance, with driver and Doctor inside. They were unaware that we were so close, and I do not think that they relished our appearance.' Major F.J. Rice RFA, CO of C Battery, 82nd Brigade, also in 18th Division, defined the mood of the moment in a letter to his parents written just two days earlier: 'The war seems to be going very well. We have had a very strenuous time, but we can all stick more if we are advancing.'

* * *

One and a half kilometres to the north of the town of Péronne, set back from the road to Bapaume in a tiny village, the sturdy statue of an Australian soldier in his distinctive swept-back cap, standing feet astride on a substantial plinth, catches the eye of the driver heading along that busy route nationale – the N17. The road's gentle rise from Péronne, aided by a curtain of roadside trees, obscures the fact that the statue is on the apex of a hill which dominates the open ground falling away to the west. The hill is known as Mont St Quentin (a name unconnected with the city of St Quentin thirty kilometres to the south) and in the late summer of 1918 it was a key strong point in a major defence line established by the Germans after they had been pushed back across the River Somme. With its daunting frontage of barbed wire and maze of interconnecting trenches, at that time entirely bare of trees and commanding ground bereft of cover, it was considered by its defenders to be impregnable. This was not the view of the Australians, however, a thousand of whom, on 31 August, 'yelling like a lot of bushrangers' (at the inspired suggestion of one of their officers, Captain E.T. Manefield), attacked the position and overran it. The Germans, applying overwhelming force, rallied and drove the attackers back, but only to a point just below the summit. Next day, 1 September, the Australians had their revenge, seizing the hill and advancing beyond it, while at the same time they emphasized their dramatic victory by liberating most of Péronne itself. On the 2nd the advance was consolidated as they took the rest of Péronne and also made ground to the north. Summing up what he called 'this brilliant action', their official historian, C.E.W. Bean, recorded that 'without tanks or creeping barrage, the Australians at a cost of 3,000 casualties dealt a stunning blow to five German divisions.' The 'Digger' on his plinth marks this outstanding achievement.

The Australian medical officer, Major Coutts, whose base was an aid post set up in a ravine which was part of the unfinished Canal du Nord, recorded the progress of events in his diary, at intervals during the long work of caring for the inevitable mass of wounded. 'Our men had done wonders in the attack,' he noted, writing on 1 September. 'Heard that the Huns had counter-attacked early this morning, and driven the 5th Brigade out. Our men had a very bad time from shelling all through the night, and we had a good many killed; but today they attacked up the hill against deadly machine-gun fire, and the village was captured about 11 a.m.' The success had meant unremitting work by himself and his medical team: 'Continued dressing wounded all day, until about 9.30 p.m. The Battalion stretcher-bearers have done wonderful work. Some of them have done seven or eight trips between the village and the ravine.' Afterwards he would recommend twelve of them for the Military Medal. Meanwhile, although the ravine might be safe from the enemy's high explosives, it was not secure from that other frequent artillery hazard – gas shells: 'During the night, the Hun gassed us. The ravine got full of gas, and it got into all the dugouts. We had to wear our masks nearly all night.'

It was not until the 5th that he was at last able to visit the site of the recent fighting: 'Got up at dawn and walked to Mont St Quentin. Found the dugout where one of our men had captured twenty Huns. There were machine-guns everywhere, and dead Huns lying round them. There was a high brick wall along the main street, with machine-guns everywhere, and all around the village were wire entanglements. Lots of Hun material about and plenty of good souvenirs. Hun began to shell village whilst I was there, so I left.' He returned to his battalion: 'a very small one now, all the men have been terribly knocked out, but in good spirits.' Their morale was happily bolstered on the following day when the survivors withdrew to return to their billets. As Coutts described it, 'about 10 o'clock the band came out and met us, and played the battalion back all the way to Cappy. We marched all along the Somme Canal.'

The 24th Battalion was awarded many decorations following this action, among them numerous Military Medals, so presumably some at least of Coutts's recommendations were accepted. The battalion's authorized history also states: 'Major D.D. Coutts, the Battalion's medical officer, who had displayed marked valour and devotion in many engagements, was awarded the DSO.'

Of the memorial itself the battalion history claims that 'it marks the scene of one of the greatest victories of the AIF'.

* * *

Just to the north of Mont St Quentin on the N17 lies the little village of Bouchavesnes. Its one remaining relic of the war is a statue of Foch, also plinthed like that of the Australian a kilometre or two to the south; head held high, uniformed as a Marshal of France, the figure stares imperiously in the direction of the great advance of 1918. But in that victorious final campaign this was the scene of fierce fighting conducted not by the French, but by the British, in an attack which both helped and benefited from the Australian success just described. A.R. Armfield, at that time a twenty-year-old second lieutenant, has left a remarkable account of the action, from which it is evident that the set-piece 'over the top' attack, seen as the norm in the years of trench warfare and of virtually all battles from Neuve Chapelle to Third Ypres, could still take place, and could still be as sacrificial, in 1918. Looking back with a much later perspective but with a vivid recall of sensation and detail, Armfield would write of this aspect of First World War experience:

Only those who have gone 'over the top' understand the full meaning of the term. In the cold light of dawn, or in the darkness and confusion of night, deliberately to climb out of the comparative safety of the trench exposed to a sheet of flying metal – sharp, jagged deadly metal – coming from a determined, skilful enemy in hidden, prepared positions, is an ordeal to test the morale of the strongest, and one that none who endured it and survived ever forgot. Each attack was an unspectacular 'Charge of the Light Brigade'. To repeat this ordeal once, twice or three times, at short intervals, was to test courage, self-sacrifice and human endurance to the uttermost. Yet this was the lot of all those British Infantry Divisions that were engaged, particularly on the Somme, at this time, and it was the final instalment of the price of Victory in 1918.

Armfield's battalion was the 2/4th Battalion, London Regiment, 47th (London) Division, he himself being in command of a platoon in 'D' Company. Three battalions were involved; the 2/4th to the right, the 3rd London on the left, with the 2/2nd Londons in support. The attack, timed for 1 September, was to be made behind a creeping shrapnel barrage: 'To get the full benefit of this type of barrage the advancing infantry had to be positioned, throughout the operation, almost beneath the exploding shells.' Enemy defence was in depth: 'Forward of their front line were irregularly sited isolated machine-gun posts in shallow gun-pits protected by barbed-wire entanglements – veritable suicide positions from which to inflict heavy loss upon us before receiving their own "coup de grâce".' These 'condemned men', Armfield commented, would perform their assigned tasks courageously. This kind of tactic was a notable phenomenon of the 1918 campaign that produced a high casualty toll on both sides. Failure to 'mop up' thoroughly in such circumstances could mean that many men were ignominiously shot down from the rear as they concentrated on their forward advance. On the German side, the chances of survival of such machine-gun teams were arguably as great as that of the Japanese Kamikaze pilots of the Second World War.

Zero-hour, on a cold but fine and clear morning, was at 5.30:

I watched the minute hand moving slowly to the appointed time then, drawing my revolver, I called 'Here we go, lads!' and clambered out of the trench followed by my platoon, well aware that wherever I went they would faithfully follow for as long as they could stand on their feet. That certainty rested on complete trust and understanding between the infantry officer and his men in the field.

The ground was grass-covered and flat, without trees, sloping gently up to the rubble that had once been the town of Bouch-avesnes. Attack formation at this time was in 'blobs' – small sections, or parties, or four or five men moving forward at walking pace at about 20 yards interval from each other. Thus if one section was held up the others would go forward independently under their own section leader. There was no cover whatever: even had there been we were not expected to take advantage of it – that was implicit in the provision of a creeping barrage. The troops were expected to move steadily to their objective or until shot down or halted temporarily by heavy machine-gun fire or other fire from directly ahead, when sections on right and left would continue to advance, and bring fire to bear from the flanks upon the enemy point of resistance.

Soon after leaving the assembly trench and advancing over this open, gently rising ground, a runner came forward to tell me that a single enemy shell had wiped out the Company Commander (2nd Lieut. Prince) and his entire headquarters party, and that I was now in command. I acknowledged the message, and continued to advance with my platoon. In my right hand I carried a drawn revolver, my single offensive weapon. The men carried rifles with fixed bayonets, each platoon including a Lewis gun section. Heavy machine-gun fire was opened right ahead of my 'blob' and I paused and rested on one knee to survey the position and to direct the fire of my Lewis gunner.

Quarter right I saw Capt. Griffiths, Officer commanding 'A' Company, striding ahead of the advancing line to encourage his men, waving his walking stick above his head in a manner befitting a knight of old calling 'For St. George and Merrie England'. But I expect he was shouting fire orders.

Soon both the remaining platoon commanders, 2nd Lieuts Gant and Gilson, were killed. Captain Griffiths then moved forward to take over personal command of the remnants of his three leading platoons in order to ensure that the advance was maintained.

Griffiths was the senior officer among the advancing troops and, I believe, felt that no sacrifice on his part was too great to ensure the success of the operation. Deliberately he made himself conspicuous to his men, showing his complete disregard for danger, thus encouraging and inspiring in them a similar spirit. I believe his splendid example was an inspiration to all around him. Unfortunately he was equally conspicuous to the enemy and fell mortally wounded, but not before he and his party had succeeded in overcoming the machine-gun post that barred their way.

More officers fell until it seemed to Armfield, as he looked along the steadily advancing but thinning lines of men, that he was the only one left in the whole battalion. Shortly afterwards there occurred a strange, intense moment of battle that would remain always with him:

So that I might survey the forward position I had stopped in a very shallow depression about seven feet in diameter, the forward lip of which was then lined, in prone position, by my Lewis gun section of three men. After a few moments, I ordered the section to follow me forward. They did not stir, and when I turned towards them, my eyes looked through a gaping hole in a steel helmet, into a bloody mass that had been a human brain. All three men were dead. I recalled that as I was scanning ahead, I thought I had seen out of the corner of my eye the head of one gunner fall gently forward, without a sound; or perhaps no human cry could be heard amid the clatter of shrapnel shells overhead, the crump of high explosives on the ground, the rattle of machine-guns and the crack of rifle fire.

Pulling the Lewis gun from beneath the dead gunner, I cleaned his life's blood from the butt of the gun on to the green, understanding French grass, and handed the gun and drum of ammunition to two other soldiers who had now come up and joined me.

The advance continued, the men moving forward steadily, undismayed and undeterred alike by the shells and bullets as by the sight of comrades stricken down at their side, some men firing their rifles from the hip as they walked. Their splendid indifference to danger made a vivid and lasting impression on my mind; I have always remembered with great pride the fine conduct of my troops during this attack. Nothing would have prevented them from reaching their objective except death or a wound.

We passed on and quickly reached the objective, a line of trenches along the crest of slightly elevated ground. I jumped down into the German trench followed by an NCO and about eight men. The trench was deserted except for some bodies of dead Germans. Later, I noticed the sad manner of the death of one of these. Evidently a piece of shell had carried away the whole calf of his leg, baring it to the bone. He had dragged half of his body into a 'cubby-hole' at the bottom of the trench side, there to die quietly, in the dark, his face hidden from the world. He was respected and grieved for, in death, by at least one enemy soldier.

The battalion would undertake a further attack just over a week later, on 10 September; although its casualties were lighter on this occasion it would emerge so reduced in numbers that it would shortly be disbanded, its surviving personnel being incorporated in the 2/2nd battalion. The attack of 1 September, resulting in the taking of many prisoners and guns, and an advance of 3,000 yards over bullet-swept, shrapnel-strewn, shell-torn open land would remain the battalion's finest, as it was also its final, action. Yet, to Armfield's distress, no decorations were awarded for it; in the hurry and confusion of so strenuous a time such matters as the conferring of honours for individual deeds of valour could, he admitted, almost seem on the level of triviality. But he was particularly sad at the failure to reward the memory of one fine, brave young officer: 'I have always felt that 2nd Lieutenant, Acting Captain F.J. Griffiths, aged 23 years, showed in his conduct that day something beyond the standard of courage normally expected of all soldiers. For his devotion to duty, determination to ensure the success of the operation and disregard for his own life, I would have awarded him then, as I would now, the highest decoration, although it must, alas! have been posthumous.'

* * *

On the same day as the Bouchavesnes attack, Lance-Corporal Frank Earley – he had recently been promoted – wrote two letters home.

In the first, to his two young sisters, Win and Louie, and dated 'Sunday morning 1 Sept. 1918', he was his typically cheerful self, making the best of things, seeing the positive side of the less than luxurious conditions in which he found himself:

I received your two letters last night, and sat reading them until about eleven o'clock, they were so long. Would you like to know where I read them? It was in my little dugout, my home these last two or three days. I am in a narrow trench about four feet deep, and my dugout is a hole scooped out of the trench side and roofed over with a piece of corrugated iron. When, at night, we settle to rest, and hang up the oilsheets at the openings, and light our candle, we are quite comfortable, and happy. You must know that we have good companions – fine, big earwigs, who run about the walls all day and night. They are much bigger than those you know at home, and look very fierce. I like to watch them crawling about, and running out of the way of the big field spiders. See what grand amusement I have!

Later he wrote a second letter, dated 'Sunday afternoon 1 Sept 1918'. This time there was no conversational preamble; instead he went straight to the heart of the serious reflections uppermost in his mind. The following is its complete text:

My dear Father,

It is a strange feeling to me, but a very real one, that every letter now that I write home to you or to the little sisters may be the last that I shall write and you read. I do not want you to think that I am depressed; indeed on the contrary, I am very cheerful. But out here, in odd moments, the realization comes to me how very close death is to us. A week ago I was talking with a man, a Catholic, from Preston, who had been out here for nearly four years, untouched. He was looking forward with certainty to going on leave soon. And now he is dead – killed in a moment during our last advance. Well it was God's will.

I say this to you because I hope that you will realise, as I do, the possibility of the like happening to myself. I feel very glad that I can look the fact in the face without fear or misgiving. Much as I hope to live thro' it all for your sakes and my little sisters, I am quite prepared to give my life, as so many have done before me. All I can do is to put myself in God's hands for him to decide. And you and the little ones pray for me to the Sacred Heart and Our Lady.

I hope that you will not have to move out of the old house

yet. Write and let me know when anything happens. I see that
you went to Weston a few days ago. It seems years and years
since I tried to get drowned in the canal.

Well, I have not much time left and I must end.

With my dear love. Pray for me.

> Your son,
> Frank

Documents retained with his letters indicate that next day he suffered
a severe wound to the chest and, some hours later, died of wounds
at a casualty clearing station. He was aged nineteen. The Official
History shows that his battalion was caught under severe shell fire
on 2 September when waiting to make an attack. Whether it was a
sense of premonition or, more simply, the awareness of yet another
impending action that drove him to write to his father in such
sombre terms it is impossible to say.

Earley was a conscientious and intelligent soldier who had given
much thought to what would happen, and what attitudes might
prevail, once the war was won. These last letters will not be his final
contribution to this narrative.

* * *

On 2 September it was the Canadians' turn as in the northern sector
to the east of Arras they smashed through the elaborate defences of
an outwork, or offshoot, of the Hindenburg Line, labelled in English
terminology the 'Drocourt-Quéant Switch', and reached the open
country beyond. The Germans' somewhat more accessible name for
it was Wotan, and there were other lines or sub-lines facing the
advancing Allies with similar Wagnerian connotations: among them
Siegfried, Hagen, Alberich, Brünnhilde. It is curiously ironic that all
these names were taken from the final opera of Wagner's *Ring*:
Götterdämmerung, known in English as 'The Twilight of the Gods'.
No doubt there was an overtone of Teutonic defiance in the choice
of such resonant titles, though an alternative interpretation might be
that it was as though there was a recognition that the German
Valhalla was in imminent danger of collapse, and that if such were
the case the only way to face the inevitable was by striking the
grand, heroic gesture, and by proclaiming an unflinching faith in

their country's enduring cultural values. In such a context it is perhaps not irrelevant to quote the final sentence of Ernst Jünger's *Storm of Steel*: 'Though force without and barbarity within conglomerate in sombre clouds, yet as long as the blade of a sword will strike a spark in the night may it be said: Germany lives and Germany shall never go under!'

Jünger's words, of course, relate to the situation of two months later, when the curtain had come down on Germany's war. For the moment there was still much hard fighting to be done. 'We have been going hammer and tongs since August 20th and we are all a bit battered and exhausted.' So wrote, in somewhat earthier terms, Lieutenant Harry Siepmann of 400th Battery RFA, 31st Division, in a note in his diary on 7 September.

Each branch of the service had its problems as the armies settled into the new, unfamiliar war of movement, with endless shifts to fresh ground creating immense difficulties, not least in the matter of supply. There was a constant requirement to sustain the guns, the men, and – pre-eminently, in Siepmann's case – the horses; in effect the living muscles of the artillery, on which all its weapons (apart from the very heaviest, which were moved by tractors) depended for everything except such minimal manoeuvres as could be achieved by manpower. But ammunition, food and fodder were not the only requirements. His diary note continued:

> The great problem for me has been water. My horses use 10 gallons a day each and I have to find the water for the men as well, and for the little washing that we do. Most wells are dry and all pumping installations are hammered to pieces by our shell fire. The country is parched and thirsty and I have been at my wits' end. Of course the wastage of all sorts has been tremendous. I started the battle over-equipped. I am now threadbare. I have lost my saddlers, and my harness is getting useless for want of repair. My vehicles are shaken to pieces and all the wheels are loose. And my poor horses, that looked so well! My own dear little chestnut has been killed and my groom is wounded. Yesterday I had a man killed by one of those infernal machines that the enemy manage to leave behind them in a hurry. Still, it has been a great battle and a pretty notable victory, and I would not have missed it for anything.

It was indeed a time for which so many had dreamed, for now the Germans were, if not on the run, certainly conceding much ground and showing distinct signs of disarray. 'It is very strenuous in the front line just now,' Lieutenant-Colonel Walter Vignoles had written just three days earlier, on 4 September, 'continually chasing the Boche, moving forward every day, no billets, no shelters; everyone sleeping under hedges or in shell holes. The Boche is burning all the farms, and as three-quarters of a French farm is wood it doesn't leave much. There is no doubt that Fritz is in a great mess.'

Sometimes, indeed, he was retreating so fast he was not even there. A letter of early September by Private Frederick Noakes, now with the 1st Coldstream Guards, describes an attack that signally failed to find its intended target:

> The arrangement was that we were to attack about midday, relieving another battalion which had gone 'over the top' at dawn. When we arrived at the front line, however, there was no sign of Fritz or of our men, and even the guns were silent. Fritz had not waited for the attack, but had made off during the night! We, following, were marching for the best part of the day, and only towards evening did we get anywhere near the new positions. It was a most strange day. We kept meeting men coming back, and every time their reply was the same: 'We can't find the enemy'; 'We've lost Fritz.' There were scarcely any dead on the field. I only remember seeing three, and I didn't see a wounded man all day. I wish all battles were like that.

Yet there was still plenty of fight in the Germans and it was clear that much hard campaigning lay ahead, so much so that there was no general assumption that the war was rapidly approaching its conclusion. Vignoles, for example, had written of the enemy as September began: 'I think we should settle him next year'; adding, in terms which must have been widely used at this period: 'If only the Yanks had been fully trained and organized now, I think we could have finished it this year, but we'll give him something pretty hot next spring, I expect.'

*   *   *

In fact the 'Yanks' were now becoming increasingly involved, and before many days were out the American Expeditionary Force would acquire its proudest battle honour of the war with its offensive at St Mihiel.

The essence of this action was that it was an attempt to take out a salient – a 'pocket', as the Americans tended to call it – of German-held territory to the south-east of Verdun. St Mihiel's occupancy by the enemy had taunted the French ever since 1914; shown on maps of the Western Front as a triangular sector obtruding noticeably into the sacred soil of France so near to the especially sacred soil of Verdun, it cried out for attention now that the Allies were at last dictating the terms. It fell to the Americans, if with strong French support in men and *matériel*, to undertake the necessary task.

The attack was launched on 12 September, with Pershing in command. The strike force consisted of twelve American divisions, making a total of 550,000 men; the French provided 110,000. The battle opened at 1 a.m. with an artillery bombardment by over 3,000 guns, none of them, as it happened, of American manufacture, though over half – 1,681 – were manned by American crews. The main American attack, on the southern face of the salient, went in at 5 a.m.; the Franco-American attack, on its western face, followed three hours later. The day went well, with the taking of 15,000 prisoners and 460 guns, though at the expense of 7,000 American casualties. A somewhat irresolute defence by the Germans contributed to the American victory, but victory nevertheless it was. For Pershing this was a vindication of his policy of fighting as a distinct national army. Among the accolades which flowed in were tributes from Foch, Haig and the American President, whose enthusiastic endorsement – 'The boys have done what we expected of them and done it in a way we most admire' – precisely reflected the mood of the nation back home.

'Our attack was a complete success,' wrote Private Sam Ross of the 42nd (Rainbow) Division on 21 September, adding: 'The Huns' defence was very feeble, our artillery took all the fight out of them and then the boys advanced so quickly that the "Dutchmen" [as ever Ross wrote Dutchmen for Deutschers] never even got started. We captured thousands of prisoners and they were glad to be captured too, there was a continuous stream of them passing us all the time day and night.'

Achievement had been duly followed by celebration: 'We went for thirty-six hours without eating, we were dug in outside a small town that had been occupied by the Huns two days previous. Three of us went into the town and cooked up the meal of our lives, we had a rabbit each, beans, onions, barley pan cakes, jam and coffee, all German stuff and after that we fed mostly off the Dutch supplies – they left enough behind to keep us all going for some time.'

The Machine Gun Battalion CO Major Leland B. Garretson, was also involved in this action, though only peripherally. He would make light of his contribution in a letter written just after the Armistice: 'On the night of September 13th we and one of the Infantry Regiments went into the St Mihiel salient, to cut off and clean up the so-called "pocket". We bussed and marched for three days and nights, and in our wanderings practically crossed the upper part of the salient, but as a fight it was a joke, for we never fired a shot and all we saw were many destroyed Boche trenches and dugouts, and any quantity of hungry Austrians who were anxious to do anything in the world but fight, and whose favourite form of sport was eating.'

But there was harder fighting to come. Garretson's letter continued: 'Our next effort was on September 26th, at least it began on that day and we came out seventeen days later.'

He was referring to a battle which would provide as hard a challenge as, by contrast, the fight for St Mihiel had been, relatively, an easy one. This was not, however, an action on its own; it was part of the great last heave which would bring all the Allied armies engaged – British, French, American, Belgian – to a sudden, astonishing, if undoubtedly sacrificial, victory.

However, before turning to that final Western Front campaign, it is time to look at the situation elsewhere in the last months and weeks of war, and also at an aspect touched on only lightly so far, the response of civilians to the pressures and anxieties of 1918.

9

CIVILIANS AND SIDESHOWS

'THINGS BEGIN TO LOOK ever so much brighter than they did, and everyone is going about with a much lighter step and a much lighter heart.' So commented Mrs Ethel Bilborough in her diary following the Allied success in August. Her next entry was not written until the end of October, by which time her mood had changed from one of relief mixed with cautious optimism to one of happy and amazed incredulity: 'This has been a most eventful month, and it seems impossible to believe that the end is in sight at last. Is it really true that after these four interminable years of uphill fighting, and grappling against tremendous odds, we are finally *going to win*?'

If it had been a long haul for the soldiers, it had also been a time of great trial for the civilians. Indeed, it could almost seem that, for the first time in any war, there was little distinction between the two roles. A year earlier, in the dark days of November 1917, commenting angrily on the air raids that had become such a regular phenomenon of the domestic scene, Mrs Bilborough had written: 'But as someone said the other day, "There are no civilians now, we are all soldiers."'

She had, however, added to that statement: 'Still, soldiers have the power to *hit back*, but what chance have poor frightened folk in their beds?'

Cheerfully coping with shortages was one way of helping the national cause that did not occur to everybody, but it did to Mrs Bilborough in the difficult months before rationing resolved the difficult situation of food shortages. She had written in January 1918: 'Meat is getting scarce and we have had no butter or margarine for a fortnight! I am rather glad, because when one is struggling with a slice of horrid dry toast that rebels against going down, one really feels one is at last taking part in the War!!' Initially suspicious of the introduction of rationing, she had settled to it with a will; hence this comment in June following the premature death of the man responsible for imposing the scheme, Viscount Rhondda, the Welsh colliery owner and former Liberal MP:

> Lord Rhondda, the great Food Controller, has just died. Poor man! he had rationed himself too severely, and when he got ill with pleurisy or something, he had no strength left to fight against it. But he will be much missed, for he worked out the appalling problem of placing England under food rations, with amazing skill and foresight. It was he who introduced the ration cards which every soul has had: no one could get any meat or butter or bacon or poultry without presenting in exchange an absurd little coupon. Neither at a restaurant nor an hotel may one procure meat without one, though a 'half portion' is permitted, in which case the coupon is divided! In years to come people will hardly believe that such things really *were*, and yet they not only exist at the present day, but the whole scheme has succeeded wonderfully well, in spite of the stupendous difficulties that had to be overcome.

She allowed herself a certain amount of spleen, however, about one decision of which she strongly disapproved: 'Why in the world should we adopt the French word "coupon" I wonder? And the funny thing is that the French have adopted an *English* one for the same thing, and talk about their "teekets".' This reaction, however, might well be put at the door of the upsurge of antipathy to both aliens and allies in the uneasy middle months of the year (see Chapter 7, p. 174).

For Robert Saunders, headmaster of the village school at Fletching, Sussex, the best means of hitting back at the enemy was to join with a will the national campaign to make the country more self-sufficient. The King had set an example months before by digging potatoes, and, in a pledge of 1917 which his subjects were invited to endorse, had publicly renounced 'all unnecessary consumption of grain' as being 'the surest and most effectual means of defeating the devices of our enemies, and thereby of bringing the War to a speedy and successful termination'. Posters of the time suggested how the public might respond: on the one hand 'Save Wheat and Help the Fleet: Eat less Bread': on the other 'Grow More Food'. Saunders took the latter injunction conscientiously to heart. A valuable commentator on the war by virtue of the fact that throughout it he wrote regular letters explaining home conditions to a son in Canada, he provides a useful barometer of the volatile, ever changing moods of 1918. The letter he wrote on Sunday 12 May dealt with the two matters then uppermost in his mind; the first, by now almost an obsession, was his and his school's garden:

> We have had a much better week for gardening and have been able to make better progress. On Monday the ground was still very wet but still it was possible to do something. On Tuesday it rained most of the day. All the rest of the week was fine and dry and the sun was very strong, so that you got very hot at work, though out of the sun the wind was very cold. I had a headache on Thursday so couldn't do anything beyond get through school as well as I could. On Friday I was all right and yesterday I had a good day and finished digging to the bottom of the garden. Now I have only to fine the ground down and sow some cauliflowers, broccoli, savoys, onions for salad, radish, etc. then I shall only have the trimming up to do.
>
> I wish I could say the same of the school garden which, at present, is a kind of nightmare. I put in a lot of extra time last week with the boys, but the ground wants so much preparation before being fit and we only managed to get in three rows of potatoes and four rows of onions. The rows are thirty feet across. This week if the weather is suitable I want to get in carrots, beet, parsnips, beans and the various cabbage for the autumn and winter, then I can rest content to enjoy Whitsun without worrying about seeds that ought to be in.

The other matter on his mind was the ever present, unavoidable war: 'We can't get away from the War even on the most peaceful day. Aeroplanes or Airships passing over, distant guns rumbling, or the nearer practice of Bombs, Mines and Machine Guns at the camp at Maresfield. Every day we hear of casualties among people we know, this week Wally Gordon and F. Brooks missing, P. Triggs wounded, W. Triggs gassed, L. Davidson prisoner, Chapman wounds, etc.'

A letter of 16 June reported unhappily that 'taking the spring right through it has been a most unfavourable one for the garden'.

Apples were also showing signs of failing: 'A farmer at Piltdown who has a big orchard of apples says he won't get a bushel. The papers are advising people to grow marrows for jam to make up for the fruit shortage, but I don't think anything can take the place of apples.' However, his next letter, written on 23 June, recorded a heartening success on his own patch: 'I dug up some potatoes, "Sharpe's Express", just one root and found thirteen. Now I shall have no peace unless I keep digging.'

*   *   *

For many young women there had been other ways of helping the cause ever since the beginning of the war. They had served as nurses and ambulance drivers, and as members of the forces in uniform.

Several moving accounts relating specifically to 1918 have survived written by women who played a valuable supporting role close to the line, while still essentially retaining their civilian status.

Alison Strathy was born in 1891 in Montreal, Canada, the daughter of Lieutenant-Colonel Strathy of the 5th Royal Scots, aide de camp to Lord Aberdeen, then Governor-General. Though from a distinctly privileged background – 'there were seven servants to run our house, and we had four horses mainly to run the family coach' – she had no qualms at immersing herself in the demanding circumstances of the Western Front. Her motivation and the nature of her work are evident from the opening entries in her diary, begun in the last days of May:

> At this time the Germans were advancing on Paris again, and they were not sending women over unless necessary. It was through the kindness of a family friend, Col. Gerald Birks, that I was given my papers.
>
> Marguerite had told me there were many jobs – just to get over there.
>
> In the last two years, May 1916 to 1918, we have lost fifty friends killed in action, not counting those wounded, or prisoners.
>
> *May 29th.* Left for France – saw myself off.
>
> *May 30th.* 3.00 a.m. dropped anchor off Le Havre.
>   8.00 a.m. on shore.
>   The train left Le Havre at 5.30 p.m. and we arrived in Paris at

10.15 p.m. Couldn't find Marguerite so went to the Hotel Petrograd, Rue Caumartin.

Got to my room just as the hotel lights were switched off, and the sirens started an air raid warning. I opened my window, the raid was on, and I could see shrapnel bursting from the bombs in the sky. I unlocked my bag, dropped my clothes, got into bed in the dark and went to sleep.

May 31st. Marguerite came in from St. Cloud. We went round (at her suggestion) to the American Red Cross and I have a job as 'Nurse's Aide'. It is a new job to tide over the present rush of wounded. One nurse and one aide make a team. We must both speak French and will be lent to the *'Service de Santé'*. We shall be sent to French hospitals where American boys may be sent as patients. As there is not time for me to order a uniform I may wear my navy blue suit with a *'brassard'* (armband).

It was some weeks before Alison Strathy encountered the harsh realities for which her role had been devised. To begin with her diary was filled with descriptions of pleasing social engagements and moments of high spirits; as for example when – literally – in the field towards the end of June: 'One night when all our world had gone to sleep, the moonlight was so enticing, Bea suggested we should go out and dance among the corn stalks, stacked in high pyramids. So we put a chair by the window and climbed over the sill – it was warm and still and lovely – so we danced like fairies. Fairies only wear wings! – but what if *Le Patron* (the old farmer) had wakened and looked out of the upper window – I think he would have had a fit.' On another occasion she and a colleague were offered a lift by, of all people, General Pétain, an episode which resulted over some weeks in a gallant exchange of correspondence and compliments. But things changed markedly with the start of the Battle of the Marne:

July 20th. GAS. Young chap prised his eyes open and remarked: *'que vous êtes jeune!'* [how young you are!]. I even got *'que vous êtes jolie!'* [how pretty you are!]. Bea was busy all day with the wounded. My legs ache!

July 21st. Just busy, all day.

July 22nd. 8–8 p.m. again. One of the negroes died from gas.

Most of them are slight cases, and much better after their eyes are washed free of matter, and they are beginning to walk about. Some of the orderlies have been on duty for 48 hours.

July 23rd. Another gas case died, a young French lad. He was out of his head most of the time and quite violent – twice he tried to escape out of the window.

The bad cases suffer terribly, coughing their lungs out.

This a.m. a pneumonia case died in another hut.

July 26th. Yesterday I was as sick as the dickens and felt awful – maybe the gas? But managed to go this a.m. and found another empty bed in Barrack 7 – the sergeant had died at 4.30 a.m. I think it was to his sister I said 'Don't leave him'. His parents had to return to Paris as they were working people.

The little 20-year-old is still fighting hard for his life. He suffers terribly – the doctors don't think there is much hope. This afternoon we gave a couple of non-commissioned officers a meal – they were hungry and had got separated from their battalion.

July 27th. When I got to the hospital this a.m. they told me the little lad had died in the night. There are three others – and not much hope, as not one but both lungs are burnt out in each of them. Another man was brought into my hut tonight – it is for the '*grands malades*' [the serious cases]. I still have occasional spasms of cramps – they say it is the gas – the corporal and an orderly (medical) both have the same thing – sore throat, vomiting and cramps. Dr. Rattier, my ward doctor, said to go into the fresh air as often as possible. He has to leave the ward sometimes to go out and vomit from the gas he breathes in from the patients.

July 28th. This a.m. I found three others had died. One man told me 'it was nice to see a demoiselle again, after being so long in the trenches' – he died two hours later.

Dr. Rattier is sweet and gentle and was a children's doctor before the war. He asked me to make him a cover for his stethoscope to prevent the patients coughing on it. The next day I turned up with one of the shoe bags I had made for our trip to Switzerland! He was pleased and surprised at my prompt service.

Margaret Mercer was a war widow. Born in 1890 to a well-to-do family in Essex, she had married in 1913 and promptly sailed to India, where her husband was to take up a posting as an officer in the Dorset Regiment. Despatched with his battalion to do battle with the Turks following their entry into the war in October 1914, he had lost his life in one of the first actions of the Mesopotamian campaign, being shot and killed instantly while leading his men over open desert at Sahil on 17 November. Their daughter was born just thirteen days later. By 1918 Mrs Mercer felt able to devote herself to some form of war work, and made two extensive visits to France to assist a family friend, Clara Heinemann, who was serving as a volunteer helper attached to a hospital in the French sector. The extracts that follow are from the diary of her second, more intensive visit, covering the period from late August to December:

29th August. Set off again for France. This time I take only what can be carried, as I know I shall be pushed off to the front at once. Daddy sees me off, travel with a VAD and rather a remarkable American woman, Mrs B. Witacre, who has been at the front in a French Ambulance since 1914. As she has been going to and fro ever since, I allow myself to be taken charge of, and sail along under her protection. Reach Paris 10.30.

30th August. Call on Noni [a friend just recovering from influenza], she is surprised to see me, looks very seedy. To the Barraque together, interview with Miss Wyld. I am to go to Meaux tomorrow en route to join Clara at some new 'cantine' she is starting at the front through Château-Thierry, at a place called Coincy. Lunch with Noni at a restaurant in Avenue Matignon, decide to go into Hotel M. afterwards. I have delicious shampoo, last clean before going off to the wilds.

1st September. Clara meets me at Château-Thierry, where the Boches were so lately, it is all very battered and the bridge blown up and we motor out through the town and over a very narrow, temporary bridge. Clara is most indignant at the amount of my luggage, though I thought it was extraordinarily little! We go out to Coincy in an American ambulance, bumping along on very hard seats. The fields are full of shell holes and the villages in ruins, just as one imagines it and where I never expected to be!

Coincy is a ruined village, our hospital is in a château and also in tents across the Meaux road and a little railway made by the Boches. Clara and I share a room over the stables, it used, I suppose, to be a loft, and the only place to put things is on the shelves where the apples used to be. Our windows are all broken and there is a huge unexploded shell in the yard outside. Our mess-room, where we feed with the nurses, is a sort of Indian wigwam in the yard and the kitchen is almost underneath our bedroom, in what was the coach-house. Fleas, of course, abound – if I did not keep them within limits by masses of Keating's powder, I should have to retreat to Paris.

Their place of work was the so-called '*triage*'; in effect a clearing station where the wounded were categorized according to their condition and their prospects of survival. The volunteers' job was to help clean up the men and offer them a mix of refreshment and good cheer, following a code of practice not always easy to enforce:

Thursday 5th September. I spend the morning at the *triage*. At 11.30 *blessés* (wounded) begin coming in and, after this, we are really busy, especially from 1.30 onwards. Am nervous at this new sort of job but, no doubt, shall soon get hardened. We get the men straight from the battle, they have been bandaged at a *Poste de Secours* (First Aid Post), but get here, of course, covered with mud and blood. They come into the *triage* to be sorted out and often stay for ages. I dread the *grands blessés* as they are nearly all waiting to be operated on so must not have drinks, and lie groaning on their stretchers, imploring me to give them something '*à boire*'. I long to run away but try to nerve myself to wash the blood off their faces etcetera – and after seeing men in this condition, one feels one ought never to complain.

Friday, 6th September. Provide a lot of drinks this afternoon, not only for the men in here, but orderlies come from all over the hospital with jugs to be filled. It is awfully nice to have lots to do and feel the *oeuvre* (work) is being made use of.

Sunday, 8th September. Five Boches brought in today – one a very nice looking boy, who dies in the night from shock, though he is not seriously wounded – it must be awful to be wounded and among a hostile crowd.

The St Mihiel attack of 12 September by the Americans, with French support, produced a crisis, and some chaos, at the hospital at Coincy. There was a 'feverish' (Margaret Mercer's word) attempt to clear existing wounded in order to cope with the inevitable 'fresh crowd' shortly to arrive:

> *Saturday 14 September.* At about 9 a.m. the wounded started coming in with hardly a pause and, after some hours, the *triage* is very much my idea of hell – on one side groaning figures on stretchers, smothered in mud and blood and bandages, on the other side rows of *poilus* huddled up on benches or propped against the wall. They stay here for hours, it is perfectly awful, the hospital staff is utterly inefficient to deal with them – we are so short of stretcher-bearers in here that Clara and I have to cart a man across to a stretcher ourselves, because he is too tired to sit up and, much as I dislike the dreadfulness of it all, I am glad to be here, as I do feel that the hot drinks and very inadequate *petits soins* (small attentions) that we give them really do something to redeem the horror of the wait.
>
> Things seem to go from bad to worse – a train is sent off full of wounded, lots of them the ones who came in today, still crying with pain, having had nothing done to them. And there is often not enough food to go round, so that often they've only had what we have given them.
>
> *Sunday, 15th September.* Clara still at it when I turn up about 6.30; has had a hectic night, she goes off absolutely worn out. It is a perfect morning, pale sky and pink clouds, and certainly one feels that 'only man is vile' who torture each other at so much expense of life and money. I deal with one lot and then, to my relief, there is a pause. The shed is swept and the sun streams in and, at least, there is time to breathe before it begins to fill up again.

Annah Peck, a native of Chicago, worked from September onwards as a volunteer with an American Red Cross Mobile Canteen, serving with the French and American armies on the Champagne front, and moving forward with them as they advanced in the final weeks of the war. Notably older than the two women already quoted, having been born in 1870, she was nevertheless clearly an energetic, outgoing and extremely attractive personality. From the account of her experiences, written shortly after she finished her assignment, it is evident that she and her colleagues had been immensely popular; known – by virtue of the commodity which they dispensed more than any other – as *'les dames au chocolat'*, they had gladdened the hearts of countless battle-weary soldiers as they went about their business.

The canteen's basic task, as suggested by its title, was to provide a flexible variant of the work fulfilled at stationary hospitals by such as Margaret Mercer and her colleagues. It would base itself at a set point in some appropriate building, usually in a village rather than a town, but it would also cast its net elsewhere according to perceived requirements and the initiative and enterprise of its staff. This is Miss Peck's typically upbeat explanation of their dual role:

> When, on the morning of our arrival, we were told what our duties were to be, they made such a delightful program, that it was hard to believe that it was work, especially after the monotony of a big canteen which we had all experienced. It consisted of one person opening a small canteen in the village, morning and evening, and, during the busy time, in the afternoon, when we served hot chocolate, cold lemonade, and the inevitable cigarettes. With the help of a piano, a gramophone, some picture papers and games, this proved a great success, and before the opening hour the street outside was thronged with soldiers waiting for it to open.
>
> We had two motors, a touring car belonging to the *Directrice* which she always drove, and a Ford Camionette which was supplied by the American Red Cross and was driven by one of the other women. This held three people in front and had very good accommodation in back [*sic*] for supplies or extra people as the situation required, for there were bench seats along the side of the car which could be let down if necessary. We would fill these cars with chocolate and cigarettes and then go to the rest camps dotted about the country, where the men were too far away to go to any village or find the least distraction from the daily routine of camp life.
>
> Every evening we went to the neighbouring railway station to meet the soldiers who were coming to take the leave trains, and

they were always glad of cigarettes and something hot to drink before starting on their journey, for they had usually walked miles to the stations from either the trenches or rest camps and then often had a long wait before their train left.

Remarkably, the women were even allowed to visit the trenches, in quiet times and by arrangement:

> To do this we were obliged to leave our car in some secluded spot quite far back, and a soldier would show us the way, for even when we reached the communication trenches, it was impossible to tell which way to turn, and made one appreciate the many stories one hears of men getting lost in the trenches and going the wrong direction. For these excursions we could only take cigarettes, but the *Poilus* seemed to enjoy them more than anything, and also the novelty of seeing us there.

However, there were soon signs of imminent action, the roads being lined for miles with 'convoys of cannons, motors and every conceivable accessory of war'. After this build-up had been going on for some days, the women learned that the infantry were beginning to come up at night. They decided to take out the Ford Camionette, with urns of hot chocolate and baskets of cigarettes in the back, to meet them:

> It was only necessary to pull in at the side of some main road, and before long a faint blur in the distance would appear accompanied by the unmistakable tramp of soldiers marching. At their approach, we would ask the officer in charge if his men would like a cup of hot chocolate, and explain that it could be served from the back of the car as they passed. He would invariably allow them to have it and it was a joy, especially on a rainy night, to see these men change from tired men, marching apparently on without a word or thought, just tramping on, to cheery human beings, so glad to break the monotony of a night's march that they treated the little incident as a festive occasion.
>
> What seemed to amuse the Frenchmen more than anything was to see women near the front, and they would never fail to make some remarks about it, but always with the light touch which was often funny but never offensive. A *Poilu* called out to one of the women who was driving her car past a convoy nearing

Verdun during one of the many times when the situation was serious, *'Maintenant la France est Sauvée'* ['Now France is saved.'], and then with a smile they all waved as she passed.

Much admired by the French, Annah Peck and her colleagues became virtual icons to the Americans, for whom the sight of a woman was amazing, of an American woman something near to a miracle. On one occasion a member of the American Red Cross came to the canteen and asked if a member of their group would accompany him to a nearby village, to make hot chocolate for some American soldiers billeted there:

One of us could usually be spared, so I went up with him and visited two Field Hospitals on the way, arriving at Pauvre early in the afternoon. It did not take long to start the chocolate making, but before we had been there half an hour, we saw the courtyard outside literally packed with men. They were crowded around the door, and peering in like schoolboys, and an officer came to the kitchen to tell us that the men had heard that there was an American woman there and they all wanted to see her. In fact, they seemed to care more about that than the chocolate and cigarettes, so after the first lot was made I left the directions for making more and went out to talk to the men. While we were talking and looking at the photographs that every soldier carries about tucked away in his pocket, one man interrupted the group I was talking to, suggesting that I should stand on a table and speak to them all, as a lot of the men had not even seen me. I did not feel equal to that, but the thought was rather touching, and it was always the same whenever we met Americans, we were always impressed by the real joy they showed at seeing American women. The afternoon passed in no time, and it was almost impossible to get away as I had to shake hands with all the men who were standing near the car and some of them kept coming back to say good-bye again.

In telling the history of this remarkable year it is fitting that tribute should be paid to the important, easily overlooked, contribution of such gallant and compassionate women as Alison Strathy, Margaret Mercer and Annah Peck, representative of many others who offered unselfish and often exhausting service for scant or no reward at this time.

*   *   *

What, meanwhile, of the lesser theatres, the so-called 'sideshows', as 1918 moved into its final months? Inevitably the prime focus of this narrative has been on the Western Front, but there were thousands of men – and indeed women – elsewhere hoping to contribute in what ways they could to the conclusion of this apparently endless war, and their role, albeit inevitably a supporting one, should not be overlooked.

For most of those far from home in these almost forgotten campaigns this had been a mixed and less than satisfactory year. Major Alfred Bundy, who had been in Salonika, base for the Macedonian front, since the previous October, chronicled a time more notable for frustration than achievement. 'Am getting tired of the humdrum monotony of life here,' he had written in his diary in early March, after serving considerably longer than he wanted to at the Summerhill Camp's new School of Instruction near Salonika city: 'Had talk with the CO and cautiously sounded him of the possibility of a spell up the line. He was not at all pleased and after expressing the view that I was doing invaluable work plainly told me he would refuse to let me go. I was disappointed but not shaken from my determination to get away as soon as possible.'

Yet this period also had its moments of undoubted humour, as when towards the end of that same month he had been persuaded to join a somewhat amateurish shooting expedition:

Party of us went to Lake Laganze today (10 kilometres) to try for some duck that rumour says are so plentiful there. The Motor Transport people lent us a lorry and the British Red Cross Society sent us sporting guns and 1000 cartridges. It was great fun. None of us has had any experience of shooting 'game'. When we arrived near the lake we advanced across the rather broken ground in extended line, and soon started up a fine hare which moved in leisurely fashion along our front and disappeared before anyone thought of firing at it. Our extended line tactics brought us no more luck so we separated to try our individual chance. We never even saw a single duck and the total bag was one emaciated crow that the Doctor said he shot, although it was clear that if he hadn't shot it it would have soon died from old age.

A week later Bundy at last got his way and received orders to join the 2nd Battalion, King's Own Royal Lancaster Regiment, 28th Division, in the line. Now his diary grew more eloquent, with, for example, a description of the 'wonderful panorama of the Struma Valley with the town of Seres on the right and the River Struma winding through a vast green plain as flat as a billiard table'. It was perhaps a simile more apt than he realized, for he soon found that in this sector games rather than active campaigning made up the routine agenda, against a background of war-weariness of a quite different kind from the one he had encountered in late 1916 on the Somme. 'Inspected men,' he noted on 20 March. 'They seemed stale and listless. Some have been here for two years without leave! This place must be very monotonous though of course safer than France. The men play football and cricket on No Man's Land and the Bulgars never interfere, so I am told, but the least sign of military training brings shells over.'

Abrupt changes of climate were also a prime part of the Salonika/Macedonia experience. Under April 11th–15th, he commented: 'The days are getting insufferably hot and with no rain the beautiful flowers and greenery are all drying up. The Bulgars now use a searchlight at night and every few minutes they sweep No Man's Land with it. Perhaps they are windy though I know of no reason for extra vigilance on their part.'

Some two weeks later there was a flurry of activity, but of a curious kind, underlining rather than contradicting the sense of languor and lack of purpose which pervaded the whole campaign:

May 1st. Last night we had a real thrill. I had returned to my dugout at 2.15 a.m. after inspecting posts and was just going to bed when a trip-wire bomb exploded followed immediately by the rapid concussion of hand bombs and rifle fire. I rushed out in the direction of the sound and found the parapets manned by my excited and expectant troops, but the explosions had ceased and not a sign was to be seen of the enemy. I fired Very lights but could detect no movement in front of our wire. After waiting about fifteen minutes I sent out a sergeant and six men to examine the ground in front and covered them as best I could with my Lewis gun and as many of my garrison as I could spare with bombs and rifles. In about 30 minutes the sergeant and the party returned bringing a number of crudely printed handbills placed in cleft sticks that had been stuck in the ground about 100 yards in front of our position. The bills read

> I am Boris the Bulgar
> The man with the knife
> The pride of Sofia
> The taker of life.
> Good gracious, how spacious
> And deep are the cuts
> Of Boris the Bulgar
> The knifer, the knut.

Dear Englishman

We are singing these words to your pretty tune called Gilbert the Filbert. Will you join us tonight and sing heartily?

On the reverse side of one of the handbills was written in pencil –

Dear Englishman

Why are you so foolish as to continue this war? Rumania has been beaten and you will soon lose also. Why not put aside your weapons and be friends? We like you and do not want to fight you, but if you will not be friends we will show you what we will do with our bayonets.

Yours truly

Boris the Bulgar.

Boris after delivering these billets doux had hurriedly departed without trying his luck against our defences.

May 2nd. Today my men mounted the parapet and sang the Bulgar song at the top of their voices and coming back was the distant sound of enemy voices also but it was impossible to tell whether they were also singing the song. I am preparing a reception tonight if we should have another visitation.

But no visitation came, they were shortly moved to a camp behind the lines and the doldrum campaign continued as before.

What shook this front awake was a change of command in June

which replaced the competent but relatively unambitious General Guillaumat with the fiery, thrusting General Franchet d'Esperey – soon dubbed 'Desperate Frankie' by the British component of this French-dominated Allied force (which also included Serbs, Greeks, Italians and Czechs). He, like General Duchêne, had emerged from the Chemin des Dames battle somewhat under a cloud, but, sent to Salonika by way of punishment, he set about retrieving his reputation with determination and energy. His message to his troops on his arrival – 'I expect from you savage vigour' – heralded a time of intensive build-up for a new offensive. Permission, from Paris, London and Rome, to reactivate a campaign which had been largely dormant was not easy to obtain, with the British and the Italians being particularly reluctant to agree. (Lloyd George had always favoured a peripheral, sideshow strategy, but with the Western Front at last yielding high dividends this did not seem its most appropriate hour.) Once given the required approval, Franchet d'Esperey prepared two major parallel strikes against the Bulgars; one on his centre-left by the Serbs and French, to be supported by a second on his right by the Greeks (a new arrival on the Allied side) and the British – this largely to forestall any attempt by the enemy to switch troops from an unthreatened to a threatened sector. The second strike's target would be the high ground above Lake Doiran, an area already attacked twice with heavy losses in 1917. Major Bundy recorded the progress of events from the British point of view:

Aug. 28th–Sept. 11th. Rejoined battalion at Doiran after two days on ration lorry. Preparing trenches for an advance but the Greeks have to do the dirty work and we are to be in reserve.

Sept. 12th. Greeks took over trenches today. They look surprisingly tough and seem quite determined. The Bulgars evidently have wind of an attack for they have shelled us unceasingly for 48 hours. We have had many deserters and from these we learn that the Bulgars are finished and will not stand up to an attack. I have heard that sort of thing before and I shall certainly be surprised if the Greeks are successful. I should be more disposed to back the Serbs who are attacking to our left. They are splendid soldiers and are definitely keen on killing Bulgars. In any case the general conditions appear to be favourable for a breakthrough, for according to reports the Germans are on the run in France and the Bulgars must be dispirited.

We are all keyed up and the British are elated because for once they are looking on instead of fighting, though if the Greeks fail and fall back we've got to support them so God knows what the future holds for us.

Sept. 14th. Zero hour is 5 a.m. tomorrow and my battalion are 3,000 yards back on high ground but the Bulgars are getting some heavy shells over.

Sept. 15th. What an experience. At 4.45 the Greeks could not stay and started going over the top. They were mowed down by machine-gun fire but pressed on. It was amazing. I would never have believed they had the courage. By 5.30 they had captured the Bulgar front line and we could see the enemy bolting away like rabbits. We have had orders to go forward to support the Greeks. The Bulgars have broken at last!

Sept. 18th. What a disappointment. I have to return to Summer-hill. Am told there will be no more fighting as the road to Sofia is open. There are rumours of an armistice. Surely this is too good to be true.

In both these statements Bundy was certainly correct. An armistice was not far off but there would be some fierce, sacrificial warfare in between. Of the fighting dated 20–21 September which would become known as the Battle of Doiran (or Dojran), the Official History would write: 'In the two days the losses of the 22nd Division, plus the attached 77th Brigade and the portion of the 83rd which was also attached, were 165 officers and 3,155 other ranks. More than one battalion lost over 70 per cent of the numbers which went into action.' Seeking for a suitable comparison the History turned not to the Western Front but the American Civil War: 'It is doubtful if [such losses] were exceeded at Spottsylvania or Fredericksburg.'

An anonymous document subsequently printed in Guy Chapman's *Vain Glory* provides a vivid, even angry account of this débâcle, all the more tragic because it was so near to the final closedown of this always unsatisfactory sideshow. The anger stemmed from the claim that there was no contemporary report of their effort in any English newspaper, that the despatch of the British commander, Sir George Milne, did not appear in *The Times* until 23 January 1919 and then only in truncated form, and that even the name of the battle was unknown to most Englishmen: 'And yet, in singularity of horror and in tragedy of defeated heroism, it is unique among the record of British arms.' These are brief extracts from it:

> Our attack on the Pip Ridge was led by the 12th Cheshire.... Almost immediately the advancing battalion was overwhelmed in a deadly stream of bullets which came whipping and whistling down the open slopes. Those who survived were followed by a battalion of Lancashire men, and a remnant of this undaunted infantry fought its way over the first and second line of trenches – if, indeed, the term 'line' can be applied to a highly complicated and irregular system of defence, taking advantage of every fold or contortion of the ground. In its turn, a Shropshire battalion ascended the fatal ridge....
>
> At the same time the Welsh Brigade was advancing towards the Grand Couronné.
>
> No feat of arms can ever surpass the glorious bravery of those Welshmen. There was lingering gas in the Jumeaux Ravine (probably our own gas) and some of the men had to fight in respirators.
>
> Imagine, if you can, what it means to fight up a hillside under a deadly fire, wearing a hot mask over your face, dimly staring through a pair of clouded goggles, and sucking the end of a rubber nozzle in your mouth. At the same time, heat is pouring down upon you from a brazen sky. In this plight you are called upon to endure the blast of the machine-gun fire, the pointed steel or bursting shell of the enemy. Nor are you called on to endure alone; you must vigorously fire back, and vigorously assail with your own bayonet. It is as much like hell as anything you can think of.

And the product of all this?

> We had gained only the unimportant ruins of Doiran Town and a cluster of hills immediately above it, never of any value to the enemy or strongly defended. The fortress of Grand Couronné

was unshaken, with crumpled bodies of men and a litter of awful wreckage above it.

On 25 September, Bulgaria formally asked for the armistice which Bundy had anticipated; it was signed on the 29th. Her exit from the war was the fall of first domino, or, as it has been described, the 'first prop' of the great German alliance. However, arguably the prime cause of this fall was the fact that Germany herself – the undoubted prop of her weaker allies – was so pressed on the Western Front that she had neither power nor will to do anything to prevent it. As Ludendorff himself would admit: 'We were not strong enough to hold our line in the West and at the same time to establish in the Balkans a German front to replace the Bulgarian, which we should have had to do if we were to hold that front in the long run.'

* * *

The Palestine 'sideshow' was also approaching close-down at this time.

The Egyptian (originally Middle-Eastern) Expeditionary Force's prime function in the earlier part of the war had been to safeguard the Suez Canal. It later raised its sights to include the invasion of Palestine and the seizure of Jerusalem. Its final task was to clear the Turks out of Palestine and Syria altogether, in the hope that this would result in, or at least assist in, removing Turkey from the war. Under its third and final commander, General Sir Edmund Allenby, it was able to bring about most of what was asked of it. (Reluctant at first at being sent to the Middle East, deeming it a reflection on his performance on the Western Front, Allenby, like Franchet d'Esperey, was a general who came into his own in a sideshow.) It might have done so much earlier, however, but for the German spring offensive, for Allenby's 1918 plans were immediately put on hold while several of his best divisions were despatched to France. Eventually his force was restored to its desired strength, thanks largely to a massive injection from the Indian Army. Inevitably, however, this led to some months of marking time, with the result that the intended offensive, to quote the Official History, 'was delayed until the tide of victory had begun to flow almost everywhere else, and Turkey's elimination did not take place until all Britain's foes were on the high road to being eliminated also'.

This should not detract from Allenby's and the EEF's actual achievement, for when the Palestine offensive did take place, it shared the qualities of careful preparation, clever deception and shrewd strategic insight that characterized Britain's Western Front fighting in 1918, and proved an overwhelming victory. The commander-in-chief marshalled his various forces for what would be the decisive battle – infantry, cavalry, artillery, air, British, Indian, Australian – with such skill that when they struck on 20 September the enemy was totally unaware as to where the attack was to be launched. The Official History cites as proof of Allenby's success an enemy intelligence map of 17 September captured at Turkish headquarters at Nazareth: 'This shows Desert Mounted Corps headquarters in its old position at Tal'at ed Damm; the 4th Cavalry Division is queried at Jericho, the Australian Mounted Division shown holding the northern front of the Jordan Valley sector, the 60th Division still east of the Nablus road. There is no sign of any concentration on the coast. The enemy was thoroughly deceived, wholly unaware of the devastating blow about to be dealt him.'

The action of 20–21 September which produced this virtual knock-out blow would become known as the Battle of Megiddo, or alternatively, on account of its Biblical location and overtones – not to mention its role as a culminating act of a long campaign – Armageddon. Though successful, it was very hard fought. Some sense of the rigour with which the attack was pressed home, and of the demanding conditions of heat, dust and exhaustion endemic in this theatre, survives in an account by Lieutenant-Colonel H. J. H. Davson, 3/154th Infantry Battalion, one of the numerous senior officers of the Indian Army now serving under Allenby's command. Davson was a soldier of considerable if varied experience; among other things he had been a participant in what was undoubtedly the Indian Army's cruellest episode of the war, the siege of Kut in 1915–16. As a company commander of the 82nd Punjabis, he had been a member of the relief force which had tried valiantly, but vainly, to save Kut's starving garrison, and which had had miserably to withdraw down the Tigris while most of the survivors of that grim siege departed on a long march to captivity in Turkey which many did not survive.

This is Davson's description of the fighting of 21st September, written in his diary, though a diary which was in effect a long letter home:

I'll start at the end; we attacked a very high hill after an advance of 5,000 yards in the open. The attack was splendid and might have been a cinema rehearsal. When I saw how it was going I nearly sat down and cried. It had been a most awful strain on me. At night the Div. General told me to congratulate my Bn. on the fine show they had put up. The Brigadier was still more complimentary. His words were 'A most dramatic show equal to the best work I have seen by Indian Troops.'

My boys were splendid. I don't know how they got such untrained material to follow them. I could not have asked for more from my old regiment.

The hill was about 2,500 feet high, very steep, and it was the heat of the day. There was very heavy machine-gun fire and some shelling. We captured a village en route and had to bomb the Turks out of a few houses. The hill was so steep and the men so done about three-quarters of the way men fell down and could not get up. If the Turks had counter-attacked we should have had a bad time. I was so done myself that if a Turk had come for me I think I should have been too tired to shoot.

I lost about 80 men.

I think we have about broken the Turkish Army. My boys were so splendid. They have pulled me through. All the COs of other regiments have been awfully nice to me and congratulated me. You cannot imagine my feelings. I told you all along I had a topping lot of boys.

Once we had got the position and were safe I collapsed, absolutely done. The next thing I remember is one of my lads trying to fix up something to shade me from the sun. He was done in himself.

By the beginning of October, Damascus had fallen. On the 30th of that month Turkey signed an armistice with the Allied powers. Summing up the EEF's role in this achievement, the Official History states: 'It was not primarily responsible for driving Turkey out of the war, but it contributed notably to that end.' Since the jury is still out as to whether the 1918 Palestine campaign should have been fought at all [see Notes and References p. 363], this was probably as reasonable a verdict as its members could have wished or hoped for.

* * *

Although Italy had been a focus of crisis and anxiety in late 1917, it had subsequently become remarkably quiet as a war theatre. Senior commanders sent there at that time – Generals Fayolle and Maistre from France, General Plumer from Britain, General von Below from Germany – soon returned to the Western Front. So did four of six French divisions, two of five British, and all seven German. In addition, two Italian divisions found themselves despatched to France.

'It's piping hot here now,' wrote Captain Vere Cotton as the Italian summer imposed its grip, 'and we are all feeling lazy in consequence.' But on 15 June the Austrians suddenly attacked along the whole Italian front, from the mountains to the sea. Three days later Cotton wrote home from Teolo: 'As you will have seen from the papers, this front has at last woken up a bit and scrapping has become general, so I am told. As a matter of fact I know probably less about it than you do, for in this secluded region we hear very little of what goes on and except for the distant rumble of the guns we know nothing of what is afoot.'

The Austrians made their heaviest thrust against the French and British on the Asiago plateau: an arena of relatively flat ground reasonably fit for fighting in an up-and-down mountain landscape – utterly different from the battlefields of the north – where trenches had virtually to be hewn out of the rock, thick woods inhibited visibility and where considerable stretches of the front were virtually, or in some cases actually, impassable. The French threw the Austrians back at once; against the British they made an advance of half a mile on a narrow sector, but they were not to hold their gain for long. Writing on 18 June, Lieutenant-Colonel R.J. Clarke, CO of the 1/4th Battalion, Royal Berkshire Regiment, 48th (South Midland) Division, summed up the pros and cons – with more of the former than the latter – of their part in the action: 'The Austrians attacked on the 15th and we had a hard day. They were driven back by the night, and we took 3 guns, about 50 M.Gs., over 700 prisoners, and the killed etc. were extra. A good day for the Division!' He added, however: 'The Austrian barrage was really good, and they brought up a large quantity of guns. I always heard these guns were good, and they are.'

A second letter some weeks later showed how effective, for their part, the British guns had been:

The Division that took over from us has been finding dead Austrians by the dozen in the woods. It was in that part of the battle that a battery of 4.5 howitzers and two 18-pounders were firing 'over the sights' (i.e. at point blank range) and two of our M.Gs. were going hard for some hours. The woods are fairly thick just there, and it is difficult to see anything or anyone. I told you how some of the guns fought; three teams were surrounded about 8 a.m. and held on till 4.30 p.m., and then smashed their guns, and fought their way back to join the next line. It was a good performance, and I think we have done the Austrians a lot of harm.

The division's efforts had been suitably recognized: 'We did well for awards – 2 MC, 2 DCM, 4 MM, and 2 Italian as well.'

The Austrians had achieved better success against the Italians on the front of the River Piave, and an Italian collapse briefly seemed a possibility. However, with their attempted crossing of the river harassed by Royal Air Force attacks on their boats and pontoon bridges, the Austrians stalled and their Emperor decided on a fatal withdrawal. Desertions and a loss of morale followed. For Austria, this, as one historian has put it, came as 'a fearful calamity'.

The obvious response was a major Italian counter-attack. It was very slow in coming, even when successes elsewhere might have suggested that the omens could not have been more favourable. Thus Captain Cotton again on 30 September: 'The succession of victories on every front is overpowering, one only wonders how long it can go on. If only the Italians would join in I should have nothing to complain of, as it is one feels ashamed of saying one has come from the Italian front where nothing ever happens. They were so pleased with themselves for having resisted the Austrians in June that they think they have done their share and can just sit still and do nothing.'

On 1 October the Italian leadership agreed that their moment was come, though it was not until 23 October that serious business began. This time the British fought on two sectors. The main thrust, with a combined Italian–British force – styled the Tenth Army – under General Lord Cavan, crossed the Piave in a series of daring actions and sent the Austrians reeling back. Named the Battle of Vittorio Veneto after the target town captured on 30 October, this was a fitting revenge for the disaster at Caporetto of one year earlier. The British fought with particular gallantry and resourcefulness, with the infantry at one point wading across the fast flowing Piave with arms linked, only a handful of men being swept away and drowned. The Official History quotes the Austrian account of the battle as stating: 'The appearance of the British created universal terror (*löste einen Massenschreck*).'

On the Asiago plateau the fighting did not begin until 1 November, with an attack against an enemy who had already decided on withdrawal, so that scouting parties in several sectors came back with reports of abandoned and unoccupied lines. Yet when the Sixth Army of six Italian divisions, one British and one French, made their strike there was at first a vigorous response. Then suddenly the Austrians broke and what had started as an offensive rapidly mutated into a pursuit. Lieutenant-Colonel Clarke's 48th Division was again in action; in a mood of high triumph he wrote from Austrian territory on 6 November:

> Life has been very full for the last week and I can't tell you all we have done. I would not have missed it for anything. Now I know what the rout of an Army means. It has been a wonderful show for the Division, and after looking at the mountains for many months, at last we broke through and fought our way through to Val Sugano, the 'Land of Promise' as the Italians call it.
>
> I only hope the authorities will give us the credit due to us, for we were the point of the attack, and all the rest followed us.
>
> The men were wonderful.

By the time Clarke was writing, Austria had been out of the war for two days; meanwhile on 1 November Hungary had pulled out of the collapsing Austro-Hungarian Empire and declared its independence.

* * *

There was one other 'sideshow' of this last year of the war which would not close down for some time, and indeed would surge malevolently at the very time that hopes were rising day by day for an early end to hostilities.

The first signs of the visitation of the 'Spanish Flu' of 1918 have already been chronicled (see Chapter 7). Now it suddenly reappeared. The diarist Frederick Robinson, in his entry for 28 October, after lamenting the high number of casualties occurring regularly on the Western Front, continued: 'To crown it all there is a very serious outbreak of influenza which is claiming thousands of victims.'

Once the disease returned, it did so with a vengeance; its severest consequences were the product of this later stage. Once again it struck London, where as many as 18,000 citizens perished in a matter of weeks. Mrs Barnett of Walthamstow reported the state of events to her soldier husband, still far off in Mesopotamia. On the same day that Robinson wrote his diary entry in the small town of Cobham in rural Surrey, she despatched a letter from what might seem a considerably more vulnerable East End, admitting an earlier contact with the disease that she had not previously divulged:

> Things here are in a terrible state, this new flu as they term it is quite a plague and taking people off as they walk along the streets, in fact the undertakers can't turn the coffins out or bury the people quick enough. There's families of 6 or 7 in one house lying dead, it's really terrible dear and makes one nervous of going out, nearly every house along here the doctors are on constant call but so far we have escaped and I do pray that we shall be spared it for your dear sake. I had a dose in July and don't want it any more.

Yet statistics show that the disease was as rife in the more fashionable parts of the capital as in its poorer ones; prosperous Chelsea and Westminster suffered as severely as the slum dwellers of Bermondsey and Bethnal Green. Perhaps even more surprisingly, the elegant spa town of Bath fared worse than industrial Birmingham. Also against expectation, the principal victims were not the elderly; indeed, a considerable majority were under thirty-five. There were, however, numerous local variations. Thus the schoolmaster Robert Saunders, writing on 27 October, reported a high incidence of mortality among another category in his rural part of Sussex: 'There have been several distressing deaths in this district, of mothers, who while nursing other members of the family, suddenly died of heart failure caused by Influenza.' He added: 'Everybody is trying some remedy or other, the Chemists are flourishing, but after all the only safeguard is bed and nourishing food. It is remarkable though what a Fetish people make of Medicine and will have it. I'm sure Dr Gravely often chuckles over the fuss some of his patients make over their medicine.' All this was an indication of the panic which this mysterious lethal plague induced wherever it appeared.

As in July there were numerous deaths in England's north-east, some of which predated the surge in the south. Writing on 13 October from his training camp in Northumberland, Captain Charles Carrington told his mother of a desperately sad situation pertaining there. Disease had struck the camp, claiming as victims a number of young conscripts called up to further the prosecution of the war whose deaths were the result not of enemy action on a foreign field but of a dismal misfortune on home ground:

> We've had rather a tragic week. They sent us three or four hundred boys from Cornwall and Devon to train in this Arctic climate and they began as usual by being very well and truly vaccinated. Then another epidemic of the 'Spanish Influenza' came and caught them. It was precious cold and damp after Devonshire and they all got the flu. Four of the poor kids have died and they are continually being seized with it.

A week later he reported again: 'This epidemic of flu is still very serious. We've had 17 or 18 deaths in the Battalion and 200 or 300 cases, nearly all raw and unhardened recruits from the West of England. We, who've done winters in the trenches, feel pretty safe against little things like this.' He added, in brackets, 'I'm touching wood.'

Yet the hope that seasoned warriors would be proof against the disease was not always realized. One of Canada's VCs, admittedly her youngest at 19, died of the disease, while London's most famous local hero, Captain W. Leefe Robinson VC, the pilot who had shot down the first Zeppelin to fall on British soil back in September 1916, also fell victim. Sometime after his exploit he became a prisoner of war, and he had recently been repatriated; it was ironic that his triumphal return should be followed so soon by so unhappy an outcome. In his case the trials of being a prisoner, and by all accounts an extremely recalcitrant one, had arguably left him somewhat vulnerable, but there was no such contributory cause in the case of the deaths from influenza reported by the artillery officer and artist Wyndham Lewis, in the period immediately after the cessation of hostilities. In the military hospital in which he was being treated for double pneumonia, Lewis noted, 'enormous Anzacs, the flower of colonial England, were dying like flies, having escaped all the hazards of war'.

*   *   *

One particularly moving example of the depredations of this 'fearful plague', as Wyndham Lewis dubbed it, survives in the archives of the Imperial War Museum.

When new ration books were issued in October 1918 they carried slogans and messages of various kinds printed on the reverse of the pages of coupons. Since they were to be sent to every home in the land they were seen as providing a useful medium for promotion and propaganda; appeals to grow more food or new war-bond schemes were among a number of key causes advertised in this way. On the reverse of the nation's coupons for lard was an appeal by the Secretary of a newly established institution then based in offices in Great George Street, Westminster. It read as follows:

> The Imperial War Museum desires to receive for permanent preservation photographs and biographical material, printed or in manuscript, of all officers and men who have lost their lives or won distinction during the War; also original letters, sketches, poems and other interesting documents sent from any of the war areas, as well as documents taken from prisoners and all kinds of mementoes, even of trifling character, which may be of interest in connection with the War.

On 6 November a letter written the previous day was received at the Museum's offices, its author a young private of a reserve battalion stationed at Bramshott, Hampshire. It told as sad a tale as any to emerge out of the troubled year that was 1918:

The Secretary,
IWM

I was reading on the back of the new ration books that you are interested in stories of compassion due to this great war. Well, maybe this will interest you.

In the year 1916 seven boys of a Can[adian] Battn wrote to the *Daily Mirror* and would like seven lonely girls to correspond with them. Well, one [soldier] went to France and came to the Battn I was in. Well I told him one evening while sitting in a dugout that I had a scanty mail supply. So he had one of these seven girls who took up the correspondence through the *Mirror* write me. Well we wrote and got letters from one another until I received a Blighty touch on April 9th [1917] at Vimy which sent me back to this country. She came to see me and of course it was a real case of love at first sight. We were married in Feb 1918 and our life as man and wife started. She was 19, me 20. The Influenza plague that we are having now took her away a week last Sunday to regions unknown. I am now left a widower. The war is drawing to a successful conclusion now and I dread it for when Peace comes to the world it will not bring peace to my heart and mind. The horrors of war are nothing compared with this so we must finish this war so that men never have to be separated from their loved ones again. The end of the war means for the world at large peace and happiness where it means for me desolation and sorrow.

Hoping you will consider this privately confidential, and keep our life in your mind, a remembrance of a romance in the great war. I am

Sincerely yours

G.V. Salisbury

Married Feb. 16th/Died Oct 27th/Buried Nov 2nd, 1918.

Thus in the war's final days the tragic wild card of the year of victory continued to wreak its havoc. It would be part of the world scene until well into 1919.

Meanwhile the long struggle on the Western Front, the theatre where, more than any other, the war would be lost and won, had now moved into its dramatic last act.

10

ALLIED ADVANCE: THE FINAL PHASE

ATTEMPTING TO IMPOSE some pattern on the vast, continuously shifting kaleidoscope of events which would result in the Armistice, the British Official History isolates the period 26 September to 11 November as 'the final phase of the War on the Western Front' and offers this lucid analysis of it:

> In these seven weeks, the greatest advance of the War in breadth and depth was achieved. For the first time in the War all the Allied Armies on the Western Front from the Meuse to the sea were on the move together, and they continued advancing, with short intermissions, either attacking or pursuing, until the end. Previous operations, like that of the Somme 1916, the Chemin des Dames (General Nivelle's), with Arras–Vimy as subsidiary, in April 1917, and Third Ypres July–November 1917, to mention only the more important, had been, so to say, isolated operations, and the enemy had thus been able to concentrate large forces and employ substantial reserves to parry them. Now he was attacked everywhere at once, was forced to disperse his reserves, and, although the Allied margin of numerical superiority was not very great, he was, in the result, nowhere strong enough to hold his ground.

Yet, as the History makes equally clear, this was an advance beset with difficulties. Apart from the hazards of enemy fire – from artillery but also, in episode after episode, from tenaciously held machine-gun positions – the Allies were limited by an almost total ignorance, except for the basic information provided by often inadequate maps, of the ground over which they were moving: a territory crossed by rivers, canals and dykes, and littered with innumerable farms, villages and small towns as well as a handful of major cities. More, the enemy was intermixed – in places, it could seem, almost inextricably – with an anxious and repressed civilian population whom it was the Allies' mission to liberate with minimum suffering. Smoke, fog and fatigue also made their negative contributions, while with an advance that was virtually unceasing the Allies were beset by constant problems of supply, as those charged with managing the complex infrastructure of this substantial array of armies strove to keep the soldiers spearheading the offensive watered, fed and equipped with the necessary arms and ammunition. It is a great tribute to the often maligned staff that this was very largely achieved, in that the means of war, food and even letters and parcels from home regularly made their way to troops who were rarely in the same place for more than two or three days at a time. Yet some confusion and difficulties were inevitable, and, with an enemy who was as alert as he was courageous – and by direct order of the German High Command, intentionally and ruthlessly destructive – nothing could be taken for granted and no one involved in the fighting could relax. Deserting its usually austere, understated style, the History adds: 'The stumbling in the mud and darkness, the cries and curses of the excited troops and the roar of the barrage must be imagined. Noise and darkness, either natural or artificial, were the features of the fighting. It must be borne in mind too, throughout, that in daylight the battlefields themselves seemed almost empty; for it was fatal for either bodies of troops or tanks to be seen, and little of the artillery could be moved forward until the infantry had made a substantial advance.'

The offensive began with four great blows on four successive days. The American First Army and the French Fourth Army opened the campaign on the 26th between the Meuse and Reims. On the 27th the British Third Army struck in the Cambrai sector. On the 28th the British Second Army and the Belgian Army, aided by what would shortly become the French Sixth Army, attacked in Flanders. On the 29th the British Fourth Army and the French First Army went for the Hindenburg Line in the region of the St Quentin Canal. Thus it came about that, overall, twelve Armies, shortly to be joined by a second American one, formed in effect one long fighting front. It was like the slow pulling of a huge curtain across a stage, bringing to an end, with increasing certainty as the weeks went by, the colossal four-year drama.

This final phase would give rise to a concept which arguably deserves rather more notice than it has had: that of the 'Hundred Days' – the time it took, starting with Amiens, to wind up this most intractable of conflicts. Strictly, the count was even more favourable: ninety-six. But there is a better ring to the accepted term, which should really stand alongside, say, the 182 days of the Somme or the 143 days of Passchendaele in Britain's assessment of the Great War, with the gloss that this was a period with an incontrovertibly positive outcome.

* * *

One of the most spectacular achievements of this final phase was a resourceful feat of arms by the 46th (North Midland) Division, Fourth Army; a division that was deemed to have failed on the first day of the Somme two years earlier but was now to gain considerable acclaim.

In the latter part of September Major H. J. C. Marshall, a Royal Engineer officer of that division, returned to France from leave. After a slow two-day train journey, most of it across the ravaged former battlefields of 1916 and of early 1918, he eventually reached Brie, the railhead. Thanks to the pleasing coincidence that the Railway Transport Officer at the railhead was a personal friend, Marshall spent the night in quarters in the château at Brie – as he described it, 'a much battered round-towered castle, looking like Conway on a very tiny scale'. Next morning he reported to Divisional Headquarters at Vraignes, some five miles further on. The date was 24 September and he found everyone urgently preparing for an imminent offensive against the complex of German defences known as the Hindenburg Line. As an Engineer, Marshall was soon heavily involved, for the attack which the 46th Division was to undertake was to have as its prime task the crossing of the St Quentin Canal, which ran like a surgical incision across the generally flat, rolling landscape of northern France. (The canal might almost be described as a kind of elongated moat, to the fore of the Hindenburg Line's highly sophisticated defence systems.) In effect this was to be, most unusually for the Western Front war, an amphibious operation, for which exceptional measures were required if it were to be successfully carried out.

Exceptional measures were being duly prepared. Marshall described some of them, admiringly:

> The troops had to be got across the canal somehow, and, if all else failed, it was suggested that they should swim it. So some genius thought of the lifebelts on the leave boats, and a lorry load was brought in from Boulogne. Experiments had been tried in the Somme to convince the battalions participating in the attack that a fully armed man, with no knowledge of swimming, was safe from drowning while wearing one of these belts. Lieutenant Page was in charge of this exhibition by non-swimmers, and the result was most successful, giving the men perfect confidence.

In places the depth of water the soldiers would have to cope with was between six and eight feet, though elsewhere there were areas of congested, malodorous mud where life-belts would be useless. This hazard too had been allowed for, by the provision of specially made reed and canvas mats, which were to be unrolled across the mud in front of the attacking troops.

Yet however ingenious the means to be adopted, the task ahead would be formidable. In addition to the canal's natural strength the whole length of its banks, heavily wired, bristled with well-sited concrete and steel machine-gun emplacements. Marshall commented: 'We knew from German prisoners that they considered the position impregnable.'

There was one other element which might have deterred the 46th Division: the assumption that the task assigned to them was little more than a 'sacrificial stunt', while the main attack was to be delivered to their north, in the area where the canal ran through the three-mile long Bellicourt Tunnel (whose entrance is still topped by a large stone plaque claiming Napoleon as the inspirer of this impressive piece of military and commercial engineering). This sector was to be attacked by the Americans, with Australians in support. 'At the best,' wrote Marshall, 'we might get a foothold on the further bank, but at a cost which would leave us no longer a fighting force. The Division was indeed well used to these affairs, having in past years been given attacks to carry out over belts of uncut wire, in which it had suffered severely. At the present, however, its morale was very high – we had had a pleasant and recent view of our adversaries' backs and had felt ourselves to be definitely their superiors.'

The attack went ahead on 29 September. Marshall described the day, which, as in the case of so many operations in 1918, began in conditions of distinctly limited visibility:

> The fateful morning dawned, cold and misty, but with a promise of sun later. I was up betimes, and secured a copy of the *Daily Mail* from a motor-cyclist just in from Amiens. I was reading this when General Boyd [GOC of 46th Division] came along, looking very calm considering what he had on hand. I felt very 'bucked' at being able to offer him the latest paper in such an out of the way place.
>
> At 5.50 a.m. (zero hour) a cyclone of shells descended upon the German lines, under cover of which our men dashed to the nearest trenches where nearly 1,000 Germans were found dead mostly from the fire of the 800 machine-guns, which had been arranged to rake these trenches immediately the attack commenced.
>
> Our men, by hook or by crook, got across the Canal. My friend Capt. Teeton (killed four days later) was much disgusted to find that he had swum the Canal in ice-cold water while a tiny footbridge existed within ten yards of him which had been invisible, owing to the mist. From every gun position sprang continuous streams of fire, while a perfect tornado of sound rent the air.
>
> The bridge at Riqueval, which the Germans were too late to destroy, proved of the greatest use in getting our artillery forward, whilst the R.E.s built two other bridges, suitable for field artillery, on the concrete dams across the Canal bed.

The division did not stop at the Canal, but pressed forward into the heart of the German defences beyond. Marshall eloquently described the gratifying results of this remarkable effort: 'Suddenly the mist rose and the sun of our "Austerlitz" appeared, strong and refulgent. Over the brow of the rise opposite to us came a great grey column. Half an hour later a similar column appeared, and then

19. *Left:* Private, later Guardsman, Frederick 'Fen' Noakes, Coldstream Guards, who wrote on 13 November 1918: 'I feel as if a great black cloud has been lifted from the world, and that the sun is shining again for the first time for years.'

20. *Right:* Lance-Corporal William Sharpe, 2/8th Lancashire Fusiliers, 66th Division. His postwar memoir written for his son, entitled 'What Did You Do in the War, Daddy?', gives a searing account of the German attack of 21 March 1918, in the course of which he became a prisoner of war.

21. *Below:* Lieutenant, later Captain, Douglas McMurtrie, 7th Battalion Somerset Light Infantry, 20th (Light) Division, who had the tragic experience of seeing his beloved company destroyed during the March Retreat. He too, like Lance-Corporal Sharpe, spent the rest of the war as a prisoner in Germany.

22. *Above:* Major Leland B. Garretson, CO 314th, later 315th Machine Battalion, 80th Division, American Expeditionary Force. He wrote on Armistice Day: 'We all realize that our Division is not an old campaigning Division when compared to the French and British veterans, but during the short time we were at it we were made to pay our precious toll and came to the thorough realization that modern war is the most wholly awful thing ever conceived by the mind of man.'

23. Lieutenant Philip Ledward, Staff Captain, 8th Division, later 15th Battalion, Hampshire Regiment, 41st Division. A powerful and sometimes critical chronicler of the events of 1918.

24. Lieutenant, later Captain, Edwin 'Ted' Trundle, Australian Imperial Force. His letters to his wife vividly portray the powerful Australian contribution to the campaigns of 1918.

25. Major Alfred Bundy, Middlesex Regiment (photographed when first commissioned). A veteran of the Somme, he served in Salonika in 1918. The war affected his outlook and attitudes for the rest of his life.

26. *Left:* The grave, at Vadencourt Military Cemetery near St Quentin, of Lieutenant-Colonel J.H.S. Dimmer, VC, MC, killed in action on the first day of the first German offensive, 21 March, while leading his battalion, the 2/4th Royal Berkshires, 61st Division, Fifth Army, in a valiant but unsuccesful counter-attack. Dimmer, who had risen from the ranks, had gained his VC in the First Battle of Ypres in 1914. He was one of fourteen battalion commanders who lost their lives in the 21 March fighting.

27. *Right:* The wartime cross on the grave of Private E.J. 'Ted' Poole, killed in action, 13 October, aged eighteen, Naves communal extension cemetery, near Cambrai. One of the countless young conscripts who made the supreme sacrifice in 1918.

28. *Right:* Captain Norman Austin Taylor, 1st Surrey Rifles, also known as the 1/21st Battalion, London Regiment, 47th (2nd London) Division. He was wounded on 24 March and died in hospital two days later. His sister later wrote of him: 'Five foot ten of a beautiful young Englishman under French soil. Never a joke, never a look, never a word more to add to my store of memories. The book is shut up for ever and as the years pass I shall remember less and less, till he becomes a vague personality; a stereotyped photograph.'

He whom this scroll commemorates was numbered among those who, at the call of King and Country, left all that was dear to them, endured hardness, faced danger, and finally passed out of the sight of men by the path of duty and self-sacrifice, giving up their own lives that others might live in freedom. Let those who come after see to it that his name be not forgotten.

Pte. Edward John Poole
London Regt.

29. *Left:* The memorial scroll in the name of Private E.J. Poole. Such scrolls were sent to the next of kin of all servicemen and women who lost their lives in the war.

30 and 31. Official Photograph and Certificate of Accreditation to the French War Emergency Fund, in the name of Mrs Margaret Mercer; a war widow whose husband had been killed in Mesopotamia in 1914, she worked as an assistant at hospitals in the French Sector. Her 1918 diary offers an eloquent and compassionate response to the suffering of the wounded who came into her care.

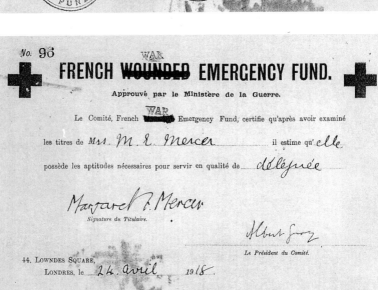

32. Losers: Hindenburg, Kaiser Wilhelm and Ludendorff in conference.

33. Victors: Field Marshal Haig and his senior Generals, 11 November, 1918; a photograph taken at Cambrai while they were being 'cinemaed'. Front row, left to right: Plumer, Haig, Rawlinson; second row: Byng, Birdwood, Horne.

INFLUENZA, THE TRAGIC 'WILD CARD' OF 1918, KILLER OF MANY MILLIONS WORLDWIDE.

34. Famous victim: Captain William Leefe Robinson VC, who had become a national hero when he shot down the first Zeppelin to fall on British soil at Cuffley, Hertfordshire, in September 1916. Later a prisoner of war, he was repatriated, and died of influenza on the last day of 1918.

35. Advertisement for Formamint, *The Sphere*, 16 November. One of the many ineffective anti-flu medicines recommended at the time.

Why catch their Influenza?

YOU need not! Just carry Formamint with you and suck these delicious tablets whenever you are in danger of being infected by other people.

"Suck at least four or five a day"—so says Dr. Hopkirk in his standard work "Influenza"—for "in Formamint we possess the best means of preventing the infective processes which, if neglected, may lead to serious complications."

Seeing that such complications often lead to Pneumonia, Bronchitis, and other dangerous diseases, it is surely worth while to protect yourself by this safe, certain, and inexpensive means. Protect the children, too, for their delicate little organisms are very exposed to germ-attack, especially during school-epidemics. Be careful, however, not to confuse Formamint with so-called formalin tablets, but see that it bears the name of the sole manufacturers: Genatosan, Limited (British Purchasers of Sanatogen Co.), 12, Chenies Street, London, W.C. 1. (Chairman : The Viscountess Rhondda.)

"Attack the germs before they attack you!"

Though genuine Formamint is scarce your chemist can still obtain it for you at the pre-war price—2/3 per bottle. Order it to-day.

Formamint
THE GERM KILLING THROAT TABLET

another and another. We had broken the Hindenburg Line, and 4,200 prisoners, seventy cannon and more than 1,000 machine-guns were the trophies of the fight gathered by our single division!'

The Americans and Australians to the north had a day of more mixed fortunes. The Doughboys' inexperience, and a shortage of their officers – many of whom were still detached at schools of instruction – combined with the confusion caused by the fog to produce an attack strong in bravery but somewhat less so in professional expertise. As Hubert Essame, historian and participant soldier of this final year (already quoted elsewhere), would later write: 'Like the British on the Somme in 1916, they had not yet realised the need for "mopping up". When they had passed, Germans oozed from the ground behind them and began to shoot them in the back.' Thus when the Australians came forward to carry on the attack they found a battlefield in disarray and suffered what one of their number called 'terrific casualties – Australians murdered because the Yanks failed to obey orders'.

The author of this statement was Captain O.H. Woodward of the 1st Australian Tunnelling Company whose satisfaction at the breakthrough at Amiens on 8 August has been quoted earlier; his critical account of 29 September continued: 'Probably as individuals the Americans were not to be blamed, but their behaviour under fire showed clearly that in modern warfare it was of little avail to launch an attack with men untrained in war even though the bravery of the individual may not be questioned. In effect so far as the Americans were concerned it was a case of a mob let loose, all plans forgotten and no definite objective in view. No wonder the German machine-gunners had a field day. They must have felt like poor sportsmen shooting sitting game.'

Significantly, Major Marshall, commenting on this aspect of the day in his account of the 46th Division's performance, wrote of one particular German machine-gunner: 'One gentleman left a note to say that he had bagged thirty Americans.'

That there was some justice in much that has been said or written about this episode would seem to be undeniable, but it should be commented that later research, such as that by the Australian historians Robin Prior and Trevor Wilson, tends to discount the generally accepted interpretation of events and to take a much less censorious view of the American performance. They claim that the confusion and the heavy casualties were 'the consequence of an attempt to advance against strongly defended positions without artillery protection', adding: 'There were any number of precedents in this war for failure under such circumstances.' Naming the British and Australian commanders concerned, they state: 'On this occasion the originators were not the hapless American troops or their commanders but Rawlinson and Monash.'

Be all this as it may, 29 September was also a significant date on the German side. It was on that day that, shaken by the success at St Quentin, and also, perhaps even more importantly, by the breaking of the defences of the Canal du Nord by the Canadian Corps, Ludendorff, Hindenburg and other members of the German High Command, meeting at Spa, found themselves facing the unavoidable conclusion that the war was lost.

* * *

Now as the attack broadened and strengthened, famous names began to appear among the list of places reclaimed. Writing on 30 September (as it happened in transit from Italy to northern France), Captain Vere Cotton expressed particular satisfaction at the achievements of his former GOC, General Plumer: 'The fact that Plumer has got back Messines and all the old ground by Ypres pleases me more than all the other news altogether. The old boy has fought there in fair weather and foul ever since '14 and I believe he loves every inch of that pestilential salient.' Passchendaele too was a notable prize at this time, though in view of the long struggle of the British and Canadians to reach it in 1917, there was perhaps some irony in the fact that in 1918 it was the Belgians who actually reclaimed it, even though it was strictly just outside the Belgian sector.

Away to the south 9 October brought the fall of Cambrai, as Third Army patrols from the south met with Canadians of the First Army entering from the north. They found a strange ghostlike city, empty, pillaged and burning. Photographs of Canadian soldiers strolling casually among the squares against a background of smoking buildings almost suggest a scene of the Second World War, of a bombed and battered Europe liberated a second time twenty-seven years on. The Commander-in-Chief himself, Field Marshal Haig, on a visit to the Third Army front, arrived to assess the situation. He noted in his diary: 'It was only yesterday that the enemy was driven from this great fortress, and yet I was able to walk about today, 24 hours later, almost out of hearing of his guns.'

Corporal James Murrell of the 2/4th York and Lancasters, 62nd Division, had, in a sense, anticipated Cambrai's fall several days earlier when he entered a deserted house in its vicinity belonging to an agricultural merchant of the city, one Octave Labbe, vendor of '*graines, huiles,* and *tourteaux*': i.e. seeds, oils (such as linseed oil), and oil cakes for cattle. Murrell had left his letter paper with his pack several miles back, so he peeled off several pages from the departed owner's stylishly printed memorandum-pad, bearing the above details, to write to his 'dear Mum and Dad'. Although it began with a variation of the standard Tommy's formula of reassurance, this was no routine letter home: rather it was in its laid-back soldierly way a virtual message of triumph:

> I hope these few lines will find you all in the best of health as it leaves me quite well. No doubt you have been wondering how I have got on during this big push we are in the midst of just now. Well so far everything is alright [*sic*], I have been in the thick of the fighting from the commencement and am now out for a rest which we well deserve. It has been a hard task of endurance as well as the fighting and really wants a strong will to carry one through it all but thank God we are made of the right stuff, Jerry is now beginning to realise that we are the master, and before many more weeks he will cry out for mercy, just now it is hell upon earth for him, and it's a wonder he is sticking it so long, the prisoners we take are a very dejected lot and are absolutely fed up with it, they say down with the Kaiser.

He added an important personal paragraph:

> Well I have a little bit of news about myself, but I am not one to brag about what I do, but I know you would be pleased to hear all about why I have been recommended for the Military Medal and another stripe. We were ordered to take a village which we took easily with very small losses, but when we got through that village we were held up by an enemy machine-gun which was knocking our boys out wholesale, so I at once volunteered to go

forward on my own and capture it, which I did, killing the five Jerrys [*sic*] that were working the gun and therefore capturing the gun. I took my section through all this fight without one of them getting wounded or killed, very lucky I can assure you.

It is evident that Corporal Murrell was not without 'the right stuff' himself. (See Foreword p. xxiii and Notes and References, pp. 351–2)

Almost as if to underline his message that the Allies were the masters now, he added that he would soon be 'forwarding a souvenir I got off a Jerry, it is the iron cross, 2nd class'.

* * *

The enemy, however, was still extremely reluctant to concede that mastery and was determined where possible to extract maximum vengeance. Some British accounts describe heavy losses in the course of the advance. One such is that by A. J. Abraham, eighteen in 1918, who had volunteered although in a reserved occupation, and had crossed to France with a draft on 1 April. Now a Lance-Corporal in the 8th Queens, 24th Division, he took part on 11 October in an attack launched from positions near Rieux, a village in the vicinity of Cambrai. German resistance was fierce; almost half of his company went down, he personally witnessing the violent death of several of his close comrades. The following night the battalion attempted to secure a bridgehead across the River Selle, provoking in reply a bombardment of gas shells. As a result Abraham and a number of his comrades became temporarily, though agonizingly, blinded, presenting, as they struggled to the rear, the kind of scene subsequently depicted in one of the war's most famous paintings – itself a product of a visit to the Front in 1918 – John Singer Sargent's *Gassed*. It would be many months before his eyes recovered from the effects of this gassing, while he would also have to cope with an attack of pulmonary TB; he would in fact be unable to resume civilian work until 1923. Necessarily his is an account written well after the event, though substantiated by contemporary diaries up to the time of his withdrawal from effective participation in the fighting. His description of this episode (written with a frankness of speech extremely rare in accounts at the time) shows how vulnerable men were in such a condition: on the one hand they could receive the tenderest care;

on the other they were open to exploitation by some at least of those whose duty it was to do all in their power to help them.

It was after the worst of the bombardment was over that Abraham, with a fellow Lance-Corporal, Cornell, and numerous others of his company, scrambled into hurriedly dug holes in a dry ditch by a sunken road in the hope of snatching some long overdue rest:

We were very tired by now and dimly I heard someone say 'Gas?' Someone else said 'Fuck the gas', and then I must have fallen asleep. We were all so exhausted that even nearby shell bursts went unnoticed and I had lost all count of time.

I woke up just as the sky was beginning to lighten, feeling pretty rough. I cannot remember whether Cornell or I was the first to emerge but we climbed out of our hole and both vomited on the road. Cornell looked at me and said 'Christ, you look a mess.' I looked at him and replied 'Well, you're no bloody oil painting'. Our eyes looked like oysters in buckets of blood and it was obvious that we had been gassed.

As it grew lighter it became evident that the whole of what was left of 'A' Company after the previous day's action outside Rieux had now been gassed. Although our road was only slightly sunken it lay at the foot of a gentle slope and thus acted as a gas trap. Our Colonel and our Medical Officer had both been affected by the stuff and during the morning they were carried away on stretchers. The rest of us stayed out there all day, coughing and retching and gradually going blind.

During the morning food was brought to them – a few loaves of bread and some tins of bully beef carried on a stretcher – but none of them could face it and it was just dumped on the road and left. Relieved in the late afternoon, they set out on the road back to Rieux: 'We could hardly see at all by this time and the march was sheer agony; never had ten kilometres seemed so long.' There was, however, genuine, caring help awaiting them on arrival:

I shall never forget the gentle kindness of our Quartermaster Sergeant when at last we reached our destination. He was like a mother to us, guiding us to a place to lie down, bringing each of us tea to drink and generally doing everything in his power to make us more comfortable. We just lay on the floor of a large

room, possibly a school room, but we could not see well enough
by now to distinguish our surroundings and I was past caring.
We just lay there, thankful to have finished marching and fighting. Our kind old QMS brought a doctor from some other unit
to see us; he came into the room, had a look at us and said, 'Well
boys, I can't do anything for you now, have a good sleep and
we'll get you down the line in the morning.' We spent the night
coughing and retching, but that magic phrase 'down the line in
the morning' had acted like a tonic for me and I felt I could face
anything now.

There was in fact worse to face than he imagined. When morning
came they were quite unable to see – 'our blistered eyelids had stuck
together' – and could only whisper. They packed their few possessions in their pockets – 'knife, fork, spoon, razor, comb and later
brush and any other little things we didn't want to part with; I think
I must have dumped my Hindenburg Line souvenirs at this stage' –
and prepared to leave:

> The doctor hung a label on each of us, and equipped with nothing
> but our tin hats and gas masks, ha ha, we groped our way outside
> with the QMS leading and each of us hanging on to the tail of
> the jacket of the man in front of him. We set off in a long
> crocodile for the Casualty Clearing Station. We had gone a long
> way like this when we heard a horseman approaching. The rider
> pulled up and said, 'Who the hell is responsible for sending these
> men like this, QM?' Our guide told him where we had come
> from and where we were bound for and he said, 'Fall out the
> men at once, QM, and I will see that they have transport.' As the
> owner of the voice galloped away QM said, 'Well boys, that was
> the General.' I never knew which General this was, but I am
> eternally grateful to him. It was not long before a fleet of motor
> ambulances rattled up and we were loaded into them and wheeled
> to the CCS, which, by the sound of things, was in a marquee.

Abraham found the CCS orderlies very considerate; they helped
them to strip and take a bath, issued them with towel, socks and
pyjamas, and guided them to their stretchers. Later, however, they
were taken to a Field Hospital further away from the line, and here
an incident took place which made him bitterly angry with certain

members of the RAMC who lived up to the worst of that Corps's part excellent, part invidious reputation. Carried from his bed to a motor ambulance en route for a hospital train, he realized that he had left his money belt under his pillow: 'I asked the stretcher-bearers if one of them would get it for me and a voice, which I recognized as that of their sergeant, said "I'll get it". There was a lot of rustling, accompanied by sniggering from the stretcher-bearers, before the sergeant said "I've put it in your bag for you" and we moved off.' Arrived at the No 2 Canadian Hospital at Le Tréport, he groped in his bag for something he wanted, to find that his belt was missing while in its place was 'a ragged-feeling cricket belt with the usual snake fastener'. His own had been a good one with a leather buckle and a money pouch containing some thirty-five francs; it had also been decorated with a few regimental badges that he had acquired:

> I now realized what had happened when I was leaving the field hospital; the significance of all that rustling and sniggering dawned on me. That swinish sergeant had exchanged his scruffy old cricket belt for my money belt and I was now without a franc to call my own. It sickened me to think that, in all probability, that revolting man made a habit of robbing others who were blind or otherwise incapable of looking after their possessions, but I was in no condition to do anything about it. Here, for me, was practical proof that the infantryman's interpretation of RAMC as 'Rob All My Comrades' was based on bitter experience.

* * *

Lieutenant Philip Ledward had returned to his regiment after his months as a staff officer in 8th Division, and was now a Company Commander in the 15th Hampshires, 41st Division, Second Army. As such he took part in the major attack of 14 October in Flanders which would become known as the Battle of Courtrai. He would later write vividly of the tremendous artillery onslaught with which the battle began:

> I feel as if I should always remember the opening of that barrage. The signal was one shot fired from a 15-inch Naval gun many

miles behind the line, and it broke an utter silence with the great crack of it speeding overhead, followed by the queer echoing roar of its passage growing less and less, till, just as it had about ceased to be audible, the barrage burst out with one tremendous crash. It was like some stupendous orchestra, grand, inspiring, exhilarating, beyond imagination. I remember standing up with my back to the barrage and Sergeant-Major Cross beside me, and making exactly the same gesture to the troops that Hugh Allen used to make to the chorus of the Bach Choir when it was time for it to stand up. Of course no word of command could possibly have been heard. The barrage was marked at every 100 yards or so by phosphorous shells, which burst in the air, pouring out a golden rain like fireworks, and it was by the guidance of these that we followed.

Private H.T. Pope of the 2nd Civil Service Rifles, 30th Division, also took part in this attack. This is his remarkable diary account of going into action on that same day, 14 October:

With the first streaks of light our guns leaped out. It was one continuous bang, bang, bang. I was told we had 900 guns along our small strip of front. We immediately got word to go forward, so – with the encumbrance of a Lewis gun – we started. We were very excited and there was a lot of noise. Kept expecting to be knocked out by a shell but wasn't. We went across ditches and through wire, getting more soaked and torn. Occasionally we stopped at a pill-box to collect prisoners but there was no resistance. Feeling don't care we lighted cigarettes as we went forward. Mash threw a bomb in a place in which we thought were Germans but instantly a big firework display started – it was a Very light store. The place, made of thin timber, caught fire. One lot of prisoners Holt took back. The prisoners were quite meek and mild. In one dugout Palmer found a Jerry parcel containing a very nice cake so we devoured this going forward. It was good. Very heavy mist this morning and we lost direction a bit and went far past our object so had to sort ourselves out. We came across numbers of stranded Germans who gave themselves up after being threatened. Eventually we found our line and settled ourselves in a ditch while Jerry commenced to register on us and strafe. I dug myself a nice funk-hole, but was shifted out by an officer whereupon Capt. Whitting 'C' Company promptly

pinched it. I came back for it later but apparently he thought the
life of a Company Commander was more valuable to the military
authorities than that of a mere private, besides it was easier than
digging one himself. I was nearly laid out soon after by a shell.
We were in a pretty fine mess: filthy dirty, all mud, soaking wet
up to the thighs and clothes all torn. Brooks was killed in the
advance and I heard that Holt was wounded by a shell. Sgt-Mjr
Dyer who had been gassed got knocked out by a shell going
down on an ambulance and was killed.

For Private Pope there was more fighting to come but this was
the last action of the war for Lieutenant Ledward. Wounded, though
not seriously, he followed on behind the barrage at a slow walk. But
loss of blood caused him to faint and when he came round the battle
had moved on and all was quiet. He walked back to Battalion HQ
where he made a report and where his wound was given a field
dressing. 'I believe I slept for a bit, and then walked out. I have
always regretted that I didn't return to the troops, as I perfectly well
could have done. I think I was just tired out and only half conscious.
I had had no sleep for about 80 hours, and had been at full stretch
all the time.' His servant accompanied him as far as a Canadian
Casualty Clearing Station, where his wound was dressed by a nurse
with a voice similar to a lady acquaintance of his in Blighty. 'She
was very pretty too, and I have understood ever since then why
soldiers and nurses were apt to fall in love. Next day I reached
England.' It was a curiously low-key exit from a campaign in which
he had served for many months with considerable distinction. He
consoled himself with the thought that if his departure from the
field had been premature he had nevertheless made a significant
contribution to the success of the operation overall:

As there is no false modesty in this account, I may as well say
that I think I was directly responsible in this last battle, not only
for my own Company's arriving at the right spot at the right
time and knowing exactly what to do, but also for the whole of
my battalion doing likewise; and that if I had not been there,
there would probably have been a muddle and possibly a fiasco.
I really do not think that anybody could have done my small job
on that occasion better than I did.

But I ought not to have come out when I did. Sergeant-Major Cross came through without a scratch and got another medal. He was a wonder.

* * *

Some way to the south Second Lieutenant Clifford Carter's 2nd York and Lancasters of 6th Division, Fourth Army, were advancing across ground over which the British had retreated in the first weeks of the war more than four years earlier. Carter had been among the first volunteers, having joined the Hull Commercials (to all intents and purposes a 'Pals' battalion) in September 1914. After surviving numerous hazards including the first day of the Somme – he had been out cutting barbed wire on the night before the attack but had been in reserve on the day itself – he was now fighting his first campaign as a newly commissioned officer. On 17 October he was involved in an attack north-eastwards from Vieux Andigny, as part of an offensive that included Le Cateau among its targets. For someone who had been so long in uniform and so much on the Western Front it was curious that this was his first major, full-blooded attack. It would remain vividly in his memory:

Oct. 17th. Attacked at 7 a.m. This was a real battle – such as a civilian would imagine a battle to be.

I was in charge of 9 Platoon, C Company. We took up our position at the edge of a wood at 6 a.m. There was a dense fog and we had no idea who or what was in front of us. We had to rely entirely on map-readings and compasses. Promptly at 7 our bombardment started up and the guns put up a perfect barrage – a real wall of fire – just ahead. It was too near to be pleasant and we had to lie flat with our faces in the grass. After a few minutes the barrage advanced 100 yards and we were just preparing to follow it when a great shout went up from behind and three tanks came lumbering out of the wood. We dashed after them seeing nothing but fog, fog, fog, fog and not knowing when we should come across the enemy. But the guns had done their work and only a few Germans popped up here and there out of shell holes and dugouts. If they seemed prepared to put up a fight our fellows gave them three rounds 'rapid' – most of them just put

up their hands and surrendered, crying 'Kamerad'. We soon
collected a score or so and after depriving them of bayonets,
knives and so forth, I sent them marching off with an NCO and
two men. Suddenly ahead I saw a German officer preparing to
fire with his pistol. I quickly aimed at him and he as quickly put
up one hand, still holding his pistol in the other. We shouted to
him to drop it – and seeing he had no chance, he did so. I pinched
his field-glasses and iron-pointed stick and still prize them as
mementoes of the occasion.

Shortly afterwards we reached our objective and immediately
dug a trench as protection from counter-attack.

*   *   *

As the offensive moved forward it freed from occupation a mass of
communities, from cities to hamlets and farmsteads, whose inhabitants had been virtual prisoners since the summer of 1914. Second
Lieutenant Frank Warren, having recovered from the wound he had
received in March (a 'clean Blighty', as he called it, with no after-
effects) was now with the 4th King's Royal Rifle Corps in 5th
Division, Third Army. He described the satisfactions of liberation in
a letter of 15 October:

> We are passing through French villages now released from the
> German yoke. It is a pleasure to find many villages little damaged,
> as compared with the wilderness created by the Hun in his spring
> retreat of 1917. Often we are greeted with cries of '*La Victoire*'
> and 'Foch'; everywhere German street names and notices survive,
> with a big crop of 'Verbotens' and 'Achtungs', a complement of
> autocratic rule. I have spoken with the village folk who seem to
> have been treated fairly by the Germans, or at least by the
> officers, who paid for what they took. But all are delighted to be
> '*livrés*' and look forward now to white bread, sugar and '*beau-
> coup de viande*' [literally 'lots of meat']. I am told that one or
> two girls left a village arm in arm with the German soldiers; even
> if it is true, it is not very surprising, seeing that the same troops
> have been in occupation for about four years.

Liberation was now a standard theme along virtually all of the
advancing front. It was about this time that the Chemin des Dames

was cleared of the enemy by a vigorous and forthright attack mounted by General Mangin, while Laon to its north, German headquarters in this sector for many months, was at last restored to its inhabitants. A striking citadel of a city, splendidly walled and rising superbly above the northern French plain, with its beautiful five-towered cathedral as its dominant feature, Laon was a prime prize for the French and its seizure was appropriately celebrated. No Tommies were in this sector now, so it was left to such as a correspondent of *The Times* to report on the event to the British public. He attended what he described as 'an extraordinarily moving service' at the markedly unscarred cathedral, at which a 'Te Deum' was sung for the city's deliverance. 'I shall never forget', he wrote, in a report published on 15 October, 'the sight of that large congregation thronging the building in the evening gloom, lit only by the twinkling lights of the altar, while the organ, which somehow managed to make music in spite of the absence of many of its pipes, crashed out the great chords of thanksgiving.'

But liberation did not yet mean cessation of war. Second Lieutenant Warren wisely added a caution against reading too much into the good news he was passing on: 'I hope you people at home are not madly optimistic about the chances of an early peace. Personally I think that Germany will very soon find herself isolated. But there is much hard fighting to be done before she is brought to her knees, and only by the occupation of German soil can we actually impose unconditional acceptance of our terms of peace.'

On 18 October, however, three days after Second Lieutenant Warren wrote his letter, Crown Prince Rupprecht of Bavaria, an Army Group Commander and one of the ablest and longest-serving of German military leaders, put his name to a letter which, had his British opponents been aware of it, might have significantly moderated their views. It was virtually an admission of defeat. The following are among its keynote sentences;

> Our troops are exhausted and their numbers have dwindled terribly. The numbers of infantry in an Active division is seldom as much as 3,000. In general, the infantry of a division can be treated as equivalent to one or two battalions, and in certain cases as only equivalent to two or three companies. Quantities of

machine-guns have been lost and there is a lack of machine-gun teams. The artillery has also lost a great number of guns and suffers from a lack of trained gun layers. In certain Armies fifty per cent of the guns are without horses. There is also a lack of ammunition. . . .

The morale of the troops has suffered seriously and their power of resistance diminishes daily. They surrender in hordes whenever the enemy attacks, and thousands of plunderers infest the districts around the bases. We have no more prepared lines, and no more can be dug. There is a shortage of fuel for the lorries, and when the Austrians desert us, and we get no more petrol from Rumania, two months will put a stop to our aviation. . . .

I do not believe there is any possibility of holding out over December, particularly as the Americans are drawing about 300,000 men monthly from beyond the ocean. I should like to add that our situation is already exceedingly dangerous, and that under certain circumstances a catastrophe can occur overnight.

Ludendorff does not realize the whole seriousness of the situation. Whatever happens, we must obtain peace before the enemy breaks through into Germany; if he does, woe on us!

* * *

A significant factor in Crown Prince Rupprecht's analysis is his reference to the Americans. At the beginning of the year the German hope had been that the war might be won before the enemy from 'beyond the ocean' could bring his potentially massive pressure to bear. The Prince's letter makes clear that Germany's worst fears had now been realized. What of the experience and achievements of the Americans in the the war's final stage?

As already stated at the beginning of this chapter, the Americans took part in the first move of this final phase, in that, on 26 September, in collaboration with the French, they attacked in the region of the Argonne. Compared with their earlier success at St Mihiel, this was a much harder battle to fight and success was a long time in coming. A labyrinthine country of hills and forest, packed with German defences honed over more than four years, this was not an area into which to cram men and guns in the hope that a breakthrough would be achieved simply by sheer weight of numbers.

This was, however, Pershing's basic plan, and at first it met with some success. There was a speedy first advance, one notable 'scalp' being the little town of Varennes, captured by Lieutenant-Colonel George S. Patton, to become famous as one of the most thrusting commanders of the Second World War. (This town had had a notable earlier moment of history during the French Revolution, in that it was here that a stop had been put to the escape attempt of the dethroned Bourbon king, Louis XVI, and his ill-fated queen, Marie Antoinette.) But thereafter there was stalemate, with little ground gained as the casualty lists grew. Pershing himself chose this moment to delegate command of the US First Army to his best field general, Liggett, while he activated a Second Army under another general, Bullard, at St Mihiel, himself becoming Army Group Commander and Commander-in-Chief. General Hunter Liggett – a commander who has been seen as one in the Montgomery mould – demanded time to reorganize his forces before he struck again, and when he did so, on 1 November, a momentum was created which took the Americans massively forward, being brought to a standstill only by the cessation of hostilities.

Private Sam Ross of the 42nd (Rainbow) Division was wounded in the Argonne fighting, though not badly. On 18 October – the date of the Crown Prince's letter quoted above – he wrote a letter to his grandmother in New York. At this stage the outcome of the battle was far from certain, but he clearly felt that enough commitment and courage had been shown by his fellow countrymen for the claim to be made that they were making an honourable and valid contribution to the war. He also took the opportunity to assess his own state of mind, and to look forward to what he saw as, despite temporary setbacks, an early and successful outcome to the campaign:

> I have now been over here almost a year and do not regret it. The hardships and dangers I have been through have helped me to find myself, to find out my good and bad, mostly bad points.
>
> You see by the papers that the Yanks are showing the Huns the kind of stuff we are made of and that in a short time now this

great war will come to its end, and all the boys will come home and the homes whose boys have been away the longest will be the happiest and the boys will appreciate their homes and parents more than ever. You never miss anything until you lose it and when you have lost a thing for a while and it is suddenly restored it is almost like the dead returning; so the joy and happiness we will all have in a few short months' time will be greater than all the suffering we have had in the last year.

As to the event which had taken him out of action: 'I was hit on the side of the left hand, it was a very slight wound, just enough to earn me a few days rest and a sleep between sheets.' It was enough, however, effectively to end his war, which was not particularly to his liking, for he had been promoted Corporal some time earlier and had then lost his stripes owing to some minor misdemeanour. His wound prevented a promised visit to the Machine Gun Company School from which he would almost certainly have emerged as a sergeant. Thus he would arrive in Europe and depart from it as Private Ross.

Meanwhile Major Garretson and his 315th Machine Gun Battalion had found themselves engaged in sustained and arduous campaigning that would continue, with only brief intermissions, to the moment of the Armistice. He wrote after the first of several surges of fighting:

Of course any specific military talk is taboo, but you probably gathered from my cable mailed yesterday that we have been fairly active of late. In fact I managed to cram as much living, and as many new sensations, into those three days as my somewhat varied career had thus far experienced. But relief came and we withdrew from the front line and now we only have the keenest satisfaction of having done in our first battle what we set out to do, in a manner which those in high command say was entirely to their liking. My battalion did good work from beginning to end, and considering what they had to do, their casualties were, thank God, light. Now they are rested up, fed, and dried out, and as soon as I have a few deficiencies patched up in equipment, will be ready to go out again.

One of the curious notions a fellow gets in one of these affairs, is that he himself is doing the trick as an individual which will turn the tide of history. Then you begin to think of the vastness of the whole thing, and you realize what a thoroughly insignificant bit of the mass you are.

He had the highest praise for his troops' fortitude and resilience: 'The men are marvels, nothing comes too hard for them and they do not know what danger means. Above all not a one has uttered a word of complaint throughout the whole show.'

He had also been greatly moved by evidence of the sheer goodness of the ordinary soldier, man to man:

Here is a sample of the Christianity of the battlefield. I was going along the road near a dressing station when I came on two woebegone-looking 'blessés' who were staggering along towards the rear. I stopped and asked what their wounds were, and one told me a machine-gun had gotten him in the shoulder. When I asked the second his trouble he said he had a rifle bullet in the lung. I started to help the latter along but he promptly stopped me saying, 'Help him Captain, he is gassed and should not walk.' When I got to the dressing station there was an ambulance there and I ordered the surgeon to put them both on board at once. There was only one seat and as soon as the man with the lung heard it, down he sat and refused to go aboard at the expense of his friend. His reward came soon in the shape of another ambulance, but believe me even if he does not know it, that man is a first-class Christian.

And for first-class nerve commend me to the kids who drive the ambulances. Late the same day I was ambling down a particularly unhealthy road, and had just counted the fourth upturned ambulance in about 1/4 of a km. when I heard 'Honk, Honk' behind me, along came two more going as tight as they could put it straight up to the firing line. It is all very well to go ambling around this countryside with a young arsenal strapped to you, for it gives you a sense of security, but not to be allowed any firearms and to depend solely on your speed and your knowledge that the Boche specializes in shelling all ambulances on sight, is quite a different proposition.

* * *

As is evident from Garretson's references to ambulances and casualties, such success as was being achieved in this final thrust of the war was not without a high price. As well as the catalogue of victories, there was the parallel catalogue of deaths.

Bombardier Charlie Stone, C Battery, 82nd Brigade, RFA (18th Division), died on 23 September at No 3 Stationary Hospital, Rouen, from wounds received in action five days earlier. He was twenty-four. Some weeks later a package arrived for his commanding officer, Major F.J. Rice, from the young soldier's family. Rice was so impressed by its contents that he sent them on to his own mother, with a covering letter explaining the situation:

> Will you please put the enclosed away for me somewhere safe? I have always got nice letters back from parents whose sons have been killed in my battery but these seemed exceptionally grateful for my letter and sent me a photo of Bombardier Stone and a sort of memorial ribbon. He was badly wounded during the barrage we fired on Sept. 18th when we were shelled from 5-15 to 6-45 a.m. and we had to go on firing our guns all the time. We had ten casualties during that time (six killed). It was the worst hour and a half I have ever had.

The ribbon, of fine white silk with its memorial message immaculately printed, described the fallen soldier as 'the dearly beloved Son of Robert and Prudence Stone' and commemorated him with a poem typical of the sentiments of the time:

> How little we thought when we said good-bye,
> We were parted for ever, and he was to die;
> Oh, the grief that we feel words can never tell,
> For we could not be with him to bid him farewell;
> But Christ will clasp the broken chain
> Closer when we meet again.

The message concluded with the reassuring assertion, possibly based rather more on hope than certainty in view of the often anodyne tone of letters informing relatives of the circumstances of soldiers' deaths: 'His end was peace'. Both photograph and ribbon would be carefully preserved with Major Rice's wartime letters.

This was but one fatality among many thousands at this stage. In his diary entry of 28 October (already quoted in the previous chapter on the subject of influenza), Frederick Robinson, who had recorded the daily casualty count in *The Times* ever since the first weeks of the Battle of the Somme two years earlier, commented with considerable concern:

> The casualties reported today are 253 Officers and 6,000 men. Our casualties for many weeks past have been enormous. They must have averaged some 30,000 to 40,000 per week. The hospitals are full to overflowing. Volunteer Orderlies of the Red Cross who unload hospital trains are kept at it all hours of the day and night, in some cases working twelve or more hours at a stretch. One of these self-sacrificing men told the writer recently that he had worked for eighteen hours without a break, and that some of the cases sent over were so bad, they were actually 'packed in boxes'. This is the dreadful side of it, and makes one long for the time to come when these horrors shall cease.

*   *   *

Late October and early November saw the most dramatic period in the military career of Major C.H. Dudley Ward, 1st Welsh Guards, Guards Division.

He had tended to play a sound but secondary role, winning a reputation as a reliable and intelligent officer with a cool head and a good nose for priorities. At one point earlier in the year an offer to join the Staff was floated before him, but though the idea had its attractions he had turned it down, partly because it would result in serious financial loss, though it seems possible he might have reconsidered his position if his status continued indefinitely to be that of an understudy. He was precisely that once again in early October when the battalion was ordered up to the River Selle; he was held back with the 'details' – that core of a unit kept back out of battle so that there would be a foundation on which to build should it suffer heavy casualties. As a result he spent a wretched period of waiting, cut off from news from the front and, since the mail went forward to the fighting companies, also contact with home. On 19 October, however, the battalion CO unexpectedly went on leave and Dudley Ward found himself projected into a position of high responsibility with virtually no time in

which to prepare. That afternoon he was away from the line, again
with the 'details', supervising the task of clearing camp before
the next move forward, when at about three o'clock he received a
note in the hand of a fellow officer, Guy Darrell, informing
him that he was to prepare to return to battalion headquarters at
once:

> This was followed by Guy himself who told me that Dick Ball
> was going on leave and I was to take over command. 'This is all
> very well,' said I, 'but I hear there is a battle tonight.' Guy said
> he would tell me all about it later – very discreet. In due course
> we left in the motor and then Guy said he thought everyone was
> mad. The attack had been arranged hurriedly on the 18th and
> no word of Ball going was heard until the morning of the 19th.
> The Brigade Major, Tiny Buchanan, was going too – all very
> hurried and on the very eve of battle. It seemed to be running
> great risks.

Battalion Headquarters was at a village called St Hilaire, where they
arrived at 5 p.m.:

> I saw Ball who was able to give me half an hour before going to
> catch his train. It was to be a night attack over ground which no
> one had ever seen, and he had done all he could to prepare the
> battalion. It appears he was only told that morning that he was
> to be left out and so rather than stay at details he applied for
> special leave. The thing was not his fault. Tiny then came to fetch
> him with a car and told me how sorry he was I had such short
> notice – and so they both went off. I was left without a map and
> waiting for a guide to take me to the battalion.
>   I did not reach the battalion till eight, knowing very little
> indeed, and with no map. I dined and had the company com-
> manders to see me. They knew the details of the attack better
> than I, and had looked at the map, but no one had seen the
> country.
>   The battle was to start at 2 a.m. with the Grenadiers in front
> (they were already on their jumping off place which was a
> railway) and we were to cross the railway at 2.10 a.m.

All this might have been a cause for panic in less phlegmatic an
officer, but, having assessed the situation and found that he had been

left with only one order to give – to fix the time at which the battalion would advance; he chose 1 a.m. – Dudley Ward found himself taking a remarkably relaxed view of the situation: 'I was not in any way excited over command – there seemed to be nothing to command. I could see no one and could not get to them. In fact one's interest seemed to slip away in a curious fashion. Vaguely I wondered if the leading companies were over the railway – but if they were I could not help them.'

If this was a curiously muted start to his period of high responsibility, there was much more direct involvement and satisfaction on his part in the battalion's next 'show', on 6 November. On this occasion he found himself, in effect, personally orchestrating the attack. It was an exhilarating and satisfying role, the more so because of the show's evident success, and, for him, its gratifying outcome. The battalion was based at a small village not far from the German-held town of Bavay:

> The village street was continually swept by machine-gun bullets and two light guns were shelling us badly, but it was exciting trying to direct the advance by directing the fire of our three guns together with four machine-guns. The fat little howitzer was squatting in the middle of the street, the two field guns in a field close to the house I had made my HQ, machine-guns were firing through the windows of other houses and the noise was most stimulating. After a while we silenced some of the machine-gun fire also the enemy field guns, but they kept moving their machine-guns and there were a tremendous number of them. Vickery, who commands the 74th RFA Brigade, came up to see me and gave me a second reaction. He was most cheery and told his officers to put in some of their 'snappiest shells', telling them 'Keep on firing – you are young, me boy! – work does you good'. Raining like blazes all the time and a horrid day for battle.
>
> I think I worked everything all right at my end. Before the day was out every arm and every man was holding on to something – even Battn HQ. The only trouble I had was from Coleman with No 2 Coy and he, through ignorance, would not get on.
>
> For 'Squiff' Ellis I have nothing but the highest praise. He led his Coy by dashing forward alone and waving them on with a

walking stick and really ran the whole battle in the front line. Wonderful little man.

We did not do all that had been marked on the map but fought all day and reached a further objective than the G. Guards on our right, and the whole time we were shot in the back from Bavay! An inky black night finished all fighting.

Next day Bavay fell to the British and Dudley Ward decided to visit the town. There he witnessed something of the raw and mixed emotions of a populace suddenly released after four years of repressive occupation:

I took Percy Battye, Jacky and six men with me and had a most amusing morning. The moment we entered the town the civilians came crowding out – we could not get on at all. We were kissed and handshaken and cried over – a fearful business. Working our way down a side street from the square there was a commotion. Women began to scream and run about, a clear way was made down the street and we saw some French civilians pointing – and then half a dozen Huns suddenly appeared and put their hands up. The men dashed forward – Percy brandishing an empty rifle he had picked up – and then the crowd closed round again and everyone began to talk. The Huns were having their packs pulled off them by the civilians who were calling them names, brutes, robbers, etc. I got hold of Sergt Ham and told him to have the Huns fall in which eventually he did. One of them was a young officer and he refused to fall in with his men which occasioned a bit of pushing about, but we got some sort of order and pursued our way.

Dudley Ward was subsequently amused, if also gratified, to find himself christened 'the captor of Bavay'.

This was one success of many at this time, creating a pattern of achievement across the front of the advance that led to a great sense of pride among the British in respect of their contribution to the war's final phase. So much is evident in a letter written on 3 November by Lieutenant J.T. Capron, 109 Battery RFA, 56th Division. He told his mother: 'It is satisfactory to feel that the *British* are doing the greater part of the victorious pushing, and not as some of us expected the Americans!', adding that the attacks being mounted, which he described as 'comparatively speaking light work', were 'a great reward after the long time of defensive'. Such a comment should be seen in the context of the view which had once been held in many quarters that the best way of winning the war was simply to hold on and wait for the Americans to force the issue by their sheer weight of numbers. That policy could only have produced a victory in 1919. In fact the victory was unquestionably going to happen in 1918, and, even as Capron was writing his letter – at a time when rumours of peace feelers from the Germans were gaining increasing momentum – was only eight days away.

* * *

'Victory was in the air breathed by the allies in the west. Not even the smell of decay, of high explosive, or the sickening sweetness of mustard gas could disguise it.' So wrote Cyril Falls, historian and soldier, who had himself been in France, serving as a Liaison Officer with French forces, during the last phase of the war.

But the authentic voice of this hectic and, despite the tang of imminent victory, still uncertain period surely belongs to the men at the spearhead, carrying the campaign forward day after day with the threat of wounding or death still ever present, a threat all the more alarming because the hour of deliverance now seemed so tantalizingly near.

'Sweating on the top line' was a phrase much used by the British Tommy. It came from the gambling game 'House', a favourite with both the Army and the Navy; when the top line of cards was nearly filled, success was in sight. Soldiers often described themselves as 'sweating on the top line for leave'; it was the anxiety that you might not survive to go on that longed-for, much-dreamed-of visit to Blighty that brought out the sweat. Now there was a new variant for the changing times. The Royal Field Artillery signaller W.R. Acklam used it in his diary for 4 November: 'Sweating on the top line for the armistice but it doesn't seem to come.'

'Wind-up' was another phrase that occurs in Acklam's diary at this time. 'Wind-up' meant fear: but 'to have the wind-up' generally meant no disgrace; it was something a soldier could admit to, though when he did so it was usually in reference to events in the past. Now the phrase went into Acklam's diary twice in one entry; this is his description of events on 30 October:

> Set off last night just before 12 and wandered along till 3 a.m. when we got to a place which put the wind up me. Just got the guns in and unloading ammo. when Fritz put whizz-bangs all round us and we nipped out damn quick. Spent the day at wagon lines and after tea two guns and two wagons set off for gun line. Of course we put one gun in the ditch before we had well started. Finally we got it out and went on all right till we met 'A' battery returning and got jammed. Everybody did a lot of shouting and all at once came shells like raindrops right on the side of the road. Horses were tangled up and men ran all over the place, but we got clear somehow, with very bad wind-up.

Wind-up would never be far away until the die was finally cast.

Private J.W. Drury, a signaller in the 3rd Battalion Grenadier Guards, aged nineteen in 1918, wrote his account of the war's final phase in the following year. Although the tension and anxiety of the countdown to the Armistice were then behind him, his memories of that harrowing time were still raw and vivid. Thus of the first day of November: '"Armistice rumours" became frequent and everyone became more "edgy" about "getting a packet" near the finish and so took no risks. It was said two German generals were to cross the line that night re a possible Armistice. The strain was terrific. Everyone was fearful of a bad wound, blinding, or death, so near the end. Reckless men became cautious, taking no risks.'

On the 2nd they heard that they were to go over in attack: in fact they were to spend much of the following days in more or less continuing action, frequently almost within eyeball to eyeball contact with an enemy determined to extract maximum cost as he was forced to withdraw. The toll of casualties and fatalities forms a constant theme in Drury's telling account:

> By short rushes we reached a sunken road down the slope and under cover of this I got in communication with HQrs asking for Support Company. Men were being hit wholesale.
> Two stretcher-bearers near the Sergeant-Major were killed by a heavy, literally 'blown to bits'. We advanced from the road to

the valley bottom over a stream to behind an old barn. We stayed here a time but soon he opened up with 17 ins [shells] and the whole ground seemed to be going up in the air.

We had covered four miles but had still seven miles to do. Our hearts fell at the news. We moved up Jerry's hill (as he withdrew) on to another sunken road and cut our way through a hedge. Two Jerries opened fire with a machine-gun only 120 yards away in the orchard and three men dropped. Pearce was one – four years in France and killed just before the Armistice!

We passed alongside a hedge between two machine-gun-swept turnip fields, with no cover, to a slit trench fifty yards or so long. We got up to it in rushes, but had a job to get in. When I was only a bare five yards off the man in front was killed and two more lay out wounded. It made me both 'windy' and careful.

I lifted and dropped quickly. Snipers' bullets whistled over me and I was up and in before he repeated fire.

A 2nd Lt. of No 2 Coy was hit on the parapet and fell in. He died within two minutes. A machine-gun was fired from a wood on the left and down a cart track. It had the slit trench pin-pointed and seven out of twelve more men following were hit whilst attempting the 'get-in'.

We were having a very bad time and had suffered very severe casualties.

That the knife-edge anxiety of the fighting troops at this time could be understood elsewhere is clear from the letters of the staff officer of 40th Division, Captain Harry Graham. He wrote to his wife on 3 November: 'How I wish the Hun would chuck it before we lose thousands more valuable lives. I can imagine the man in the trenches being very disinclined to pop the parapet, with peace so close at hand.' In a second letter the same day he expressed the hope that a similar wisdom might be shown by 'the powers that be'. He prefaced his comment with the statement: 'Oh, I am weary of this war!' It was as though what was happening was merely killing for the sake of it.

Yet there were others for whom this period was offering just the kind of exhilarating fight for which they had long been hoping, and who would have been devastated if they had not had their chance to share in it. One such was Lieutenant Alex Wilkinson of the Coldstream Guards, who had been in England recovering from wounds ever since the Battle of Cambrai and who could hardly conceal his delight when he was at last cleared to return to the front. He wrote to his young sister on 29 October: 'I am back with the Bn, in fact, home again. So henceforth please write to the familiar address, 2nd Bn Coldstream Guards BEF. It is too splendid being back, and I haven't been so happy for a long time.' For him rumours of imminent peace were less than welcome: 'It will be such a pity if we accept anything less than absolute surrender. The Hun has fought in such a filthy manner that he deserves all he gets. And you can't trust the brute a yard. Even so I feel fairly confident that we shall have another good battle or so before it is all over. I would be very disappointed if we didn't.'

Wilkinson was not to be disappointed. He wrote to his father on 6 November that the battle from which he had just emerged was 'the best I have ever had and I would not have missed it for anything':

> We were right on top of the Huns before he could get his MGs to work and we got a nice few prisoners and MGs straight away. And a nice few Huns were killed here too. I had sworn to shoot the first one I saw, but I could not bring myself to it. I am a sentimental ass. Having sent the prisoners back, on we went at a tremendous pace. The men were perfectly splendid, and showed amazing skill in the use of their Lewis Guns and rifles. It was amusing to see practically every man smoking a cigar after we passed the first objective.

Peace was indeed, Wilkinson recognized, now part of the agenda, but it was the Germans who were putting it on the table: 'I think it is safe to say that it cannot be much longer. The Huns we met were certainly nothing to fear, and they thought of nothing but peace. They fully realize that they were absolutely beat to the world.' Wilkinson's too is the authentic voice of this remarkable time.

* * *

On the front of the Fourth Army, the last action of the war was the Battle of the Sambre, of which a crucial part was the crossing of the Sambre–Oise Canal. This was achieved, if, in some sectors at least, at high cost, and Monday 4 November, the battle's first day, was notable for some significant fatalities. Several divisions were involved, among them the 32nd. Two of the division's battalions assigned to the operation were the 16th Lancashire Fusiliers and the 2nd Manchesters; they were to attack side by side to the north of the village of Ors.

The 16th Lancashire Fusiliers was commanded by a temporary lieutenant-colonel with the substantive rank of Major, one James Neville Marshall. Having family friends in Belgium he had offered his services to that country on the outbreak of war, and had fought with the Belgian 1st Regiment of Artillery until early 1915, when, having been wounded several times, he was honourably discharged as unfit for further service. He had subsequently been awarded a Belgian Croix de Guerre and appointed a 'Chevalier de l'Ordre Leopold'. After several months of convalescence he had volunteered for service in the British Army, had been accepted, and was commissioned in the Irish Guards in time to take part in the Battle of the Somme. By late 1918 he had won the Military Cross and Bar and had been mentioned in despatches three times. He had also acquired ten wounds, and the soubriquet of 'Mad Major'. As an officer famed for his discipline, energy and courage, he had been detached from his own regiment to command the Lancashire battalion, which had suffered heavy casualties and was in need of building up following the recent fighting.

The attack of 4 November would gain him the ultimate accolade of the Victoria Cross, but it would be awarded posthumously. Seeing that his men were failing, under withering fire from the opposite bank, to force their way across the canal on the improvised rafts provided for the operation, he took charge himself, emboldening his men by encouragement and example, and was killed half way across that lethal stretch of water. He had earlier protested that his battalion's task would be all but impossible if the German machine-gunners on the eastern bank were to survive the torrential opening bombardment intended to eliminate all enemy resistance; overruled, he had paid the price of others' misplaced confidence. Of two officers of the Manchester battalion who died that morning, in the same stretch of canal and for the same reason, one, a Second Lieutenant James Kirk, was also awarded the VC for conspicuous bravery; while the other, hit either on the bank when urging on his men, or also on a raft out on the water, was a Second Lieutenant W.E.S. Owen, better known as the poet, thought by many to be the greatest of the war, Wilfred Owen. He also would receive a posthumous award, of a Military Cross, though for gallantry in an earlier action, in October. All three would be buried in the tiny military extension cemetery attached to the municipal cemetery at Ors.

Elsewhere, however, there was great success that day. 'The enemy has melted away before us like snow', was the comment of one officer, later to become well known as Lieutenant-General Sir John Glubb of the Arab Legion.

Also on 4 November German soldiers sent to Kiel to suppress a mutiny in the German High Seas Fleet fraternized with the mutineers instead. The mutiny had been prompted by the proposal to send the fleet to sea for a last heroic do-or-die battle with the British Grand Fleet, something for which the Royal Navy, and in particular the Grand Fleet's flamboyant Commander-in-Chief, Admiral Sir David Beatty, had been craving ever since Jutland. The Kaiser's sailors saw no virtue in such a futile exercise, and, responding to the atmosphere of anger and disillusion spreading across the Fatherland, acted accordingly. Beatty did not get his longed-for second Trafalgar.

But the need for one was now over, for Imperial Germany was coming apart at the seams. Ludendorff, having published without the Kaiser's permission an order of the day declaring an armistice unacceptable, had already gone, having resigned his post on 26 October. On the night of 7–8 November, a German delegation crossed the front line en route for Marshal Foch's Advanced Head-quarters at Senlis, in search of the very outcome which Ludendorff had denounced. On the 9th Germany was proclaimed a republic. On the same day the Kaiser's abdication was announced: he himself made his departure on the 10th, being whisked away by the Army to what would become twenty-three years of exile in Holland; he did not die until the third year of the Second World War.

Meanwhile at the front, the fighting and the eleventh-hour killings continued. The 18th Division artillery officer Major F.J. Rice (already quoted in this chapter), mourning the death, on 30 October, of his much admired brigade commander, Colonel Thorp, suddenly found himself a lonely and a marked man. As he would write, looking back on this time not many months later: 'I was the only officer left in the brigade who had come to France with the Division and had not been killed or wounded or gassed or evacuated sick, and I felt that if the War did not end pretty soon I was just about due to join the majority in some way or other.' Colonel Thorp was buried on 2 November. On the 4th – that same historic Monday – there was another death which hit Rice hard: 'About lunch time we got some sickening news. Apparently Major Prentice had gone forward with my subaltern Lieutenant Lamb, and had walked along a road without taking any particular precautions to find out how far our infantry had advanced, and they had been opened on by a Boche machine-gun at pretty close range. Lamb was killed instantly, and Prentice had an arm and leg broken. As this took place after (as it turned out) we had fired our last shot it was extremely sad.'

But the advance was now unstoppable, and there was clearly much exhilaration, not to mention stunned amazement, as the enemy's will to fight back began to wilt. In a letter to a family friend in Washington DC, a young Corporal, George Tizard, of the 236th Canadian Battalion, described the disbelief with which he and his comrades received the news that the war was all but over. This was on 10 November, by which date the Canadian Corps, serving with the British First Army, was between Jemappes and Mons – a name of great resonance ever since 1914 and now again to have its moment of history: 'About 3.30 Mr Livesey a Canadian correspondent, came along and told us that next day would be the last day of the war. We naturally told him that we had not just joined up and asked him to give us some news that sounded a little more reasonable. He insisted that what he had told us was true.'

Also in First Army, in 55 Division, was the 2/5th Lancashire Fusiliers, under the command of Lieutenant-Colonel Stanley Brighten. The following is his exuberant description of what turned out to be the last days of the campaign, during which his battalion was part of a flying column specially formed of all arms 'to chase the Hun': in effect to follow the retreating enemy in hot pursuit:

It was really most interesting. Very hard marching as we were the only infantry, and in addition to marching in the day and keeping up with cavalry, we had to find outposts, and fight as well. The men were simply splendid, and not one fell out.

During the advance we got the most wonderful receptions in the towns, the moment the Germans had gone, and we arrived, flags everywhere. The Battn looked like an army of flags. Received officially by the Mayors etc. We had the funeral of some of our men who were killed, and the people gave a wonderful show, they made the coffins, and all turned out with a band, heaps of flowers. The Burgomaster read a very nice little eulogy, chiefly about what England had done.

In fact, when this letter was written, the war was over. The main thrust of Brighten's letter was to express his delight to his 'dearest Father and Mother' at what had finally been achieved: 'Well, isn't it wonderful? I can't realise it yet. It is of course more or less unconditional surrender, an absolute abject defeat. Of course they have had their internal troubles, but it is the military defeat which has forced and won the situation. What more complete victory could have been desired?'

11

'THE GREATEST DAY':
ARMISTICE DAY 1918

MONDAY 11 NOVEMBER was the 1,568th day of the Great War. It was just after 2 a.m. when the German delegation agreed to sign the instrument of armistice, which provided that hostilities on all fronts were to cease at 11 a.m. that morning. The setting of this event was a carriage of Marshal Foch's personal train standing in a gun siding in the heart of the Compiègne Forest; a restaurant car of the International *Wagon-Lits* Company, specially adapted for across-the-table confrontation. No German war leader of importance was present. By a turn of events that would offer an alibi to the departed militarists, it was left to representatives of a virtually non-existent German democracy to do the deed which the next generation of militarists could thus denounce and disown. (In effect, the leader of the German delegation, Matthias Erzberger, was signing his own death warrant; he would be assassinated as a symbol of 'defeatism' by right-wing extremists three years later in Berlin.) Foch and his Chief-of-Staff General Weygand headed the Allied delegation; Britain was represented by two admirals. There were no delegates from Belgium, Italy, or (with hindsight arguably the greatest omission of all) the United States. The terms, tough and humiliating, were discussed point by point and the document was finally signed at 5 a.m. Signals announcing the imminent cease-fire then began to flow in all directions.

And so at last the moment came: at the eleventh hour on the eleventh day of the eleventh month of the fifth year of (at that time) the greatest war in the world's history.

The occasion was not graced with good weather; it was wet, dank and cold.

Men heard the news of the Armistice in all sorts of places and circumstances.

Lieutenant R.G. Dixon, of 251 Siege Battery, 53rd Brigade RGA, First Army, was on a leave ship crossing the Channel. As the boat entered Folkestone harbour about midday every craft possessing a siren began to sound it and continued to do so. The first reaction of those on board was to ask 'what was all the fuss about?' But when to the din of the sirens was added the cheering and waving of crews on all the ships in the harbour, they 'tumbled to it':

'Dickie,' said Captain Brown, 'the bloody war's over! It's over!'

And it was. We had left France with a war on and arrived in Blighty with a peace on! And all those ships letting off those sirens for us, as if we were a lot of conquering heroes coming home, that was the first intimation we had of it.

While we were going through the formalities of disembarking, a strange and unreal thought was running through my mind. I had a future. It took some getting used to, this knowledge. There was a future ahead for me, something I had not imagined for some years. I said as much to Captain Brown. He smiled at me; he was a man of about forty. 'Yes', he agreed. 'You've got a future now, Dickie. And so have I. I wonder what we'll do with it, and what it will be like. Because, you know, things are not going to be the same as they were.'

But for the moment it was enough simply to think of what it was to which the announcement of the armistice had put an end:

No more slaughter, no more maiming, no more mud and blood, and no more killing and disembowelling of horses and mules – which was what I found most difficult to bear. No more of those hopeless dawns with the rain chilling the spirits, no more crouching in inadequate dugouts scooped out of trench walls, no more dodging of snipers' bullets, no more of that terrible shell-fire. No more shovelling up bits of men's bodies and dumping them into sandbags; no more cries of 'Stretcher-bear-ERS!', and no more of those beastly gas-masks and the odious smell of pear-drops which was deadly to the lungs, and no more writing of those dreadfully difficult letters to the next-of-kin of the dead.

There was silence along the miles and miles of the thundering battle-fronts from the North Sea to the borders of Switzerland. There would be silence in Ypres, and over the whole haunted area of the dreaded Salient this silence must seem positively uncanny. At long last that tormented city with the appalling ruins of its once-lovely Cloth Hall was freed from the menace of the Hun, at long last its innumerable defenders were justified and those who died in its defence could be appeased. The City of Fear was no longer the City of Fear, and doubtless out of her ruins would rise another city, a city of the new times we had hoped we were fighting for. The ancient ramparts at the infamous Menin Gate would no longer harbour our troops. The whole vast business of the war was finished. It was over.

Another member of the Royal Garrison Artillery, Gunner Sidney Edwards, was also on board ship, crossing from Le Havre to Southampton, having at last been adjudged a Blighty case on account of the burns to his legs, caused by a malfunction during firing; he had struggled on for several days after the event but had eventually managed to get a somewhat reluctant MO to take appropriate action. On the night of the 10th–11th he and the rest of the wounded on board had received a gift, presented with the compliments of the Union Castle Line and best wishes for a speedy recovery: a small box containing a pipe, a two-ounce tin of Capstan Medium Tobacco and four packets of Woodbine Cigarettes. Cheered by this, he had managed a reasonable, if abbreviated, night's sleep on a mattress below decks. At 4 a.m. on the 11th the ship dropped anchor, with disembarkation beginning four hours later. Edwards recorded in his diary:

As I stood waiting in the queue to leave the vessel, news was brought aboard that ARMISTICE had been declared. *What* a day to reach 'Blighty'!

On landing, we were taken to the train. Our destination was, to us, unknown. Scenes along the line were indescribable. Excitement was rife. Church bells were ringing and flags flying. News of the Armistice having been signed had brought people from their homes who were gathered talking excitedly, whilst children ran wildly about.

On arrival at Eastleigh, the wounded detrained and were

walked – I cannot say marched – through the streets to a near suburb where the Temporary Hospital was situated. Sympathetic remarks were made as we straggled along in our 'Blues', carrying little bundles containing all that was left of our possessions. It was a *Great* Day for everyone. For myself, although my wounds were still painful, they were but slight (as compared with those which had brought me back to Blighty in 1917) and I was ONCE AGAIN IN THE 'OLD' COUNTRY.

Satisfaction was equally evident among those wounded who had not been granted the favour of a 'ticket to Blighty'. Private Frederick 'Fen' Noakes of the Coldstream Guards was in his convalescent camp at Cayeux, another soldier recovering from his second wound of the year, when the news came through. Over the next day or so he sent a series of jubilant letters to his family, at 3 p.m. and 11 p.m. on the 11th, on the 12th, and again on the 13th. When he and his fellow patients were summoned on parade early in the afternoon of the 11th, they guessed at once what it was for. The announcement made, they sang 'God Save the King' and 'Tipperary', then the CO waving his cap, called for three cheers for the end of the war: 'we almost cracked the clouds!' After a thanksgiving service, a session at the cinema, two concerts and a brief visit to a dance, he watched the Kaiser being burnt in effigy 'with the usual honours, the band marching round and the troops doing war dances'. But as ever Noakes had more serious thoughts to offer along with the levity. As in the case of Lieutenant Dixon already quoted, he harked back to what he and his comrades had been through, intensely glad that such things were now of the past: 'To think that all those black times are over – no more shells, no more bombs, no more gas, mud, bombardments, going over the top – it seems too wonderful to bear thinking about. Every now and again I say to myself, "The War is over!" and it sends a "goosey" feeling down the back of my neck right into the soles of my boots! Now doesn't that sound "soft"? Well, the whole British, French and American Armies are feeling "soft" at the present moment.'

At the front, perhaps the most memorable place to be that day was Mons. Corporal George Tizard's 236th Battalion, Canadian Expeditionary Force, had reached the outskirts of the town by

4 a.m.; when his company halted as they marched up the Grand
Boulevard, they found themselves surrounded and delightedly
embraced by men, women and children. He himself, invited into a
house for a cup of coffee, was pleased and surprised to find his
hostess spoke excellent English: 'I soon got over my amazement
and had a long talk with Madam. She told me that her mother was
a Londoner and her father had studied science at Edinburgh.' Now
firmly convinced of the imminent armistice, he told 'Madam' and
her family of it 'to cheer them up': 'They said they could believe
anything now, since the English had routed the Huns from Mons,
an undertaking declared by the Germans to be impossible.' As the
troops moved on into the town the mood became increasingly
celebratory: 'I was enjoying myself smoking a good cigar and had
two very nice looking girls as companions, one on each arm,
everywhere you looked you saw soldiers and girls walking arm in
arm.' Strictly, they were still at war, but the news they were now
certain would come was not long in arriving: 'About 9 o'clock the
5th Lancers came through us but returned an hour later. 10 o'c
came and we were still going forward when our signalling officer
rode up and halted us and read us a few words from a message just
received: "*All Hostilities will cease at eleven o'clock.*" ' The cheers
they raised brought out the local people, including the sisters from
a nearby convent, and soon saucepans of coffee, wine, cognac,
cakes, biscuits and apples provided the basis for a victory feast.
'How on earth they had kept them away from the Huns is a
mystery to me. Anyway everybody was happy and that was the
main thing.'

Equally content with the day's outcome was First Army's
GOC, General Sir Henry Horne. Horne had been at Mons before
the famous retreat in August 1914 and it was particularly pleasing
to be there again after a sustained and successful advance almost four
and a half years later. But it was the date of the occasion that had
the greatest resonance for him, for it recalled an even more important
episode of that now far off year; the First Battle of Ypres, in which
the BEF's I Corps, under the command of Sir Douglas Haig, had
stopped Germany's efforts to reach the Channel coast in a crucial
encounter with some of her most formidable soldiers. He wrote to
his wife:

I think we may well regard Nov. 11 1918 as a red letter day, and it was on Nov. 11 1914 that the I Corps, in which I had the appointment of Brigadier General Royal Artillery, defeated the great attack of the Prussian Guard – an attack which was planned to break down the British resistance and to open the road to Calais! Now the mighty German nation is completely humbled and the great German Army, which regarded itself as the most powerful fighting machine in the world, is in retreat to its own frontiers, broken and defeated!

Sergeant Arthur Vigurs, 6th Somerset Light Infantry, also heard the news of the Armistice in the vicinity of the Front, if in a relatively inactive sector, early enough to begin a letter to his fiancée at 10.55 a.m. Relief at survival was part of his message also:

My dear Olive

Hip. Hip. Another 5 mins and the war is nappoo – at least we all hope so. I have not heard a shot fired yet this morning, and, so the order goes, we cease hostilities. It's a glorious ending to the war, anyway, and everyone must be extremely glad we are on the winning side.

11.1 a.m.

Not even a parting shot from the artillery and so the war ends up in peace and quietness.

Well, unless we are all extremely unlucky, we shall all see Blighty again after all.

Second Lieutenant Clifford Carter, 2nd York and Lancasters, 6th Division, had been much involved in the final fighting, but was engaged in somewhat less dramatic activities when the news of the Armistice arrived:

I had just marched my platoon to 'Baths', and was wandering aimlessly about the roads, waiting till they had finished, when I saw a Signaller leap out of his billet and fix a notice to the wall outside: 'Hostilities will cease at 11.00 today' etc. It was one of the pleasantest duties of my Army life to return to the Baths and report the news to the men – adding that they would not have to return to the front that night as had been expected.

It is quite impossible to describe the feeling of relief. Only those who were there can appreciate it fully.

The night was given over to revelry, in which the French joined. Bonfires were lit at every street corner and the whole countryside was ablaze with fires and star shells.

He wrote the above account sometime later. In a letter written on the day he stated: 'What a famous date this will be – the date on which the fighting ceases. I am pleased I am out here for the finish.'

That the Front was the place to be was also the view of Lieutenant Alex Wilkinson of the 2nd Coldstream Guards. As one of that remarkably substantial band of fighting men who had thoroughly enjoyed their war, he found himself facing the suddenly changed future with ambiguous feelings, mixing satisfaction at victory with a distinct regret that the 'show' was over. In a letter of 12 November he told his young sister, Sidney:

The jolly old war has come to an end at last, and a good end too. For peace I don't care one bit, but I am exceedingly glad that we have won the war. That is the point. And thank heavens I had a really good battle before the end. I would not have missed it for anything in the whole world, but I only just got back in time. It was really nice to be actually in the line when hostilities ceased. It is where I really wanted to be, and one was able to appreciate it there as nowhere else.

In the case of Sergeant Guy Buckeridge, whose Royal Engineers unit of 37th Division was advancing through drenching rain to a newly liberated town, Caudry, it took some time for him and his comrades to take in the significance of the event. As they entered the town a voice shouted 'Cheer up boys, an armistice has been signed.' At first the men trudged on automatically: 'We were all too tired to appreciate what it meant and there was no sign of enthusiasm at all. However a meal and later a double rum issue revived our dormant faculties and by evening we gave expression to our feelings more exuberantly, I am sure, than people at home.' Using a term coined in 1900 to describe the extravagant behaviour of the London crowds following the relief of Mafeking during the Boer War, he continued: 'The Battalion bands played and we danced with the civilians, sang, fired off Very lights, put ground flares about and lighted, got a speech out of the Brigadier and "Mafficked" until we broke down absolutely exhausted.'

Yet in many cases reactions were muted. Major F.J. Rice and his officers showed little excitement, though they did go so far as to buy a bottle of port from a nearby anti-aircraft battery. 'We then went round the gun park and harness sheds, and told the NCOs and men. As an example of the calmness with which it was received, when we met Sgt. Goodall walking across the gun park and told him, he merely halted, saluted, said "Very good, sir", and walked on!'

'There had been so much talk of an armistice,' wrote Captain J.C. Dunn of the 2nd Royal Welsh Fusiliers, 'that a Brigade message in the morning telling us of its having been signed at 8 o'clock, and that hostilities were to cease at 11, fell somewhat flat. The event was anticlimax relieved by some spasmodic cheering when the news got about, by the general atmosphere of "slacking off for the day", and by the notes of a lively band in the late afternoon.' A voluntary service of thanksgiving was held in a cinema built by the Germans during the occupation: 'the spacious building,' Dunn reported, 'was quite full.' By contrast, the local French civilians were overjoyed, and had Allied flags up and flying 'in astonishingly quick time'. But it was the sudden cessation of the constant noise which would remain in the minds of many in the van of the advance on 11 November. A Lieutenant Evans of the same battalion would write: 'To me the most remarkable feature of that day and night was the uncanny silence that prevailed. No rumbling of guns, no staccato of machine-guns, nor did the roar of exploding dumps break into the night as it had so often done. The War was over.'

Yet in other ways there was no change, with business continuing exactly as usual. Captain Dunn noted, in reference to the notoriously teetotal division, the 33rd, to which his battalion had previously belonged: 'Not even on this day did the GOC allow his men a tot of rum.'

Lieutenant-Colonel Rowland Feilding, CO of the 6th Connaught Rangers, 16th Division, reported the playing of another, no doubt equally lively, band, but did so with considerable frustration. He described his feelings in a letter to his wife, written from the Officers' Club newly established in the Hotel Royal, Lille:

Yesterday, we were to have pushed on and captured another town – Ath – which would have been a bloodless victory, since the enemy was retreating so fast that it was difficult to keep pace with him; and since my battalion had been detailed as advanced guard, the day would unquestionably have provided plenty of amusement. A screen of cavalry (19th Hussars) was to have advanced in front of us, and this in itself would have been a novel experience, being the first time, I imagine, since 1914, that such a thing has been possible in the war – I mean, of course, on the Western Front.

However, a stop was put to proceedings by the signing of the Armistice, which took place in the morning, as you know, and my orders were countermanded, and the battalion sent to La Tombe. As we marched away the band played a tune well known to the men, who are accustomed to accompany it with the following words:

> When this ruddy war is over,
> Oh! how happy I shall be!

This, no doubt, was very appropriate, but nevertheless, what a thousand pities that we should have had to draw off at such a moment – just as we had the enemy cold.

Captain Harry Siepmann of the Royal Field Artillery was also far from happy when his battery received the appropriate signal – as it happened some time after the ceasefire had come into force. The reason for his distress was not so much that the Allies 'had the enemy cold', as that he was one who sensed hazards ahead if the war were to end in an ambiguous, inconclusive manner, with much important business unfinished. The signal was delivered by a despatch rider who drove noisily up to their position and got a severe reprimand for doing so. When he defended himself by attempting to explain the nature of the message he had brought, a subaltern rounded on him in anger to the effect that there had been a great deal of silly talk of that sort and that people who went around spreading that kind of story ought to be put in the guardroom: 'It was not until he had gone that we opened the envelope and found that it did indeed contain the hated news. It was poor compensation to reflect that, in spite of the Armistice, we had been in action at a few minutes to one o'clock on 11th November 1918.'

One whose thoughts ranged far and wide on 11 November was

Private Arthur Wrench, of the 51st (Highland) Division, long returned from Blighty after being wounded in the first German offensive back in the spring. The previous Friday, 8 November, had been the first anniversary of the death of his younger brother, Bill, killed almost before he reached the front, whereas he, by contrast, had come through any number of hazards: 'To think poor Bill paid the penalty of patriotism so soon! I wonder what thanks he'll get for it, and we who survive too.' Armistice Day produced a substantial entry in Wrench's ever eloquent diary, in one section of which he echoed the sentiments of three days earlier. His part of the front was one where celebrations were such that he could describe them as 'a riot of enthusiasm' – 'it is pandemonium and I am sure we must all be mad'; but this had inspired him to comment: 'While we are letting ourselves get loose it is certain that each one of us has time to give a thought of regret for our late pals who have "gone west" and have not been spared to go mad like us. It is yet to be seen whether the price they have paid will be in vain or will be truly honoured and appreciated.'

He also wrote, with an irony of which he could not have been remotely conscious at the time: 'I think it is quite hopeless to describe what today means to us all. We who will return to tell people what war really is surely hope that 11 a.m. this day will be of great significance to generations to come. Surely this is the last war that will ever be between civilized nations.'

*   *   *

At certain points there was severe fighting, not despite, but because of, the imminence of the Armistice, as attempts were made to seize every final inch of German-held territory before the ceasefire came into force. At 10.58 a.m., at a canal crossing between Havre and Ville-sur-Haine on the outskirts of Mons, an attack was mounted towards a row of miners' houses by troops of the 28th North West Battalion, 2nd Canadian Division. In the attack Private George Lawrence Price was killed. Officially named as the last Canadian soldier to die on the Western Front in the First World War, he was honoured fifty years later, on 11 November 1968, by a memorial plaque placed by his surviving comrades on the wall of one of the houses. These having subsequently been demolished, the plaque is now preserved in the local Hôtel de Ville. Price was interred in a cemetery originally developed by the Germans at the nearby village of St Symphorien, where he was laid to rest less than twenty yards from the grave of a soldier killed during Britain's first action of the war, on 23 August 1914. Across a tiny piece of groomed Belgian turf the two headstones face each other, two points of demarcation defining the beginning and the end of the British Empire's involvement in the great European war of 1914–1918.

* * *

Armistice Day found Field Marshal Sir Douglas Haig based well forward of his normal GHQ, in his official train temporarily stationed at Cambrai. At 11 a.m. he held a meeting with his five Army Commanders and the General commanding the Cavalry Corps. He explained that for the moment his orders were that the British were to advance to a sector of the German frontier thirty-two miles wide extending from Verviers in the north to Houffalize in the south, and he indicated his proposed disposition of the various armies. 'I then pointed out', he noted in his diary, 'the importance of looking after the troops during the period following the cessation of hostilities – very often the best fighters are the most difficult to deal with in periods of quiet! I suggested a number of ways in which men can be kept occupied. It is as much the duty of all Officers to keep their men amused, as it is to train them for war.'

It was a day on which the media of the time was allowed to occupy, however briefly, the attentions of the high and the mighty, so that the occasion might be recorded for posterity. Haig noted: 'After the Conference, we were all taken on the Cinema. General Plumer, whom I told to "go off and be cinemaed" went off most obediently and stood before the camera trying to look his best, while Byng and others near him were chaffing the old man and trying to make him laugh.' The film survives, as does a historic photograph taken at the same time (see illustration 33).

* * *

At Streatham Secondary School in south London, thirteen-year-old Olive Wells of form Lower 5 Alpha wrote an account of the day in immaculate copybook handwriting:

We came to school this morning hardly realising what a great day this was going to be.

Miss Bassett told us that the Armistice was signed – we had received the news about 5 o'clock a.m. We cheered until we were hoarse.

At 11 a.m. the guns were fired, the church-bells were rung, the sirens were blown – we did not think of air raids as we would have done any other day.

We went out into the road and cheered. The Union Jack was sent up the staff and there it fluttered in the breeze.

Our home-work was excused for the week.

It was not a bright day but very damp.

The guns are booming while I write this.

We are coming out of school at 12.30 p.m. instead of 12.45 p.m. this morning.

Wherever we go, we see flags flying – big ones and small ones.

This has started as a day of rejoicing and I am sure will end as happily.

Yet for some children celebration did not seem appropriate. At one elementary school the daughter of a soldier who had died in the war refused to stand up for the singing of the National Anthem. Describing the event many years later, her own daughter wrote: 'For such outrageous behaviour she was hauled before the headmaster who demanded an explanation. Breaking into loud sobs she told him that all the other little boys' and girls' daddies would be coming home now, but her daddy would never come home again. In those less enlightened days this did not save her from the cane, but the headmaster was a kindly man and he did stay his hand to lighten the blows a little.' Adding poignancy to the story is the fact the soldier in question, Gunner James Bennett (whose diary is quoted in Chapter 1, p. 11), had been a late volunteer at the age of thirty-seven, only enlisting after a furious argument with his wife during which she had 'suddenly spat out that he was nothing but a coward and that if he were half a man he would be away in France, where the brave men were, defending his country'. He had died of wounds in October 1917 after sixty weeks away from home, having had only one brief leave in the course of his service. In the month following the Armistice a fellow gunner would visit Bennett's home and add a moving postscript to his former comrade's diary: 'Dec 14th 1918 greatest Victory of all time due to the works and efforts of Dear old Jim. J. A. Thomas. When others forget I can never.'

* * *

For one Yorkshire family 11 November was spent in deep anxiety as to the fate of one of its members. This was Private Mark Yewdall, the reluctant soldier of the Artists Rifles, who had written so vividly and bitterly about the conditions at Passchendaele a year earlier (see Chapter 1, page 12), and who was suddenly taken ill while undertaking a Signals Course in France in the war's final days. His sister Ellen recorded the progress of events in her diary:

> *Sunday Nov 10.* Had a postcard from Mark saying he was on the way to hospital – said not bad.
>
> *Tues 12.* To Rawdon when I got back a telegram had come saying Mark was very bad with influenza. On the Sat before Father came in at dinner time from Leeds – as he opened the front door he said 'Mark is all right, there will be no more fighting'. Sun we got the p.c. Monday the Armistice was signed, buzzers went, church bells rang, people rejoiced – but washed dusters in the cellar – hated the noise and cried out that it had come so late. How I wept and prayed as I worked but felt somehow it was too late – could somehow see that now it was starting again everything still to be settled the war had made this worse and worse and done no good at all.
>
> Tuesday the telegram – Father telegraphed and wrote and asked for permission to go out [to France] – but no word till Saturday, when a telegram came to say that all was over on Wed 13th.

A fellow member of the Artists Rifles who had been on the same course who heard the tragic news when he returned to his battalion on the 19th made the appropriate and inevitable comment: 'It seemed so impossible and monstrous that the "old chap" should jog along through the wretched business and then when all is over quietly drop out of the story.'

* * *

In London on Armistice Day the crowds celebrated with extravagant and sustained enthusiasm. 'The unceasing drizzle', commented *The Times* in its edition of the following day, 'was powerless to dampen the high spirits of the people. . . . The air was full of the intoxicating spirit of joy.' Theatres were packed, with audiences everywhere 'a-quiver with half suppressed feeling, and ready to give it vent as fully and as often as they could'. The national anthem was sung at the slightest pretext, and there were ready cheers for the King, notably at the Coliseum, where a young subaltern took the lead. Underground trains were crammed, giving rise to pleasantries which even the nation's staidest newspaper felt no shame in reporting. 'A soldier at Charing Cross,' one of its correspondents noted, 'after two attempts to squeeze himself into a westbound train, was heard to say to a comrade, "I suppose we shall get used to the horrors of peace presently". A woman made the comment that "This jam ain't rationed at any rate".'

'Triumphant pandemonium' was Winston's Churchill's summing up of the moment when, as the hour struck eleven, 'flags appeared as if by magic' and in almost no time 'hundreds, nay thousands' of people began to swarm through the 'strict, war-straitened, regulated streets'. Together with his wife he attempted to drive from his office in the Admiralty to the residence of the Prime Minister, to offer their congratulations to the leader 'on whom the central impact of the home struggle had fallen, in his hour of recompense'. But this was to be no easy rite of passage. 'No sooner had we entered our car than twenty people mounted upon it, and in the midst of a wildly cheering multitude we were impelled slowly forward through White-hall.' Inevitably Churchill's thoughts went back to the rejoicing throng of four and a half years earlier, on the day when the war had begun. 'We had driven together the opposite way along the same road on the afternoon of the ultimatum. There had been the same crowd and almost the same enthusiasm.'

Another observer of the day's celebrations who saw the shadows of the past behind the reality of the present was Osbert Sitwell, then an officer in the Grenadier Guards. In a moving passage in his autobiographical *Laughter in the Next Room* he would write:

> So that night it was impossible to drive through Trafalgar Square: because the crowd danced under lights turned up for the first

time in four years – danced so thickly that the heads, the faces, were like a field of golden corn moving in a dark wind. The last occasion I had seen the London crowd was when it had cheered for its own death outside Buckingham Palace on the evening of the 4th of August 1914; most of the men who had composed it were now dead. Their heirs were dancing because life had been given back to them. . . . A long nightmare was over, and there were many soldiers, sailors and airmen in the crowd which, sometimes joining up, linking hands, dashed like the waves of the sea against the sides of the Square, against the railings of the National Gallery, sweeping up so far as beyond the shallow stone steps of St. Martin-in-the-Fields. . . . It was an honest, happy crowd, good-natured, possessed of a kind of wisdom or philosophy, as well as of a perseverance which few races knew. . . .

One notable witness – at last, if only in a minor way, a participant as opposed to a commentator from the side-lines – was the diarist Frederick Arthur Robinson. This was an occasion he had dreamed of for many months, and he had come up to London from his Surrey fastness to savour it:

Nov. 11. A day never to be forgotten! The day has come at last which we have lived for these long four years and three months. The horrible thing is over! The last of our enemies is beaten, and her once mighty Emperor is a fugitive and his Empire crumbling to the dust. It is difficult to believe all this, but it is true.

Practically all work was suspended, and the streets became packed with people, including great numbers of soldiers on leave and thousands in hospital blue – most of these, accompanied by their lady friends, shouted themselves hoarse and waved flags, made many loud noises on improvised instruments, others danced informal quadrilles – all was one vast pandemonium. Perhaps such crowds have never been seen in London.

In the Mall was an exhibition of hundreds of cannon captured from the enemy which formed a very appropriate background to the crowds here assembled. In front of Buckingham Palace was one vast flock of people, many of whom had found positions of advantage on Queen Victoria's monument just opposite, and when the King and Queen appeared from time to time on the balcony of the Palace, the enthusiasm simply knew no bounds.

Later, when the King, Queen and Princess Mary (dressed as a VAD) drove down the Mall in an open carriage (where the writer saw them) the people simply went wild with delight. No Bolshevism here!

As darkness drew on it was realized that the lighting regulations had been withdrawn, and though there had not been time to clean the black shading off most of the street lamps, this had been done in many cases, and the streets, particularly Piccadilly, were comparatively well lighted. The clubs and hotels had their outside lights on and their blinds up which added to the general brightness.

Passing the Houses of Parliament on our way home, we saw the great clock once more illuminated and heard the thundering tones of Big Ben reverberating the great fact of peace.

If Robinson's response to the Armistice was immediate and unalloyed, by contrast, Robert Saunders, the headmaster of Fletching, Sussex, did not write to his son in Canada until several days later, and when he did a reflective, even a sombre tone, dominated his account of events. He began breezily enough with lively details of how the news was received in his village; of children cheering 'loud enough to be heard all over the parish', of everyone putting up flags and colours, and then, despite the general excitement, of a curious sensation of 'no noise till a scratch team started to ring the Bells'. He had swiftly decided that normal lessons would not be appropriate that afternoon, 'so I gave an address on the War and the Armistice after which we sang patriotic songs'. At 6 p.m. the Church clock, which had been silent since 1914, struck the hour, 'and has continued striking day and night. It may seem a little thing to you,' he told his son, 'but to all here it meant much, and sounded like the voice of an old friend returning from the grave.' Yet he had to admit that there was another aspect to what had seemed to so many so happy an occasion:

The War has pressed more heavily on us than is generally thought, even by ourselves, and I am afraid has aged us more than the 4½ years warrant as regards time. I think most people feel that some time must elapse before we can properly celebrate peace, our feelings have been too much harassed and our sympathies too often called forth, for the losses of our friends and neighbours. As I look back I can see so many tragedies in families I know well, and I can see so many of my old boys who are dead or wounded, or dying of consumption, and recall them as boys at school where I used to urge on them the duty of patriotism, so that at present it doesn't seem right that those who have escaped shall give themselves up to Joy days.

There were numerous others who thought that the end of so much suffering and sacrifice offered small pretext for heady rejoicing. One notable example was Colonel Alan Brooke, who had served in France, with much distinction, as an artillery officer, and who, as Lord Alanbrooke, would become Britain's senior soldier in the next war. He would write of the celebrations of 11 November: 'That wild evening jarred on my feelings. I felt untold relief at the end being there at last, but was swamped with floods of memories of those years of struggle. I was filled with gloom that evening, and retired to sleep early.'

A similar attitude was taken by the future scholar and writer C.S. Lewis, at that time a Second Lieutenant of the Somerset Light Infantry, recuperating in England from the effects of a shell, fired as it happened by British guns, which had killed one of his closest friends at the same time as it wounded him. A little over a year earlier he had trained as an officer at Keble College, Oxford, with a group of young men who had fared disproportionately badly in their brief time at the Front. Resorting like Sergeant Buckeridge to that now long-unused coinage from the Boer War, Lewis wrote to his father in the week following the Armistice: 'The man who can give way to mafficking at such a time is more than indecent – he is mad. I remember five of us at Keble, and I am the only survivor: I think of Mr Sutton, a widower with five sons, all of whom have gone. One cannot help wondering why. Let us be silent and thankful.'

* * *

London was not, of course, the only place to see 'wild' celebrations in the wake of the Armistice.

In New York bells rang, whistles blew, cannons boomed and all the steam sirens and fog-horns of the city added to 'the carnival of noise'. Reporting this, a British magazine noted: 'Flags and banners appeared in the streets, which were filled with rejoicing crowds who early abandoned all ideas of work for the day.' There was also much use of ticker-tape, clearly a phenomenon unfamiliar to British readers, for its reporter added: 'A feature of the celebrations was the avalanche of torn-up paper which descended from the tops of lofty buildings, and the streets beneath were littered almost to the extent of a foot in depth.'

Alison Strathy, the Canadian-born 'Nurse's Aide' attached to the American Red Cross, was in Paris on 11 November. She witnessed the slow growth of the city's enthusiasm as the news began to spread:

The cannon went off at 11 a.m. – this was to be the signal for 'Armistice signed'.

I was standing on the corner of the Place de l'Opera by myself – there was almost a silence – the significance of what it meant was overwhelming – PEACE. Then here and there excited little groups gathered – then a mob came down the Avenue de l'Opera – it developed into a procession. At its head marched Latin Quarter students (wearing large black ties) carrying the flags of the Allied countries. They were followed by soldiers, sailors, midinettes [a term for young part-time milliners or dressmakers], members of the Red Cross, the YMCA civilians and more soldiers. As they marched they were joined on all sides. In front of the Opera the procession seemed to hesitate for a moment, then with one accord they broke into the 'La Marseillaise.' It was like a match to a bonfire, now we were a seething crowd celebrating VICTORY! VICTORY! VICTORY!

I joined in and found myself arm in arm with poilus I had never seen before. I forget where we went, we toured the streets and sang and sang and the procession kept growing longer and longer. Finally, we ended up at the Place de la Concorde and stopped before the statue to the 'City of Lille'. The statue was draped with flags and loaded with laurel leaves – it had been just liberated from German hands by the British. The statue to the 'City of Strasbourg' was similarly decorated, as it had been recaptured by the Americans.

Before we separated we sang 'La Marseillaise' again, and more than one Frenchman had tears in his eyes.

That evening Miss Strathy and several of her colleagues dined at a little restaurant, the *Henriette*, in the Latin Quarter. They found themselves witnesses of a small but moving occasion:

> With us was a blind '*sous-officier*' [a French NCO]. After numerous toasts and speeches by 'all and sundry', our young soldier stood up, steadied himself by the table, and without a word launched forth into a patriotic song. It was in gratitude for the deliverance of Lille, and for Lille he had given his sight! We kissed him goodbye and he returned to his hospital and his thoughts, and we to the crowds.

Also in Paris that day was an American Medical Officer, Major F.J. Sharp; in a letter written from, as he put it, 'Over There' to his mother in far-off Salt Lake City, he stated:

> I am so happy tonight for peace is certain with the signing of the armistice. The French people are wild with joy and one can hardly blame them, for they have suffered terribly. 2½ million of her best men, they say, have paid the price of the supreme sacrifice. This of course seems to me to be the greatest loss. Towns that are destroyed can be restored but lives are lost. She has cause to rejoice and the United States has cause to rejoice that it is over so quickly for them. Her sons have shown a willingness for sacrifice that compares with France. Many of our best have paid the extreme sacrifice but not like France in numbers. We will probably be friends with the French for ever.

*   *   *

In the region of the Argonne, Sharp's fellow countryman, Major Leland Garretson, having been in action almost until the moment of cease-fire, wrote in a letter home a thoughtful, emotive assessment of the contribution of his division, and by implication of his country, to the outcome of the campaign:

> Peace at last reigns over this weary war-scarred land. Although all of us are of course ready to toss our hats into the air and howl with joy, under it all I believe most of us find ourselves thanking God over and over again that this terrible thing is really and truly over. It is hard to realize that the harvest of all our efforts for the

past year and a half is actually at hand, and that our aims are nearly accomplished. While of course we still have no end of work to do, the fact remains that the pent-up horrors of Imperialism are forever dead, and I thank God for one that I was allowed to do my very humble part in bringing it about.

We all realize that our Division is not an old campaigning Division when compared to the French and British veterans, but during the short time we were at it we were made to pay our precious toll and came to the thorough realization that modern war is the most wholly awful thing ever conceived by the mind of man, and that the Boche besides being a very worthy foe is the arch master of it all. We try not to boast but do find gratification in the fact that our work was satisfactory to the Powers that Be.

The American Red Cross volunteer Annah Peck, still serving among the French forces, also finished her war in the region of the Argonne. She had not been actively involved in relief work for long, but she had become so caught up in its stresses and challenges that she found the Armistice too overwhelming an event for straightforward rejoicing:

When the news reached us the first impression was that a curious pall seemed to fall over everything and no one knew whether to believe it or not, for although the announcement was quite official, the fact seemed too big to grasp. It was as if one had been holding fast to something all these years, holding on with a grip that one never dared to slacken, and suddenly one was told to let go, and as the tired muscles relaxed they seemed to hurt more than when one was holding on. It hurt in many ways, as big events must do, but the joy of peace was there too, and as the men realized it one saw the change. That night in the Canteen they sang as they had never sung before, not the banal songs to pass the time, but the *Marseillaise* and *Madelon* and the songs that they really loved. One man from the Opera with a magnificent voice sang the verses and when the chorus came all the Poilus joined in and seemed to sing with open throats and hearts. It was wonderful, and that evening we did not close the Canteen and put the lights out at nine o'clock, which was the rule at the front, but let them sing until they were too hoarse to go on any longer, and we stayed and listened, thrilled – for at last some expression had been given to the pent-up feelings of the day.

The English volunteer Margaret Mercer, now based at Reims, heard the news with a similar mix of emotion. For her, however, the day ended not in celebrations (of which there appeared to be very few so near to the fighting zone), but in a flurry of work facing one of the less happy consequences of the sudden peace:

11th November, Monday. They say the armistice is signed but I dare not believe it until 'Puck' [the nickname of their group leader] comes down and says it is official and a flag is flying on the Cathedral. I just want to weep with thankfulness and relief that these ghastly years are over at last, and especially that it has been so worth while, and that we have achieved the complete and overwhelming victory. One cannot rejoice at such a victory, the price has been far too terrible, but at least it has not been paid in vain. And surely, even Germany will learn by this awful lesson that war is mad and terrible, and that there are things in the world stronger and more powerful than Krupp's cannon.

I am lucky to be so much in the thick of the French Army for this wonderful day, but am surprised at the calm everywhere, there are flags on the battered houses and on most of the camions, but there is no singing or shouting. I think we are still too near the horrors of war here for any show of high spirits with the Hospital full as ever of crippled and dying men. There is more a feeling of immense relief than anything, and *enfin on ne se tue pas* ('at last the killing has stopped') is the commonest expression which truly expresses the heart of the situation.

We are busier than usual and have hardly time to think or realize at all that this is the day we have been praying for, for four and a half years. We have an invasion of dreadful old women this evening who have been driven from a hospice that was shelled and set on fire by the retreating Boches. They've been in German hands for four and a half years and are all half mad, either from old age or shock. It is a most trying party to cope with, far worse than hundreds of *poilus*.

* * *

What of reactions in the war's sideshows? Distance from the centre of the stage did not necessarily reduce the sense of relief and even delight with which the Armistice announcement was welcomed. At Kerman in Persia Captain Tom Sherwood of the South Persia Rifles wrote to his wife, mother of the recently born son whom he had not yet seen, in terms of the greatest enthusiasm:

> Isn't this just wonderful news, simply surprise after surprise. I shall never forget the last few days as long as I live, can hardly realize the situation, complete and total collapse, what must England have been like, unbelievable scenes I suppose. I know we simply went mad here, can't you realize it? And now I suppose your one and only thought is when shall we have that lovely reunion. I can think of nothing else.
>
> Wild excitement prevails amongst us all, it is most difficult to calm oneself and behave like a rational being, just think of it 'The War is over', and a few weeks ago who could possibly have foreseen it all. But darling what a great thing it is to know that it *is* over, in dark moments I have thought the War would last for years and years, oh! what rejoicing for everybody at home, no more anxiety for you brave girls, and mothers of boys at the front.

Private William Knott, Royal Army Medical Corps, was in Palestine with the 165th Combined Field Ambulance, 10th Division, when hostilities ended. His reaction was that of a man of deep religious faith who had served uncomplainingly and without rancour through hard times and often atrocious conditions in the Middle East ever since his posting to Gallipoli three years earlier:

> As soon as I heard the news I silently knelt in my bivouac and praised God for His answer to the prayers of Christ's Church on earth. I believe it is through faithful prayer this moment has come. God has given us victory as the most righteous cause, but we must continue to pray for the cleansing of our land, for still a Saviour is needed for the masses of ungodly. Now more than ever must the gospel of God's saving grace be published throughout every nation. Enmity must not arise against olden foes, international striving for the souls of men must be the motto of the Church of God.

There was a modestly triumphal event on the 12th in which Knott happily joined, as is evident from his detailed account in his diary:

> The Colonel sent three men to Ludd with 4000 piastres to buy a dinner for the Englishmen on celebration of peace. So at 5 o'clock we sat down in three marquees joined together as one, to a very creditable repast for field cookery. Chicken pie with peas and beans and tomato sauce followed by pineapples and rice with milk. The teetotallers were provided with tea in lieu of beer. The CO came in during the feasting, and thanked the troops for their excellent work and co-operation.

From Major Alfred Bundy in Salonika there was a more muted response. 'So the war is over at last!', he noted in his diary, adding in view of what he sensed would be a long task of clearing up before there was any prospect of returning home: 'It looks as though I shall have to stay on here, for some time to come.'

* * *

What of the German reaction to these events?

Princess Evelyn Blücher, English but married to a German aristocrat, reported a nation in bewilderment and dismay, especially in the high-connected circles in Berlin in which she moved: 'Amongst the aristocracy the grief at the breakdown of their country, more than at the personal fall of the Kaiser, is quite heart-rending to see. I have seen some of our friends, strong men, sit down and sob at the news, while others seemed to shrink to half their size and were struck dumb with pain.' Although no advocate of the fallen monarch, she nevertheless felt that his treatment by his own countrymen had been unduly vicious: 'I must confess that I myself feel shocked and surprised at the universal rejoicing manifested at the abdication of the Kaiser. They could not be more jubilant if they had won the war! *Vox populi, vox dei!* He may deserve his fate, but it seems very hard and cruel to throw stones at him at such a moment, when he must be enduring untold anguish and sorrow.'

She had great sympathy for the mass of the populace, victims rather than architects of their nation's fall:

> I never felt so deeply for the German people as I do now, when I see them bravely and persistently trying to redress the wrongs of

the war, for which they were in truth never responsible. The greater part of them were men fighting blindly to guard an ideal, the 'Heimat', some patch of mother earth, a small cottage half hidden in its sheltering fruit trees, ploughed fields rising on the slope of a hill up to the dark forest of pines, maybe, or a wide stretch of flat country where the golden corn-fields sway and wave in the wind as far as the eye can reach.

This everything, that meant 'home' to them, they were told was in danger, and this they went out to save.

Underneath she hoped that the bitter experience which her adopted country was now undergoing might somehow produce a positive and benign outcome: 'Truly, a great storm is passing over the land, and princes are falling from their thrones like ripe fruit from a tree, but everyone seems to be acting under a divine law which is leading the German nation to a new phase of development.'

How was the Armistice seen by Germany's soldiers in the field? The artillery officer Herbert Sulzbach noted in his diary on 11 November: 'The war is over.... How we looked forward to *this* moment; how we used to picture it as the most splendid event of our lives; and here we are now, humbled, our souls torn and bleeding, and know that we've surrendered. Germany has surrendered to the Entente!'

He also, significantly, wrote the following, two days later:

In spite of it all, we can be proud of the performance we have put up, and we shall always be proud of it. Never before has a nation, a single army, had the whole world against it and stood its ground against such overwhelming odds; had it been the other way round, this heroic performance could never have been achieved by any other nation. We protected our homeland from her enemies – they never pushed as far as German territory.

*   *   *

The eleventh day of the eleventh month of the final year of the Great War would become one of the landmark dates of the century, and it has gained rather than lost its impact as the decades have gone by. Queen Mary's instinct to call it 'the greatest day in the world's history' caught the mood of countless people at the time, though, sensing what could only be an ambivalent mood after so much suffering, she wisely added: 'A day full of emotion and thankfulness – tinged with regret at the many lives who have fallen in this ghastly war.'

At the fighting fronts, as soon as the news had been taken in and digested, one pre-eminent subject dominated the agenda so far as the soldiers who had done so much to bring about the Armistice were concerned. Sergeant Vigurs raised it in his letter of 11 November, writing within minutes of the actual moment of cease-fire: 'The question on everyone's tongue is "When shall we get home?" '

12

'Till the Boys Come Home'

'CHEER-HO! the war is coming to an end now, and it will not be long now "till the boys come home".'

So Private Frederick Noakes had written in mid-October, with three weeks or so of fighting yet to come. *The 'Better Times'* – the final incarnation of the famous trench magazine *The Wipers Times* – was swift to broach this vital subject of homecoming, than which none was closer to the heart of the soldier, in its penultimate edition published in November. It included the following brief item, under the title 'EXTRACT FROM THE BOOK OF TOMAR-SAT-KINS':

> And it came to pass at eleven hours of the eleventh day of the eleventh month there was silence throughout the Land of the Westernfront. And no-one did loose a gun, no, not so much as a pip-squeak did go off. And the heart of Tomar-Sat-Kins was glad in him so that he did give praise saying 'Wotto, no tarf, and the Land of Blighty shall know me *some* more'. For he did know that the time of Hunnites was come, and that peace would shortly come throughout the land.

Which being interpreted meant that Tommy Atkins, having gone to war, had now completed (in his view) his terms of contract, and wished to go home. For thousands, however, there would not be the easy, happy return they dreamed of; it would take many months before they were back in their hoped-for destination of 'Civvy Street', and 'Blighty' would remain 'Shangri-La' for a frustratingly long time.

For the vast majority of men in uniform the switch from concentrating on fighting the war to focusing on reaping the benefits of the peace was virtually immediate. Having defined in his letter of 11 November 'the question on everyone's tongue' as 'When shall we get home?' (see opposite page), Sergeant Vigurs continued: 'When

the war was in full swing everyone used to say that as long as the
war was on it didn't matter how long we stopped out here, and now
everyone wishes to be back home 2 mins after hostilities have ceased.
Tommy is a funny animal – never satisfied and always grumbling.'
In other words: mobilization had had its day, and far too long a one
at that; now and immediately, its opposite, demobilization, was the
current issue. There would be a great deal of grumbling over the
following weeks and months, some of it spilling over into active
protest, before this most difficult of problems was resolved.

A prime cause of friction was that it was soon realized that the
Government's emphasis was more on what it deemed to be the
nation's interest, rather than on the wishes of those who had fought
the nation's cause. It saw as its first priority the release of what it
called 'pivotal men' – people who could be returned with immediate
effect to the running of the nation's economy. But this in effect
meant: last in, first out, since clearly those who had only recently
vacated their civilian employment could be slotted back into peacetime work far more swiftly and conveniently than those who had
been out of the frame for several years. The latter inevitably felt this
was not fair; indeed, even before the Government's policy was established, those who had been the longest in uniform were protesting
their right for the earliest consideration for repatriation and release.
Thus Captain Tom Sherwood, in his 'Armistice' letter written on 17
November from Persia, stated: 'My contract of three years or the
duration has expired and all who joined when I did, "The First
Hundred Thousand", are surely entitled to our discharge first.'

Some commanding officers decided simply to ignore the government's instructions. Major H.J.C. Marshall, Royal Engineers, who
had assisted at the crossing of the St Quentin Canal by his 46th
(North Midland) Division in September, found himself in early 1919
successively in charge of two RE Field Companies, the 466th and
the 468th. In a passage in his postwar memoir which focused on this
crucial nub of the demobilization process he would write:

> Demobilizing these Companies was a terrible task. In an RE
> Company almost everyone had jobs waiting for them and wanted
> to be the next to go home. Major Hardman and I disregarded the
> regulations and demobilized our men by the length of service

abroad, which the men themselves considered the fairer way. Of course the last joined men, having just left a job, could easily go back to it. Very possibly this job had originally belonged to a man who had joined up in 1914, who would in this way be done out of his old job, and be penalised for patriotism. This was the weak point of the official scheme of demobilization.

I am sure that every officer who demobilized a Unit ought to have had the DSO. It was the hardest job of the war.

What complicated the issue, and led to much resentment, even anger, was the fact that changes of attitude among the troops were not immediately matched among those who commanded them. The latter expected business as usual but without the fighting. The men by contrast felt they were entitled to relax, to take things easy. The job was done; they were going home sooner or later; why should they be treated as though they were still engaged in an active campaign? As early as 12 November the artillery signaller W.R. Acklam commented in his diary: 'Everybody rather happy today in spite of harness cleaning, as the weather was fine and no signs of war about, but all the same there is a noticeable beginning to tighten the screw in such matters as parades and stables. I am hoping this will meet with opposition, if they do much of it, now that the war is over.'

The postwar memoir of Sergeant Guy Buckeridge, Royal Engineers, (quoted in the previous chapter), shows clearly that that 'tightening of the screw' did indeed continue, giving rise to the upsurge of a volatile and indignant mood of a kind that Gunner Acklam had feared. After 'a few days' rest, new clothes and a general refit', the march eastwards that had been interrupted by the cease-fire continued, but the troops were not happy: 'There was a riot in our Division here. The fellows declined to march and carry full packs. The War was over for them and they declined to be pack animals any longer.' In this case, fortunately, those in charge were quick to recognize their misjudgement: 'It all seemed very foolish to me but the authorities very wisely conceded what was asked for and in the end spare gear was carried for us.'

Buckeridge saw further evidence of disaffection when some weeks later he left his division to go home on leave:

On 13th December my leave warrant was handed to me. The 14th found me at Bavay where I stayed in charge of a billet until the 17th. The weather was awful and the men fractious. Rations were bad. They hated being delayed in reaching their homes and the transport commandant had a difficult and thankless task. There were several riots and he eventually appealed to all NCOs to help to make things go. But it was hopeless. The continual rain and lack of amusement gave the fellows no chance of getting outside their immediate grievances.

The 18th found me at Cambrai, where we were put in the barracks. The feeling was not better there and I was glad to leave. It seemed as though the whole Army had become imbued with a spirit of revolt against the system which had held the individual for so long.

For Buckeridge release was in fact near at hand, though not until after a somewhat dismal return. 'On the 21st I reached Boulogne and that evening I reached home. I was too unwell to do anything. The usual Christmas depression was stronger than ever. On the 27th I roused myself and made enquiry and on the 28th I was demobbed and became a free man again.' A former member of the National Telephone Company, later the Post Office, he had left what was virtually a reserved occupation when he volunteered in 1915, and in his case his employers were happy to re-employ him despite the length of his time of absence.

John McIlwain was a thirty-eight-year-old Warrant Officer in the Connaught Rangers with eight years of service in India behind him (from 1899 to 1907), as well as a Mention in Despatches for gallant service in Gallipoli. His diary for November–December 1918 mentions several brushes with the authorities which clearly rankled in the case of a soldier with so long and distinguished a record. Thus on 23 November: 'Went with others to 2nd Lieutenant Caldicott to protest about circular re punishment for not shaving, etc.' The basic reason for the anxieties of his superiors is evident from the next entry in his diary: 'Two days after, lecture by Lt.Col. Carstairs our CO about Bolshevism. British Prussianism afraid of being upset.'

All this was while the battalion was still at the Front. By 5 December they were back at the base. Summing up the time they spent there, McIlwain wrote: 'Have fairly pleasant time in Rouen from now onwards. Light work. Walks in evening with Atkinson (Munsters). YMCA Library, Place Carnot. Introduced to Brontë books. I take prominent part in agitation for demobilization and am branded Bolshie.'

Fear of the contagion of Bolshevism spreading from Russia undoubtedly complicated the whole demobilization issue, with some eminent persons in high authority – notable among them Winston Churchill – all too ready to interpret troop protest as ideologically motivated. The truth seems to be that political pressures played virtually no part at all; when Tommy said he wanted to go back to Blighty, he meant precisely that and no more. He was far more likely to strike up that favourite, plaintive song of the trench years 'I want to Go Home', than to break into the 'International', with the tune, words and sentiments of which he was most unlikely to be even remotely acquainted. As Keith Jeffrey has pointedly written: 'The demobilisation chaos made citizen soldiers bloody-minded, not revolutionary.'

Disaffection was not confined to the British – or Irish – 'other ranks' at this time. Following a spell in hospital the Australian infantry officer, Ted Trundle, was back with his Brigade, where the facts that he had reverted to Lieutenant from his wartime rank of Captain and that his battalion had been abruptly amalgamated with another had done nothing to improve his general temper. On the contrary this had brought out a natural 'Aussie' tendency to look sceptically at some of the more pompous rituals of the imperial motherland. He wrote to his wife on 4 December:

> Last Sunday, the day after I rejoined, the whole Brigade was turned out in style and we went through the ordeal of being reviewed by the King, the Prince of Wales, Prince Albert, and God knows how many more 'fish-heads' – about twenty all told. We have very little to do here other than a little salvaging and the blowing up of old Boche mines and dumps. Everyone is absolutely fed up with soldiering now that the blanky old war is over – and we have only one objective in view and that is to get home.

It might be thought that such sentiments were not shared by his British counterparts. However, this was not necessarily the case. For example, the end of November found Lieutenant George Havard

Thomas and his 8th Sherwood Foresters of 46th Division at Landrecies, on the edge of the Forest of Mormal, through which the BEF
had famously retreated in August 1914. The seizure of such historic
territory made it almost inevitable that some of the royal party
described by Lieutenant Trundle would duly make its appearance
there. Writing on Sunday the 1st – the same day as Trundle's
Australian parade – Havard Thomas reported laconically to his
parents: 'Today the King came to see us and the town. He got out
of his car and walked down the road with Prince Albert and part of
his staff, it was very cold but it didn't last long. There was a great
deal of cheering and flag-waving.' However, the main purpose of his
letter was to air his dismay at what he saw as a demobilization
process becoming increasingly absurd. 'Everyone is anxious to get
back home,' he wrote, 'and yesterday twenty-five coalminers went
from my company.' Clearly by any standards these were 'pivotal
men', so that he could have had little objection on that score; what
was so baffling was the nature of the traffic coming the other way:

> Today I had two new officers join the company. I cannot in the
> name of common sense understand why they are sending people
> out from England now. Flocks of people are coming out who
> have been well dug in in some job at home, there is nothing for
> them to do, either! I have now seven officers and when we were
> fighting about a month ago I had two.
>
>   I am quite fed up with the Army now. The job is finished and
> one put up with a great deal of things when there was a necessity
> to help beat the Boche, but now a lot of things simply irritate me.
> Two days ago I had to design a Xmas card. I had about an hour
> to do it in and nothing to draw from. These people have a very
> queer idea of art, they now ask me to design some memorial for
> Bellenglise with a suitable inscription [a reference to the crossing
> of the St Quentin Canal in September]. The said design to be in
> to Bn Hqrs by 6.30 p.m. I told them to go to Hell, General and
> all.

He speculated pessimistically as to what might be his chances of
early release, wondering whether – being in fact by vocation a
sculptor – he might be wise to attempt a change of category: 'I do
not know when on earth they will let me go as my trade is not of

national importance. I believe I can get back much quicker in the grade of a student.'

A pre-Christmas letter two weeks later carried a similarly despondent message:

> Nobody has as yet been demobilized except coalminers and they are going as fast as the authorities can print new forms. There are extremely few men who have any desire to remain in the Army; all are anxious to discard their khaki now that the job is finished.
>
> I trust you will all have a very merry Xmas. I fear there is no hope of my being there with you this time, better luck next time.

Protest at the unfairness of the demobilization procedure took many forms at this time, varying according to the tradition and nature of the unit concerned. A battalion which had always prided itself on its excellent internal relations, the 1st London Rifle Brigade, registered its complaint at a Christmas concert. Christmas Day had produced a happy regimental occasion, with officers waiting on the troops at dinner before going for a drink in the Sergeants' Mess, the sergeants then being invited back for similar hospitality at the Officers' Mess. But on Boxing Day the first man from the battalion to be demobilized was sent on his way to Blighty – a Yorkshire miner who had only had two months' active service. The aggrieved battalion Transport Section, which included at least a dozen men who had been out since early 1915, decided to interrupt the proceedings at the battalion concert to be held a few days later. Their noisy barracking so enraged the officers, who were the principal performers, that they finally stormed off the stage. But no disciplinary action was taken, doubtless because (in a regiment whose most recent history is fittingly entitled *Gentlemen and Officers*) those in command, despite deploring the culprits' behaviour, understood and sympathized with the frustration which lay behind it.

* * *

The Western Front was far from being the only theatre where disaffection sprang up following the Armistice. In Salonika Major Alfred Bundy noted an immediate rise in indiscipline; indeed, his diary entries for the last weeks of 1918 chronicled a situation on the verge of outright disorder:

Nov. 15th. I have now to adapt the camp for demobilization. Tomorrow my first batch of men for demobilization comes in.

Nov. 16th. First arrival of about 600 men, and they are difficult to handle.

Nov. 17th – Dec 24th. Hundreds of men have arrived daily. Strangely enough now that the war is over, numbers of the men refuse to obey orders or rather they show a certain amount of independence that is most disconcerting. I had to talk to a whole company that were disgracefully abusive to their officers. I realized that any show of military authority would be fatal so I reasoned with them and told them that for the benefit of all and in order to facilitate the movement of those who were anxious to get back to England, it was necessary that they should still behave as disciplined soldiers. My remarks were greeted by cat-calls and rude noises but I knew that there must be a large proportion of the men who were anxious to assist me in the performance of my duty and in facilitating the return to England, so I announced that I would look to the men themselves for co-operation and that if there was obstruction I should have the offenders arrested and kept back. There was then almost complete silence and I had no further difficulty.

But further difficulties there were, with the added hazards of a breakdown of law and order in the surrounding community. Summing up the period 26 December to 6 February 1919, Bundy commented in some disillusion, if with a touch of irony: 'Men coming and going. Nothing exciting except reports of murder, robbery and rioting. If this is peace – war is better!'

He was also concerned for himself. 'Applied today for leave to England – the hoped for preliminary to demobilization,' he wrote on 7 February. 'Most of my old battalion colleagues have gone, as well as about half the Salonika army. It seems unfair that I, a married man, should be detained on duties that might be performed equally well by one without home ties.' He received the necessary papers next day, and left on the 9th, his mood somewhat chastened by a desperately slow train journey and a very high temperature. This was perhaps an unfortunate omen, in that he was to discover that he had not, as he had hoped, finally shaken the dust of Salonika from his feet. He would in fact be sent back for further service and would not be demobilized until 26 October 1919.

Egypt was the scene of even more rebellious behaviour. In March 1919 Private William Knott, Royal Army Medical Corps, released from service in Palestine, found himself kicking his heels in the huge camp at Kantara, on the Suez Canal, allegedly awaiting demobilization. By nature far from a troublemaker, indeed a soldier who had fought hard to retain a non-combatant status on account of his fervent Christian faith, he was nevertheless instantly sympathetic when he heard of the grievances – rife throughout the camp, and indeed the whole Egyptian Expeditionary Force – of men who felt they had been 'fooled for long enough' by the military authorities. He used this phrase in his diary on 3 April, and two days later recorded 'a mass meeting of some 800 men who are protesting against the treatment of soldiers in the EEF'. On 20 April unrest reached such a point that 'the whole camp walked off parade and massed on the football field, formed up in fours and paraded before the CO presenting their demands.' These not being met, the troops went 'on strike' and the camp was at a standstill for a week until the authorities at last gave way. No longer an observer but now an actual participant in the protest, Knott described the progress of events:

Sat Apr 26th. At the meeting this morning General Lloyd's message was read after his return from Cairo. But the answer was neither yes nor no to our demands but an assurance that reinforcements were on the way and demobilization would start when these arrived. We have heard these idle promises before but they are not good enough this time.

Sun Apr 27th. At the meeting this morning the strike was declared finished and thanks to the abilities of the leader, McCarthy, has been brought to a successful finish. So the whole [camp] marched back on to the parade ground presenting themselves for duty! Though the authorities have not come on bended knees (none expected them to) yet their assurances are almost immediate despatch of troops.

Mon Apr 28th. We are now all waiting patiently for a home draft to be called out and be away to those we love.

Knott embarked on the liner *Caledonia* en route for Marseilles on 1 May, and, after a train journey across France, reached England on the 16th. Demobilization followed at once. He concluded his diary, which he had faithfully kept throughout his four and a half years of service, on that same day, with a comment typical of many in its several hundreds of pages: 'Thus I close my army career, with no tinge of sorrow or regret, but praising God for his wondrous love and strengthening of my spiritual eyesight. To Him be the glory!'

* * *

Further afield still the desire for home assumed even more urgent proportions as men came to fear that having survived war they might become the victims of disease. Writing on 4 December 1918 Captain Tom Sherwood reported from Kerman in Persia 'a visit from "Spanish Flu" of a most virulent type [causing] hundreds and hundreds of deaths.' He told his wife:

> I had 150 cases of it in the Regiment in 24 hours and 30 deaths. The doctors at the hospital struggled manfully with it, only 3 of them, then they all went down with it and fresh cases occurring had to be dealt with in Barracks. By this time half the BOs [British Officers] were down too. I was all right so started my hospital for my men in barracks, had no Persian officers, all in bed, so up to the hospital I went for medicine and thermometers. For 3 days I struggled along, treating the poor beggars, then I collapsed. Simply had to give in, went to bed, temp 104! Had just 7 days of it, got up yesterday, am quite all right again, just a bit groggy on my pins.

A friendly civilian and his wife, a Mr and Mrs Taylor, wrote Sherwood, 'saved our lives', during his seven days of sickness: 'There we were in bed in our quarters, *all* the servants and cooks down with it. Mrs Taylor took over the situation and got soup for us. I don't know what we would have done without her. Then a servant crawled back to duty, so I was all right. It has been an experience I don't wish to repeat.'

But there was one unhappy development elsewhere in the East that he could not conceal from his wife:

I have one dreadfully bad bit of news for you. Dear old Carr on his way to India got this 'Flu' in Sirjan, pneumonia set in and he died on the 26th. I can't believe it, it has been a shocking blow to me, we were more than brothers to each other, and how he used to talk of meeting you and Boy, almost the last thing he mentioned was the present for Boy he was going to send from Bombay. And now he's gone. Oh! it's a terrible tragedy, to have lived through the War as he did, to have escaped death as he did in France, and then to be bowled over by Spanish Flu in Sirjan!

The basic anxiety of men far from home and retained in a dangerous climate was well expressed by a Private W. Clutterbuck of the Royal Army Ordnance Corps, writing in the diary he kept throughout his year and a half in Mesopotamia, most of that period subsequent to the Armistice: 'The War is over and the fighting is finished for the chaps in Europe, but us chaps have to go on fighting day and night about 7 or 8 different diseases, any one of which may prove fatal. If I get back to my wife and children again I shall go down on my knees and thank God for sparing me through this awful time.'

Here the principal menace was not from influenza but malaria. Clutterbuck described his own fight with it, which began after taking two of his 'mates' to the nearby 40th military hospital:

When I came back the fever came on me, I got to bed about 10 o/c but I was sick and bad and had a temperature of 105. I lay awake all night absolutely in a pool of sweat, my bed was sopping wet in the morning. I went to the MO, he took my temperature, 102. I was more dead than alive for 3 or 4 days. Weak as a child and as ill as I could be. Some huts nearly empty out of just over 200 men in the depot. 110 are in dock, nearly all with malaria. Chaps dying every day. Indians at one hospital dying at the rate of 30 a week. Oh it's a terrible time for us boys now, and we can't help but get the wind up. And it makes us think seriously if we shall ever see our home and wife and children again. I thought to myself when I wrote my last letter home, if my little Nell knew how ill I was, she would never know a minute's peace.

And there was another dreaded disease to add to the toll: 'Our little MO went in dock himself this morning. I went over there with one of my Arabs, and they told me that the doctor had been taken away with cholera.'

All this was in the summer of 1919; Clutterbuck and his comrades would not reach home until February 1920, after a brief final period of service in India. His pithy comment as they waited for their final release doubtless summed up the attitude of them all: 'Very near fed up with Demob. Parading here and being buggered about everywhere.' Nor was their voyage without its troubles. Storms in the Mediterranean knocked out some of the men with seasickness: 'Poor devils they have suffered, they did not care if the blooming ship went down or otherwise, that's how they felt.' And the old enemy was back: 'The Flu has been very bad too, and they have been giving a second lot of inoculation, but as I am feeling pretty well myself I have not troubled about it.' There was even a last-minute delay to their disembarkation at Devonport. His diary's last, laconic entry reads: '*Feb. 26th*. Was paraded on deck from 8 o/c in the morning and did not leave the boat till 2 o/c. All hanging about here in the docks. Sent a wire to Nell.'

By this time Captain Sherwood had long been home – though overall his service in eastern theatres had been far more extensive than Clutterbuck's, including Gallipoli from September 1915 until the evacuation, Salonika from June 1917, and, following a period as an officer cadet at Emmanuel College, Cambridge, Persia from November 1917. His motives for early repatriation had been greatly multiplied by a passionate marriage contracted while training for his commission, and the birth of a son, Baby Jim, or Boy, whom he had not seen. After recovering from his bout of flu he had been sent to convalesce in Bombay in India. This had worried him; he was well aware that there were two standard patterns for officers in India when their leave-ticket came up: home leave, or local leave. The latter might be fine for an unencumbered subaltern eager for exotic adventure, but for Sherwood the married man, this was simply not an acceptable option; he would even go so far as to defy the authorities. During his transit to India he had written to his wife from on board ship (where he had had little to do except 'slack about all day on deck, play bridge, etc.', and – though this is implicit rather than stated – dream of his homecoming): 'If I don't get English leave I am going to kick and hard too, what does it matter if

I am cashiered, have quite decided to refuse to return to Persia if ordered to.'

Five days later, now in the Colaba Hospital in Bombay – 'a huge Palace, owned by some Rajah, a wonderful place, on the sea, lovely grounds, *every* convenience', but clearly not where he wanted to be – he wrote again, in a thoroughly unhappy mood: 'The chatter from other Officers here is very depressing – no one goes home unless dying! One only gets leave in India, isn't it awful? I've met three Officers here today who, like me, have yet to see their Baby, and they have been based in India since 1914, not a hope of getting away, there must be thousands of separated couples at present.'

But he was determined that he would not be thwarted: 'Chin up, my dear, I get home this year.'

His best hope lay in his dubious state of health, but he knew that even so the cards were stacked against him. Increasingly obsessed by his situation, he wrote an even more forceful letter on 17 February:

Treasure Wife of Mine
    Here I am still in hospital waiting for my papers to be written up for a Board – as far as I can see I'm likely to be here for about a fortnight before my fate is decided. Two things can happen: 1. leave to England (10 to 1 against, I'm afraid) 2. leave in India. If No 2 is my fate I shall employ my time in doing all I know to either be demobilized here or returned to England for that purpose. I may have to go to Delhi and Simla to try and get somebody to take an interest in my case. You know, Princess, it is most awfully difficult for me to do anything here. I don't know a soul of importance. I'm a mere cypher – never felt so lost in my life. Have quite decided not to return to Persia even if I'm forced to adopt extreme measures. I am quite entitled to discharge, if anyone is – 4½ years have I put in, 3 of which have been on Active Service.

His next letter, dated 12 March, gives the happy denouement to his story: 'What glorious news! am coming home! Last Friday I appeared before the Medical Board, results out this morning – I am sent to England on 3 months leave, am in a state of wild delight as you can well imagine, can hardly realise it is true, just think of it! Two other Officers were boarded with me, both expected England, both got leave in India. My luck has held and back I am coming to you and Boy Jim.'

* * *

Disease was obviously a greater hazard in the dangerous climates of the East, but it also continued its depredations on the Western Front well into 1919. A series of letters preserved with the papers of a Major R.D. Russell, of D Battery, 162nd Brigade, Royal Field Artillery, 33rd Division, unfolds an unhappy and wasteful episode.

Early in February one of Russell's subalterns, Lieutenant Charles Bennet, who had been in France for at least a year and had distinguished himself during the fighting in the previous April, set off to go home on leave. The weather was at its Western Front worst, and the transport system at its most incompetent. After a series of hazards and delays Bennet finally reached his home in Northam, Devon, in such a condition that his father, himself a retired Colonel, Royal Engineers, wrote to Major Russell the next day, 9 February:

> My son wishes to let you know that he arrived home safely yesterday (Saturday) after 5 days travelling. Whether he wishes me to add that he arrived with a temperature of 104° and went straight to bed where he now lies I don't know, but so it is, a sharp attack of 'flu', and no wonder after 7 hours in an open cattle truck from 3.30 a.m. to 11.30 in a snow storm and then 24 hours on board ship from Dieppe to Tilbury with the men on deck all the time. I fancy he was not fit when he started and so was liable to catch the 'flu'. I don't expect he will be fit to return at the end of his leave, but I know he will be anxious to get back as soon as the Dr. allows. His temperature still keeps at 104° and he is rather restless but I hope for an improvement tomorrow. The Drs have had lots of practice with the epidemic.

Nine days later Colonel Bennet wrote again: 'My son is still alive but I fear cannot last much longer, he has had a terrible time of it the last 10 days, his wandering mind constantly dwells on his Battery, the horses, etc., he seems to be talking on the telephone: "All right then I will send up 82 pairs of horses and 82 men," etc., etc. Constant Oxygen, Strychnine, etc., keep him alive, but as I said it cannot continue.'

The inevitable next letter is dated 25 February: 'My poor boy died this morning after 17 days suffering. I am writing to *The Times* about it as it is scandalous that so many valuable lives should be wasted by exposure in cattle trucks in the journeys home and out. His end was peaceful and he was more or less conscious all the time but we could not hear what he said the last few days.'

Colonel Bennet's letter duly appeared in *The Times* on 27 February. It was brief and undramatic, its core being extracts from his son's diary covering the period of his journey, followed by the simple concluding sentence (echoing his letter to Major Russell): 'He died of pneumonia on February 25, after 17 days of suffering.' Its justification lay in the Colonel's opening statement: that he was sending the diary extracts to the newspaper in the hope that by so doing 'it may be productive of good for others'.

Some consolation was subsequently offered by Major Russell when he forwarded to Colonel Bennet an account of his son's extreme gallantry during heavy fighting at a point called Siege Farm near Kemmel on 25 April of the previous year, as a consequence of which he was being put up for a Military Cross. The form of recommendation is preserved with Colonel Bennet's letters. A later hand has written what reads like a pathetic footnote to an already tragic story: 'But he did not get it.'

* * *

Meanwhile a different kind of soldier had been attempting, somehow or other, and from a wide range of starting-points, to get back home. The account by the American Mobile Canteen volunteer, Annah Peck, contains the following entry, undated, but referring to the period just following the Armistice:

> One day we had not gone very far before we saw hundreds of men coming towards us on the road. They were an extraordinary sight for instead of the mass blue or khaki that one expected to meet, we saw a straggling line of men wearing every kind of uniform that the Allies had used since 1914. One would see many khaki figures of English Tommies and American Dough-boys tramping along side by side with French *poilus* in blue and Italians in their greeny-grey uniforms, and then to our surprise a

Frenchman would appear with the old red cap and trousers, and sprinkled among all of these were men in the drab looking uniforms worn by the Allied prisoners in Germany. We were particularly struck with the appearance of the English prisoners, for on the whole they looked much worse than the others. Many of them were worn and thin and some looked very ill. It would be hard to find a more dreary sight than these men presented, for they had been turned out of the German prisons in Belgium and had just managed to exist on the food given them by the Belgians, who doubtless had been obliged to go without food themselves in order to feed so many. We were very glad to have some bar chocolate with us, which we had been keeping up to the time of the Armistice for the men in hospitals, for we broke it all up and gave out all we had in the car.

Private Thomas Bickerton of the Essex Regiment, captured the previous April, was one of such a crowd of prisoners, some 500 to 600 strong, in this instance all British, which set off just before the Armistice to march from the vicinity of Freiburg towards the French lines, though, as he admitted in the account he later wrote for his family, 'we did not know where we were going'. He was, however, 'determined to go home' and did his best to maintain a cheerful spirit among this motley crowd of men, of whom some, since they were being accompanied by a number of German guards on horse-back, believed that they were simply being moved forward to be placed between the bayonets of the advancing Allies and those of the retreating Germans. But by now the balance of war had shifted and this time their escort would prove benign. Bickerton's account continues:

We marched all day and the going was hard. Most of us had only got squares of rag to take the place of socks and our boots were in bad shape. We were also very weak from starvation, and the company soon got straggled out miles down the road, our mounted guard stopping from time to time for the stragglers to catch up. After a day's march we pulled up and slept in a barn for the night, and received a reasonable amount of food. We probably marched around twenty miles that day. The stragglers came in during the night and the following morning we set out again. We could see that we were getting towards the rear of what had been the German front line, and we were all terrified when we had to pass close to a large ammunition dump which the Germans set on fire. Shells were bursting in all directions; bullets seemed to be flying all over the place – it was a real inferno and we were all very much afraid we might be injured. Fortunately we got past safely and continued on our way.

When we were within about five miles of the French front the mounted Germans pulled up until a lot of stragglers had caught up with us, and then waved us towards the front and said, '*Alle weg*', meaning 'Off you go', or that is what I understood it to mean.

My heart sang; I knew that the hour of release was near.

Eventually we reached the French front line and of course they knew nothing about our repatriation. I should think there were only about thirty of us out of 400 or 500 to reach the line in a group. One of our party spoke French and the French officer came out and they held a parley. As soon as they realized we were returning British prisoners of war they came out to greet us. We were escorted through the front lines. It was now dark but they made a great fuss of us. They formed us up and we all felt we would show them how British soldiers could march, and even after our exhausting journey we formed up into fours and marched proudly down the road singing 'It's a long way to Tipperary' at the tops of our voices.

The now ex-prisoners were housed in a barn and fed with iron rations, and then taken by military transport to a large French army barracks in Nancy, spending one night on the way in a camp where they were extremely well fed by the hosts – 'of course we made pigs of ourselves, that was only natural, and suffered the next day in consequence'. At Nancy a double guard was posted to keep them from wandering through the town, but they ignored the sentries on the gate and went out and made friends with the citizenry, being especially welcome because they had now been issued with plenty of food, including the much sought-after British bully beef. An officer and some NCOs from the nearest British unit, a detachment of the Independent Air Force, were detailed to look after them, helping them to clean up and reclothing them prior to their return to

England. Meanwhile the barracks soon became full to capacity as other ex-prisoners began arriving in their hundreds, 'or I should think probably thousands':

> The condition of some of these prisoners was pitiful, but we all had one idea and that was to get home. The small number of officers and NCOs were soon swamped and if they came into the square to form us up for any purpose, chaos ensued; those men coming out last and forming on the right being afraid that they would be left behind and rushing to the other side. How quickly the thin veneer of civilisation falls away from us under duress; it was obvious that strict discipline would be necessary.

Bickerton's group having been the first to arrive, they were the first to be ready to depart:

> The difficulty was to get us out without the others knowing about it. We were isolated and were warned that we would be called out at night, that we must not on any account leave the barracks and that we must stay in our quarters. During the night we were awakened and told to get dressed as quietly as possible and to move without making any noise. We entrained in a hospital train and soon found ourselves at Calais, where we naturally expected to be put aboard ship without any delay.
>
> We were terribly disappointed to find that we were taken to a repatriation camp. But here discipline was good and we were soon told why we must stay at this camp for 48 hours. We were again thoroughly cleaned up and given a bath with change of clothing. I managed to keep my greatcoat, which was an Air Force one, and I was very proud of it. And then the last thrilling stage of our journey! A boat crammed full with men – our destination Dover. When we arrived there, all the harbour boats sounded their sirens. We were some of the first prisoners to reach England; flags were out everywhere and the people gave us a wonderful welcome. We were formed up and marched up the hill to Dover Castle in great style. We were again disappointed; we had expected to go right on to the boat train for Victoria, but when we arrived at the Castle we were fed and informed that we must have a medical inspection and stay there one night before we went home.

Bickerton had suffered intensely from irritation caused by lice and had septic sores on his chest and down his legs. The doctor, however, anxious not to retain someone who had been through so much and was so eager for his release, asked him whether if he were sent home he would be able to have proper medical attention. 'I said, "Yes sir, I am quite sure I can – there is a military hospital near St Albans; my father is a foreman joiner at this hospital and I am quite sure this can be easily arranged." I was very glad when he said "Righto, young man, you can go home." '

His father was waiting for him at the station and the day of his return was 1 December, his mother's birthday; she would always say afterwards that this was the best birthday present she had ever had. He was given his demobilization papers and twenty-one days' leave, and his army career ended with a brief visit to the Essex regimental depot. His discharge papers and a 'suit of civvies' were sent after him. He was out of uniform and ready to resume an interrupted apprenticeship before Christmas.

* * *

Of the other prisoners of war whose capture has been described in this narrative, neither Captain McMurtrie nor Private Sharpe experienced the kind of hazardous homecoming endured by Bickerton and his fellows.

At McMurtrie's camp for officers at Graudenz, the inmates had sensed a sudden change of fortune in their favour on the eve of what they would come to know as the date of the Armistice. On 10 November they had seen the camp's officers and men straggling on to the parade ground, where there was much agitated talking and what looked like voting, with much showing of hands, and the prisoners were subsequently informed that the soldiers had told the officers that their powers were suspended and that each company had appointed a representative to help run the camp. Badges of rank instantly came off – 'any who objected were helped' – and the mood became almost jocular: 'That night everyone, English and German, prisoner and guard, were very happy. The sentries sang and joked on their beats.' Next day they heard the news of the Armistice and saw the terms in the papers. 'From then on we were given our parcels as soon as they came in, letters were not censored and a great many of the annoyances we had suffered from came to an end. We all started collecting souvenirs – cockades, eagles off helmets, swords, daggers, etc. Everyone thought and talked only of the probable date of departure and the way we should go.'

From Monday 25 November they were allowed to wander freely about the town: 'We all went, going into hotels and restaurants, Boche waiters would rush up and take your gloves, cap and coat. It was priceless being able to walk where we liked without a guard. On Tuesday we went down to Graudenz again, went to a cinema and rode back to the camp on a tram.' Several French officers were invited to dinner that evening, which also saw the last performance of the camp theatre: 'All the stage and theatre were trimmed with red, white and blue. We had just had the first turn when the Boche reported that a party of two hundred officers (we were in it) was to parade at 10.30 that night and so the performance came to an end, but not before we had sung "God Save the King" and "The Marseillaise".'

In fact 10.30 was soon changed to 4.30 a.m. and then 4.30 a.m. was also 'washed out'. They were finally ordered to parade at 8.15 p.m.: 'We marched out of the camp for the last time, down to the station and left Graudenz very happy about 10.30 p.m. that night in 2nd and 3rd class carriages.' Their destination was Danzig, which they reached, after a tediously slow, uncomfortable journey, to find a liner waiting for them; as the officers went on board the ship's band played 'Let's all Go Down the Strand.' With two others McMurtrie shared 'a "top-hole" little cabin and entered civilisation once more'.

There were 200 officers and 1,500 men on board; 'some of the men had been taken in 1914, some in the March offensive. We were excited enough after nine months – what must those, who had been taken in 1914, have thought.' As they headed for home, pausing briefly at Copenhagen, they were vociferously cheered from about fifteen British destroyers entering the Baltic to ensure that the terms of the Armistice were being carried out. They reached Leith to a tremendous welcome on Sunday 1 December, the same day that Private Bickerton disembarked at Dover.

Lance-Corporal Sharpe's period of captivity had been considerably less arduous than that of many soldiers of non-commissioned rank. After some time in hospital and various moves here and there he been put to agricultural work in eastern Germany, alongside a mixture of nationalities including Russians. Of a deep Christian conviction, he had been able to visit the local church and had found much solace in the company of a minister's family, to which he had become greatly attached. His worst sufferings had been from dreadful nightmares, during which he saw 'dead men and skeletons get up under heavy shell fire and run in all directions'. Repatriation was slow; he finally came out via Copenhagen in January 1919, and, after several months of regimental duty, he was discharged in July.

It was at that point that, finally restored to his family, he decided, for the benefit of his young son, to face what would be the boy's inevitable question as he grew older: 'What Did You Do in the War, Daddy?' The following, from his long, always thoughtful and often eloquent narrative, is his exuberant account of his final day in khaki:

> *July 6th 1919.* Wake in the Army hut very early, but wake in the Army but not of it. A civilian again at last.
>
> It was 11 o'clock before I got my final papers, B2079 (discharge certificate), railway warrant and food vouchers etc., and I left Litherland camp with buoyant steps and cheerful heart – for NOW I was on my way HOME for all times.
>
> I caught the 12.55 p.m. train from Liverpool and arrived in Leicester at 4.15 p.m. after 3 years 12 days service with His Majesty's Forces and 196 days as an attested man under the Derby Scheme.
>
> And that, my son, is 'The Answer'.

* * *

The returning prisoners of war detailed so far came from Germany, but there were others who had been held by the Austrians.

Miss Colina Campbell was a VAD driver based in northern France who helped many such as they came through en route for the Channel ports. In a letter to her mother written on 2 December she told the moving story of one man who never did reach home:

> Such a sad thing happened about a week ago. I drove one of our British sailors who had been a prisoner in the hands of the

Austrians for 26 months, and he had just come through on his way to England. He was so looking forward to seeing his people once more, he had been captured off a submarine. Well he had a temp. and I took him into hospital and saw the Dr. and asked him not to keep him a moment more than necessary as the man was pining to go home. Well, I heard yesterday the lad had died. I just could not sleep all night thinking of him and he is only one case out of many.

The general condition of these ex-prisoners was such that even if they managed to escape serious illness they found it hard to cope with a sudden return to normality: 'Our prisoners coming through just make your heart bleed, they look at you with such pathetic eyes and say "You're a woman, we could not even begin to tell you the things we have suffered." Many of them are in such a weak condition that the first food (which people give them out of the kindness of their hearts) knocks them over, their stomachs are too weak to stand anything.'

Of the vast number she helped on their way who had arrived by the more standard route via Belgium, she added: 'One and all say that if it had not been for the kindness of the Belgian women few of them would be here at all.'

* * *

It is worth commenting, in relation to the Australians, that, whether their undoubtedly formidable, if somewhat buccaneering, reputation was justified or not, their demobilization was conducted, on the whole, with remarkable success, and without the disciplinary problems which occurred in the British Army. This was largely because their commander, Lieutenant-General Sir John Monash, accepted the principle, passionately held by his soldiers, of 'first come, first go', and was instrumental in persuading the Australian Prime Minister, W.M. Hughes, to agree to its implementation. In the words of their distinguished official historian, C.E.W. Bean: 'Monash ordered each division to classify its men in order of their length of service in "quotas" of 1000 each – that being a normal trainload, a normal shipload, and also a number readily organised as a battalion. ... Of the 155,000 Australian troops based in England, by the end of September only 10,000 were left.' 'Our demob is going on very steadily,' wrote Corporal Oswald Blows in the spring of 1919, in a diary comment wholeheartedly endorsing his country's official policy: 'The system is very fair, and upheld owing to that fairness by all the boys.'

There was briefly the threat of trouble when some troops on arriving transports were quarantined because of the suspicion that a handful of their number might be suffering from influenza, but good sense and an understanding reaction on the part of the authorities ensured that the matter did not get out of hand. Citing a report of the British Ministry of Health which named Australia 'as the only country which escaped, for at least some months, the terrifying type of influenza which, from October to November 1918, raged elsewhere', Bean claimed that 'the soldiers' tolerance of this last trial was possibly of great value to their nation'.

Blows' account of his return adds an amusing footnote to the story. His troopship dropped anchor close to another ship which had recently arrived full of married couples – Australian soldiers who had married English wives. 'The nights were hot,' he recorded, 'and the couples slept outside on the decks, side by side: husband and wife, ditto, ditto. Of course it caused amusement to men on my transport and wonderment if mistakes were made during the night and any of the spouses turned the wrong way for love and comfort.'

* * *

There was, however, another substantial category of men for whom an early departure from the service was not even an option when hostilities came to an end. These were the members of those divisions set aside to become part of the Allied occupation force in Germany.

By the terms of the Armistice the German Army was under obligation to withdraw within fifteen days from all the territories it had seized during the war – the occupied parts of France and Belgium, plus Luxembourg – and from Alsace-Lorraine, which had been ceded to Germany following France's defeat in the Franco-Prussian War of 1870–71. During the subsequent sixteen days they were to evacuate all German territory west of the Rhine, together with three key bridgeheads on the river's eastern bank, at Mayence, Coblenz and Cologne. The bridgeheads thus yielded were to be held by, respectively, the French, the Americans and the British.

General Sir Herbert Plumer was chosen by Field Marshal Haig to command the British contingent. On 12 December he took the salute as the main body of troops assigned to what would become the British Army of the Rhine crossed by the Hohenzollern Bridge into Cologne. The sight inspired one officer who had witnessed the very different events of nine months earlier, Major T.H. Westmacott, to comment, in a letter to his wife: 'It is difficult to remember what we were like last March and April, during the retreat of the 5th Army, and to find ourselves here as conquerors in one of the proudest cities of Germany.' Moved by the bearing of the troops as they passed, he added: 'I wish you could have seen them – each man making the most of himself, and full of pride and *élan*.'

For many soldiers, inevitably, the idea of becoming part of the occupation force was extremely unpopular. Hence the emphatic comment of Private Emrys Richards of the 63rd Machine Gun Battalion in a letter of 29 December: 'No Germany for me, thank you; I've seen quite enough of Germans.' Others, such as Private J.W. Drury, were antipathetic because, like virtually everybody else quoted in this chapter, they simply wanted to get back to where they belonged. One of Drury's first thoughts on hearing of the Armistice had been of 'the prospect of meeting someone soon back in Blighty. I was keenly disappointed therefore to learn that we were transferred to the Army of Occupation with no likelihood of getting home for some time.' In a similar mood the staff officer Captain Harry Graham had written to his wife on 12 November (at which time the Rhineland was not seen as the only foreign posting on offer): 'There is talk of the 1st seven Divisions going to Germany or to India! The only place *I* want to go to is 11, Gloster Place!'

Yet the prospect was received by some without dismay, indeed in certain cases with positive delight. 'Wonderful news' was the reaction of Second Lieutenant Clifford Carter, when he heard on 13 November that his division was under orders to march to the Rhine. He was to enjoy his life in Germany so much that while being pleased to receive his demobilization papers in the following spring he was also sad to leave. He had enjoyed the sheer fact of travel, the sightseeing in which he had been able to indulge, the culture – particularly the operas, comic or serious, at the city's various theatres – and he had come greatly to value his relations with ordinary

German people. He had become especially friendly with the German family with whom he was billeted. Returning from leave with a bad cold in early February he was overwhelmed by his landlady's kindness: 'No sooner had I reached my billet than she ordered me "a hot bath and off to bed"! Then she plied me with hot milk and honey, cough mixture and so forth and was delighted to find next morning that the cold had gone. And yet we didn't understand each other's language! Kindness is universal.' Thus it came about that for his last entry in his diary covering his time in Germany he wrote: '*April 14*. Goodbye to dear old Cologne.'

Another who welcomed the prospect of visiting the country of the defeated enemy was former Private, now 'Guardsman' Fen Noakes (he announced the new title in a letter of 15 December, adding the terse, one-word comment 'SWANK!') On the 18th he wrote, enthusiastically:

> Here I am at last, at the goal of all our hopes, the banks of the Rhine! I arrived in Cologne (or Köln, as the German name is) last night.
>
> I woke up just in time for crossing the German frontier. We stopped at Aachen (Aix-la-Chapelle) a large junction for the old Paris–Berlin–Petrograd expresses, and again at Düren. When we got to Cologne we detrained and waited for three hours on the platform. Then might be seen how the Guards invaded Germany and fried bacon in Cologne station, for we made fires and cooked our supper. At last we moved off and entered Cologne singing 'Good-bye-ee', the song that has taken the place of 'Tipperary' in the Army now. It was a great moment! At last the goal of our ambitions is reached, and our victory is demonstrated. The Rhine – *der Deutscher Rhein* – is now guarded by British troops and the Union Jack flies over Cologne. Instead of the Kaiser eating his Christmas dinner in London, we shall eat ours in the heart of Germany. What a change!

Noakes was much gratified by the reaction of the citizens:

> The inhabitants do not seem at all hostile; indeed, I was greatly surprised at the pleasant manner in which we were received. They are not enthusiastic – one could not expect it – but they are very polite and seem anxious to please us. In the shops they serve us

with many smiles and are strictly honest in changing French or English money. The language does not present such a difficulty as in France, owing to the similarity between German and English, and, also, many of the Germans speak English quite well.

Even so he was equally delighted when on 20 February 1919 he could write: 'The Guards are coming home!!!' Yet that was not the end of his story, for over the following months he became increasingly frustrated as the prospects of demobilization seemed to come and go like a mirage. Thus as late as 8 October he was writing, from Warley Barracks, Essex: 'I am waiting—waiting—waiting. Almost any hour now I may have the order to parade for demob. There are 53 of us on the list who are all complete, papers filled up, etc., and all that is now delaying us is an official paper from Headquarters. In the demob office they are expecting it at any time, and then we shall go "*toute suite*". But, oh! it's a weary job waiting!'

At last at 1.56 p.m. on 9 October he was able to hand in a telegram at Charing Cross with the triumphant massage: 'SHALL ARRIVE FIVE OCLOCK DEMOBBED. CHEERIO.'

*   *   *

One concept often on soldiers' lips and in their writings in the preceding years had been the idea of the war as a game; or, more grandly, as the 'Great Game'. It might be thought that such a notion would have been long played out by the time the fighting stopped and the survivors finally came home. Yet when, for example, Gunner C.P. Straw, Royal Garrison Artillery, was demobilized in February 1919, he received a letter of thanks from a senior officer couched in the following heroic terms:

> You take away with you the priceless knowledge that you have played a man's part in the great War for freedom and fair play. You will take away with you also your remembrances of your comrades, your pride in your Regiment, and your love for your country.
>
> You have played the game; go on playing it, and all will be well with the great Empire, which you have helped to save.

AFTERWORD

A VICTORY WON:
A VICTORY IMPERILLED

SO THE GREAT WAR WAS OVER, a victory had been achieved, and the 'boys' – those who had not remained to become part of a foreign field – had at last come home.

Looking back on the war produced an infinite range of reactions. For many who had worn uniform it had given them an experience they would never forget, and never regret. Alex Wilkinson, very much a front-line soldier throughout his career (during which he also saw active service in the Second World War in Sicily and Italy), would always remain true to the sentiments he expressed immediately after the Armistice in November 1918: 'The jolly old war has come to an end at last, and a good end too.... And thank heavens I had a really good battle before the end. I would not have missed it for anything in the whole world.'

A similar attitude was that of Sidney Rogerson, fellow staff-officer of Lieutenant Philip Ledward on the Chemin des Dames front and author of *The Last of the Ebb* (quoted in Chapter 5). In a statement not from that book but from its predecessor, *Twelve Days* (about the last period of the Somme battle in 1916), Rogerson wrote: 'The pacifist may inveigh against war's hideousness, leagues and societies may condemn it in vigorous resolutions and solemnly declare that "there must be no more war," yet the fact remains that, terrifying as they sometimes, and uncomfortable as they often were, the war years will stand out in the memories of vast numbers of those who fought as the happiest period of their lives.'

For Charles Carrington, who had feared that he would be 'at a loss' when the war ended, there followed the best part of a decade in which he would be virtually locked into his wartime experiences. He would later write: 'I could not escape from the comradeship of the trenches which had become a mental internment camp, or should I say a soldiers' home. I might as well have been in Chelsea Hospital.' Central to this situation, and giving it positive value, was the fact that he had been, if not in 1918, one of that band of brothers, 'the soldiers at the front, mostly volunteers, who were sustained by a dogged unreasoning pride', and between whom and the rest, the non-combatants, there lay 'a psychological barrier which perhaps grew more impenetrable with time'. (In essence, this was a St Crispin's day mentality, with distinct Shakespearean echoes, as though it were no coincidence that Henry V's army of knights and bowmen had marched through the Somme country on its way to its famous encounter with the French at Agincourt.) A tall, handsome man with an erect, military bearing, he would serve again in the second war and remain a soldier in spirit for the rest of his long life.

Yet for many others there was no glory, little or no hint of the swagger and bravado with which the first to respond to the nation's call had gone so blithely to enlist back in 1914 (echoes of which had certainly survived into 1918, as in the case of Lance-Corporal Frank Earley). Accounts the very writing of which meant that their authors had to confront and relive often grim and shattering experiences could produce solemn and heartfelt conclusions. This was certainly so in the case of former Lance-Corporal William Sharpe. His 'Answer' to the question 'What did you do in the Great War, Daddy' ultimately became, in effect, a gesture of warning. His final summing-up paragraph reads: 'Memories of the late war MUST never fade. Let everything about it be known. Teach it to our children: make it lurid, emphasize it, preach it, *glorify* it as the Biggest and Best Argument for Peace evermore.'

An equally forthright statement, in this case a foreword as opposed to a conclusion, occurs in the brief memoir, much of it referring to his experiences in Gallipoli, by former Private Ernest Lye of the Duke of Wellington's West Riding Regiment (not quoted elsewhere in this book): 'If every man who fought in the Great War was to take up a pen and put his impressions on paper we should get no two stories alike, yet I venture to predict that one and all who saw the hideousness and horror and walked hand in hand with Death for months at a time, would be in agreement that nothing whatever can justify WAR and that the greatest advocate against WAR is

WAR itself. If we who have tasted war's bitter cup could impress that upon the coming generation, our sacrifices will not have been in vain.'

Even more pointed, and poignant, was his memoir's dedication: 'For my sons I write of my experiences, in the hope that, after having read them, they will forever work for peace.'

* * *

For countless ex-servicemen, however, there was no desire to relive their war by setting down their experiences in writing. There were those, perhaps the majority, who shrugged off the past cheerfully or otherwise, resumed their normal lives and went on trying to make the best of things like everybody else. (In many cases the sheer attempt to find work in a world allegedly fit for heroes was enough to concentrate the mind wonderfully, and thus displace any absorption in the things of war.) Yet there were those whose attempts to ignore what had happened failed, because it had left too strong a mark. Of these many refused to, or were simply unable to, even so much as speak of what they had gone through. Instinctively or by deliberate decision they shut the war years away entirely, banishing them, as it were, to a locked room of the mind. Some did so successfully, but for others the most they could achieve was a kind of angry silence, which could have a potent impact on youngsters of the next generation, who, as time went by, came to realize that they might soon have to follow in their elders' footsteps. Hence this comment by Alan Brodrick, of Leyland, Lancashire, himself a participant in the second war (from a letter to the author written in 1997):

> I was born in 1921, and those who did not grow up between the Wars cannot imagine how 'The War' hung over us. Young as we were, we knew that something terrible had happened, a long time ago, of course, but crippled, blind and disfigured men were a common sight in our streets, and if we asked a relative or a friend about a photograph of a young man in uniform, we would be told casually, and apparently without sadness: 'Oh aye; that were our Bert; he were killed in t'War, tha knows.' Our fathers and uncles were young men in their thirties who had their lives to

lead and families to raise: they spoke little about the War, but it was obvious that those who had seen the most said the least and kept quiet if they saw that we were listening, but we learned from their guarded conversations to learn 'It was no picnic there, I can tell you.'

Uncle Mark had joined up when he was still only fourteen. His two older brothers had gone in that first enthusiastic rush, and Mark persuaded his widowed mother to let him go. A fine big lad, the Army took him. Smiling, they wrote the lie: 'aged nineteen years', and Mark was only fifteen when he was present at Loos in 1915. His brothers were both killed. Mark ended the war as a nineteen-year-old sergeant, and was a silent and embittered man for the rest of his life.

※   ※   ※

There were yet others whom the end of the war left stranded in a kind of personal limbo, relieved and glad that the fighting was over but marooned in a chronic emotional uncertainty. 'Desperately confused over war and peace' was how the soldier-poet Edmund Blunden would describe himself, looking back later at the period 1918–19. 'Clearly,' he wrote, 'no man who knew and felt could wish for a second that the war should have lasted for a second longer. But, where it was not, and where the traditions and government which it had called into being had ceased to be, we who had been brought up to it were lost men. Strangers surrounded me. No tried values existed now.' A 'soul grown strange in France', he called himself in a poem of 1919, its very title – 'The Estrangement' – underlining his sense of being caught in a new category of No Man's Land, cut off from his former life, unable to reconcile himself to a different one.

Blunden would never, in fact, entirely shake off the shadows of the war, and it would remain a recurring theme, overtly or covertly, in his writings for the rest of his life; he would write a poem entitled 'Ancre Sunshine' – as it happened his last – as late as 1966, in his seventieth year. (Poet as he was, there was no Shakespearean nostalgia in his cast of mind, nor in that of others of this strange legion of the lost.) Moreover, a desperate urge to ensure that the horrors of the Great War were not visited on the next generation would make him an instinctive supporter of appeasement in the late 1930s, and drive him to use every effort to create a better fellow-feeling between Britain and Germany. This led to his being surrounded by a certain amount of suspicion when war broke out, only dispersed when he effectively abandoned his personal resistance to the war and became a map-reading instructor with an honorary rank of captain in 1942.

A similar course was followed by Major Alfred Bundy, as, marked by the draining frustrations of his two years in Salonika as well as by his earlier harrowing experiences on the Somme, he resumed a career in advertising. Sympathy with the enemy he had fought grew from what he saw as the injustices and dangers inherent in the Treaty of Versailles; he made no secret of his admiration for Germany's recovery and travelled there frequently in the interwar years. Thus as the European skies darkened again in the late 1930s, there were those who considered him politically suspect. As his daughter has written: 'Not surprising really – he wore a swastika lapel badge, employed Austrian maids, kept a German Shepherd dog whose kennel was labelled "Prince's Schloss", and subscribed to Sir Oswald Mosley's weekly newsletter. But loyalty to his country should not have been doubted – sympathy for a cause is a far cry from treachery, and he was soon in any case to become disillusioned. In the run-up to the war some people, of course, were happy to believe anything; for example, father was said to have signalled to enemy aircraft from the woods with a hand torch – absolutely absurd, but I understand that for this reason he was asked to resign from the Home Guard!'

In this respect, Bundy's experience was not far removed from that of the novelist Henry Williamson, whose pro-Germanism and benign attitude to Hitler would, in the eyes of some, put his reputation, and henceforth even his writing, under a cloud of suspicion for many years. Yet for both these men the basic motivation was the same; somehow to secure that there would not be a return to what they saw as the inhuman, destructive, internationally poisonous conflict of 1914–1918.

* * *

Inevitably a war of such dimensions had to be chronicled, on the grand scale at one extreme, while, at the other, there was infinite scope for the focused eye-view of the 'ordinary' individual. The British Official History of the Western Front, frequently quoted in this book, was to make its majestic appearance part by part, under its running title *Military Operations in France and Flanders*, over the next thirty years; it was not until 1947 that its the last two 1918 volumes were published. Meanwhile the other theatres and arms were similarly memorialized, with works on the various sideshows and, of course, the war of the air and the war at sea.

In the medium range, and very soon, there was a spate of works of varying calibre recording the history of divisions, regiments, battalions, air squadrons, ships, sometimes with the task of chronicling the achievements of the unit concerned entrusted to a member or former member. Such commissions were by no means easy, for they had serious constraints; particularly, perhaps, because they could impose a kind of automatic censorship on the author, who naturally felt the need to put forward the best possible case on behalf of his former comrades-in-arms. It was almost inevitable, indeed, that he should adopt as much a propagandist's as a historian's role.

An interesting example is that of Major C.H. Dudley Ward, 1st Welsh Guards, much quoted in this book, who rose finally to the role of acting commander of his battalion. The Welsh Guards were a product of the war, having been founded in February 1915; it was a proud boast that they had mounted guard at Buckingham Palace just three days after formation on 1 March, St David's Day. As it happened, Ward had anticipated, with some acerbity, the problems any postwar chronicler would face long before hostilities were over. Writing on 22 May 1918, at a time when the outcome of the series of German attacks was still far from certain, he stated (in a letter to the unidentified 'Beloved' to whom all his correspondence was directed): 'No one will ever write the true history of this war, we have not the courage to punish negligence and will certainly not have the courage even to condemn when all is over, because, in spite of all, we shall win, or at least not lose and then negligence will be forgotten, incompetence forgiven, and fools, criminal fools, will be heroes.'

Discharged from the Army on 12 August 1919, Ward found himself almost at once engaged in the task of compiling the Welsh Guards' regimental history. He set to with speed and vigour, and his book, a meticulous, competently written, but essentially uncritical, work, making much use of personal evidence, especially his own, was published in 1920. A recent scholarly report, when comparing Ward's wartime letters with his postwar account, made this telling comment: 'It is ironic that within eighteen months of writing [the above] words Charles Dudley Ward had produced just such a history in which he omits all reference to the damning criticisms he had once confided to his journal.' Whether it was that his wartime anger had cooled with the piping days of peace, or that he saw no option other than to write the kind of history that would bind up old wounds and present a fair face to the world, it is impossible to say; at the least a certain realism must have told him that a seriously critical history of a brand-new regiment would be less than acceptable in the atmosphere of the time. As it was, his *History of the Welsh Guards* was so well received that he went on to publish more volumes in the same vein: such as a history of the 56th Division in 1921, of the 74th (Yeomanry) Division in 1922, and of the 53rd (Welsh) Division in 1927, not to mention the *Regimental Records of the Royal Welch Fusiliers*, quoted in Chapter Four.

Such works inevitably might be seen as reinforcing what would now be called an establishment view of the conduct of the war. Their role in helping to prime what would become ultimately a powerful counter-culture of protest – or, to use the key word of the time, 'disenchantment' – is impossible to quantify, but there can be little doubt that histories which became, if with the best will in the world, virtual 'apologias', suppressing all doubts and salvaging often dubious reputations, could produce a strong reaction among those who felt that they failed to express the true nature of the war experience. Also fuelling such a response was the mass of other works – biographies, autobiographies, reminiscences, essays, part-works, etc. – covering every field of activity and every theatre of war, which, continuing a trend which had started during the war itself, appeared in a steady stream in the years following the Armistice. In the wake of an undoubted victory, it was perhaps inevitable that the first fruits in this field should be largely triumphalist in tone. Significantly, it was in response to this mass of published material that, as quoted in the Foreword, F.E. Noakes made his eloquent plea on behalf of the contemporary letter, believing it to be closer to the realities of war than works based substantially on hindsight. Significantly, too, Mark

VII, the pseudonymous author of *A Subaltern on the Somme*, published in 1927, one of the first books to take a more critical stance in relation to the war and its conduct, when questioned as to why he had written it, cited the following as a principal motive: 'I wrote the book first in the hope of helping to stay the inevitable tide of glamour and romance that gathers about all great events.'

In fairness, it should also be stated that he continued: 'and second to perpetuate the memory of heroic spirits who, it seemed, would have no other recorded memorial'; and that by then Max Plowman, to give Mark VII his real name, had become a noted pacifist.

Yet the urge to strip the war of glamour and romance was a powerful one. Thus when the next, very different, harvest began about 1929, its most noted crop was a number of often superbly written so-called 'anti-war books', which, by the candour and quality of their descriptions, tended, whether intentionally or otherwise, to prompt questionings not only as to whether the war had been fought as well as it might have been, but even as to whether it should have been fought at all. Such questionings could seem to have special resonance at a time when it looked as though all hopes of seeing the brave new world for which men had fought and died were doomed to disappointment; an assumption, it should be added, likely to breed doubts in the minds of ex-servicemen who would never dream of reading a single word by Erich Maria Remarque, Siegfried Sassoon, Wilfred Owen or Robert Graves. Had it not all been a terrible mistake, a wanton waste of life, a massive exercise in futility, even – to take a worst-case scenario – a wicked indulgence all round by equally guilty imperialist powers? Disturbed by such suggestions some old soldiers would begin to question their own motives and the justification of their own involvement.

By contrast others would see such questions as misjudging the nature of their experience entirely, stalwartly, even angrily, maintaining that what they had done had been from the best possible motives, and that, if there had been little romance and glamour, there had been much hardihood, heroism and the finest companionship. This response would produce its own crop of writings of quality in support, among them Charles Carrington's *A Subaltern's War* in 1929, Sidney Rogerson's *Twelve Days* (as cited above) in 1930, or Graham Greenwell's *An Infant in Arms* in 1935. In this way a cultural battle was joined every bit as ferocious as the war which prompted it; a conflict still unresolved after seventy years.

Such questions would come into even sharper focus after the Second World War, the purpose of which, in the light of the aims and philosophy of Nazi Germany, Fascist Italy and Imperial Japan, few would fail to endorse, with the exception of those who took the stance of outright pacifism. The former Archbishop of Canterbury, Lord Runcie, himself a tank commander of distinction in the 1939–45 conflict, once stated, in a simple but telling sentence: 'A war that closed down Belsen was a war worth fighting.' So, there is a strong, indeed, virtually an irrefutable case for the later war, in which the anti-Fascist alliance is generally seen as having convincingly occupied the moral high ground. But what of the earlier war?

Former Lieutenant R.G. Dixon (quoted in Chapter 11 on the significance of Armistice Day), writing a half-century later, and therefore after the Second World War, was vehement in arguing the case for the defence of the First:

There is a tendency nowadays among the smug, easy-chair and roll-top desk brigade, to ask what it was all for, and was it not a colossal waste for nothing which should have been avoided. Indeed, I have met folk who regard us of that 1914–18 generation rather in the light of poor, deluded fools.

To such I would reply that they do not know their history, nor, because they did not live through these events, are they capable of assessing the peculiar circumstances of the time – nor the mood – correctly. Only we of that generation that was 'lost' can tell them something of those things. Reviewing all the facts, and with hindsight added, it is entirely possible to sympathise with King George V when he said to the American Ambassador: 'In God's name, Mr Paige, what else could we have done?' And I am sure that history will echo indeed, 'What else?'

I think we saw quite clearly enough what we were doing, and that we had a filthy job on hand that had to be done. But I can testify to our feelings by 1918, and these feelings were practically universal among the fighting troops, and commonly expressed. We were quite sure we were going to win the war, but, we said, 'the politicians will lose it for us afterwards'.

And at Versailles, sure enough, they did. . . . The Treaty of

Versailles contained within its provisions the seeds of the next conflict, which it made inevitable.

As to whether the Allied effort of 1914–18 was as defensible as was its successor of 1939–45, a justification can surely be found in the similarity of the basic 'plot'. To look at just one key aspect: in the Second World War Nazi Germany occupied a vast amount of Europe which, by general agreement among her opponents, even among most neutrals, had to be returned to its rightful owners. In the First World War Imperial Germany in a similar manner seized a substantial amount of the territory of north-west Europe, including Luxembourg, most of Belgium and much of the industrial heartland of France; a situation which in common justice surely required a similar solution. The inhabitants of occupied Brussels, or Lille, or Laon, were as much prisoners in their own countries between 1914 and 1918 as were the inhabitants of the territories seized by the Nazis between 1940 and 1945. (Indeed, the descriptions of scenes of liberation in this book's Chapter 10 could easily have come from a book about 1944–45.) The fact that that earlier war is now seen as being especially horrific – particularly in its manifestations on the Western Front – does not mean that it should not have been fought to a conclusion or that attempts should not have been made to achieve at least the most honourable of its aims. For, granted that the Kaiser's Second Reich was not in the same league for evil as Hitler's Third, the prospect of a twentieth-century Europe dominated by her autocracies as opposed to her democracies was not one that invited acceptance. Whether the conflict might have been avoided, or whether it was inevitable, were, and remain, serious and important questions, but once the frontiers had been crossed – once, as it were, the burglars were in the house – the obligation to respond became mandatory. In a word, the war might be monstrous, but it had to be waged, and, if possible, won.

* * *

But, after that, what then?

As the world knows, the year 1918 saw a victory gained, which, over the following two decades, was to become a victory tarnished. The very fact that there was a second war shows that the first one, in effect, for all the huge effort and sacrifice which went into it, ultimately failed. Indeed, it can be argued that the essential futility of that war is to be found not so much in the war itself as in its tragic aftermath.

As early as 1919, sensing that the Peace Conference in Paris was unlikely to achieve its prime aim of securing a stable future, Field Marshal Foch allegedly made the prophetic statement: 'This is not Peace. It is an Armistice for twenty years.' Similarly Colonel A.P. Wavell, the future Field Marshal and Viceroy of India, has been quoted as stating, in the light of the vindictive tone of the postwar treaties: 'After the war to end war, they seem to have been pretty successful at making a Peace to end Peace.' [See, however, pp. xvi and 366.]

This is not the place to discuss the misjudgements and mistakes of the would-be peacemakers of Paris and Versailles, but it is perhaps valuable to show what one or two of the soldiers featured in this book thought as they approached the end of the conflict, and wondered what would be done with the victory they were helping to achieve.

Lance-Corporal Frank Earley, enthusiastic warrior of 1918 (already referred to in this Afterword), died of wounds on 2 September, 1918, aged nineteen (see p. 217). Since he was by trade a journalist – he had started his career when only seventeen, as a pupil in the literary department of the *Derby Daily Telegraph*, where he had much impressed his seniors – it is not surprising to find among his papers attempts to set down his observations other than in the routine format of letters home. There is thus a sharp, but also witty and humorous, account of his period of basic training as a conscript, under the title 'Sketches of Life in the New Army' (a not unworthy predecessor in its modest way of such notable efforts at enshrining the mysteries of induction into the armed forces of the Crown as T.E. Lawrence's documentary novel *The Mint* or Arnold Wesker's play *Chips with Everything*). This was duly printed as a major feature article in his own newspaper, occupying much of four columns, under the authorship of 'A Boy of Eighteen'.

There is also a long essay in typescript, apparently unpublished, entitled 'An Eye for an Eye', written under his trade name of Francis T. Earley. Undated, it appears to have been a product of the queasy summer of 1918, at the time of the surge of vituperative anti-

Germanism that was then sweeping Britain. His aims in writing it are clear: to endorse the widely held belief that those most guilty should be duly punished, but to resist any demand for a return to 'the old law of an eye for an eye, and a tooth for a tooth', which he saw as 'but the primitive expression of a primitive instinct'. He defined the increasingly vocal clamour of the time as follows:

> This is the cry: – 'For every town, for every village sacked and spoiled in France or Belgium, let a town and a village be sacked and spoiled and burned by the Allied armies. Let cities be held hostages for cities. If Laon is destroyed, let Cologne lie in ashes; if Bruges and Ghent are destroyed, let Trèves and Freiburg be destroyed likewise. For every cathedral ruined in France, let one be ruined in Germany; for every church, for every castle, for every house, for every barn damaged or pillaged in France, let a church, a castle, a house, a barn be similarly damaged and pillaged in Germany.' And so on. This is the cry; the cry for retaliation, for vengeance in kind, for the exaction of an eye for an eye, a tooth for a tooth; it is a cry from the heart, but not from the soul.
>
> For consider. It is justly the proud boast of the Allies that their fight is for liberty and honour, justice and civilization; that their cause is the cause of the world, a cause upheld on behalf of future ages and unborn generations. Civilization against barbarism, that is the cause. Would that cause be upheld worthily? Could the Allies truly say that it was the cause of Civilization, if what the Germans did in France, Belgium, Poland, was done also by their opponents in Bavaria, Rhineland, Silesia? There is but one answer to this. Destruction there must be in every war, it is unavoidable; but wanton destruction by way of ignoble revenge is avoidable; more than that, it is criminal, it is hunnish, it is hellish.
>
> No; this thing must not be. The only result of a policy of retaliation in kind would be that the world would suffer a greater loss than it has yet suffered, and that future ages would have to mourn a double destruction.

As for the guilty, Earley was not against their receiving the ultimate punishment, even supporting the popular notion of having 'him of Potsdam' – meaning the Kaiser – publicly hanged before the towers of Reims, or his advisers and counsellors – by which he doubtless meant such as Ludendorff and Hindenburg – being similarly disposed of before the ruins of Louvain or Ypres. Before questioning any possible inconsistency in his dual argument, it is perhaps worth remembering that this was more or less precisely the dispensation – of restraint in dealing with a defeated country, combined with the sternest punishments for its most important leaders – that was enforced by the victors of the Second War at Nuremberg a quarter of a century later, with the difference that the executions were not carried out in public.

* * *

A less polemical discussion of the problems of the postwar world (Earley was obviously writing with a newspaper's audience in mind) occurs in a letter by Frederick 'Fen' Noakes, written on 17 October, from his convalescent camp at Cayeux, where he was recovering from his second wound of 1918:

> Do you think Germany is really in earnest over the Armistice? The Allies certainly don't seem inclined to let her down gently – nor do I think they should. But at the same time, they must be careful not to allow the elation of victory to run away with them. In my opinion, this is a most critical and dangerous time for us – the greatest danger we have yet faced. *For it is now not the danger of defeat, it is the peril of victory.* [Author's italics]
>
> In the enthusiasm of success, will England remember the ideals for which we went to war; will she be true to the principles she professes? It is so very possible that in the first glow of unlimited power for good or evil, she may yield to the 'Junker' element of the nation, and cast aside the unselfish aims of justice and freedom for which so many thousands have laid down their lives.
>
> A lasting peace it must be, but it must also be an absolutely *clean* peace. Otherwise, the war has been in vain.

This was far from being a popular, or a general, view at this time. There were many who supported the concept of punishing Germany so severely that she would never be able to hold up her head in the international community again. By contrast, Field Marshal Sir Douglas Haig wrote on 26 October: '... it is most important that our

Statesmen should think over the situation carefully and not so to humiliate Germany as to produce a desire for revenge in years to come.' In this, it is interesting to note, Commander-in-Chief and humble 'ordinary soldier' were magnanimously at one.

Private, later Guardsman, F.E. Noakes, Coldstream Guards, has become something of a minor hero in this narrative (providing, among other things, part of the theme and title of this Afterword). Perhaps therefore, in the situation of a twentieth-century Europe about which no last words are possible even now, the final statement might be left to him.

In 1952 Noakes published, privately, a memoir which he entitled *The Distant Drum*, with the sub-title *The personal history of a Guardsman in the Great War* (in which he used extracts from some – though he might have with advantage used more – of his fine wartime letters). As stated in the previous chapter, Noakes became for a time a member of the British Occupation Force based in Cologne. Looking back on that period from the standpoint of the 1950s, well aware that such hopes as he had entertained at that time had been dashed in the most violent possible manner, he wrote:

> The people welcomed us, not as conquerors, but as deliverers from war. That was the universal feeling: relief that the war was over, at any price. Also, our presence was a safeguard against the tide of revolution, which was rampant in the rest of Germany. And our men, by their correct behaviour and lack of 'Prussian' swagger, soon became genuinely popular.
>
> During that Christmas-tide of 1918 I think that, could matters have been left to the soldiers and the common people, such a Peace of reconciliation and mutual good-will could have been made which would not only have fulfilled the ideals for which millions had died, but would have secured a lasting friendship between the erstwhile enemies. The men who had fought and suffered, on both sides, had had their fill of war, and were ready for a peace based on Christian concord without malice. But the soldiers were virtually disenfranchised, the politicians took control and imposed a vindictive treaty the like of which was never seen in the modern world before. All our subsequent troubles and frustrations date from that; the supreme opportunity was thrown away.

The harsh realities of politics have a way of clashing with the romantic dreams of the rank and file; nevertheless this quotation by F.E. Noakes can perhaps be seen as offering a positive and heartening way in which to conclude this account of the remarkable year of darkness and light that was 1918. For a year that began so grimly, it is good to acknowledge that at its end there could be a glimmer, if only a faint one, of the concept of reconciliation which – though it would take another generation and another war before it could become a viable reality, and even then would have its times of doubt and difficulty – has been a crucial part of the culture of Western Europe for the past fifty years.

Notes and References

For sources of quotations by participants, whether service personnel or civilians, see Index of Contributors. For publication details of books referred to, see Bibliography. In the interests of brevity, the British Official History is referred to as *O.H.* followed by the appropriate Volume number: e.g. *O.H. 1918*, Volume I; again for full details see Bibliography.

Foreword – A Year of Darkness and Light

page xxi – F.A. Robinson's unpublished four-volume war diary, held in the IWM's Department of Documents, which provides a remarkable day by day commentary on the war from 4 August 1914 to the Armistice, has already been quoted in my *IWM Book of the First World War* and *IWM Book of the Somme*. See also Index of Contributors.

page xxii – Queen Mary's comment on Armistice Day; James Pope-Hennessy, *Queen Mary*, p. 509.

pages xxii–xxiii – Information about the work of the British Official Photographer, David McClellan; from Jane Carmichael, *First World War Photographers*, pp. 72, 74.

page xxiii – Quotation by the Official Historian of the 46th Division; from Major R.E. Priestley, *Breaking the Hindenburg Line: The Story of the 46th (North Midland) Division*, p. 31.

Comment on the achievement of the 46th Division by John Terraine; *To Win a War*, pp. 173–4.

page xxiv – The 'right stuff'; American astronauts are the subject of Tom Wolfe's best-selling book *The Right Stuff*, first published in Britain (by Jonathan Cape) in 1979. The phrase was already is use in relation to American Air Force test pilots before being applied to the heroes of the space race. Wolfe assumes the phrase as given, offering no hint of its previous usage.

In respect of such earlier use, enquiries among friends and colleagues have produced the following examples:

In a military context: from Eric Partridge's *A Dictionary of Slang*, edited by Paul Beale, 1984:

> Stuff: Men as fighting material: coll.: *Manchester Examiner*, 24 Nov. 1883 'The army of Ibrahim included a good deal of tougher stuff than the ordinary fellah of Egypt' (OED); T. Gowing, writing early 1880s of the Crimean War, 'We had some of the right sort of stuff with the Fusiliers'; by 1930 virtually standard English.

Curiously, in view of this work's authorship, no reference to the phrase occurs in Brophy and Partridge's *The Long Trail, Soldiers Songs & Slang 1914–18*. Clearly, however, Corporal Murrell is not the term's inventor; he uses it (writing to civilians, not soldiers) as though it were a well-understood formula of the time.

A search through American dictionaries of military slang has also produced no sightings, but a not dissimilar usage with an American provenance and in a 1918 context has been found in a book entitled *Some Letters, written to Maude Gray and Marian Wickes, 1917–1918*, by Katherine Blake, New York, privately printed, 1920. Under the date 12 August 1918, Miss Blake wrote: 'Today we have the great British victory to read about; a victory which does my heart good, for the English are our brothers and our race. They have tasted the bitterness of defeat in March and they have been able to prove of what stuff they are made.'

In a non-military context: I have been offered a fascinating, much earlier example in *The World of Ice*, by R.M. Ballantyne (1825–94), author of such famous Victorian boys' stories as *The Coral Island*, *The Dog Crusoe* and *Martin Rattler*. The context is a conversation in a whaling ship in which two members of the crew are discussing the qualities of the captain: '"It's my opinion," remarked Buzzby to Singleton one day, as they stood at the weather gangway watching the foam that spread from the vessel's bow as she breasted the waves of the Atlantic gallantly – "it's my opinion that our skipper is made o' the right stuff."' It would seem possible, indeed probable, from this that Corporal Murrell's use of the phrase stemmed from the highly popular culture of nineteenth-century adventure books for boys.

page xxiv – The statement 'We all have one great ambition' etc., by a Tommy on the Somme in 1915, is from a letter by Private Sidney Appleyard, Queen Victoria's Rifles; it is quoted, twice, in my *Imperial War Museum Book of the Somme*, pp. 7 and 342.

page xxv – Quotation by CQMS W.E. Bates; from the Foreword (p. vii) to *Ten Years Ago*, by R.H. Mottram, subtitled *Armistice & Other Memories, Forming a Pendant to 'The Spanish Farm Trilogy'*, published in 1928.

page xxvi – Details from the British Official History of the action involving the 1/2nd London Regiment (56th Division); *O.H. 1918*, Volume V, pp. 262–3.

page xxviii – Frederick Noakes's privately printed memoir is entitled *The Distant Drum*; for details see Bibliography. See also p. xv and Afterword pp. 348–9.

page xxix – Charles Carrington's reference to chivalrous moments on the Somme is from an unpublished monograph on the first day of the Somme, quoted in my *Imperial War Museum Book of the Somme*, p. 283.

page xxx – The recently published book on the air war: *Tumult in the Clouds*, by Nigel Steel and Peter Hart, Hodder & Stoughton, 1997, Coronet, 1998.

1. THE UNENDING WAR

pages 1–4 – Details about 1 January 1918; contemporary newspapers, notably *The Times* and *The Daily Mirror*.

page 4 – Quotation by Desmond Allhusen; IWM Department of Documents, quoted in my *Imperial War Museum Book of the First World War*, pp. 272–3.

pages 4–5 – Quotation by Hubert Essame; from his book *The Battle for Europe 1918*, p. 11.

page 6 – Comparison of the sufferings of the Canadians at Passchendaele to those of Christ: Captain Harwood Steele MC, *Canadians in France 1915–18*, p. 181.

page 8 – Quotation on anti-submarine campaign; Cyril Falls, *The First World War*, p. 275.

page 9 – Sir Maurice Hankey quotations; Stephen Roskill, *Hankey, Man of Ideas*, Volume I, Collins, 1970, pp. 470, 443.

Statistics of air raids for 1917; from Appendix on Raid Records 1914–1918, in H.C. Castle, *Fire over England*.

pages 9–10 – Lord Northcliffe quotation; A.J.P. Taylor, *The First World War: An Illustrated History*, p. 211.

pages 12–13 – Quotations by General Sir Henry Rawlinson; Robin Prior and Trevor Wilson, *Command on the Western Front*, p. 273.

page 14 – Pecksniff: Dickens' archetypal hypocrite, as portrayed in *Martin Chuzzlewit*.

page 16 – Background to the Derby scheme; see Trevor Wilson, *The Myriad Faces of War*, pp. 167–8.

pages 22–3 – Quotation from Princess Blücher; from her book *A Woman in Berlin*, p. 185. See Index of Contributors.

page 23 – New Year comment by Herbert Sulzbach; from his book *With the German Guns*, pp. 140, 141. See Index of Contributors.

pages 23–4 – Hermann Hesse quotation: from *If the War Goes On . . . Reflections on War and Politics*.

page 24 – Editorial from *The B.E.F. Times*; edition of 22 January 1918, compilation edition published by Peter Davies, pp. 271–2. The title *The 'New Church' Times* dates from the period when the editors, officers of the 12th Sherwood Foresters, were based at Neuve Église.

2. WAITING FOR THE INFERNO

page 25 – Chapter titles on the 'menacing pause' before the German March offensive: 'Calm before the Storm' is from Roskill's *Hankey, Man of Secrets*; 'The Eve of the Storm' is from Trevor Wilson's *The Myriad Faces of War*; 'Before the Storm' is from Martin Middlebrook's *The Kaiser's Battle*; 'The Wrath to Come' is from H. Essame's *The Battle for Europe, 1918*.

pages 26–7 – Memorandum by General J.C. Smuts, as quoted in the British Official History of the War; *O.H. 1918*, Volume I, pp. 40–41.

pages 27–8 – Details of Forward and Battle Zones, etc, and of the reorganization of the BEF; from Martin Middlebrook; *The Kaiser's Battle*, pp. 74–5 and 86–8.

page 35 – Quotation by Martin Middlebrook; ibid., p. 29.

pages 35–6 – References to dissidence in the German Army; Hew Strachan, Chapter 28 of *Facing Armageddon*, pp. 383–98.

page 37 – Ernst Jünger quotation; *The Storm of Steel*, p. 242.

pages 37–8 – Correlli Barnett quotation; *The Swordbearers*, p. 288.

pages 38, 39 – Stephen Westman quotations; *Surgeon with the Kaiser's Army*, pp. 154, 160–61.

page 39 – Field Marshal Haig to his Army commanders; *The Private Papers of Douglas Haig, 1914–19*, p. 291.

page 40 – Field Marshal Haig to his wife; ibid., p. 294.

Quotation by David French; *The Strategy of the Lloyd George Coalition*, pp. 223–4.

3. SPRING OFFENSIVE: MARCH

page 48 – Details of opening bombardment, 21 March; John Terraine, op.cit., p. 59–60

Gough quotation; Gough, *The Fifth Army*, Hodder & Stoughton, 1931, p. 260 (quoted John Terraine, op. cit., p. 59)

pages 48–9 – Churchill's response to 21 March bombardment; Martin Gilbert, *Winston S. Churchill*, Volume IV, pp. 77, 79.

page 49 – Details of shattered battalions and quotations from war diaries; p. 313, in the invaluable chapter 'An Analysis', in *The Kaiser's Battle*, by Martin Middlebrook.

Fate of troops in Forward Zone of 153rd Brigade, 51st (Highland) Division; *O.H. 1918*, Volume I. p,221.

pages 49–50 – Quotation by Ernst Jünger; op.cit., p. 250.

page 50 – Quotation by Lieutenant-Colonel Rowland Feilding; *War Letters to a Wife*, p. 262.

pages 50–1 – Casualty statistics, 21 March; Trevor Wilson, *The Myriad Faces of War*, p. 560, citing Middlebrook, qv.

page 51 – Quotation by Ernst Jünger, op. cit., pp. 254–9, *passim.*

pages 51–2 – The diary of Max Walter Weber is held in a Miscellaneous German collection in the IWM Department of Documents; see also Index of Contributors.

page 58 – For the sake of accuracy it might be mentioned that Lieutenant Ledward's account of seeing French troops throwing away their rifles as they 'crossed the river going into the village' of Moreuil does not quite make sense geographically, as the river, the Avre, is on Moreuil's further, western side; however, this in no way invalidates the nature of the disturbing, indeed in military terms shocking, event he was describing.

page 60 – Peter Simkins quotation; *World War I, 1914–1918: The Western Front*, pp. 188–9.

page 61 – Reference to the performance of the 51st (Highland) Division in March attack; details from *O.H. 1918*, Volume I, p. 224.

The newspaper story quoted is from the papers of Corporal S. Bradbury, IWM Department of Documents.

pages 69–70 – Closeness of Ludendorff to achieving success; see David French, *The Strategy of the Lloyd George Coalition*, p. 224.

page 70 – Response of Lloyd George to the Spring Offensive; Trevor Wilson, *The Myriad Faces of War*, pp. 565–6.

pages 70–1 – Doullens and Beauvais agreements; text quotations from Cyril Falls, *The First World War*, p. 318.

page 71 – Comment on General Rawlinson's note on papers handed to him by General Gough; Robin Prior and Trevor Wilson, *Command on the Western Front*, p. 282

page 72 – Official History comment on 'a strange but fitting Nemesis'; *O.H. 1918*, Volume I, p. 533.

German comment re 'the Somme desert'; ibid., p. 533.

page 73 – Account by Captain Rudolf Binding; from his book *A Fatalist at War*, pp. 209–10, quoted Terraine, op.cit., p. 62.

pages 75–6 – Vimy attack; Cyril Falls quotations; op.cit., p. 319.

pages 79–80 – Captain Cosmo Clark's encounter with Churchill and Clemenceau; quoted from my *Imperial War Museum Book of the Western Front*, pp. 219–20.

page 80 – Churchill quotations; from Martin Gilbert, Volume IV, pp. 102, 104.

pages 80–1 – Quotation from J.H. Johnson; *Stalemate*, p. 212.

page 81 – Quotation from Trevor Wilson; op.cit., p. 564.

4. Spring Offensive: April

page 83 – Wartime history of Armentières; Rose E.B. Coombs, *Before Endeavours Fade*, p. 63.

Armentières described as 'much battered'; *O.H. 1918* Volume II, p. 159.

page 84 – Major J.D. Wyatt was a soldier of much experience in this sector; he had been present there as far back as Christmas 1914, when he was a participant in the Christmas Truce.

Official History quotations on the state of the ground in the Lys area: *O.H. 1918*, Volume II, p. 147.

Ludendorff quotation: ibid., p. 153n.

page 84ff – The Portuguese have always come in for censure for their inadequate performance on the Western Front. For a defence of their role by a distinguished student of the war, see C.E.W. Bean, the Official

Australian Historian, *From Anzac to Amiens*, p. 427. Referring to their abrupt retreat in April 1918, he wrote: 'The Portuguese melted – why they should have been expected to fight so formidable an enemy in a cause of which they knew little is a question on which military and political leaders might well have pondered.'

page 85 – Captain R.G.C. Dartford's description is quoted at greater length in my *Imperial War Museum Book of the Western Front*. pp. 221–2.

Captain C.L. Overton, 1/4th King's Own Royal Lancasters, is also quoted at greater length in ibid. p. 222.

pages 85–6 – Brigadier-General F.P. Crozier; the quotation is from his memoir *A Brass Hat in No Man's Land*, 1930, pp. 200–201.

pages 90–1 – Details regarding General Plumer's reaction to the need to withdraw from Messines and the Ypres Salient; Geoffrey Powell, *Plumer, The Soldier's General*, pp. 263–4.

page 96 – Vera Brittain as a VAD: A VAD – strictly a 'Voluntary Aid Detachment' – was a trained but not a professional helper who had volunteered for hospital or similar service either in Britain or abroad; the term carried with it a hint of superior social class, being part of the long English love affair with the concept of the talented but unpaid amateur.

Vera Brittain's 'fear of losing the war'; *Testament of Youth*, p. 411; her reaction to Haig's Special Order; ibid., p. 420.

page 97 – Cyril Falls quotation, from *The First World War*, p. 321.

Charles Carrington quotation, from *Soldier from the Wars Returning*, published in 1965, p. 237.

Comment by Lieutenant-General Alexander Godley; Geoffrey Powell, op. cit., p. 263.

Captain Stephen Roskill's comment on Haig's Special Order; *Hankey, Man of Secrets*, Volume I, p. 524.

page 98 – A Lieutenant and later historian; H. Essame, *The Battle for Europe 1918*, 1972, p. 48.

pages 98–9 – Quotation by Private H. Baumber from Peter Bryant, *Grimsby Chums*, p. 168.

page 99 – Quotation by Captain J.C. Dunn, *The War the Infantry Knew*, p. 468.

Comment by Brigadier-General John Charteris; John Terraine, *Douglas Haig, The Educated Soldier*, p. 433.

page 100 – Official History verdict on Haig's message; *O.H. 1918*, Volume II, p. 249. Australian subaltern's order; ibid., p. 249n.

pages 100–1 – Drunken behaviour by German troops; Stephen Westman, *Surgeon with the Kaiser's Army*, pp. 158–9.

page 101 – 38th (Welsh) Division's move to the Somme front; Lieutenant-Colonel J.E. Munby, *A History of the 38th (Welsh) Division*, by the GSOs I of the Division.

page 102 – Fall of the Hanging Virgin of Albert; Captain Moore's description and Captain J.C. Dunn's comment are from *The War the Infantry Knew*, pp. 468–9.

pages 102–3 – Attack by 113th Brigade; Major C.H. Dudley Ward, *Regimental Records of the Royal Welch Fusiliers*, p. 421. It will be noticed that Major Dudley Ward's contemporary letters are much quoted in this book. See also Afterword, pp. 340–1.

page 103 – 16th RWF battalion war diary: Public Record Office document, WO95 2556.

page 106 – Fate of two companies of 20th Middlesex: *OH 1918*, Volume II, p. 173n.

pages 107–8 – Death of Captain Norman Taylor; the remarkable April 1919 letter by his sister, Joyce Taylor, was first published in my *IWM Book of the First World War*, p. 282. I am pleased to have the opportunity to reprint it here, in context, and with extracts from other letters held in the Taylor collection.

page 112 – Death of Baron Manfred von Richthofen; Trevor Wilson, *Myriad Faces*, pp. 614–16.

pages 112–13 – Details of the Ostend and Zeebrugge raids; ibid., pp. 630–32.

page 113 – Zeebrugge raid modelled at Wembley Exhibition; Stephen Roskill, *Admiral of the Fleet Earl Beatty*, Collins, 1980, p. 256.

pages 113–14, and 115 – The history of the 'Chemin des Dames'; Richard Holmes, *Fatal Avenue*, p. 327. As 'sanatorium of the Western Front', ibid., p. 329.

page 114 – The young soldier quoted is Private William Hall; see Index of Contributors and next chapter.

5. Spring Offensive: May

page 116 – Description of Chemin des Dames area; Sidney Rogerson, *The Last of the Ebb*, pp. 3–4.

page 117 – References to Nivelle offensive; Cyril Falls, *The First World War* p. 261; see also *O.H. 1917*, Volume II, p. 503.

Reference to 'a holocaust of tanks'; Falls, op. cit., p. 260.

Trenches as 'arbours covered with rambling roses'; C.T. Atkinson, *The Devonshire Regiment, 1914–1918*, p. 349.

pages 119–20 – Account by Major-General von Unruh; by invitation this account was included as a special appendix to Sidney Rogerson's *The Last of the Ebb*; the extracts quoted are from pp. 123–5.

page 121 – British anxieties regarding General Duchêne's strategy at Chemin des Dames; *O.H. 1918*, Volume III, pp. 43–4.

pages 123–4 – German monograph on Chemin des Dames bombardment quoted by the Official History: ibid., pp. 48–9.

page 140 – References to the last stand of the Devons; C.T. Atkinson, *The Devonshire Regiment, 1914–1918*, pp. 352–3.

pages 140–1 – Quotations by Major-General von Unruh; Rogerson, op.cit., pp. 133 and 146.

6. 'Over Here': Enter 'Uncle Sam'

page 143 – Cantigny attack: *O.H. 1918*, Volume III, p. 115n.

'Doughboys', or 'Dough-Boys', as preferred nickname to 'Yanks or Sammies'; John Brophy and Eric Partridge, *The Long Trail*, p. 93.

Details of Belleau Military Cemetery; R.E.B. Coombs, op.cit., p. 160.

John Terraine quotation; op.cit., p. 73.

pages 143–4 – References to American songs, and quotation about the pre-war American Army; James Cooke, 'The American Soldier in France, 1917–1919', in *Facing Armageddon* p. 243.

pages 145–7 – Pressures on General Pershing and the terms of his mission; Frank Vandiver, 'Haig and Pershing', ibid., pp. 73–4.

page 146 – Quotation from Marshall's biographer; Forrest C. Pogue, *George C. Marshall: Education of a General 1880–1929*, p. 169.

page 159 – American casualties in the Second Battle of the Marne; see Cyril Falls, *The First World War*, pp. 332–3.

pages 161–2 – For Brophy and Partridge on 'Yanks', etc., see *The Long Trail*, p. 185.

pages 162–5 – The story of the raid in which Ensign Keyes took part is told in H.A. Jones, *The War in the Air*, Volume VI, pp. 361–3.

7. UNEASY SUMMER

page 166 – 'Long Max'; details from John Terraine, *White Heat*, p. 306; Rose E. B. Coombs, op. cit., p. 132.

Churchill quotations: *World Crisis*, Volume II, NEL edition, p. 901.

pages 167–8 – Details of air raids; H.G. Castle, *Fire over England*, Appendix on Raid Records 1914–1918. Quotations from Sir Maurice Hankey and War Cabinet discussions; Roskill, *Hankey: Man of Secrets*, pp. 559–60.

pages 168–70 – Details of Influenza epidemic; Richard Collier, *The Plague of the Spanish Lady, passim*; Trevor Wilson, op.cit., pp. 650–5.

page 169 – Impact of influenza on Washington DC: Geoffrey C. Ward, *A First-Class Temperament, The Emergence of Franklin Roosevelt*, New York, Harper Row, 1980, p. 414.

page 171 – Flu' and 'Flanders fever' on the Western Front; Cyril Falls, op.cit., p. 330.

Impact of influenza on the Royal Navy; Stephen Roskill, *Hankey: Man of Secrets*, p. 569.

page 172 – Camphor; a well-known catch, sung to the tune of 'John Brown's Body', suggests one of camphor's basic usages, as follows:

> John Brown's baby's got a cold upon his chest,
> John Brown's baby's got a cold upon his chest,
> John Brown's baby's got a cold upon his chest,
>   So we rubbed it with camphorated oil.

Inevitably, this kind of popular ditty was too much for the men in khaki to resist. Brophy and Partridge quote a Tommy version in their collection of songs sung on the march (*The Long Trail*, p. 34):

> John Brown's baby's got a pimple on his – shush!

John Brown's baby's got a pimple on his – shush!
John Brown's baby's got a pimple on his – shush!
The poor kid can't sit down.

Advertisements for Oxo and Formamint; see for example *The Sphere*, editions of 9 and 16 November. The *Evening Standard*'s 11 November edition carried a front-page advertisement praising the anti-influenza virtue of Brand's Beef Essence. *The Sphere* advertisement is reproduced as Illustration 35.

pages 172–3 – Quotation from Guy Chapman; *A Passionate Prodigality*, p. 337.

pages 173–4 – Chilwell disaster: speech by Mr Kellaway, Parliamentary Secretary to the Minister of Munitions; *The Times*, 9 July 1918; see also Diana Condell and Jean Lidiard, *Working for Victory*, p. 105; Churchill telegram and other details. The principal source for this section is the collection of contemporary papers relating to the Chilwell disaster held in the Department of Documents, IWM.

pages 174–5 – Upsurge of xenophobia and strikes in UK; see Trevor Wilson, *The Myriad Faces of War*, p. 656.

pages 176–8 – This moving letter came to the IWM with the papers of WI Prothero, RAF, in 1976.

page 179 – 'Peaceful Penetration'; C.E.W. Bean, *Anzac to Amiens*, p. 445.

pages 179–80 – 'A more recent Australian historian'; Bill Gamage, *The Broken Years*, p. 198.

pages 182–30 – Quotation on war's 'compelling fascination'; Guy Chapman, *A Passionate Prodigality*, p. 226.

page 188 – Clemenceau quotation 'a lamentable rout'; C.E.W. Bean, op. cit., p. 447.

C.E.W. Bean's phrase 'Pétain's prudent policy in defence'; ibid, p. 463. His comparison of Ludendorff to Mr Micawber; ibid., p. 465.

8. ALLIED ADVANCE: AUGUST AND AFTER

page 190 – References to and quotation from Ernst Jünger; *The Storm of Steel*, pp. 298, 303–4, 318.

Quotation by Ludendorff: Gregory Blaxland, *Amiens, 1918*, pp. 163–4.

page 192 – 'The Fourth Army's answer to Bruchmüller'; Peter Simkins, *World War I, The Western Front*, p. 204. Much of the material on British preparedness before Amiens is adapted from this source.

pages 192–6, and 199–201 – H.L. Witherby's account. A footnote might be added to these remarkable reminiscences, written, as stated in the text, in hospital just a few months later. Asked when an old man in the 1960s by his nephew about his 'notes' on his wartime career, Witherby denied all knowledge of them. Perhaps the sheer fact of setting down his undoubtedly searing experiences had achieved the catharsis of deleting them from his memory.

page 196 – Major-General Salmond and RAF deception techniques: see H. Essame, *The Battle for Europe 1918*, p. 124.

page 197 – Sir John Monash's description of the opening of the Amiens battle; from his book *The Australian Victories in 1918*, p. 132.

page 205 – Rawlinson's comment to Sir Henry Wilson on the success of the Amiens offensive, 9 August; Trevor Wilson, *The Myriad Faces of War*, p. 582.

page 206 – Gregory Blaxland quotation; op. cit., p. 205. The quotations by Foch and Haig in this section are from the same source, pp. 203–5.

pages 207–8 – Quotations by Barrie Pitt; from his *1918 – The Last Act*, p. 211.

page 208 – Book by F.J. Hedges; *Men of 18 in 1918*, pp. 147, 143.

page 209 – The Australian statue at Mont St Quentin is a substitute for the original, to which the Germans objected when they occupied northern France in 1940, since it showed an Australian triumphantly bayoneting a German eagle. The current statue shows Australian pride and confidence, without insulting German pride.

pages 209–11 – 'Yelling ... like bushrangers'; some of the details in this section, including the bushranger quotation, are taken from the official plaque at Mont St Quentin describing the Australian success of 1 September 1918. Other material from C.E.W. Bean, *Anzac to Amiens*, pp. 479–83.

page 211 – Details of the awards given to the 24th Battalion and to Major Coutts are taken from *The Red and White Diamond*, an 'authorised history' of the battalion by one of its sergeants, W.J. Harvey MM.

page 218 – Quotation by Ernst Jünger; op. cit., p. 319.

9. Civilians and Sideshows

pages 236–7 – Details of the efforts of General Franchet d'Esperey to arouse the Salonika theatre; from Trevor Wilson, *The Myriad Faces of War*, pp. 619–20; see also *The Gardeners of Salonika*, by Alan Palmer.

pages 288–9 – The Battle of Doiran is described in *O.H. Macedonia*, Volume II, pp. 163–72. Anonymous account in *Vain Glory*: 'The Battle of Doiran', pp. 666–9.

pages 242–3 – E.E.F.'s role in bringing about defeat of Turkey; *O.H. Egypt and Palestine*, Volume II, p. 633. For a recent discussion as to whether the Palestine campaign was necessary, see Matthew Hughes, 'Lloyd George, the generals and the Palestine campaign, 1917–1918', *IWM Review*, No. 11, 1997.

page 244 – Austrian defeat 'a fearful calamity'; Cyril Falls, *The First World War*, p. 365.

page 245 – Austrian account quoted in the Official History; *O.H., Italy*, p. 296.

page 248 – Wyndham Lewis's reference to 'enormous Anzacs . . . dying like flies' from influenza is from his book *Blasting and Bombardiering*, p. 206.

10. Allied Advance: The Final Phase

page 250 – Description of the final phase of fighting: *O.H. 1918*, Volume V: Preface p. iv.

page 251 – Description of fighting conditions in the final phase: ibid., p. vii.

page 255 – Description of American performance by H. Essame; *The Battle for Europe 1918*, p. 188.

pages 255–6 – Comments on the American–Australian attack of 29 September by Robin Prior and Trevor Wilson; *Command on the Western Front*, published in 1992, p. 375.

page 256 – Irony of the Belgians capturing Passchendaele, even though it was strictly just outside the Belgian sector; on this see John Terraine, *To Win a War*, p. 160.

Photographs of Canadians in Cambrai: e.g. CO 3373: illustration 14 in the first section of photographs.

pages 256–7 – Comment by Haig on Cambrai after its capture; John Terraine, *To Win a War*, p. 190; quoted from Terraine's own papers, ibid., 231.

pages 261–2 – For details of the Battle of Courtrai, as described by Lieutenant Ledward; see *O.H. 1918*, Volume V, pp. 272 and 285.

pages 264–5 – For background to the attack described by Second Lieutenant Clifford Carter; see ibid., p. 303.

pages 266–7 – Letter of Crown Prince Rupprecht, 18 October: ibid. pp. 327–8.

page 267 – Cyril Falls quotation re victory in the air; op. cit., p. 386.

For the meaning of 'sweating on the top line', and 'wind-up'; see John Brophy and Eric Partridge, *The Long Trail*, Glossary of Soldiers' Slang.

page 281 – Quotation by Sir John Glubb; John Terraine, op. cit., p. 238.

Keil mutiny, ibid., p. 242.

11. 'THE GREATEST DAY': ARMISTICE DAY 1918

page 291 – Quotations by Captain J.C. Dunn; from *The War the Infantry Knew*, pp. 567–8. The teetotal GOC of 33rd Divsion was Major-General Sir Reginald Pinney.

pages 291–2 – Letter by Lieutenant-Colonel Rowland Feilding, from *War Letters to a Wife*, pp. 351–2.

pages 293–4 – Details of death of Private G.L. Price; Rose E.B. Coombs, *Before Endeavours Fade*, p. 94.

page 294 – Quotations from Field Marshal Haig; *The Private Papers of Sir Douglas Haig*, p. 340.

page 297 – Churchill description of Armistice Day; *World Crisis*, Volume II, p. 949.

pages 297–8 – Quotation from Osbert Sitwell, *Laughter in the Next Room*, pp. 3–4.

page 300 – Lord Alanbrooke quotation; David Fraser, *Alanbrooke*, p. 81.

C.S. Lewis quotation; *Letters of C.S. Lewis*, p. 96.

pages 306–7 – Princess Blücher quotation; op.cit., pp. 289–90.

page 307 – Herbert Sulzbach quotation; *With the German Guns*, pp. 248, 250 *pages 307–8* – Queen Mary quotation; James Pope-Hennessy, *Queen Mary*, p. 509.

12. 'TILL THE BOYS COME HOME'

page 309 – Quotation from The *'Better Times'* (the final incarnation of *The Wipers Times*); facsimile edition, p. 308.

pages 310 et seq – For an excellent essay which deals with, among other subjects, the problems of demobilization, see Keith Jeffrey, 'The post-war army' in *A Nation in Arms*, edited by Ian F.W. Beckett and Keith Simpson. For details of soldiers' unrest in Britain and elsewhere see Andrew Rothstein, *The Soldiers' Strikes of 1919*. Including much material culled from newspapers, this book is filled with numerous graphic accounts.

page 313 – Quotation by Keith Jeffrey; op.cit., p. 227.

pages 315 – Post-Christmas protest of the 1st London Rifle Brigade; K.W. Mitchinson, *Gentlemen and Officers, The Impact and Experience of War on a Territorial Regiment*, pp. 245–6.

page 330 – C.E.W. Bean quotations; *Anzac to Amiens*, pp. 515–19.

pages 331–2 – Details of Armistice terms re occupation of Rhineland, and Plumer's appointment to command the British occupation force, etc.; Geoffrey Powell, *Plumer, The Soldier's General*, p. 284.

page 332 – The comment by Major T.H. Westmacott, Deputy Assistant Provost Marshal in 24th Division, is quoted in my *Imperial War Museum Book of the Western Front*, pp. 258–9.

AFTERWORD – A VICTORY WON: A VICTORY IMPERILLED

page 335 – Sidney Rogerson quotation; *Twelve Days*, pp. 59–60.

pages 335–6 – Charles Carrington quotations; *Soldier from the Wars Returning*, p. 280, p. 18.

pages 337–8 – Comments by Alan Brodrick, of Leyland, Lancashire; letter to the author, 11 June 1997.

pages 338–9 – The Edmund Blunden quotation 'desperately confused over war and peace', etc., and details of his poem 'The Estrangement' are taken from *Overtones of War*, introduced and edited by Martin Taylor, p. 10. Blunden's last poem, 'Ancre Sunshine', dated 3 September 1966, appears on p. 211 of the same work.

page 339 – The later career of Major Alfred Bundy; details from letters from his daughter, Mrs Gloria Siggins.

page 341 – Report on the wartime letters of Major C.H. Dudley Ward; by Ann Commander (Mrs Ann Brooks), IWM Department of Documents, 1996.

Regimental Histories by Major C.H. Dudley Ward; dates as given in the text, all published by John Murray.

pages 341–2 – Mark VII, *A Subaltern on the Somme*; the quotation is from my Introduction to the IWM facsimile edition, 1996, which also includes a facsimile of the actual letter quoted, dated 21 January 1928.

page 343 – Quotation by former Archbishop of Canterbury, Lord Runcie; from a speech at a conference to announce the IWM's Holocaust Exhibition, 23 April 1996.

page 345 – Foch quotation: Winston Churchill, *History of the Second World War*, Volume I, p. 7.; also Alistair Horne, *To Lose a Battle*, p. 18. Horne writes: 'Foch boycotted the signature of the Treaty, grumbling in disgust and with some accuracy: "This is not peace. It is an armistice for twenty years."' I have retained this quotation in spite of the failure to find a French source, as discussed on p. xvi.

Source for Wavell quotation: epigraph to *A Peace to End All Peace*, by David Fromkin, André Deutsch, 1989. (This quotation is undated in the source attributed though clearly seems contemporary.)

pages 345–6 – On the matter of Lance-Corporal Earley's proposals for justice in postwar Europe compared with those of 1945, it is worth commenting that the deliberate reduction of German real estate was, of course, scarcely an option in 1945, since that had already taken place, partly as a result of area bombing, partly because of the three-fold invasion in force, from the south, the west, and, most destructively of all, from the east, which finally brought hostilities to an end. However, the whole approach of the Allies of 1945 – at least the western ones, the Soviets having their own quite distinctive agenda – was far more creative and positive than that of 1919, leading to infinitely happier results.

pages 347–8 – Field Marshal Haig quotation; from John Terraine, Foreword to *Sir Douglas Haig's Despatches*, p. ix.

page 348 – Quotation from F.E. Noakes's *The Distant Drum*; I find this eloquent comment on a crucial opportunity lost movingly reminiscent of a famous parallel, the statement on the failure of the postwar settlement in the powerful Introductory Chapter to *Seven Pillars of Wisdom*, by T.E. Lawrence; wartime soldier (as liaison officer to Arab forces in the Middle

East), and himself a participant in the Paris Peace Conference as political aide to Prince Feisal. Speaking not only for those involved in his own struggle, he wrote: 'We lived many lives in those whirling campaigns, never sparing ourselves: yet when we achieved and the new world dawned, the old men came out again and took our victory to re-make in the likeness of the world they knew. Youth could win, but had not learned to keep: and was pitiably weak against age. We stammered that we had worked for a new heaven and a new earth, and they thanked us kindly and made their peace.' Lawrence, of course, was writing without the knowledge that that peace would be very short-lived.

BIBLIOGRAPHY

All books published in London unless otherwise stated.

C.T. Atkinson, *The Devonshire Regiment 1914–1918*, Exeter, Eland Brothers, 1926

Correlli Barnett, *The Swordbearers*, Eyre & Spottiswoode, 1963

C.E.W. Bean, *Anzac to Amiens*, Canberra, Australian War Memorial, 1946

Ian F.W. Beckett and Keith Simpson (editors), *A Nation in Arms*, Manchester, Manchester University Press, 1985, Tom Donovan, 1990

Paul Berry and Mark Bostridge, *Vera Brittain, A Life*, Chatto & Windus, 1995

Edmund Blunden, *Overtones of War, Poems of the First World War,* edited with an introduction by Martin Taylor, Duckworth, 1996

British Official History *History of the Great War*
—*Military Operations, France and Belgium, 1918*, Volume I, 1935
—*Military Operations, France and Belgium, 1918*, Volume II, 1937
—*Military Operations, France and Belgium, 1918*, Volume III, 1939
—*Military Operations, France and Belgium, 1918*, Volume IV, 1947
—*Military Operations, France and Belgium, 1918*, Volume V, 1947
—*Military Operations, Italy*, 1949
—*Military Operations, Egypt and Palestine*, Volume II, 1930
—*Military Operations, Macedonia*, Volume II, 1935
   All volumes recently republished jointly by the Imperial War Museum and the Battery Press, Nashville, Tennessee, USA

Vera Brittain, *Testament of Youth*, Gollancz, 1933, Virago, 1978

John Brophy and Eric Partridge, *The Long Trail*, André Deutsch, 1965, Sphere Books, 1969

Peter Bryant, *Grimsby Chums: The Story of the 10th Lincolnshires in the Great War*, Hull, Humberside Leisure Services, 1990

Jane Carmichael, *First World War Photographers*, Routledge, 1989

Charles Carrington, *Soldier from the Wars Returning*, Hutchinson, 1965, Arrow Books, 1970

H.C. Castle, *Fire over England*, Leo Cooper in association with Secker & Warburg, 1982

Hugh Cecil and Peter H. Liddle (editors), *Facing Armageddon*, Leo Cooper, 1996

Guy Chapman, *A Passionate Prodigality*, Ivor Nicholson & Watson, 1933
—— *Vain Glory*, Cassell, 1937
Winston Churchill, *The World Crisis 1911–1918*, Thornton Butterworth, 1927, two-volume edition, Odhams Press, 1938, NEL Mentor paperback edition, 1968
Richard Collier, *The Plague of the Spanish Lady*, Macmillan 1974, Allison & Busby 1996
Rose E.B. Coombs, *Before Endeavours Fade*, After the Battle Publications, 1976, revised edition, 1994
F.P. Crozier, *A Brass Hat in No Man's Land*, Jonathan Cape, 1930
Frank Davies & Graham Maddocks, *Bloody Red Tabs: General Officer Casualties of the Great War*, Leo Cooper, 1995
Major C.H. Dudley Ward, *Regimental Records of the Royal Welch Fusiliers*, Forster Groom, 1928
Captain J.C. Dunn, *The War the Infantry Knew*, P.S. King, 1938 (private edition), Jane's Publishing Company, 1987, Cardinal, 1989
H. Essame, *The Battle for Europe 1918*, B.T. Batsford, 1972
Cyril Falls, *The First World War*, Longmans, 1960
—— *War Books*, Peter Davies, 1930
Rowland Feilding, *War Letters to a Wife*, Medici, 1929
David Fraser, *Alanbrooke*, Collins, 1983, Hamlyn, 1984
David French, *The Strategy of the Lloyd George Coalition*, Oxford, Clarendon Press, 1995
Martin Gilbert, *Winston S. Churchill*, Volume IV, 1916–1922, Heinemann, 1975
Sir Douglas Haig's Despatches, first published 1919, reissued by J.M. Dent, with foreword by John Terraine, 1975
The Private Papers of Douglas Haig, 1914–19, edited by Robert Blake, Eyre & Spottiswoode, 1952
Sergeant W.J. Harvey MM, *The Red and White Diamond*: *Authorised History of the Twenty-fourth Battalion A.I.F.*, Melbourne, 1920
Frederick James Hedges, *Men of 18 in 1918*, Ilfracombe, Devon, Arthur H. Stockwell Ltd, 1988
Hermann Hesse, *If the War Goes On . . . Reflections on War and Politics*, first published in German in 1946; English translation by Ralph Manheim, Jonathan Cape 1972, Triad/Panther 1985, Triad Paladin Paperbacks, 1990
Richard Holmes, *Fatal Avenue*, Jonathan Cape, 1992, Pimlico, 1993
J.H. Johnson, *Stalemate*, Arms and Armour Press, 1995
H.A. Jones, *The War in the Air*, Volume VI, Oxford, Clarendon Press, 1937
Ernst Jünger, *The Storm of Steel*, first English edition, Chatto & Windus, 1929, new edition, with introduction by Paddy Griffith, Constable, 1994; first published in German as *In Stahlgewittern*, 1920; latest German edition (39th), Klett-Cotta, Stuttgart, 1998

Letters of C.S. Lewis, edited by W.H. Lewis, Geoffrey Bles, 1966, Fount Paperbacks, 1988

Wyndham Lewis, *Blasting and Bombardiering: An Autobiography (1914–1926)*, Eyre & Spottiswoode, 1937, reprinted (facsimile edition) Imperial War Museum, 1992

Erich von Ludendorff, *War Memories*, Hutchinson, 1920

Martin Middlebrook, *The Kaiser's Battle*, Allen Lane, 1978, Penguin, 1983

Martin and Mary Middlebrook, *The Somme Battlefields*, Viking, 1991, Penguin, 1994

K.W. Mitchinson, *Gentlemen and Officers, The Impact and Experience of War on a Territorial Regiment*, Imperial War Museum, 1995

General Sir John Monash, *The Australian Victories in France in 1918*, Melbourne and Sydney, The Lothian Book Publishing Co, 1920; Hutchinson, 1936

R.H. Mottram, *Ten Years Ago: Armistice & Other Memories, Forming a Pendant to 'The Spanish Farm Trilogy'*, Chatto & Windus, 1928

Lieutenant-Colonel J.E. Munby (editor), *A History of the 38th (Welsh) Division*, Hugh Rees, 1920

F.E. Noakes, *The Distant Drum*, privately printed, Tunbridge Wells, 1952

Barrie Pitt, *1918 – The Last Act*, Cassell, 1962

Max Plowman (Mark VII), *A Subaltern on the Somme*, J.M. Dent, 1927; reprinted (facsimile edition), Imperial War Museum, with introduction by Malcolm Brown, 1996

Forrest C. Pogue, *George C. Marshall: Education of a General, 1880–1939*, Macgibbon & Kee, 1964

James Pope-Hennessy, *Queen Mary*, Allen & Unwin, 1959

Geoffrey Powell, *Plumer, The Soldiers' General*, Leo Cooper, 1990

Major R.E. Priestley, *Breaking the Hindenburg Line: The Story of the 46th (North Midland) Division*, T. Fisher Unwin, 1919

Robin Prior and Trevor Wilson, *Command on the Western Front*, Oxford, Blackwell, 1992

Bill Ramage, *The Broken Years*, Canberra, Australian National University Press, 1974, Penguin Books, 1975

Sidney Rogerson, *Twelve Days*, Arthur Barker, 1930, reprinted Norwich, Gliddon Books, 1988

——*The Last of the Ebb*, Arthur Barker, 1937

Stephen Roskill, *Hankey: Man of Secrets*, Volume I, 1877–1918, Collins, 1970

Andrew Rothstein, *The Soldiers' Strikes of 1919*, Macmillan, 1980

Peter Simkins, *World War 1, 1914–1918: The Western Front*, Colour Library Books, 1992

Osbert Sitwell, *Laughter in the Next Room*, Macmillan, 1949, Reprint Society, 1950

Captain Harwood Steele MC, *Canadian in France 1915–18*, T. Fisher
    Unwin, 1920
Herbert Sulzbach, *With the German Guns*, Frederick Warne, 1981,
    reprinted Barnsley, Pen & Sword Books, 1998
John Terraine, *To Win a War*, Sidgwick & Jackson, 1978
——*Douglas Haig, The Educated Soldier*, Hutchinson, 1963
——*White Heat, The New Warfare 1914–18*, Sidgwick & Jackson, 1982
Stephen Westman, *Surgeon in the Kaiser's Army*, William Kimber, 1968
Trevor Wilson, *The Myriad Faces of War*, Oxford, Basil Blackwell, 1986,
    Cambridge, Polity Press, in association with Basil Blackwell, 1988
The Wipers Times, Facsimile Edition, Peter Davies, 1973

NOTE

In respect of certain published works specifically quoted in the narrative,
the author and publishers would like to make the following acknowledgements:

The two excerpts from *Testament of Youth* by Vera Brittain are included
with the permission of her literary executors, Mr Paul Berry and Mr Mark
Bostridge.

The excerpts from *The Battle for Europe 1918* by H. Essame are included
with the permission of Messrs B.T. Batsford.

The excerpts from *The Storm of Steel (In Stahlgewittern)* by Ernst Jünger
are included with the permission of its German publishers, Klett-Cotta of
Stuttgart.

The excerpt from *Laughter in the Next Room* by Sir Osbert Sitwell is
included with the permission of his literary executor, Mr Frank Magro.

The excerpts from *With the German Guns* by Herbert Sulzbach are
included with the permission of Pen & Sword Books, Barnsley.

INDEX OF CONTRIBUTORS

Ranks of soldiers are given as they were at the time of the experiences described. Full regimental details, etc., are included when available. Decorations are not shown. Senior officers are listed only if quoted from previously unpublished sources. In the case of fatalities, the date, cause of death and place of burial are given in square brackets. The generous help of the Commonwealth War Graves Commission in supplying these details is gratefully acknowledged. The names of copyright holders or donors of previously unpublished material, where known, are given in round brackets. Every effort has been made to trace such copyright holders; the author, the publishers and the Museum would be grateful for any information which might help to trace those whose identities or addresses are not known. Where the source is a published work, its title is appended; for full details of such works see Bibliography. Figures in italics refer to illustrations.

BRITISH AND BRITISH EMPIRE SERVICEMEN

AMERICAN SERVICEMEN

GENERAL INDEX

Figures in *italics* refer to illustrations. For sources of personal evidence from IWM archives see Index of Contributors.